THE PIOUS ROAD TO DEVELOPMENT

For Bjørg, Ingvild, Kai Håkon and Nina

BJØRN OLAV UTVIK

The Pious Road to Development

Islamist Economics in Egypt

HURST & COMPANY, LONDON

First published in the United Kingdom by
C. Hurst & Co. (Publishers) Ltd,
41 Great Russell Street, London WC1B 3PL

Printed in India

A catalogue record for this volume is available from the British Library.

ISBN 1–85065–760–2

CONTENTS

PREFACE AND ACKNOWLEDGEMENTS

In the mid-1980s I travelled to Egypt for the first time, to improve my Arabic and to do research for a thesis on the Egyptian economy under Sadat's open-door policy. As a nearly full-time activist in Norwegian student politics, I was also keen to explore the political scene in Egypt. Yet this proved harder than expected. Even as I gradually overcame the language barrier it became clear that the Egyptian political landscape was not easily read using the well-worn map of West-European politics. Apart from the remaining limits to political expression the difficulties of interpretation were twofold. On the one hand the setting was a society which on almost every level was overwhelmingly dominated by the state and where political power was, despite a nascent pluralism, monopolised by a closely-knit élite with roots in the 1952 revolutionary coup. In such a situation the debate on the benefits of private versus public enterprise in economic life must necessarily take on a different meaning. On the other hand there was the enigma of the Islamist movement, which by then had become well established as the most potent force of opposition. How to orient oneself? Who was "left" and who was "right"?

Out of my frustration emerged a desire to break the code to the reading of the Egyptian political field, to be able to decipher the ongoing debates. One approach seemed to be a study of the Islamic movement at the interface between its highly ideological discourse and the very real matters of economic development. The result was the doctoral dissertation[1] that forms the basis for the present work. My hope is that this effort contributes to a better understanding of the politics of Islam, and thereby of Egyptian politics. Certainly the endeavour has been personally enriching, not least in forcing me to take a second look at the role of religion in society and politics in my own part of the world.

Many people helped me on the way. The initial phases were financed by a four-year scholarship from the Faculty of Arts at the University of Oslo (UO). Not least I owe gratitude for the stimulating research environment provided by my fellow staff members at the UO's Department of East-

[1] *Independence and Development in the Name of God: The Economic Discourse of Egypt's Islamist Opposition 1984–90*, University of Oslo, 2000.

European and Oriental Studies, where I have been Associate Professor since 1996. My supervisor for the doctoral work was Kari Vogt of the Department of Cultural Studies, UO. The extent to which the work acquired clarity and cohesion, especially in the more analytical sections, owes a lot to her sharp-sighted criticism. More generally our discussions on Islam and Islamism, whether in Oslo, Cairo or Esfahan, have always added inspiration to my work. Others who read and commented on early drafts include Galāl Amīn of the American University in Cairo, François Burgat of the French Centre Nationale de la Recherche Scientifique, Tore Linné-Eriksen of the Norwegian Institute for International Affairs and Rex Sean O'Fahey at the University of Bergen. In addition there are those, too numerous to mention, who have heard me present parts of the argument at various conferences and seminars and enriched me with their views. To all I owe a debt of gratitude, while naturally assuming full responsibility for all errors of fact and of judgment that the work might still contain.

While my research was in progress, many helped in various ways with gaining access to sources and information, notably the staff at the French research centre CEDEJ in Cairo and at the library of the Egyptian People's Assembly. Thanks are also due to the people at *al-Maḥrūsa* Centre for Publication and Press Services, to Heba Handoussa of the American University in Cairo and to all those Egyptian friends who in many and long conversations helped me understand more of Egyptian society and politics.

I am also especially grateful to those members and sympathisers of the Labour Party and the Muslim Brothers who shared their time and their views with me. In particular I owe thanks to 'Ādil Ḥusayn who in 2001 passed away far too early, to Magdī Ḥusayn, to Ḥusayn Shaḥḥāta and to Iṣām al-'Iryān, who later served five years of forced labour to which he was sentenced by a military court for being an active organiser within the Society of Muslim Brothers.

Finally in Cairo there is the enduring friendship, hospitality and knowledge of Muḥammad Ḥassān, without whom my understanding of Egypt and Egyptians would have been infinitely poorer.

In the lead-up to publication Michael Dwyer, Christopher Hurst and Maria Petalidou of the publishers C. Hurst & Co. gave valuable advice and help.

My greatest debt is to Nina, who urged me on and generously provided time and space to get the work done. With Bjørg, Ingvild and Kai Håkon she lived closest to the delights and the perhaps at times more visible frustrations of producing this book. Thanks to all for your impatient patience and joyful distractions, but most of all for being there.

July 2005 B.O.U.

TECHNICAL NOTES

Transcription

Transcription from Arabic generally follows the system used in the *International Journal of Middle East Studies*. In rendering Egyptian personal names I have made some adjustment to Egyptian pronunciation, thus "Aḥmad Migāhid" rather than "Mujāhid". In cases where a person's name has become familiar to the Anglophone reader in a spelling not conforming to standard transcription, I have used the form commonly used in Western literature, such as Naguib Mahfouz, Osman Ahmad Osman, Nasser and Mubarak. The same goes for a few geographical names, notably Cairo, Alexandria and Luxor.

Currency

At the official rate 1 Egyptian pound (LE) was worth $ 1.25 in 1984 and $ 0.38 in 1990.

Abbreviations

In the references:
IJMES—International Journal of Middle East Studies.
MMS—Minutes of the People's Assembly (*Maḍābiṭ majlis al-sha'b*). The reference "*MMS*, F5, 1–15, *ṭm*, pp. 3–21" points to the Minutes from the "Fifth Legislative Period" (1987–90), First Term (1987/88), Fifteenth Meeting. "ṭm" is short for *ṭab'a mu'aqqata*, or "provisional printing".

Koran quotations

Quotations from the Koran follow the text in the translation of N. J. Dawood, *The Koran*, Penguin Books, London, 1994.

INTRODUCTION

"ISLAM IS THE SOLUTION", BUT WHAT ABOUT THE ECONOMY?

Despite the many wishful declarations made by both politicians and academicians about the "failure" and "decline" of political Islam, Islamism in its various guises remains the most potent force of popular opposition to incumbent non-democratic regimes across the Middle East and North Africa. Shielded from Western observers by the intense media focus on bin Ladin-style terrorist groups, broad-based movements for moral, social and political reform in the name of Islam form the mainstay of civil society activism in most countries. This is amply confirmed on most of those rare occasions when public opinion is given the chance to express itself through something resembling free elections.

To some extent such an occasion arose in Egypt in the parliamentary elections of 1987. These elections saw a loose coalition between the Labour Party (*Ḥizb al-'Amal*) and the Muslim Brothers (*al-Ikhwān al-Muslimūn*) emerge as the dominant opposition to the regime of President Mubarak. The Islamic Alliance, as it called itself, conducted its campaign under the slogan "*al-islām huwa al-ḥall*", ("Islam is the solution"). It demanded that Egypt be turned into an Islamic state in which the revealed law of Islam, the *Sharī'a*, would govern all spheres of human activity.[1]

Although the level of actual popular support has been harder to gauge in the less liberal climate of Egyptian politics that has emerged since then, most observers agree that the moderate Islamist trend led by the *Ikhwān* continues to constitute the main oppositional current in the country. In most of the Arab world and in a large number of non-Arab Muslim countries a similar situation obtains. Therefore, understanding Islamism is imperative if one wants to understand what makes this part of the world "tick". Consequently, an intense debate on how to interpret the Islamist phenomenon is taking place in both Arab-Muslim and Western academic

[1] See the Islamic Alliance programme for the 1987 elections, "Al-barnāmaj al-intikhābī 'alā qā'imat ḥizb al-'amal", *al-Sha'b*, 17 March 1987, Part 2.

circles. For obvious reasons this debate tends to focus on such aspects of Islamism as its attitude towards the West and towards "modernity", its position on gender relations, its view of democracy and human rights and, especially after 11 September 2001, its relation to terrorism. In short, the focus has been on issues where Islamism would appear to be in conflict with, or at least profoundly different from, dominant modern political ideas in the West.

Yet it seems clear that to gain depth the investigation of Islamism must proceed to examine and compare the ways in which various Islamist groups have translated the general message of Islamism into agendas for reform. In this respect a central issue that has been largely neglected is that of Islamist positions *vis-à-vis* the towering economic problems facing the population of the Muslim world. Indeed, the deep-seated economic problems of the countries in question are often cited as important in explaining the emergence of the Islamist movements, or at least their rapid growth in later years. But to what extent do these different movements concern themselves with the economic problems causing frustration in Muslim societies, and what remedies do they propose? This issue is treated only summarily by available works on the Islamist movements, and is the one to which the present work is devoted.

Without reducing politics to economics, it would seem almost a truism to state that the economic policy of a political party or movement is essential in determining its place and role within the broader political landscape of the society it inhabits. Therefore, a study of Islamist economic ideas is vital to deepen our understanding of the political role played locally and internationally by Islamist groups in the Middle East, the major contestants of current regime policies. Egypt is a natural place to start: it is the most populous Arab country, the political centre of the Arab world and the birthplace of modern Islamism.

The present work is built on a comprehensive study and analysis of the answers given by the two main partners in the Islamic Alliance, the Labour Party and the Muslim Brothers, to the economic problems confronting Egypt in the latter half of the 1980s. However, it should be noted that the mainstream Islamist tendency in Egyptian society does include other important voices, notably a number of independent Islamist intellectuals connected by the liberal ideology of *wasaṭiyya* or "centrism".[2] Writers like Yūsuf al-Qaraḍāwi, Fahmī Huwaydi, Muḥammad al-Ghazālī and Ṭāriq al-Bishrī exert a marked influence over both the Brothers and the Labour Party, and some of them have commented extensively on

[2] For a broad presentation and analysis of this group see Raymond William Baker, *Islam Without Fear: Egypt and the New Islamists*, Harvard University Press, 2003.

economic questions. Nevertheless, in an attempt to avoid any ambiguity, we have kept strictly to those texts and opinions produced by persons directly linked to the two organisations in question, ensuring the ideas presented in these pages really are those of the *organised* Islamist political movements.

Three main questions are raised. The first concerns the substance of the economic ideas of the Muslim Brothers and the Labour Party and how they have developed over time. Here it is argued that two main concerns direct the Islamist involvement in economic debate in Egypt, the struggle for independence and the search for development. Regarding the latter it will be shown that the Islamists were consistent advocates of economic modernisation and that this was given clear priority over the formal fulfilment of perceived "Islamic economic rules", for instance the ban on interest. Within this framework there was a definite tendency during the late 1980s, following the collapse of the communist bloc, to emphasise the desirability of private entrepreneurship and a market economy.

The second question relates to the possible particularity of the Islamist movement. In what sense does its proclaimed Islamic character determine its concrete economic policies? The answer provided is that at one level Islam (however defined) contributed a vocabulary more than it determined particular solutions to economic problems. Yet in a more circumspect way, because the struggle to achieve independence from the West, at both the real and the symbolic level, is one of Islamism's most important (and attractive) motivating forces, it is certainly predisposed to search for ways of strengthening an Islamic country's ability to move in international relations according to its own interests.

Finally, how should we properly describe the core of the Islamist phenomenon, the impulses behind it and its precise relation to modernity, and to nationalism? Our investigation has led us to believe that, while sharing the agenda of Arab (and Egyptian) nationalists in the struggle for true independence, the Islamists are also people moving from within a religious conviction to effect a thorough modernisation[3] of their society.

[3] For the purposes of this work modernisation is understood to refer to:

1, historic processes of technological and economic change underway in some areas of Europe since the 16th century and in the Middle East from the 19th, producing a society where market relations dominate production and exchange, where the cities contain the bulk of the population and where industry is the dominant branch of production; and

2, the attendant processes of social and political change; on the social level the break-up of tightly-knit traditional units dominated by family and patron-client relations within urban quarters, villages, or kinship groups, on the political level the increased mobilisation of the population and the rapid growth and centralisation of the state apparatus.

This work focuses on the period 1984–90, since this was when Egyptian Islamists enjoyed the widest possibility, and experienced the need, to express their ideas on economic questions. They enjoyed significant representation in the Egyptian Parliament, especially after the 1987 elections. The elections of 1984 signified the establishment, albeit partial, of party pluralism in the elected institutions of the country. However, the elections of 1990 meant, for all purposes, the end of that experience, and can in retrospect be seen as heralding the gradual closing of the limited space for political participation that had been opened up in the early part of Mubarak's presidency. Until 2000 the Labour Party still had considerable scope to express itself through its own press. The newspapers of the Labour Party and the Liberal Party also provided an outlet for the Muslim Brothers. Yet many of the *Ikhwān*'s central figures cited in this work spent much of the 1990s behind prison walls. Since then the Labour Party and its newspaper have been effectively shut down through government action.[4] The years from 1984 to 1990 therefore present the best opportunity to study in conjunction the different levels of discourse on economic questions produced by the mainstream Egyptian Islamists. And such a study is vital if one is to grasp fully what Islamist economic politics are all about, especially given that the struggle for independence is hardly mentioned in the broad ideological expositions of Islamic doctrine, while it is the lifeblood of Islamist participation in current debates as viewed through newspapers and parliamentary records.

Note on sources

A complete list of the primary sources utilised is provided at the end of the book. They fall into three groups.

General works on an "Islamic economy". Here we have based ourselves on writings produced by leading members of the Labour Party and the Muslim Brothers in the period 1984–90. Chosen as representative are the works of 'Ādil Ḥusayn,[5] and those of Yūsuf Kamāl. The former was the undisputed authority on questions of economic policy in the Labour Party

---

When it is stated in the following that a certain characteristic of the Islamist movement is "modernising" it is meant to suggest that it tends to speed up the processes outlined here, or at least to accommodate the population to them.

[4] The Labour Party's newspaper *al-Sha'b* continues to be published on the internet (www.alshaab.com). The Muslim Brothers mainly expresses itself through the weekly newspaper *Āfāq 'Arabiyya*, published since 1996 by the Liberal Party.

[5] Even if the major work of his that we have analysed, *Towards a New Arab Thinking*, does not explicitly set out to define an Islamic Economy. 'Ādil Ḥusayn, who was an important interlocutor in the production of this work, passed away in 2001.

while the latter was, together with Ḥusayn Shaḥḥāta and 'Abd al-Ḥamīd al-Ghazālī, the leading formulator of Muslim Brother ideas of an Islamic economy in the period under study.

Programmatic documents. To this group belongs a somewhat scant body of documents pertaining to economic questions produced by the Labour Party, the Muslim Brothers and the Islamic Alliance they formed in 1987. It is a hybrid category in the sense that it contains both very general abstract statements of the type dominating the general works on "Islamic economy" and more concrete suggestions for economic reform in the Egypt of the 1980s. More material of this type may exist, but presented here is all that is claimed by the two groups to have been produced. To make full use of these documents, a couple more produced just outside the 1984–90 timeframe have been included.

Fortunately, in respect of the Labour Party a series of six programmatic documents on questions of economic reform spread over the period 1982 to 1989 were available. But for the Muslim Brothers the only documents available were the programme of the Islamic Alliance for the 1987 elections and a document on economic reform prepared by Ḥusayn Shaḥḥāta on behalf of the Economic Commission of the Society in 1991.[6] This is partly a reflection of the fact that the Muslim Brothers have never been recognised as a political party in their own right, and therefore have never been given an opportunity to express their opinions freely. Nevertheless, this should not be taken to indicate that the Brothers were not concerned with economic questions. Throughout the period many of their members were heavily involved in both financial business and various kinds of charitable work, and from 1982 onwards circles close to the Brothers produced a monthly journal dealing with the intricacies of Islamic economics (*Majallat al-iqtiṣād al-islāmī*).

Newspaper articles and parliamentary speeches—consisting of articles from the Islamist press and speeches made in Parliament by Islamist MPs, taken from the Minutes of the People's Assembly.

The latter covers the entire session of 1984/85 and about half of each of the sessions of 1987/88 and 1989/90, in addition to a few selected debates from other sessions. Thus the first year of the period in question has been studied in full to establish a basis for discovering the potential development of Islamist positions on economic questions by 1990. The remainder concentrate on the period 1987–90, when the Islamists, as the leading opposition group, entered Parliament in force and a greater number of their leading spokesmen became MPs.

[6] Ḥusayn Shaḥḥāta, *Al-minhaj al-islāmī lil-iṣlāḥ al-iqtiṣādī* [The Islamic Road to Economic Reform], n.p., Cairo, 1991. A leading member of the Economic Commission of the Muslim Brothers, Shaḥḥāta was a professor at al-Azhar's Faculty of Commerce.

As for newspaper articles, included are a selection of around two hundred articles written by leading members of the two groups in the Islamist press of the period. One source is of course *al-Sha'b*, the newspaper of the Labour Party, which also published, particularly since 'Ādil Ḥusayn became editor in late 1985, writings of the Muslim Brothers. However, the main sources for Muslim Brother views are *al-Nūr*, the Islamic newspaper of the Liberal Party, the junior partner of the Islamic Alliance[7] (which also publishes *al-Aḥrār*), and the Islamist magazine *Liwā' al-islām*, which is also close to the Brothers.

Since this book presents itself as a discussion of an *Islamist* discourse on economic questions, a few comments on the role of the Labour Party are required, for only in 1989 did the party adopt a clear-cut Islamist platform. How, then, is it possible to include Labour Party statements from 1982 to 1988 as indications of Islamist ideas? First, in 1987 the party openly allied itself with the Muslim Brothers in an Islamic Alliance, and it seems clear that at least from this date the leadership grouped around Ibrāhīm Shukrī and 'Ādil Ḥusayn were bent on the Islamisation of the party. For 'Ādil Ḥusayn this intention was clear from as early as 1985. Secondly, when analysing party statements on economic questions before and after the establishment of the Islamic Alliance there is no discernible discontinuity. On occasion even statements made by MPs who left the party in 1989, in protest against its Islamisation, are quoted. In those cases their non-Islamist leanings are pointed out to explain their sometimes divergent views.

A question sometimes raised while discussing the discourse of Islamist movements—indeed, political movements in general—is how to distinguish between their sincerely held views and statements more or less flavoured by tactical considerations. Particularly hot issues include Islamist views on democracy, the position of women, religious minorities etc., since there appears to be contradictions between traditional interpretations of the *Sharī'a* and internationally recognised human rights.[8] Ann Elizabeth Mayer has suggested that tactical considerations certainly seem to play a role in Muslim discourse on human rights. Often the problematic points, where conflicts arise between internationally accepted rights and the *Sharī'a*, are simply avoided, or translations to Western languages are modified to appear more acceptable to Western audiences.[9]

[7] The Liberal Party officially broke with the Alliance in 1992.

[8] See Abdullahi Ahmed an-Na'im, *Toward an Islamic Reformation*, Syracuse University Press, 1990, for a catalogue of potential contradictions and an attempt to resolve them along the lines suggested by Maḥmūd Ṭāhā (see below p. 8).

[9] Ann Elizabeth Mayer, *Islam and Human Rights: Tradition and Politics*, Westview Press, Boulder, CO, 1991, pp. 93ff.

The primary sources referred to in this study are written exclusively in the Arabic language, and as such are not intended, at least primarily, to make an impression on foreign readers. Still we cannot exclude the possibility that some of the writings may have been produced with the at least partial purpose of winning over people from the leftist or liberal intelligentsia, who constitute a not wholly insignificant group within the small section of the population that do read newspapers. On the other hand it should be remembered that such tactics may point Islamists in more than one direction. Making one's ideas look good in the eyes of traditionally-minded Muslims might also be a highly significant consideration.

While, in a setting of free elections and parliamentary governments, economic policy is indeed often the most effective arena in which to woo potential voters, it is not the field where the apparent tension between traditional Islamic ideas and modern Western-inspired views is strongest (except for the question of interest, duly dealt with below). So the tactics that have to be taken into account are more of the general kind, of promising too much. The tendency, typical of opposition parties everywhere, to be against whatever the government is for, must also be kept in mind. Given that the political setting of Egypt affords little immediate chance of opposition forces taking power, the tendency to outbid other parties in search of voter support is perhaps not so marked with the Islamists. The rosy picture painted of a true Islamic economy, the general vagueness and the paucity of concrete proposals for reform might give the impression of a tactical concern to preserve the broadest possible front against the government. But a considerable amount of "blood, sweat and tears"-discourse regarding the road to reform is also evident.

Ultimately how important is the dividing line between convictions and tactically held views? If the view is abandoned that employing tactics is merely a synonym for deceit, it becomes clear that the dividing line between a person's or an organisation's tactical and strategic views or acts is very subtle indeed, and that taking up a position for tactical reasons is often the first step towards making it a strategic position once doctrine has been revised to accommodate it. Consider for instance the development of the social democrat wing of the labour movement in Europe from revolutionary socialism to moderate reformism. It would thus seem in general most fruitful, while being alert to the part tactics play in the political game, to consider apparent contradictions as signs of an ideology undergoing change, and, possibly, of factions developing within political movements.[10]

[10] See Robert Springborg, *Mubarak's Egypt: Fragmentation of the Political Order*, Westview Press, Boulder, CO, 1989, pp. 219–23, for a discussion of the unlikely idea that the Islamist movement constitutes "one, seamless web", and that the infighting factions are merely various tactical masks for various occasions and audiences.

1

THE PIOUS ROAD TO MODERNITY

UNDERSTANDING ISLAMISM

To clarify the premises of this study of the Egyptian Islamists, it is necessary to consider the question of how the Islamist movement as a phenomenon may be understood.

First of all: who are the people being discussed? For the purposes of the present work the Islamist movement is defined as those who call for the establishment of an Islamic state, and who organise themselves into political movements to achieve this. The main criterion defining such a state is that it should be governed by the *Sharī'a*, the revealed law of Islam. This definition has the practical advantage of covering a range of groups almost identical to the range of groups who refer to themselves as the Islamic (or Islamist) movement (*al-ḥaraka al-islāmiyya*).[1] It also serves to distinguish Islamism as a socio-political ideology from the related but much wider phenomenon of Islamic revival evident in later years in the form of increased mosque attendance, more widespread observance of the requirements of a pious Muslim life, increased adoption of the "Islamic code of dress", and not least a tremendous growth in Islamic religious and charitable associations.

Clearly this definition of Islamism does not cover everyone who is trying to formulate policies for modern society based on Islamic precepts. Alternative, often more liberal and open, discourses exist, like those of the *wasaṭiyya* circle mentioned above, the Sudanese ideologue Maḥmūd Ṭāhā,[2] or the "Islamic Left" proposed by the Egyptian philosopher

[1] As with all definitions there are troublesome "misfits", most prominently the Turkish Islamist movement, currently led by the governing Party of Justice and Development (AKP), which in its varying manifestations have not been calling, at least officially, for the reintroduction of the *Sharī'a*. However, on the Egyptian scene our definition works well to distinguish Islamists from all those nationalists, liberalists and even some secularists who make a point of frequently expressing their high regard for Islam and Islamic values.

[2] Ṭāhā advocated a return to the message of the Koranic *sūra*s revealed to Muhammad in Mecca, which he considered more timeless than the concrete rules established for the

Ḥasan Ḥanafī,[3] although their political role is for the moment rather insignificant. Nor does this definition include the "Islamising from above" that incumbent regimes under pressure resort to by increasing religious programmes on television and by giving the *'ulamā'* greater power to exert censorship against "blasphemous" literature; a game played by "secularist" rulers in several countries. Finally, Islamism is a modern phenomenon. As a product of Muslim societies unsettled by economic modernisation and Western colonisation, it should analytically be distinguished from pre-modern Islamic reform movements, like Wahhabism, the ideology upon which the kingdom of Saudi Arabia was built.

A comprehensive survey of the vast and ever growing literature—in both Middle Eastern and Western languages—on what is variously termed Islamism, political Islam, radical Islam or Islamic fundamentalism is not possible here. However, there follows a brief consideration of some of the main analyses on offer, and a presentation of the main points of what this study holds to be the most fruitful approach. A brief discussion is also provided of the meagre body of writing pertaining more directly to the subject at hand: the economic policies of the Islamist movement (as distinct from the general field of what has come to be known as "Islamic economics", that is the expounding of guiding principles for the economic life of an Islamic society, based on the Koran and the Sunna).

A response to economic frustration?

Should the growth of Islamism be seen as a reaction to dismal living conditions and frustrated hopes? It is true that at the beginning of the 21st century the majority of the population in most of the Muslim world, many having seen their situation deteriorate over the previous several decades, find themselves in poverty, while small groups have greatly increased their wealth in a period of economic liberalisation and opening up to the West. The radical nationalism of the previous generation, which in the 1950s and '60s was seen by many to offer hope of a better future, is now associated with corrupt oppressive ruling classes and with repeated defeat at the hands of Israel and the West.

Certainly there appears to be a link between the development of economic conditions and the growth of Islamist movements, especially con-

---

nascent Muslim state in Medina, as expressed in the Medinese *sūra*s and in much of the *Ḥadīth*. He was executed by the Numayrī regime in 1985. See Mahmoud M. Taha, *Islams annet budskap*, Universitetsforlaget, Oslo, 1983, and Abdullahi Ahmed An-Na'im, *Toward an Islamic Reformation*.

3 Cf. Ḥasan Ḥanafī, *Al-yasār al-islāmī*, Al-Markaz al-'arabī lil-baḥth wal-nashr, Cairo, 1981.

sidering the social groups supplying the bulk of the movements' active supporters: students and middle and lower ranking public servants. In Egypt the first "great moment" of the Muslim Brothers came in the late 1940s, a time when the groups in question were threatened by pauperisation. Seeking an education and government employment had been a means of social upward mobility and a guarantee of a decent standard of living. But while the number of educated people seeking a job was increasing rapidly, the post-war economic crisis reduced many of them to unemployment and economic misery.[4] In the 1950s and '60s the Nasserist system temporarily alleviated this problem by expanding the state apparatus and the public sector of economic enterprise, securing new jobs by the hundreds of thousands. At the same time the Islamist movement was harshly repressed. In the 1970s and '80s the new growth of the Islamist movement coincided with the reversal of the economic policies of the state, the so-called "economic opening", intended among other things to reduce the state's dominance over, and direct involvement in, Egypt's economic life.

Under Nasser the universities had been greatly expanded. Now state retrenchment, intensified by the evolving debt crisis, once more frustrated the hopes of the educated youth. The standard of education at the overcrowded and underfinanced universities and schools deteriorated. And although most graduates still found jobs in the vast state and public sector bureaucracies, new employees were becoming increasingly superfluous and their salaries were a heavy burden on the state. Furthermore inflation in the 1980s drastically reduced the already low purchasing-power of an average individual salary.[5] Nazih Ayubi, on the basis of this, and of similar conditions obtaining in other Muslim countries, claims that the Islamist movements "are all a manifestation of, and a reaction to, a developmental crisis in the Muslim part of the Third World" and "they are almost all movements of the upwardly mobile, formally educated and recently urbanised youth … [whose] sense of 'relative deprivation' may … explain much about their general anxiety and about the adoption of religion as a goal-replacement mechanism".[6]

It seems clear that even though the appeal of Islamism as a "symbolic revolution" cuts across classes, the growth in the movement's following is

[4] Ahmad Abdallah, *The Student Movement and National Politics in Egypt*, Al Saqi Books, London, 1985, pp. 36–7.

[5] For facts see Heba Handoussa, "The Role of the State: The Case of Egypt", paper presented at the First Annual Conference on Development Economics, Cairo, June 1993, Table A. 7.

[6] Nazih Ayubi, *Political Islam: Religion and Politics in the Arab World*, Routledge, London, 1991, p. 176.

in large part connected to the economic misery and frustrated hopes of educated youth with close ties to sections of the population still dominated by the traditional Islamic outlook. However, the economic factors can only explain the propensity of these groups for radical oppositional politics and not their "adoption of religion as a goal-replacement mechanism" (whatever that means). Rather, as is explained below, Islamism's power of appeal resides in the legitimation of its policies with reference to Islam and the coining of its message in an idiom drawing its authority from the ultimate source of legitimacy for the majority of the population—the Koran and the Sunna.

Revolt against the modern age?

Does this "return to the Holy Scriptures" mean the movements fighting for an Islamic state—in which the Islamic Law, the *Sharī'a*, rules supreme—can best be understood as part of a "world-wide reaction against modernist thought"?

This is the thesis of the book *Defenders of God: The Fundamentalist Revolt Against the Modern Age* by the American historian of religion Bruce B. Lawrence, possibly the most systematic attempt to formulate a theory of fundamentalism as a general phenomenon common to different religions. Lawrence surveys what he identifies as "fundamentalist" movements within the three major religions of Semitic origin: Judaism, Christianity (American Protestants) and Islam. In seeking to understand how fundamentalists relate to the realities of the modern world, Lawrence makes a distinction between *modernity* and *modernism. Modernity* is seen as the concrete facts of modern life: the revolutions in production and communications technology brought on by industrialism and the concurrent changes in material life and to a certain extent in social organisation. Lawrence's fundamentalists are, with the possible partial exception of the Naturei Karta group in Israel, not opposed to modernity. And they are capable of exploiting the most modern means of communication in both their campaigning and organising of activities. *Modernism* on the other hand characterises the new way of thinking about the universe, nature and society that arose in the West as a result of, or at least alongside, the industrial and scientific revolutions of early modern Europe. Modernism is marked by a strong belief in the powers of science and reason and by a basic scepticism towards any absolute truth. To the modernist mind no "truth" is immune to, or exempt from, scientific inquiry, and consequently it is always potentially subject to revision.

What Lawrence sees in the movements he studies is a religious ideology out to defend Absolute Truth, as preserved in the Holy Scriptures, from the onslaught of modernism, in other words, out to defend God.

The core contest is between two incommensurate ways of viewing the world, one which locates values in timeless scriptures, inviolate laws, and unchanging mores, the other which sees in the expansion of scientific knowledge a technological transformation of society that pluralises options both for learning and for living.[7]

Others have also tried to analyse the "last-ditch defenders of God", to use Lawrence's expression, across religions, notably the French political scientist Gilles Kepel. In his book on what he calls "the revenge of God", he examines much the same groups as Lawrence, but he also draws interesting parallels with certain movements within the Catholic Church in Italy and France. Although Kepel is less concerned than Lawrence with developing a theoretical framework for understanding these movements, he seems to agree with the general analysis of the latter. For Kepel, Islamists, ultra-orthodox Jews, American evangelists and Catholic movements like the Italian *Comunione e liberazione* share the view that humanity was led astray by the ideas of the Enlightenment. Man, or human reason, was put on a par with or replaced God. Thereby the foundation was laid for the tyranny of man over man, ultimately leading to the Gulag of Stalinist Communism. The politico-religious movements in question oppose efforts at modernising religion, advocating instead the Islamisation, Judaisation or Christianisation of modernity. They want to reconquer their secularised societies for religion; to make the state and its citizens abide by the rules laid down in holy scripture.[8]

In scope, the most ambitious study was the Fundamentalism Project organised at the University of Chicago by Martin E. Marty and R. Scott Appleby, who edited a series of mammoth volumes on a supposed "family" of fundamentalisms within all major world religions, including Buddhism, Shintoism, Confucianism, Hinduism and Sikhism as well as the Abrahamic religions. Although the programme produced a wealth of interesting studies on socio-political religious movements around the globe, as a theory-building venture it was torn apart by the sheer diversity of movements and situations under consideration. This is immediately evident from the editors' attempt to summarise the findings of Volume 1.[9]

Despite these and a flurry of later interventions on the subject, Lawrence's book remains the main comparative theorising venture to be considered. However, first the existence of a clear-cut line between

[7] Bruce B. Lawrence, *Defenders of God: The Fundamentalist Revolt Against the Modern Age*, I. B. Tauris, London, 1990, p. 232.

[8] Gilles Kepel, *La Revanche de Dieu. Chrétiens, juifs et musulmans à la reconquête du monde*, Seuil, Paris, 1991. See for instance pp. 259–60.

[9] Martin E. Marty and R. Scott Appleby, "Conclusion: An Interim Report on a Hypothetical Family" in Martin E. Marty and R. Scott Appleby (eds), *Fundamentalisms Observed*, University of Chicago Press, 1991.

secularism and reason on one side and religion and fundamentalism on the other needs to be questioned.

In his 1992 work *Postmodernism, Reason and Religion* Ernest Gellner states that in the present times there are three main currents of thought about the world: postmodernist relativism, religious fundamentalism and Enlightenment rationalism, of which he ironically declares himself a fundamentalist adherent. The existence of Objective Truth is a belief the latter two currents have in common. But while religious fundamentalists consider this truth readily accessible through revealed scriptures, rationalists believe no person or group of persons will ever possess absolute knowledge of truth. The only thing they consider absolute, says Gellner, are the rules for seeking knowledge.[10]

Gellner's division might be relevant here when looking at the subjectively-held views of the groups in question on epistemology, that is, how they themselves would explain the sources of true knowledge and the possibility of attaining it. But in regarding the *practice* of the same groups the division appears less clear-cut. Consider on the one hand the attitude to the writings of Marx and Lenin in the communist movement of the twentieth century, or the attitude towards the thought of Milton Friedman among the aspiring young economists and politicians of Eastern Europe after 1989. These are extreme, but not atypical, examples of the very strong position of "scripture" in political cultures where science has in the public mind taken the place of religion as the source of truth. Obviously in these cases truth is posited not as originating in God, but in the scientific work of outstanding human thinkers. But the difference can easily be overstated. For on the other hand we must also consider that among those defending God and the scriptures as the ultimate source of truth and (therefore) of morality, there are important groups who do not stand for a literalist interpretation and application of the message contained in the scriptures. Such people would claim that we must draw the essence from the scriptures in the form of certain general moral principles which should guide our individual and collective conduct on this earth. Regarding the Islamic scene this point will be dealt with in some greater detail below, but perhaps the appeal to the absolute truth of the Koran and Sunna serves more than anything as a shield against the universalist aspirations of Western thought in an effort to protect a separate space for Muslim thought and discourse. Either way it is important to note that the degree of literalism in the attitude towards scripture varies greatly both among self-styled secularist rationalists and among those advocating a religious interpretation of life in this world.

10 Ernest Gellner, *Postmodernism, Reason and Religion*, Routledge, London, 1992, pp. 2, 80 ff.

Somewhat related is the question of the extent to which religion and politics are two clearly separate entities. Is religion in itself apolitical? During at least ninety-nine per cent of human history this would have seemed an absurd proposition, since religion encompassed the sum total of human ideas about this world and the next, including the question of how to organise life. Every political movement would also be a religious movement, or at least have to seek religious legitimation. Needless to say, a debate on the definition of religion is not within the scope of this introduction. For the purpose of this study it is sufficient to be aware that one important aspect of the major religions is undoubtedly that they give symbolic expression to the bond between the individual and his or her fellow human beings.[11] Therefore, the specific doctrines of different religions also aim to establish rules for conduct towards other people. The number, detail and rigidity of these rules and their centrality to the doctrine of salvation differs between creeds, but they do exist. And such rules cannot avoid having political implications of one kind or another. Although in many countries those "defending God" have been pushed to the background of the political stage, and versions of certain faiths have developed to allow for the separation of religion from politics, religion in itself has not become apolitical.

In what sense can we really speak of non-religious politics? In Norway, normally considered a secularised society, the Constitution states that not only Christianity but a specific version of it remains the religion of the state. And there is a state church of which well over ninety per cent of the population automatically become members at birth. And in many European countries there are important political parties with the word 'Christian' in their name who claim to follow a line based on the tenets of the faith.

Even in relation to openly secularist states like France, and political movements with no religious references in their programmes it is important to consider in what qualitative sense they differ from their religious counterparts. Obviously they do not purport to base their policies on scriptures transmitting absolute truth from a personal, transcendent God. However, if secularist politicians were pressed for the moral imperatives guiding their search for beneficial policies, they would most likely cite basic tenets which in content do not differ principally from those claimed by religious groups on the basis of Scripture. And these basic tenets would certainly not have been deduced through scientific reasoning. Rather, they would be values that are deeply rooted in the societies in question and which were, traditionally, religiously understood.

Consequently the real significance of the Great Secularist Divide, the supposed separation of religion from politics, needs to be reconsidered.

[11] For a discussion see Bjørn Olav Utvik, "Kommunistar og Gud" [Communists and God], *Røde Fane*, no. 3/89.

Religion as an explicit reference to a transcendent God and divine scripture may have been reduced to an obscure back-bencher, as it were, but the reference to an embedded set of values, which may be debated, but nevertheless are in the main given *a priori* through cultural heritage, remains central. In fact, this type of "religion" is not absolutely new: Confucianism, to mention just one example from history, could be considered a kind of overarching set of moral values not given by a god but by a great human thinker and model.[12]

There are hardly any moral or political issues raised by religious movements that are optional and can vanish from the arena, although the explicitly religious framework for understanding them may itself disappear. Conversely, religious political activists are not really introducing new substantial issues into the political arena, but changing the language in which these issues are being discussed. Combined with the earlier observation that rigidity and flexibility of thinking are distributed equally among both secularists and those campaigning on a religious platform, this should discourage any secularist arrogance in approaching religio-political activism.

With this in mind let us ask, do the Islamists of the Middle East fit in with Lawrence's notion of a "fundamentalist revolt against the modern age", or at least against modernist thought? To answer this requires taking a closer look at the content of what seems to be their central demand—the application of the *Sharī'a* to every field of society, including economy and government.

According to the Islamist view, God made the laws once and for all. Permitting human beings to make laws is equivalent to placing man on a par with God, which means weakening the security of the individual by making his or her safety dependent on the whims of the rulers. In a part of the world which has for countless generations known autocratic rulers and military regimes, these arguments easily find resonance in the experience of the people.

Based on the idea of legislation as the sole prerogative of God, some Islamists have at times declared they are against democracy, since democracy gives sovereignty, and therefore the right to legislate, to the people.[13] But, as we will see, the matter does not end there, for what is the alternative Islamist system of legislation in practice?

[12] Stein Tønnesson, "From Confucianism to Communism, and Back? Vietnam 1925–95", unpublished paper, presented at the conference of the Norwegian Association of Development Studies, June 1993, p. 7, on Confucianism's "contempt for religion".

[13] See for instance a statement by Ali Belhaj, one of the leaders of the Algerian FIS, quoted in François Burgat and William Dowell, *The Islamic Movement in North Africa*, Center for Middle Eastern Studies, University of Texas at Austin, 1993, p. 125.

The *Sharī'a* is not a written code of law. It is based on the Koran and the example of the Prophet Muhammad as recorded in the stories (sing. *Ḥadīth*/pl. *Aḥādīth*)[14] of what he did and said during his lifetime. These *Aḥādīth* are collectively known as the Sunna of the Prophet, and in *Sunnī* Islam six collections are considered authoritative, the most prestigious being that compiled by Bukhārī and Muslim. The *Shī'a* have their own collections, in which the traditions of the infallible imams also figure prominently.

Traditionally the functioning of the *Sharī'a* has depended on the existence of a body of learned men (*'ulamā'*) specialising in jurisprudence. They would issue interpretations of the *Sharī'a* (*fatwās*) and serve as judges. These experts, known in Arabic as *fuqahā'*, would deduce the correct rulings in specific cases in accordance with certain methodological principles that had been fully developed by the ninth century. On issues where the Koran or the Sunna gave no unequivocal answer one must, according to the dominant view within classical Sunnī *fiqh*, proceed through reasoning strictly limited to analogy (*qiyās*), i.e. searching for similar cases in which the scriptures provided clear rulings. There is also a principle known as *ijmā'* (consensus). According to one *Ḥadīth*, the Prophet once said "my followers will never agree on error". This has been taken to imply that if the whole community, or at least all *fuqahā'*, agree on the legality or illegality of a certain practice, this constitutes a valid interpretation of the *Sharī'a*.

There are two important points to note regarding the way modern Islamist movements view the introduction of the *Sharī'a* as effective law in their societies, points which serve to distinguish them from a merely conservative, traditionalist reaction:

First, the necessity of codification. Traditionally the *Sharī'a* only existed in the form described above: the corpus of *fuqahā'* interpreting the holy books through certain principles and with due regard for an enormous corpus of earlier interpretations and commentaries made by *fuqahā'* through the centuries. In Saudi Arabia in principle this is still the situation—officially there are no law codes enacted by the state.[15] However, modern Islamists clearly conceive the process of introducing the *Sharī'a* as one of formulating written laws in a modern sense, based on the principles of the Koran and the Sunna. This is an important point, since written laws imply greater predictability in the rulings of courts and practice of government, but not least because it implies that some group of

[14] In Western literature the singular *Ḥadīth* is also commonly used to refer to the whole corpus, and this usage is adopted in the present work.

[15] Nathan J. Brown, *The Rule of Law in the Arab World: Courts in Egypt and the Gulf*, Cambridge University Press, 1997, p. 4.

human beings has to make decisions regarding the concrete formulation of these laws. The question is, who should take on this responsibility? The answer given by most mainstream Islamists in countries such as Egypt, Tunisia and Algeria is that it should be an elected assembly representing the population. The *'ulamā'* should play an important part either as members of the assembly or through some supervisory function, but only a minority would hold that they should have a monopoly over this legislation, or law interpretation, as the Islamists would prefer to call it.[16]

Second, the necessity of *ijtihād*. If the interpretation of law is to be conducted by an elected assembly, what scope of interpretation should be left to them? Should they copy the old masters of jurisprudence (*fiqh*) or do they have the right to reinterpret scripture? This question connects with the thousand year old debate on *ijtihād*. *Ijtihād* is short for *ijtihād al-ra'y*, that is "exercising one's opinion" in order to find the correct interpretation in cases where there are no clear rulings in the Koran and Sunna. From the tenth century onwards there seems to have been a tendency within Sunni Muslim circles to see the "gate of *ijtihād*" as closed. It was argued the great masters of *fiqh* had already found answers to all conceivable issues, and these answers were strengthened through *ijmā'*.[17] Even so there have always been trends defending the right or even the duty of *ijtihād*, that is for individual scholars to go directly to the scriptures and deduce concrete rules through independent reasoning.[18]

The Islamists strongly emphasise the need for *ijtihād* in applying the *Sharī'a*. In this sense they are heirs of the central figures of the so-called Islamic renaissance of the late 19th century, Jamāl al-Dīn al-Afghānī and Muhammad 'Abduh. These thinkers made a point of distinguishing between the essential message of the Koran and Sunna and the concrete forms of its application. Within the sphere of human relations—the *mu'āmalāt*—it was the former, the principles, that were to be taken directly from scripture. But the concrete applications would have to be adjusted to the circumstances of time and place. The same view was taken by 'Abduh's pupil Rashīd Riḍā, whose thinking was a clear inspiration for the first modern Islamist movement, the Muslim Brothers, founded in Egypt in 1928.[19] It has also been adopted by important newer trends within

16 Some speak of it as "legislation of the second order", for instance Ṭāriq al-Bishrī in Ṭāriq al-Bishrī and 'Alī al-Dīn Hilāl, "Ḥiwār ḥawla mu'assasāt al-dawla fī al-nuẓum al-islāmiyya" [Dialogue on state institutions in Islamic regimes], *Minbar al-ḥiwār*, no. 14, 1989, p. 78.

17 Joseph Schacht, *An Introduction to Islamic Law*, Clarendon Press, Oxford, 1982, pp. 70–1.

18 For a nuanced discussion cf. Knut S. Vikør, *Mellom Gud og stat: ei historie om islamsk lov og rettsvesen*, pp. 147 ff. (An English version of this work is forthcoming as *Between God and the Sultan: An Historical Introduction to Islamic Law*, Hurst, London, 2005).

19 Albert Hourani, *Arabic Thought in the Liberal Age*, Cambridge University Press, 1983, pp. 148, 233, 360.

today's Islamist landscape, such as the Labour Party in Egypt and Tunisia's *al-Nahḍa*, as well as by a number of independent Islamist-leaning thinkers.[20] This is reflected in a broad debate taking place today about how correctly to distinguish between the fixed (*al-thābit*) and the evolving (*al-mutaghayyir*) elements within the *Sharīʿa*.[21]

To sum up, the principle of *ijtihād* leaves considerable freedom of choice to legislators despite the basic constraint of having to conform to Scripture. And the Islamists, while never compromising on the idea of God as the sole legislator, nevertheless consider human agency a necessity for turning the principles of the *Sharīʿa* into law codes for modern society. According to most of them this agency should be popularly elected.[22]

Based on the foregoing discussion there are a number of critical questions to be raised regarding the usefulness of Lawrence's analysis for understanding the Islamists.

The choice of concepts is not good. "Fundamentalism" would be a good name for the Islamists in the sense that they *do* advocate a return to the fundamental bases of the faith, to the holy scriptures. In this sense the Arabic translation of fundamentalism, *uṣūliyya*, is gaining a certain currency, and is sometimes used in a positive sense by Islamists themselves. This Arabic term, incidentally, has a strong connotation of "authenticity" and does not necessarily imply a conservative stand. The Islamist sword is double-edged, it strikes not only against the impact of modern Western ideas, but also against the *ʿulamā*'s mindless repetition of old interpretations drawn up by scholars through the centuries. Consequently the term "fundamentalist" becomes problematic because, linked to its original use in a Christian context, it evokes the idea of a literalist attitude to scripture. In defining "Islamic fundamentalism" John Voll writes that its proponents adopt "an approach marked by an exclusivist and literalist interpretation of the fundamentals of Islam".[23] But the evidence suggests this is hardly typical of Islamists. On the contrary many of them would emphasise the spirit and not the letter of God's message in the Koran. John Voll's central case is the Muslim Brothers of Egypt, but studying one of

[20] See Muḥammad ʿImāra, "Hal yajūz al-ijtihād maʿa wujūd al-naṣṣ?" [Is interpretation legitimate in the presence of a text?], *Minbar al-ḥiwār*, no. 13, 1989, for a typical example of the views of this line of Islamism on the legitimacy of *ijtihād*.

[21] For one example see Ṭāriq al-Bishrī, "Shumūliyyat al-sharīʿa al-islāmiyya: ʿAnāṣir al-thabāt wal-taghyīr" [The comprehensiveness of the *Sharīʿa*: elements of constancy and of change], *Minbar al-ḥiwār*, no. 13, 1989.

[22] For the official position of the Egyptian Muslim Brothers, see Al-ikhwān al-muslimūn, "Mūjaz ʿan al-shūrā fī al-islām", *al-Shaʿb*, 19 May 1994.

[23] John O. Voll, "Fundamentalism in the Sunni Arab World: Egypt and the Sudan" in Marty and Appleby (eds), *Fundamentalisms Observed*, p. 347.

his own references we find 'Iṣām al-'Iryān—one of the central ideologues among the younger generation of Brothers—during his most militant period warning against a literal imitation of the Prophet. Although the Prophet used to clean his teeth by chewing a small piece of wood, known as *siwāk*, 'Iryān denounces those who think

> ...the most important thing is to throw away their toothbrushes and toothpaste and to clean their teeth only by chewing *siwak*. ... here the tree of *siwak* obscures the forest of Islam.[24]

In the sense that they all see belief in God as the only possible stable basis for a moral society, Islamists and Christian and Jewish fundamentalists definitely have something in common. But in the interpretation of the Divine Law the Islamists distinguish between essence and form in a manner that could not be considered to promote literalism. So Lawrence's emphasis on "the defence of Absolute Truth" also misses the point somewhat. The Islamists do indeed defend the existence of absolute truth, but their call for the application of the *Sharī'a* does not mean the defence of any particular substantial truth about politics.[25]

Finally, Lawrence's synchronic comparison of contemporary religio-political groups in countries as different as the United States and Egypt remains highly problematic, and prevents him from clearly discerning aspects central to an understanding of Islamism. There are two issues at stake here, the first related to the different positions of the two countries in the current world order. The Islamist revolt is not least a powerful reaction within former colonies marked by widespread poverty against cultural and ideological pressure from what is seen as dominant, aggressive outsiders. Protestant American fundamentalism, on the other hand, is a reaction against an ideological enemy within the same cultural sphere, taking place within the world's dominant economic and military power. And regarding US interference in areas like the Middle East, it has repeatedly allied itself with the most hawkish political tendencies.

[24] Gilles Kepel, *The Prophet and Pharaoh: Muslim Extremism in Egypt*, Al Saqi Books, London, 1985, p. 154. Cf Abdel Salam Sidahmad and Anoushiravan Ehteshami, "Introduction" in Abdel Salam Sidahmed and Anoushiravan Ehteshami (eds), *Islamic Fundamentalism*, Westview Press, Boulder, CO and Oxford, 1996, p. 3, who argue "the line of demarcation that sets the Islamist leaders and followers apart from their coreligionists is their political activism rather than a dogmatic or literalist attitude toward Holy Scripture". Cf. also Ervand Abrahamian's critique of "fundamentalism" as a label for the ideology of the Iranian revolution, which is largely relevant here, despite the particularity of the Iranian situation. See Ervand Abrahamian, *Khomeinism*, I. B. Tauris, London, 1993, pp. 13–17.

[25] Cf. Martin E. Marty and R. Scott Appleby, "Conclusion: Remaking the State: The Limits of the Fundamentalist Imagination" in Martin E. Marty and R. Scott Appleby (eds), *Fundamentalisms and the State: Remaking Polities, Economies, and Militance*, The University of Chicago Press, 1993, p. 638.

Lawrence does acknowledge this difference when he writes:

For Muslims [fundamentalism] is a third world ideology of protest; its defining characteristics relate as much to the third world socioeconomic conditions of the majority of Muslims as it does to universal Islamic creedal appeals, ... For Protestant Christians, on the other hand, fundamentalism is a first world, overtly capitalist ideology of reform.[26]

Still he does not really appreciate the profoundness of the dissemblance, the fact that in the Muslim world religion is important as a uniting factor because the perceived threat to people's livelihood and freedom comes from powers belonging to another religion and cultural sphere. Consequently, Lawrence becomes somewhat blind to one of the main aspects of Islamism, its call for cultural independence from the West.

The other issue concerns the fact that since Ḥasan al-Bannā's time Islamism has been a part of societies that are in the midst of the unsettling transition from a situation in which the overwhelming majority lived in the countryside working the land to a more modern, urban-based socio-economic set-up. The United States, on the other hand, at least since the early part of the twentieth century has been the very symbol of modernity. Consequently, current American Christian revivalism should be studied in the context of the problems raised by late modern society. In the Middle East the Islamists are reacting *to*, not *against*, the break-up of traditional social and moral structures caused by the ongoing processes of urbanisation, commercialisation, industrialisation and bureaucratisation, and forging a "new" Islam aimed at promoting modernising change while providing a moral framework to sustain social cohesion.[27]

Lawrence's insistence on discovering a cross-cultural fundamentalist essence prevents a clear view of this aspect of Islamism too. Indeed, it is a general problem that the search for such an "essence" tends to drive researchers to pursue specimens of the ideal type they constructed at the

[26] Lawrence, *Defenders of God*, p. 229.

[27] Alain Roussillon also notices that the Islamist reaction is not against the process of modernisation as such, but against its most destructuring effects, in particular with regards to social morality. But when he states that the success of the Islamists is due to their capacity "à articuler des techniques d'intervention sociale et politique 'modernes' et la prise en charge d'aspirations que, faute de mieux, on qualifiera de 'communautaires'", he misses the point that the construction of a new, thoroughly modern ideology is taking place, not a mechanical articulation of modern and traditional elements. What is at stake is not the reconstruction of a pre-modern "organic" community, but an effort which works to legitimise social change and evolving "modern" social relations within Muslim society, while simultaneously seeking to impose moral control on these same relations. Cf. Alain Roussillon, *L'Égypte et l'Algérie au péril de la libéralisation,* CEDEJ, Cairo, 1996, pp. 282–3.

outset, rather than letting them study the development and variety of real movements, as evidenced in Marty and Appleby's question: Can fundamentalism truly exist in a moderate form without being compromised in its essence?[28] Lawrence's contribution is of course not without merits. In striving to liberate themselves from Western models, to challenge the Western monopoly of access to universal truth, Islamists cannot avoid calling into question what is arguably the core of the cultural hegemony that the expanding, modernising Europe has spread throughout the world: the ideas of the Enlightenment. The Islamists certainly want to tear human reason down from the pedestal upon which it had been placed by "*les Lumières*". In seeing this as common to the Islamists and religious revivalist movements in the North, both Lawrence and Kepel are indeed right. But the question is: how essential are the similarities? What the Islamists call for is not foremost the belief in certain dogmatic truths analogous to the resurrection of Christ or his birth from a virgin, but the defence of an absolute source for ethical rules, and not least a *domestic* source, one the West does not control. In fact, we might suspect that what is resented is not primarily a high regard for human reason, but the fact that the apotheosis of reason for two hundred years has been experienced from the South as a claim for the right of European reason and power to dominate the world.

Indeed, a rationalist approach to politics quite different from that of traditionalist *'ulamā'* is in many respects represented in the writings of the Labour Party ideologue 'Ādil Ḥusayn, the Tunisian Islamist leader Rāshid al-Ghannūshī and Ḥasan al-Turābī in Sudan. To the extent that their ideas are read and debated fairly widely, they would actually encourage a modernising of political thinking among sections of the population drawn, by the Islamist movements, into national political life for the first time. To use one of François Burgat's images one might find in the end that the disturbing sounds made by the throat of Islamism come from the Muslim world swallowing, rather than throwing up, modernity.

This is linked to another issue. It is a merit of Lawrence's work that he points out that what he terms Islamic fundamentalism comes into existence as a response to the challenges raised by the process of modernisation. And he emphasises the Islamists are modern in the sense that they create a political ideology. He is also quite aware, despite the subtitle of his book, that in contrast to some of the Jewish fundamentalists he discusses, the Islamists have a positive attitude towards the technological developments of modern society. They use this technology in their work, and desire it for their countries.

[28] Marty and Appleby, "Introduction" in Marty and Appleby (eds), *Fundamentalisms and the State*, p. 5.

Still he holds on to his idea that the Islamists, along with other fundamentalists, reject *modernism*, understood as a *rationalist, scientific* way of thinking, and opt for the age-old, absolute truth of the scriptures. In reality things are rather more ambiguous. Certainly most Islamists are very restrictive when it comes to critical questioning perceived to undermine respect for the sanctity and eternal truth of the Koran, since this is felt to threaten the very cornerstone of the positive identity they seek to build for the Muslim world. On occasion one may find Islamists opposing the idea of the evolution of species. But this has never been a central issue as it has for the American fundamentalists. A man like Mortezā Motahharī, central ideologue of the Islamic revolution in Iran, elegantly incorporated Darwin into his Islamic worldview, stating God's creation is an ever continuing process. More important, there is much evidence to support the argument that the Islamists are not only actively promoting technical and economic development, but also a modern way of thinking, with their emphasis on diligent work, individual responsibility and on the practical application of science.

It might have been more fruitful for Lawrence had he conducted comparisons with religio-political movements at the time of the modern breakthrough in Europe, the Calvinists of England, the revivalists of nineteenth century Scandinavia.[29] Such comparisons would certainly corroborate the idea that the Islamist phenomenon has something to do with the advent of modernity in the Middle East. John Voll, cited above, is not so far off the mark when he states "Islamic fundamentalism" is a "distinctive mode of response to a major social and cultural change introduced either by exogenous or indigenous forces and perceived as threatening to dilute or dissolve the clear lines of Islamic identity".[30] Marty and Appleby, the directors of the Fundamentalism Project, express themselves in almost identical terms, adding that the movements in question "remain simply reactive", with no positive programme of reform.[31] However, rather than being a hostile or negative reaction to change, Islamism could be seen as on the whole an effort to promote modernisation while Islamising, domesticating and indigenising it.

29 Some tentative propositions on what might be learned from such a comparison are put forward in Bjørn Olav Utvik, "'A pervasive seriousness invaded the country …' Islamism: Cromwell's Ghost in the Middle East" in Stein Tønnesson, Juhani Koponen, Niels Steensgaard and Thommy Svensson (eds), *Between National Histories and Global History*, FHS, Helsinki, 1997. Cf. Michael Walzer, *The Revolution of the Saints: A Study in the Origins of Radical Politics*, Weidenfeld and Nicolson, London, 1966, and Berge Furre, *Soga om Lars Oftedal*, Samlaget, Oslo, 1990.

30 John O. Voll, "Fundamentalism in the Sunni Arab World", p. 347.

31 Marty and Appleby, "Conclusion: Remaking the State", pp. 620, 629.

The dual driving force of Islamism

The picture that emerges is of Islamism as the confluence of two powerful currents. One is of a social and religious nature and springs from the agonising effects of modernising change that would be felt in any society; accordingly it carries a lot of parallel traits to Christian activism in early modern Europe. The other is more cultural and political and relates to a special characteristic of Middle Eastern (and "colonial world") modernization; it has proceeded while local society has been subjugated by forces beyond the domestic cultural sphere.[32] Let us first consider the latter.

I. *Cultural nationalism, symbolic revolution*

In an effort to explain Islamism, the French political scientist François Burgat, among others, has taken as a point of departure a perceived dichotomy which splits today's Muslim societies. On the one hand there are the "modernised" élites, who have received a Western-style education and have led nationalist, Marxist or liberal regimes and opposition groups.

Socially, and not least ideologically, these élites have remained a tiny rather isolated minority. For on the other hand, the majority of the population in town and countryside is still solidly rooted in the traditional Muslim world-view and way of life.[33] Linked to this until recently "silent majority" is another élite with roots going back more than a millennium—the Islamic learned class of *'ulamā'*. They have their own distinct intellectual tradition, a common language in Arabic, and a tradition of traversing the Islamic world in search of education. In particular the thousand-year-old university of al-Azhar in Cairo is a meeting place for students and *'ulamā'* from all over the Islamic world.

Generally this "indigenous" intellectual élite has played only a secondary and belated role within the Islamist movements of *Sunnī* Islam. Typically the leaders of the Muslim Brothers and other movements have been engineers, lawyers or teachers who have received a more or less

[32] Laura Guazzone suggests the rise and spread of Islamism is due to "causes that can be traced back to two major interacting factors: (1) the cultural contradiction produced by the kind of access to modernity in the Arab world; and (2) the crisis of efficiency and legitimacy of the political ideologies and systems established after independence." While Guazzone's first point corresponds well with our analysis, her second point cannot explain Islamism at all, merely the conditions for its growth. Guazzone does not grasp the essential role played by a religio-moral reaction to the unsettling effects of modernisation. See Laura Guazzone, "Islamism and Islamists in the Contemporary Arab World" in Laura Guazzone (ed.), *The Islamist Dilemma: The Political Role of Islamist Movements in the Contemporary Arab World*, Ithaca Press, Reading, 1995, p. 4.

[33] On this point see, for example, an article by the Palestinian Maoist turned Islamist, Munīr Shafīq, "Two societies" in Anwar Abdel-Malek (ed.), *Contemporary Arab Political Thought*, Zed Books, London, 1983, pp. 236 ff.

Western-style secular education. In many instances they have even studied at universities in the United States or Europe, as is the case with the leader of the Algerian FIS, 'Abbāsī Madanī. They have been very critical of what they considered the inability of the *'ulamā'* to face up to the challenges of modern society. Still the very existence of the traditional Islamic intelligentsia has meant the continued existence of an alternative discourse, an alternative language for expressing views about the world and society.

Against this background the Islamist movement could be seen as an attempt to regain the identity and viability of contemporary Muslim societies by reconnecting with an indigenous system of references for producing meaning, thus creating a separate symbolic universe within which to debate the proper understanding of the modern world and how to tackle the problems with which it confronts Muslim societies. Islamic intellectual tradition in general, but most specifically the *fiqh*, becomes a reservoir for shaping a new political language finding its concepts and meaningful symbols in the vocabulary of the Koran and the *Ḥadīth* and its privileged references in the history of *Dār al-Islām*, especially that of the first generation of Muslims. François Burgat sees this as the essence of Islamism.[34]

Even after the Muslim countries gained political independence the model to be emulated was always the European one. Dominant élites considered the indigenous tradition was obstructing the development of modern societies with a modern economy. The discussion of politics was dominated by concepts taken from European theories and ideologies and by references to Western history. In Burgat's view a main function of the Islamist movement is to impose upon political debate (and upon the discussion of social and existential questions in general) a language taking its references from the dominant local moral system and intellectual tradition, that of Islam.

Muslims today are heirs to a civilisation and culture that has lasted for almost one and a half thousand years. For several centuries the lands of Islamic culture were the most advanced in material and intellectual achievements in the western half of Eurasia. But during the last five hundred years or so the Islamic world gradually lost ground to the growing strength of the emerging capitalist centres of Western Europe. From the 19th century onwards, first through local rulers' attempts to catch up with the European enemy through Westernising reform, then even more intensely through the policies of Western colonial rulers and the modernising

[34] See for example Burgat and Dowell, *The Islamic Movement in North Africa*, p. 41. For an earlier formulation of a similar view see Olivier Roy, *Islam and Resistance in Afghanistan*, Cambridge University Press, 1986, p. 79. Cf. Bruno Etienne, *L'islamisme radical*, Hachette, Paris, 1987, pp. 197ff.

regimes that followed them, Islamic culture was pushed to the background in its own homelands in vital areas such as education, government, legislation and later in the emerging mass media. The response has been a refocusing of attention on one's own roots, and an effort at countering the rampant Eurocentrism of intellectual and political discourse with an energetic Islamocentrism, as it were. Nazih Ayubi claims that more than anything else the Islamic resurgence represents a "quest for authenticity". Islamism is seen as a sort of "cultural nationalism" in which Islam serves "as an effective weapon against the 'cultural dependency' that often results from the Westernisation policies passed off by various Middle Eastern rulers as developmental policies".[35]

However, the term nationalism must be employed with care. On a theoretical level nationalism, in the sense of seeing the ethnic (*qawm*) or territorial nation (*waṭan*) as commanding the ultimate claim of loyalty from the individual, is strongly rejected by Islamists. It is seen as narrow and as a threat to the greater Islamic community (*al-umma al-islāmiyya*), in which all are equal irrespective of race or language. Yet Islamism is clearly akin to nationalist movements in the former colonial world in that it tries to liberate the Muslim countries from the continued economic, political and cultural dominance of the Western powers. It is a fact that despite growing international ties between Islamist movements, each conducts its fight for an Islamic state within the confines of its home country.

It is not uncommon to see Islamism as the expression of a third stage, or perhaps a third level, of resistance to the West. It is seen to extend the struggle for *political* and *economic* independence into a struggle for *cultural* independence. Burgat writes:

> [The] ideological and symbolic terrain now provides the framework for seeking a balance of power after decolonisation. … One cannot express the rejection of the West, using its language and its terminology. How better to mark the distance, how better to satisfy the demand for an identity, than to employ a language that is different from its own, along with a system of codes and symbols that seem foreign to it?[36]

As shall be seen, however, the issues of political and economic independence are not alien to the Islamists. It is only that the cultural revolt against the West is seen as a prerequisite for achieving anything lasting in these fields.

It is of course important to remember the history of Islam is rich with *various* political, spiritual, cultural and philosophical currents. A basis

[35] Ayubi, *Political Islam*, pp. 217–18.
[36] Burgat and Dowell, *The Islamic Movement in North Africa*, p. 64.

could be found in this history for advocating a whole range of divergent ideas. Even if leading Islamists promote one particular interpretation of Islamic history as the "correct" one, an effect of their political success will be that believers, as well as not-so-firm believers, are stimulated to find support in Islamic history for their own points of view. So the apparent ongoing Islamisation of Muslim societies is not the expression of *one* uniform unchanging ideology.[37]

The Islamists are increasingly forcing public discussion to take place within an Islamic framework. Their fight for re-establishing Islam as the ultimate source of truth has meant changing the rules of political discourse. Solutions must be formulated within what is conceived of as an Islamic conceptual framework instead of a Western one. Legitimation for a certain point of view can no longer be sought in quotations from Marx, Mill or Montesqieu, it must be seen to be consonant with the message transmitted by Muhammad. For Islamists this change is a prerequisite for a cultural liberation without which political and economic liberation will remain a sham. Yet by the same token they may be contributing to a much greater plurality of ideas within the Islamic framework, and potentially providing a stronger foothold for some imported ideas that are formulated in a conceptual language that has a much broader popular resonance. For "reconnecting" clearly does not mean the Islamists are somehow relaunching the "pure, original Islam", whatever that may mean. They are obviously selective in what they choose to emphasise and what they choose to lightly pass over from within the vast reservoir of the indigenous intellectual tradition of the Islamic world. The Islamists are drawing on an old vocabulary, but they are forming new sentences.[38]

II. *Change and pray: promoting modernisation under pious discipline*

Although the defence of cultural identity is essential, it is not sufficient explanation for the impetus behind Islamism. For one thing, as hinted at, similar social and political movements expressing their aims in terms of a

[37] Nor is Islamism in any sense a "necessary and logical outgrowth of inherent characteristics of the Islamic faith". For a polemical retort to this kind of cultural essentialism, see Guazzone, "Islamism and Islamists in the Contemporary Arab World", p. 5.

[38] An argument along similar lines can be found in Marty and Appleby, "Conclusion: Remaking the State", p. 638. Sometimes, however, the Islamist criticism of Western cultural domination is understood to imply a total rejection of everything Western, and by implication of any change in the position of women, of increased cultural and political plurality, and other developments connected to modernising processes, as in Salwa Ismail, "Confronting the Other: Identity, Culture, Politics, and Conservative Islamism in Egypt", *IJMES*, no. 2, 1998, p. 210. But this can only be done by letting a literalist reading of the most traditionalist fringes of Islamism represent Islamism as such, and cannot stand up to any serious investigation of mainstream Islamist discourse, as the present work will show.

return to true religion and the enforcement of God's will in the public arena, have occurred in other times and places in societies not particularly threatened by the cultural dominance of outsiders. What these societies had in common with the current Middle East was the experience of undergoing comprehensive modernising change. For another, the strong focus in movements like the Muslim Brothers on the reedification of the souls and minds of the believers, the "rigorist pursuit of sociomoral reconstruction", to use John Voll's expression,[39] is hardly reducible to the requirements of identity politics.

A review of the leading activists of the movements in question reveals they are representative of dynamic elements within the middle and lower middle classes for whom modernisation provides an opportunity for upward social mobility. They also have a very positive attitude towards economic and technological modernisation. However, the ensuing social change is rapidly breaking up the old framework of town quarter, village, kinship group and patron-client relations in which people used to lead their lives. To counter the uncertainty and fear of social chaos springing from these dissolving effects of modernisation, it is not unnatural that people from traditional religious families should look to Islam to provide both a personal feeling of safety and confidence and at the same time social cohesion. However, this call for reislamisation suggests the traditional Islam of the *'ulamā'* has not kept up with the changes. Hence the Islamists, either consciously or unconsciously, create a new version of Islam suited to giving moral guidance to a changing society, while promoting economic progress. Their Islam is marked by a new stress on individual responsibility, on the duty of the true believer to engage in a constant struggle against evil within both oneself and society, and to work hard to increase prosperity and welfare. At the same time it involves new organisational practices, in which lay people gather outside the traditional village or kinship groups in associations that study the scriptures, edify the souls and engage in social and political activism for the perceived cause of God.[40]

[39] John O. Voll, "Fundamentalism in the Sunni Arab World", p. 347.

[40] For a more thorough discussion see Bjørn Olav Utvik, "The modernising force of Islamism" in François Burgat and John Esposito (eds), *Modernizing Islam: Religion and the Public Sphere in the Middle East and Europe*, Hurst, London/Rutgers University Press, Piscataway, NJ, 2002. Cf. Andrea B. Rugh, "Reshaping Personal Relations in Egypt" in Martin E. Marty and R. Scott Appleby (eds), *Fundamentalisms and Society: Reclaiming the Sciences, the Family, and Education*, The University of Chicago Press, 1993; Marit Tjomsland, "'The Educated Way of Thinking': Individualisation and Islamism in Tunisia" in Mette Masst, Thomas Hylland Eriksen and Jo Helle-Valle, *State and Locality*, Proceedings of the NFU Annual Conference 1993, Centre for Development and the Environment, University of Oslo, 1994; Gudrun Krämer, "Cross-Links and Double Talk? Islamist Movements in the Political Process" in Guazzone (ed.), *The Islamist*

In one of their attempts to define "fundamentalism", Marty and Appleby acknowledge that it

> … intends neither an artificial imposition of archaic practices and lifestyles nor a simple return to a golden era, a sacred past, a bygone time of origins. […] Religious identity … renewed becomes the exclusive and absolute basis for a recreated political and social order that is oriented to the future rather than the past.[41]

The fact that they go on to suggest that fundamentalisms "stand in the way of individual self-determination" and "impede material advancement, progress and prosperity", has more to do with the self-imposed straitjacket of the comparative Fundamentalism Project than with careful observation of the ideology and practice of those Islamic movements they treat under the "fundamentalist" label.[42]

Some writers have construed the focus on individual compliance with religious ritual and moral teachings to be a ploy of rich "petrodollar Islamists" to make the masses concentrate on metaphysics and the afterlife and forget their socioeconomic plight, while they themselves are free to exploit opportunities for trade and currency speculation undisturbed.[43] But the fostering of a conscious, self-disciplined, responsible Muslim individual as a prerequisite for building a truly Islamic order in the modern setting has been central to Islamist ideology since the time of Ḥasan al-Bannā, and is as such intimately linked to the call for social reformist activism. This is not changed by the fact that for a time in the early 1980s some leading, often rich, members of the older generation of Muslim Brothers tended to speak little of socioeconomic issues.

This socio-religious aspect of Islamism is of course closely linked to the question of cultural identity. This becomes obvious in the thinking of the Islamist-leaning Egyptian jurist and historian Ṭāriq al-Bishrī, who has emphasised the cohesive function of religion in society.[44] He claims that

---

Dilemma, p. 54; Charles Tripp, "Islam and the Secular Logic of the State in the Middle East" in Sidahmed and Ehteshami (eds), *Islamic Fundamentalism*, pp. 61–2. A discussion of the pre-1954 Muslim Brothers in similar terms is found in Richard Mitchell, *The Society of Moslem Brothers*, Oxford University Press, London, 1969, pp. 330–1.

41 Marty and Appleby, "Introduction" in Marty and Appleby (eds), *Fundamentalisms and the State*, p. 3. Laura Guazzone also shows an affinity to the present analysis when she asserts that "the recovery of religious symbols remains the main way left open to Arab masses today to explain and control modernity, which would otherwise be seen as devastating and senseless", although she wrongly claims that this phenomenon is especially pronounced among "those who have benefited the least from … modernization". See Guazzone, *The Islamist Dilemma*, pp. 7, 11.

42 Marty and Appleby, *ibid.*, p. 7.

43 Cf. Salwa Ismail, "Confronting the Other", pp. 211–14.

44 François Burgat, "Les conditions d'un dialogue avec l'occident, entretien avec Tariq al-Bichri", *Egypte Monde Arabe*, no. 7, Cairo, 1991, p. 95.

when colonial powers and/or modernising regimes attacked Islamic Law and reduced the social position of the *'ulamā'*, of Islamic institutions of learning and of the popular Sufi orders, they simultaneously destroyed the moral ties linking individuals and local communities to state authorities in pre-modern Muslim societies.[45] It needs perhaps to be emphasised here that the issue is not whether Muslim societies before the eighteenth century were in some ideal way practising the Islamic concept of justice. The point is rather that however just or tyrannical the practices of the ruling élites might have been, there existed a commonly accepted ultimate reference for determining right and wrong, the teachings of Islam as expounded by the *'ulamā'* of the various legal schools.[46]

According to Bishrī the result of the reduction of the traditional role played by Islam was an atomisation of society and a decline in public spirit. The trend was towards a society where groups and individuals belonging to smaller solidaric entities based on kinship, local origin or religious sects tried to fend for themselves as best they could without regard for broader interests.[47] The vacuum left by religion has been filled by an increasingly corrupt bureaucracy and by police and armed forces, but without much of the population regarding the decisions of government as legitimate and morally binding. One might add that this alienation of society's base from its upper echelons is accentuated by the policies of the regimes, for instance in Egypt, where a certain degree of political pluralism is tolerated within the upper classes and the educated urban élites, while the lid is kept tightly on independent political or trade union activity among workers and farmers. Against this background the Islamist movements represent to Bishrī an attempt to reinstate that which has been eroded, namely the religious framework that held individuals and state power together in a divinely sanctioned societal order.

Political Islam: a spent force?

For some time the prominent French political scientists Olivier Roy and Gilles Kepel have both been announcing the decline of Islamism as an active force in the shaping of Muslim societies.[48] However, the evidence

[45] On the role of religion in pre-modern Muslim societies, see Ira M. Lapidus, *A History of Islamic Societies*, Cambridge University Press, 1988, pp. 253, 264.

[46] However, recent research indicates the gap between theoretical *Sharī'a* and actual judicial practice in the Ottoman Empire should not be exaggerated. See Nathan J. Brown, "Shari'a and State in the Modern Muslim Middle East", *IJMES*, no. 3, 1997, pp. 361–3.

[47] On this point cf. Rugh, "Reshaping Personal Relations in Egypt", pp. 156–7.

[48] In for instance Olivier Roy, *The Failure of Political Islam*, Harvard University Press, 1994, and Gilles Kepel, *Jihad: the Trail of Political Islam*, I. B. Tauris, London, 2002.

seems to point the other way, indicating that the zenith of Islamist influence is yet to come. The success of incumbent regimes in forcing the opposition underground by way of police oppression, and the failure of the extremist wing of Islamism in effecting the overthrow of the same regimes though violent means, should not be misread as a genuine reduction of the attractive force of the Islamist ideological option.

François Burgat criticises the idea of a general decline as being vaguely formulated and both badly and deficiently substantiated.[49] He shows that if one focuses on the moderate mainstream of the Islamist movement they have actually been strengthened rather than weakened during the period in question. According to Burgat the proponents of the decline thesis tend to argue along shifting and sometimes contradictory lines. It is generally implied that the violent "revolutionary" groups are somehow the true representatives of Islamism, such that their weakening represents a decline or at least a decay. Yet this contradicts somewhat Roy's original argument, in *The Failure of Political Islam*, that from representing a fresh and promising attempt at reappropriation of modernity from within an Islamic cultural framework, Islamism degenerated into sheer sterile neo-fundamentalism. But the representatives of this reactionary fundamentalism are precisely those groups that are otherwise said to have been weakened, not least by state counterstrategies of repression. Now the argument seems to be: as mainstream groups like the Muslim Brothers and the Turkish AKP "take over", the Islamist movements become more social-democratic and may well score greater successes, but this is no longer Islamism. Yet, as Burgat shows, the great majority of Islamists have never belonged to the violent extreme groups with their simplistic doctrines. A more objective treatment would discover a gradual maturing of what has always been the mainstream in the direction of a greater acceptance of pluralism and of a democratic system. Instead of being seen as a "decline of Islamism" this development should be understood as an indication of the potential for evolution and adaptation within the framework of Islamist ideology.

A moral economy: Islamist economic ideas

As a subject the economic policies favoured and fought for by Islamists is vastly understudied (as is the "positive programme" of the Islamist mainstream in general). It is important here to distinguish this from the more general field of Islamic economic ideas and practices. There is by now a vast literature in Arabic and other major "Muslim" languages on the

[49] François Burgat, *Face to Face with Political Islam*, I. B. Tauris, London, 2003.

concept of an Islamic economy as distinct from both capitalism and socialism.[50] There is much in English too. Western academics have analysed some of this literature and studied the experience of non-interest "Islamic banks".[51] Studies of economic ideas and practices in medieval Islamic society have also emerged.[52] However, to the best of our knowledge a systematic study is yet to be undertaken of the economic policies of the oppositional Islamist movements of the Arab world, incorporating both their general ideas on an Islamic economy and the day-to-day positions they take on current issues.

Certainly Richard Mitchell's classic work on the Muslim Brothers until their suppression in 1954 contains an exposition of their economic programme, showing it to be largely identical with the programme implemented by the Nasser regime, at least until the socialist reforms of the early 1960s. Primarily it aimed at national independence and strength, involving land reform, state-led industrialisation and the nationalisation of key foreign assets such as the Suez Canal.[53] However, studies of the movements of the more recent past are sparse. Nazih Ayubi considers the revived Islamist movement of the 1980s lacks any socio-economic vision.[54] Their enemy, he says, seems to be socialism rather than capitalism, which was under primary attack in the 1950s. He links this to the fact that the Nasserist programme, which to a large degree had been shared by the Muslim Brothers, had failed and had moreover become associated

50 See for instance Al-maṣraf al-islāmī al-duwalī lil-istithmār wal-tanmīya, *Bibliyujrāfiya al-iqtiṣād al-islāmī* [The bibliography of Islamic economy], Al-risāla lil-ṭibā'a wal-nashr, Cairo, 1987, which lists more than a thousand books and articles in the Arabic language alone.

51 See for instance Timur Kuran, "On the notion of economic justice in contemporary Islamic thought", *IJMES*, no. 2, 1989, which is based on a survey of all writings on the subject published in English between 1970 and 1987, mostly of Indo-Pakistani origin. Other relevant articles by Kuran include "The Economic Impact of Islamic Fundamentalism" in Marty and Appleby (eds), *Fundamentalisms and the State*, and "Islamic Economics and the Islamic Subeconomy", *Journal of Economic Perspectives*, vol. 9, 1995. It should be noted that the bulk of writings on Islamic economy today is the result of the establishment of the subject as an academic field in "Islamising" states such as Pakistan and Saudi Arabia. A similar development is taking place in some other Muslim countries as a result of the states' attempt to accommodate the general Islamic revival. This literature is quite distinct in style and content from that produced by the oppositional Islamist movements. See for instance Roy, *L'échec de l'islam politique*, Editions du Seuil, Paris, 1992, pp. 177–8, where he labels its vision of an Islamic economy conservative and technocratic.

52 *E.g.* Maxime Rodinson, *Islam and Capitalism*, Penguin Books, Harmondsworth, 1977.

53 Mitchell, *The Society of Moslem Brothers*, pp. 272 ff.

54 Ayubi, *Political Islam*, p. 223. For a similar view cf. Salwa Ismail, "Confronting the Other", p. 213, who states that what she terms "conservative Islamism" is supported by "the production of an Islamic identity in terms devoid of national and social content".

with an aggressive (and we might add oppressive) secularism. As we shall see, this is not altogether wrong. But in the case of Egypt, which is the basis of Ayubi's argument, he ignores the developments of the later 1980s, when the Labour Party and their Muslim Brother allies were very active critics of the regime's economic policies. Above all they were clearly concerned with national independence, untiringly attacking the influence exercised by the International Monetary Fund (IMF) and the United States on the economic practices of the regime.

Other writers, like Olivier Roy and Olivier Carré, in their works on political Islam have devoted chapters to the doctrine of an Islamic economy.[55] Their analysis seems to be based mainly on works produced by Islamists in the 1950s, and in the case of Roy mostly from Iran and Pakistan. Roy emphasises that the idea of an "Islamic economy" as a separate sphere within Islamic society is a phenomenon of the twentieth century, an innovation of the Islamists and of Western inspiration. It tends, he says, to take as its starting point the responsibility of man as God's caretaker on earth, not specific rulings in the Koran. Nevertheless, economic rulings such as the prohibition of interest and of monopoly, the payment of *zakāt*, inheritance laws and the like are incorporated into the doctrine. The end result, he says, is a sort of social-democrat vision in the sense that it acknowledges private property, but institutes checks and balances upon it. The rich are supposed to share with the poor, and to secure this the state has the right to interfere. The inheritance laws and the prohibition of interest prevent the excessive accumulation of wealth, but the doctrine is basically one of harmony between the classes, not of class struggle, which is abhorred as divisive.

A conservative tendency, expressed in the writings of the Indo-Pakistani Islamist pioneer Mawdūdī, puts the stress on the sanctity of private property and restricts the right of the state to interfere. More "statist" exponents of an "Islamic economy" base themselves heavily on the principle of the common good, *maṣlaḥa*, as the overriding concern. Carré points out that this principle was promoted by Rashīd Riḍā, forerunner and inspiration of the Muslim Brothers.[56]

Although in broad terms much of this picture is confirmed by our findings, Roy and Carré still do not grasp the dynamic development of Islamist economic doctrine in the 1980s. And neither they nor Ayubi point to the issue that arguably emerges as the central theme of the economic policy of the Egyptian Islamists in this period, namely independence. Most likely

[55] For Roy see *L'échec de l'islam politique*, pp. 167 ff., for Carré cf. *L'islam laïque ou le retour à la Grande Tradition*, Armand Colin, Paris, 1993, pp. 93 ff.
[56] *Ibid.*, p. 96.

this is because they have exclusively been studying general works on an Islamic economy, and not the Islamists' party programmes, newspaper articles and interventions in Parliament. They also ignore the works of the influential figure 'Ādil Ḥusayn, the ideologue of the Labour Party.

Finally mention should be made of Alan Richards and John Waterbury's brief treatment of Islamist economic policies in the 1996 edition of *A Political Economy of the Middle East.* They start with the question of whether Islam is the solution to the development problems of the Middle East, which they answer in the negative. Theirs is a double argument. On the one hand they agree with Ayubi that the Islamists do not possess a clear economic vision, which they attribute to a lack of interest in economic questions due to Islamism being "preeminently a politics of culture". In their view this leaves Islamists open to a pragmatic, even opportunistic line in economic questioning, which can only be bad for development prospects, since it would expose the economic policies of an Islamist government to the twists and turns of popular opinion. In addition, they state that while "successful development requires a single-minded focus on growth", "needless to say, this is most unlikely to be true of Islamists". On the other hand, to the extent that the Islamists present specific Islamic economic precepts, which Richards and Waterbury list—much like Roy above—the authors do not think much of them. Either they will not really be implemented, or they would have harmful effects. And although Richards and Waterbury do notice Islamist concern with economic independence, they consider it a part of Islamist xenophobia, and state that it will only work to encourage harmful strategies of self-sufficiency and scare off much needed foreign investment.[57]

The aim of the present study is not to answer the question raised by Richards and Waterbury of whether Islam, or Islamism for that matter, possesses the solution to the development crisis in Egypt or elsewhere. Rather it is to enhance understanding of the political and ideological position of the mainstream Islamist movements. Nevertheless, their comments might serve to illustrate the superficiality and anti-Islamist preconceptions that mar much of the writing on the subject and should be gotten rid of for the sake of insight. To Richards and Waterbury the lack of a clear-cut Islamic economic theory and programme makes the Islamists prone to pragmatism with regard to economic policies, something they consider to be negative. Yet simultaneously they warn that "every move will be scrutinized for religious rectitude", which is also negative.[58] Damned if you do, damned if you don't.

[57] Alan Richards and John Waterbury, *A Political Economy of the Middle East*, Westview Press, Boulder, CO and Oxford, 1996, pp. 351 ff.
[58] *Ibid*, p. 352.

Furthermore, if it is needless to say that Islamists would lack a "single-minded focus on growth", that is because it is a highly dubious statement at best, and can only spring from an insufficient knowledge of Islamist writings. As this study will show, it is a consistent feature of Islamist discourse on economic questions that economic development is elevated to the level of a *farīḍa*, or religious duty.

Basing themselves on a rather simplistic Smithian idea of "selfish man", Richards and Waterbury criticise Islamists for dreaming up a Utopia that would presuppose a prevalent altruism. Islamists themselves actually put great stress on Islam as a balanced "third way" that acknowledges both individual and collective interests. At the abstract level theirs would seem a more reasonable assessment of human nature than both the myopic collectivism typical of communism and the cynicist image of "Economic Man". It is true of course that Islamist propaganda contains the idealistic contention that banning interest and introducing the *zakāt* system of taxation would end all problems. But Richards and Waterbury put undue focus on such statements, and go on to dismiss any positive role for religious beliefs in inducing the kind of moral behaviour conducive to the functioning of a sustainable market economy. Such an argument would hardly stand up in a careful investigation of the role of various Protestant movements in the development of modern Western European and American society.[59] On the basis of their wrongful assessment of the European experience, the authors pass too lightly over the possibility that Islamist moralising could play a role in economic development.

Lastly Richards and Waterbury's dismissal of Islamist discourse on economic independence as xenophobia can hardly be upheld when one considers for instance the way Islamists appreciate the experience of (non-Muslim) South Korea, which represents a careful mix of protective measures and exposure to the world market as the road to realising economic growth and diversification.

In what sense is the Islamist discourse on economic questions specifically "Islamic"? Anticipating the evidence discussed below, it would appear that Islam enters the discourse in primarily two ways: first as an energising force, mobilising the population to resist the policies of the state and then galvanising it under Islamist leadership to sustain the hardships and strenuous effort inevitably connected to the development process; secondly as providing a moral framework such that the economy is made to serve the strengthening of positive values and does not degenerate into a scramble for profit and material gain.

[59] See for instance Walzer, *The Revolution of the Saints*.

As Ervand Abrahamian has pointed out, with reference to E. P. Thompson, "people do not go out to die simply because the price of bread has gone up a few percentage points, but because their sense of right and wrong, justice and injustice, legitimacy and illegitimacy—in short their moral economy—has been flagrantly violated."[60] Well aware of this, the Islamists seek to build opposition to government policies by portraying them as contradicting the true Islamic principles of economic justice. They lay heavy emphasis on their claim that Islam is the only authority that can legitimise the development effort, and that faith in God is the only force that can mobilise people for the necessary efforts. Indeed it seems likely that for instance the importance of replacing current taxation systems with a state-enforced *zakāt*, would reside mostly in the potential effects of the change in denomination. If one's contribution to society's expenses were considered as *zakāt*, paying would be a religious duty, whereas if it were called a *ḍarība*—a tax—an attempt to avoid paying might not play on one's conscience as much.

This stress on the importance of religious legitimacy is often linked to the question of people's faith in the leadership. It is claimed that people would be willing to sacrifice a lot if they believed in the moral uprightness of their leaders, and the leaders were seen to have a credible strategy for progress. The linkage may take surprising forms, as when 'Abd al-Ḥalīm 'Alam al-Dīn of the Labour Party cited the Caliph 'Umar and Mao Zedong as parallel positive examples.[61]

The Islamists certainly present an interpretation of the social message of Islam conducive to economic advance: development as a collective duty, work as an *'ibāda* and the development effort as a *jihād*. And this is all connected to an image of the life of a devout Muslim as a disciplined, purposeful and untiring use of his or her allotted time for the furtherance of good and the increase of material production.

Yet the centrality of faith is linked to the presentation of the Islamic economic system as one built on moral principles rather than material calculations. So to an extent the Islamic economy as presented by the Islamists in Egypt is a "moral economy". In a sense it belongs to the paradigm that also dominated in Europe before the Enlightenment, when first the Physiocrats, followed by liberal thinkers such as Adam Smith, sought to establish economics as a science along the lines of the natural sciences. Prior to this the idea of a good economy had been argued on moral premises of justice. However, starting with the Physiocrats, the emergent

[60] Ervand Abrahamian, *Radical Islam: The Iranian Mojahedin*, I. B. Tauris, London, 1989, p. 4. Cf. E. P. Thompson, "The Moral Economy of the English Crowd in the 18th Century", *Past and Present*, no. 50, 1971, pp. 78–9.

[61] See pp. 203–4 below.

thinking would treat it from a "neutral, objective" point of view, where observed or deducted results were what counted, not whether the means to achieve them were deemed more or less moral.[62]

The economic thought of the Islamists clearly connects with a moral position. For one thing their agitation against the unjust effects of inflation sometimes recalls what Thompson described as "the moral economy of the English crowd", where the crowd upheld the principle of "just" prices, as embedded in old legislation against that of the "natural" prices resulting from supply and demand, preached by the adherents of the new "objective economic science".[63] For another, the Islamists are eager to dissociate themselves from the idea most explicitly advanced by Marxists, that the principles of economic and social organisation are determined by the level of development of the forces of production. Islamic principles of justice, they maintain, are applicable at all times and under all circumstances. Indeed it is stated that the adoption of Islam as the ideology of the state will *produce* a certain set of social, political and economic relations.

But in discussing the "moral economy" of the Egyptian Islamists, it is important to distinguish between a "weaker" and a "stronger" understanding of the expression. In the weak sense, and here all Islamists would agree, the central point is that only a moral society will gain the strength necessary to bear the hardships that are unavoidable on the road to progress and development. And the only possible basis for a moral society is that its members are bound together in faith in God, and fear of the Judgment to come. In this regard the particular rulings of the *Sharīʻa* on economic matters are important because people think of them as just, so their implementation is necessary in order to create mutual trust within society. This view may be combined with a strong emphasis on the spirit and purpose of the *Sharīʻa*, more than on the letter of either the Scriptures or the classical *fiqh* treatises. In the most general sense, says the Tunisian Islamist leader Rāshid al-Ghannūshī, frequently writing in *al-Shaʻb*, Islam came to liberate mankind and better its conditions. Therefore devout Muslims must above all strive to achieve these goals. In exercising *ijtihād*, one should apply the principles of *istiṣlāḥ, istiḥsān* and the like, that is, in choosing between several possible interpretations of the Koran and Sunna, one must take that option which is seen to be for the public benefit (*maṣlaḥa*).[64] Ideas like this were echoed not only by ʻĀdil Ḥusayn,

[62] See Robert B. Ekelund, jr. and Robert F. Hebert, *A History of Economic Theory and Method*, McGraw-Hill, New York, 1990, pp. 73 ff. for an account of this transition.

[63] E. P. Thompson, "The Moral Economy of the English Crowd", pp. 129 ff.

[64] Rāshid al-Ghannūshī, "The Participation of Islamists in a Non-Islamic Government" in Tamimi (ed.), *Power-sharing Islam?*, pp. 54–5.

but also by 'Abd al-Ḥamīd al-Ghazālī with his emphasis on the identity between *maṣlaḥa* and God's will, and his call for Muslims to adopt all useful methods whatever their origin. Ghazālī's fellow Muslim Brothers Kamāl and Shaḥḥāta at times express similar views. It is no accident that this view tends to combine with a strong emphasis on the idea of society as God's collective deputy on earth and an assertion that "service of the people brings one close to God", as it is sometimes expressed by the Labour Party. Hence this kind of moral economy is "weak" because it allows a compromise with "man-made" economic theory in the sense that in order to choose the most beneficial interpretation one must study, through "modern scientific means", what will be the outcome of the application of a certain injunction. In fact Yūsuf Kamāl and other Islamist writers express a strong belief in economics as an "objective" science that can explain fully how the economic mechanisms work once the choice of social ideology is made.

The idea of "Islamic priorities for investment" clearly falls within the "weak" kind of moral economy. For although it refers back to the texts of classical *fiqh*, and its sequence of *ḍarūriyyāt, ḥājiyyāt* and *taḥsīniyyāt* (cf. p. 106 below), it involves stressing social effects of certain policies rather than the moral nature of the means and methods used. This is obvious in the application of the idea of priorities to criticise technically *ḥalāl* financial institutions for not investing productively, although formally they may be adopting legal Islamic methods of saving and investment. It is even suggested that one of those methods—*murābaḥa*—is no better than *ribā* (cf. p. 94 below). Conversely the positive aspect of "Islamic" banks and investment companies is found more in their ability to draw savings into the circuit of the modern economy through the attraction of running a *ḥalāl* operation, than in the superiority of the Islamic methods in and of themselves.

The "stronger" version of the moral economy insists that every rule and economic means must be moral, and not only judged by its results. Here we must remind ourselves that, at least in theory, the sole criterion for considering a given regulation as moral is its support in the text of the Koran or the *Ḥadīth* collections. Usually along with the textual evidence there goes a rational argument for the superiority of the ruling, but the text is almost always the starting point within this tendency.

Taken as a whole, the modern Islamist discourse is spread out between, and filled with the tensions between, these two positions, the moral economy in its weak and its strong varieties. This study shows mainstream Egyptian Islamists lean heavily towards the weak version, even though traces of the more rigidly scripturalist attitude are often present in Muslim Brother writings.

In either case one main target of the campaign for a moral economy, and a major reason for its gaining support, is the widespread corruption believed to exist at all levels of government. It is a widely held view among people in the Egyptian street that family links and other connections, as well as outright bribery, are used by those in high positions to gain access to subsidised goods for production or speculation, to win favourable contracts, to avoid taxes, to win import licences, to win approvals for investment projects under the Law for Foreign Investment (in order to reap tax benefits) etc. Although there is a variety of views on how best to fight corruption—whether it involves more state intervention or less—the agreement among the Islamists is that its removal is an important and major step in the direction of economic reform. This would restore public confidence in the economic activities of both the private and public sector, indispensable for mobilising savings through the credit system for investment. Furthermore, rooting out the harmful practices of *al-mufsidūn fi al-arḍ*[65] would immediately strengthen the economic performance by doing away with a lot of parasitic squandering of resources.

To increase the legitimacy and moralising appeal of their discourse Islamists often turn to religious vocabulary. ʻĀdil Ḥusayn, for one, likened the IMF and the World Bank to Satan, and stated that although economic reform was urgently needed, it must proceed according to God's commands not those of Satan, and that God's commands must be translated into a long-term strategic programme for development. But this legitimising effort, at least with regard to economic questions, is primarily found in the explicit treatises on an "Islamic economy", and in election programmes and sloganeering. In newspaper debates and especially in the People's Assembly the striking fact is rather the relative paucity of "Islamised vocabulary", especially when one considers how religious references permeate general Egyptian parlance and the fact that more often than not MPs from the government's National Democratic Party would heavily intersperse their speeches to the People's Assembly with Koranic quotations. This lack of "Islam density" in parts of Islamist discourse would seem to support the claim that Islam is important mainly as a provider of an over-arching moral legitimacy to the efforts of the Islamists, not so much as a provider of particular solutions. On the other hand it might point to the business-like attitude of the Islamists in a society where grandiose rhetoric has been the norm.

Yet, as indicated, in the more ideological statements Islamic references are certainly common. Their significance in Islamist economic discourse

[65] "Those that perpetrate corruption in the land", a Koranic expression. See for instance Koran, 38:28.

may be clarified by studying the one point of programmatic substance where a distinct Islamic commandment seems to come into play, namely the prohibition of interest on loans and bank deposits, understood by Islamists to be a form of the *ribā* condemned in the Koran.[66] Indeed Islamists do express the theoretical opinion that once interest is removed most economic and social problems would solve themselves, the parasitic class of rentiers who sap the strength of the economy would disappear and a more dynamic climate would be created in which financial means are channelled into productive purposes rather than purely speculative deals. Nevertheless, the Islamist attitude towards the practical experience of the non-*ribā* Islamic banks and investment companies shows that in real life the formal satisfaction of a Koranic injunction is less important to the Islamists than its supposed beneficial results. True, the Islamists hailed the creation of these banks and investment companies as an important experiment, and defended them against the government onslaught of the late 1980s. Still they remained thoroughly critical of their practices, in particular because the Islamic investment companies did not invest their holdings according to Islamic principles and national interests, but remained concentrated on trade and speculative ventures while the country needed resources for the development of agriculture and industry.

This critical attitude towards purportedly Islamic institutions may serve to illustrate a more general point. Despite all references to Islam as the solution to all ills, it becomes clear that the efforts of the Egyptian Islamists are focussed on the achievement of some vaguely defined, but still identifiable, goals: independence, economic development and, though perhaps to a lesser degree, social justice. The adoption of Islam as the guiding ideology of society and state is presented as a necessary means towards those ends. But the fact that proclamations of adherence to Islam are not what counts most is reflected in the scarcity of references to existing self-proclaimed Islamic institutions and even governments as ideals for emulation. Indeed South Korea was more attractive as a model for economic policy than Islamic Iran.

A lot of effort is put into arguing the superiority of the non-interest system. However, since the fact that the supposed positive result of this system is thought to be increased productive investment and social equality, the whole exercise could be seen as an instance of an Islamic reference employed for the purpose of better propagating an ethic of economic

[66] Of course we might also mention the call for the implementation of the *zakāt* as society's way of securing social welfare (this is made primarily by the Muslim Brothers). But here it is harder to say what, other than the name and the moral force connected to it, would really be different from a non-religious taxation system.

behaviour contributing to the furthering of economic development. Use of the word *ribā* would primarily serve as a symbolic reference adding legitimacy to modernising ideas, rather than as the promotion of a specific timeless content. What counted was the cultural Islamisation of the economic sphere more than a substantial systemic change.

The foregoing discussion leads to the formulation of a number of assumptions regarding the Islamist movement and its economic discourse, assumptions that, having studied the evidence produced by the investigation at hand, we will re-address in the conclusion.

At one level Islamism is a movement of revolt against a perceived Western cultural domination. It could well be seen as a continuation of nationalist aspirations for freedom and development, but it is distinguished by its emphasis on cultural independence, considered necessary to buttress the fight for political and economic independence. In a sense Islamism represents a symbolic revolution, that is, an endeavour to replace the dominance of Western models and references in political discourse with a counter-system based on the history, intellectual tradition and religious beliefs of the Islamic world. In this the target of attack is not only Western influence, but—just as important—the entrenched power of the Western-oriented local élite groups.

At another level Islamism is a reaction to the socially disruptive effects of modernising change. Islamists are not opposed to modernity: they are eager to achieve the benefits of modern economic and technological developments for their countries. What they seek is to impose a moral cohesion on a modernising society. In the process they foster a novel understanding of Islam in the form of norms and practices that can be seen to promote economic, social and political modernisation.

The growth of membership and of popular support for Islamist movements, and their increasing activism, is connected to an oppositional mood spurred on by widespread misery and a widening gap between rich and poor. But Islamism, rather than being a "movement of the disinherited", most centrally expresses the growing assertiveness of an aspiring alternative élite of upwardly mobile educated groups originating from the lower middle classes and raised in a religious environment.

2

A COUNTRY STUCK IN LIMBO

THE ECONOMIC AND POLITICAL ENVIRONMENT AND THE GROWTH OF ISLAMISM

The Egyptian economy: infitāḥ *and permanent crisis*

The political climate in which the Egyptian Islamists presented their economic views during the late 1980s was one in which almost every field of society appeared to be in crisis. The public discussion has been aptly described by one observer as "azmatology", from the Arabic word for crisis, *azma*.[1] There was talk of an *azma* of housing, one of energy, of water, of the economy, a moral *azma*, a social *azma*, a population *azma* and so on. The expression "permanent crisis"—strictly speaking a contradiction in terms—catches precisely the general mood in Egypt, where "the economic crisis" became the general term for "the economy".

A feeling that social and economic conditions were rapidly deteriorating was evident. Many linked the decline to Sadat's so-called "opening-up" of the economy initiated in the mid-1970s. There was also an acute awareness, especially among the intellectual participants in the public debate, of a perceived parallel with fateful events shaping the 19th century economic and political destiny of the country. From 1805 to 1840 Egypt, under its Ottoman governor Muḥammad 'Alī, became a regional great power in the Middle East. The French occupation of Egypt (1798–1801) had taught Muḥammad 'Alī that the precondition for building a strong, independent state in the 19th century was a modern economy. His military expansion was built on thoroughgoing economic reforms, focused on increasing state revenue and state control of the economy. A dramatic attempt was even made to introduce modern machine-driven factory industry into the country. However, the whole system was rapidly dismantled after Britain in 1840, through military threats, forced Muḥammad

[1] Muhammed Guessous interviewed by Kevin Dwyer in Kevin Dwyer, *Arab Voices: The Human Rights Debate in the Middle East*, University of California Press, 1991, p. 15.

'Alī to accept the British-Ottoman free trade agreement of 1838. The monopolies and thereby state control of the economy and the protection against foreign competition had to go. Within a few years there were no modern factories left, and except for some sugar refineries modern industry all but disappeared from the country until well after the First World War.

Consequently the Egyptian economy developed in the typical mode of a Third World monoculture. Up to a quarter of the cropped area was planted with cotton,[2] and the produce exported raw to the cotton factories of Lancashire. As late as 1950 raw cotton accounted for as much as 85 percent of the value of Egyptian exports.[3]

What is more, to finance the building of a modern infrastructure for the cotton economy, the next modernizing autocrat, Muḥammad 'Alī's grandson the Khedive Ismā'īl (1863–79), placed the country in heavy foreign debt. This resulted first in the 1870s in the country's economy being placed under administration of representatives of the European debtors, organised in the so-called *Caisse de la Dette Publique*, whose inspectors were the real leaders of the government ministries. Then in 1882, following a national uprising under Colonel 'Urābī to challenge foreign control, the country was occupied by Britain who systematically channelled its resources into paying the debt.

Eighty-five years later another radical development project, that of the Nasser regime, was abruptly ended by defeat in the June 1967 war with Israel. The war caused huge economic losses and the defeat weakened popular confidence in the government although Nasser stayed on as president until his death in 1970. Nasser's successor, Anwar al-Sādāt (Sadat), made a break with the recent past on several counts, and in 1974 he officially launched "the economic opening"—*al-infitāḥ al-iqtiṣādī*—in 1974. In a couple of years the socialist-nationalist framework in which the economy had functioned was overturned, at least in principle. Most publicity was accorded the new law of foreign investment, Law No. 43 of 1974, although judging by its results it is debatable to what extent this was the most important part of the *infitāḥ*. This law gave a number of incentives, such as tax privileges, exemptions from labour laws and guarantees against expropriation, to foreign investors[4], but with little consequence.

[2] Charles Issawi, *An Economic History of the Middle East and North Africa*, Columbia University Press, 1982, p. 120.

[3] John Waterbury, *The Egypt of Nasser and Sadat*, Princeton University Press, 1983, p. 30.

[4] Composed at the start of the post-1973 oil boom, the law distinguished between "foreign" and "Arab" investment. Eager to attract Gulf capital the law makers under the banner of "Arab integration" gave special privileges to Arab capital in some sectors of investment, like housing.

At the same time the import regime was drastically liberalised and the country was flooded with hitherto inaccessible foreign goods. Exports stood more or less still, and a heavy payment crisis and increasing debts resulted. In 1975–6, seeking to be bailed out of the crisis, the government found itself knocking desperately at the door of the International Monetary Fund (IMF).[5]

The 1980s: lost opportunities

In contrast to this gloomy image, international statistics for the period 1974–85 show Egypt with a high yearly growth in GDP. According to World Bank data, adjusted for inflation, the average real growth rate during this time span was just below 10 percent a year, with growth ranging between 5 and 15 percent in individual years.[6] However, this was almost entirely due to an increase in the income from oil exports and from certain service sectors directly dependent on the oil boom of the period and did not reflect any significant growth in other commodity-producing sectors.

Nevertheless the first eleven years of the *infitāḥ* was certainly a period of growth in some senses, and of increased wealth for quite a number of Egyptians in more than one layer of society. Liberalisation resulted in a tremendous trade boom. The handling of foreign trade was still a prerogative of Egyptian companies, but was privatised.[7] An enormous number of so-called import-export companies grew up almost overnight. Their business was mainly import, since the export of Egyptian goods, with the important exception of oil, almost stood still in the period.

In this time of feverishly-growing consumerism amongst the middle and upper middle classes, who under the old economic regime had been starved of an outlet for their purchasing-power, the import business gave rapid returns resulting in fresh wealth for many people from modest backgrounds with the initiative to exploit it. The possibilities for speculative dealings in internal trade were also great since so much of the old system remained, which meant that those able to secure stocks of subsidised goods, meant for industry or public stores, could earn large profits by selling on the open market. Since securing subsidised goods was greatly facilitated by having family or other close contacts within the public sector administration, this became a field of widespread corruption.

[5] Waterbury, *The Egypt of Nasser and Sadat*, p. 407.

[6] Heba Handoussa and Gillian Potter (eds), *Employment and Structural Adjustment: Egypt in the 1990s*, AUC Press, Cairo, 1991, p. 128, table 38.

[7] Malak Zaalouk, *Power, Class and Foreign Capital in Egypt*, Zed Books, London, 1989, pp. 119–20.

The commercial representation of foreign firms interested in operating in Egypt was also lucrative. Many from the old capitalist class, that had seen their businesses nationalised in the early 1960s, made a comeback via this avenue.[8] Corruption was rampant in this field too since so much depended on securing contracts for one's client through connections in the state apparatus. A case in point was foreign investment. To get their projects for joint ventures with Egyptian companies approved, foreign investors had to pass through a complicated bureaucratic procedure ending in the General Authority for Foreign Investment established by Law 43. Judging from the results it seems that whether the proposed project would be of service to the national economy or not was no more important in influencing the decision of those responsible for approving the project than their private interests. Centrally-placed persons might be bribed into giving their approval, or they might refuse because the proposed project could create heavy competition for a company in which they, their family, friends or colleagues had interests.[9] In any case the process of approval proceeded rather haphazardly. Some applications might not be considered for years, while at other times approvals were rushed through, as on 27 March 1977 when 'Abd al-Razzāq 'Abd al-Magīd, then head of the Investment Authority, railroaded through the approval of 102 projects in five hours.[10]

In any case there was not, as had been hoped, a concentration of foreign investment in sectors of industry stimulating technological development or in projects aimed at exporting industrial goods. Well over half the investment made under Law 43 was concentrated in the service sector, trade, tourism and banking,[11] and to the extent that it went to industry, its aim was to exploit the Egyptian market, not to export. In a number of cases, joint ventures with foreign investors were even given a monopoly over the production of certain products in the Egyptian market. Since imports were liberalised at the same time, thereby removing the dominant incentive for outsiders to invest in local production, total investment in industry was small, and that went to sectors where import was still regulated and tended to contribute little to technological development. Very often existing equipment was taken over by the joint venture as the contribution of the Egyptian partner to the shareholders' capital of the new company, and was seriously undervalued. The foreign contribution

[8] For a thorough treatment of this, see *ibid.*, pp. 129 ff.

[9] See *ibid.*, pp. 6–11, for an account of a famous example, the 'Āmiriyya textile project near Alexandria. Springborg, *Mubarak's Egypt*, pp. 83 ff. has an interesting discussion of the way creation of joint ventures was used to translate public capital into private wealth.

[10] Waterbury, *The Egypt of Nasser and Sadat*, p. 146.

[11] Utvik, *Kva kom inn den opne døra? Industrien i Egypt under Sadats nye økonomiske politikk. 1970–83* [What Came in the Open Door? Egyptian Industry under Sadat's New Economic Policy 1970–83], University of Oslo, 1990, p. 92.

remained, on average, at 30 to 40 percent. Where new production was introduced it was often merely the assembly of imported parts, as in most of the automotive industry, and in any case technological know-how was heavily guarded against Egyptian take-over by patent regulations and the like.[12]

With regards to the structure of Egyptian industry a long-time goal, in accordance with the import substitution industrialisation (ISI) strategy followed more or less since the 1930s, had been to increase the weight of those sectors producing intermediate and capital goods in relation to those producing consumer goods. In the ISI strategy the relative weight of the former branches is taken to indicate the degree of development of an independent technological basis for industrial production. A country heavily dependent on importing machinery and intermediate products for its industry remains economically and politically vulnerable. Building a local capability for producing and innovating capital goods, above all machinery, is considered the *sine qua non* of developing an independent industrial economy and thus making real political independence possible.

During the first years of the *infitāḥ* policy, there seemed to be a certain change taking place in the structure of Egyptian industry.[13] In the fiscal year 1980/81 the two traditionally dominant branches of light industry—textiles and food—accounted for more than 60 percent of industrial production. This was still a reduction of almost ten percentage points from the situation ten years earlier. And, as prescribed by the strategy, there was an increase in the relative weight of intermediate goods and capital goods. For intermediate goods this was mostly either the fruit of large-scale projects begun under Nasser, like the aluminium factory in Nag' Ḥammādī, or the resumption of full production as the currency constraints of the late 1960s were eased. However, the considerable increase in the production of capital goods, albeit from a low starting point, shown in most statistics is misleading. This is because the bulk of the apparent growth in the "capital goods sector" is accounted for by the production of durable consumer goods like cars, televisions and refrigerators. So from the point of view of the real capacity of local industry to supply the country with

[12] On this point see two articles by Muḥammad 'Abd al-Shafī' 'Īsā, "Al-taṭawwur al-tiknulūjī wa istrātījīyat al-i'timād 'alā al-dhāt fī al-tajriba al-ṣinā'iyya al-miṣriyya 1970–1980" [Technological Development and the Strategy of Relying on Oneself in the Egyptian Industrial Endeavour 1970–80], *Al-fikr al-istrātījī al-'arabī*, April 1982 and "Al-tiknulūjīya al-ṣinā'iyya al-miṣriyya fi al-thamānīniyyat—wāqi'uhā al-ḥālī wa āfāq taṭawwuriha" [The Egyptian Industrial Technology of the 1980s: Its Present State and the Horizons for its Development], *Al-fikr al-istrātījī al-'arabī*, October 1986.

[13] See Ṣabrī Aḥmad Abū Zayd, "Al-taḥawwulāt al-haykaliyya fī al-ṣinā'a al-taḥwīliyya fī miṣr 1959/60–1980/81" [Structural Changes in Egyptian Manufacturing Industries 1959/60–1980/1], *L'Egypte Contemporaine/Misr al-mu'āṣira*, no. 403, January 1986, p. 35.

equipment for production, this growth has no real significance, the more so since the sector is dominantly concerned with the assembly of imported parts

Furthermore foreign investments did not contribute in any significant way to increased industrial exports,[14] and foreign banks were channelling more Egyptian savings abroad than drawing fresh funds into the country. Indeed, the capital held by Egyptian citizens in banks outside Egypt, though variously estimated, was often claimed to be substantially larger than the country's enormous foreign debts. It is therefore, very doubtful that the *infitāḥ*, in the sense of attracting foreign capital, made a net positive contribution to ameliorating the shortage of foreign exchange.[15]

Nevertheless the period from 1975 to 1985 afforded Egypt extraordinary access to foreign exchange. Four sources were available which reduced the deficit in the current account to bearable levels, and on occasion even produced a small surplus.

The largest one, and the only one that could be directly linked to one aspect of the *infitāḥ*, was the remittances from Egyptians working abroad. Under Nasser strict limits had been put on the export of labour. Now the gates were opened wide, and the enormous increase in the wealth of the Arab oil producers—due to increased oil prices—in the Gulf and Libya, where labour was scarce, created a tremendous pull. In the period up to 1985 more than three million people—a prudent estimate—had found work abroad at one time or another. In 1987 the Central Agency for Public Mobilisation and Statistics (CAPMAS) reported that 2 million Egyptians were abroad, of which 90 percent were workers.[16] In the first ten years of the *infitāḥ* the income from migrant labour may have affected directly up to one quarter of all Egyptian households.

To many people it meant a marked increase in living standards. It also made for social turbulence, not least in rural areas, where the traditional leading families of a village would often be overtaken, in terms of wealth, by families of lower standing enjoying income from members working in the Gulf or Libya. However, this source of income did not greatly benefit the national economy. Generally it was spent on imported luxury items and on housing. Only to a limited degree did it find its way, either directly or indirectly, into productive investment, with the possible partial exception of the efforts of some of the so-called "Islamic investment companies" (discussed below, pp. 203 ff.).

[14] In 1982 the joint ventures involving foreign capital exported industrial products worth 18 million LE, while they imported capital and intermediate goods to the tune of 300 million LE. See Utvik, *Kva kom inn den opne døra?*, p. 175.

[15] For a more detailed discussion see *ibid.*, pp. 175 and 185–6.

[16] Nader Fergany, "A Characterisation of the Employment Problem in Egypt" in Handoussa and Potter (eds), *Employment and Structural Adjustment*, pp. 40–1.

Another major source of foreign exchange was oil exports. Although oil continued to be sold at subsidised prices on the local market, a subject of intense criticism from the IMF, the latter half of the 1970s saw Egypt establish itself as a medium-sized oil exporter. New oil and gas fields were opened in the Western desert and off the Delta coast, exploration activity picked up in the Red Sea and Gulf of Suez regions, and as control was regained over the Sinai so was income from the oil fields there.

The two other important hard currency earners were tourism and the Suez Canal, after its reopening in 1975. Between them the "big four" provided Egypt with 75 percent of its inflow of hard currency in 1981/82, decreasing, as a result of falling oil prices, to around 60 percent at the end of the decade.[17]

The important thing to notice is the vulnerability of these sources. Together they far outweighed all other providers of foreign currency. After the signing of peace accords with Israel in 1979 Egypt started receiving economic aid from the United States to the tune of 2 billion dollars a year, yet only the "big 4" ensured the balance of payment was not a complete disaster. However, they were all tightly linked to a single factor—the price of oil. Expatriate workers overwhelmingly worked in the oil countries, whether they were engineers, skilled or unskilled manual workers, teachers or farmers filling the gap after Iraqi peasants had been sent to the front in the 1980–8 war with Iran. Between 40 and 50 percent of tourist nights spent in Egypt in the early 1980s were spent by Arabs,[18] typically arriving from the Gulf countries to celebrate *Ramaḍān* in the somewhat laxer atmosphere of Cairo compared to the austere public night life of their own countries. And finally much of the traffic through the Suez Canal was either oil coming from, or Western goods going to, the Gulf, either directly or by way of Jordan.

When the oil price fell in 1985/86 there was a drastic fall in revenue from all the "big four".[19] And the golden years of hard currency flows had not been used to secure a productive base able to penetrate foreign markets with a broader range of products. GDP growth fell from 7.4 percent in 1984/85 to 4.2 percent in 1986/87 and to 2.1 percent in 1990/91.[20] The debt burden soared. By the time of the Gulf War Egypt had the largest

[17] Galāl Amīn, *Ma'ḍalat al-iqtiṣād al-miṣrī* [The Dilemma of the Egyptian Economy], Miṣr al-'arabiyya lil-nashr wal-tawzī', Cairo, 1994, p. 103.

[18] Central Agency for Public Mobilization and Statistics (CAPMAS), *Statistical Yearbook: Arab Republic of Egypt 1952–85*, Cairo, 1986, pp. 212–13.

[19] They fell by 30 percent from 1983/4 to 1986/7 before gradually picking up again (but still in 1989/90 the figure remained well below that of 1983/4). See Galāl Amīn, [The Dilemma of the Egyptian Economy], pp. 102–3.

[20] Heba Handoussa, *Egypt's Structural Adjustment Program and Prospects for Recovery*, report prepared for the Institute of Developing Economies, Tokyo, March 1993, p. 40.

foreign debt per inhabitant of any country in the world. It was back to square one, and to protracted negotiations with the IMF and Western creditors over a rescheduling of the debt. This process in reality only ended in 1991 with the new agreements concluded with the IMF in May and the World Bank in November of that year,[21] in which the government undertook a vigorous structural adjustment programme in line with Bretton-Woods orthodoxy. As part of the settlement, and sweetening the pill somewhat, half the foreign debt was written off.[22] This was commonly understood to be a reward for Egypt's participation in the war against Ṣaddām Ḥusayn.

One of the early results of the reform process, following a first agreement with the IMF in 1987, was the official devaluation and subsequent floating of the Egyptian pound (LE). Whatever the economic reasons for this, it meant giving up the principle that in a weak economy like that of Egypt the state needs to control the use of a limited strategic resource such as hard currency. In the same vein the IMF continued to press for a final abolition of the state policy of fixing prices for strategically important goods.

The post-1986 crisis accentuated problems that had been brewing during the whole *infitāḥ* period. When Mubarak took over as president in late 1981 it was officially recognised that the *infitāḥ* had been tilted in favour of non-productive sectors of the economy; trade and finance, with a fair amount of shady or purely speculative dealings. The new president called for a *productive infitāḥ*, but with seemingly little result, although the scandals involving corruption and speculation, which had been rampant under Sadat, became fewer for a time. Publicly-owned industry, which continued to account for 70 percent of industrial production was stagnant, with little or no investment being made. Industrial growth rates were falling and commodity exports other than oil remained very limited.

Agriculture had been stagnant for some time. In the four years from 1980 to 1984 the production of major food crops hardly grew at all,[23] while the population grew by 2.5 percent per year. The importation of food stuffs took an ever increasing share of the scarce currency resources.

[21] See Hans Löfgren, "Egypt's Program for Stabilization and Structural Adjustment: An Assessment" in *The Economics and Politics of Structural Adjustment in Egypt*, Cairo Papers in Social Science, vol. 16, no. 3, AUC Press, Cairo, 1993.

[22] The write-off was only to take effect in "instalments" over several years, subject to Egypt's compliance with IMF policy. See Louis Blin, "Un trimestre d'informations economiques", *Egypte-Monde Arabe*, no. 6, 1991, pp. 248–50. Cf. by the same author "Le renouvellement de l'accord entre l'Egypte et le Fonds Monétaire International et ses conséquences", *Egypte-Monde Arabe*, no. 15–16, pp. 300–1.

[23] CAPMAS, *Statistical Yearbook*, pp. 45–8.

Under these circumstances agriculture was less and less able to offer meaningful employment to the growing number of young people leaving school. Since such industrial activity as existed remained heavily concentrated in the regions of Greater Cairo and Alexandria,[24] as did to a large extent the jobs offered by the overstaffed bureaucracy, population congestion increased around these and other urban centres.

It is a widely held view among economists that the extraordinary foreign currency earnings of the first *infitāḥ* decade (which had little to do with the *infitāḥ*) were actually a cause of the stagnation in the productive sectors. The argument is that the inflow of currency, augmented by foreign aid, led to a real appreciation of the exchange rate, which resulted in a misallocation of investment, with a bias in favour of infrastructure and other service sectors.[25]

At least for a time a significant portion of the population had been able, through the *infitāḥ*, to improve their material standard of living. Some grew rich through involvement in more or less legal and more or less speculative trade; some through exploiting their position in the state apparatus or public sector. The living standards of millions of families improved through members working abroad. Average life expectancy rose and child mortality dropped, an indication not least of a rising per capita nutritional level. But large and important groups were falling behind. The gap between rich and poor increased. But the social malaise also grew because groups traditionally enjoying a respected status saw themselves sink into poverty while others of a traditionally lower standing grew rich. This situation was not confined to rural areas, where poor families of migrant workers overtook the old "*a ʿyān*" (notables). Similar changes were taking place in the cities, where migrant work and ingenious business initiatives lifted some out of poverty, while the modern-day *afandīya*, the amorphous class of educated people, mostly working as civil servants, was experiencing a rapid decline in both status and relative living standards.[26]

Since Nasser's day the state had guaranteed work for all university graduates. With the enormous increase in the student population in a period of economic stagnation, this guarantee became a real headache for the government. Without the expansion in industry and private service needed to give these graduates employment commensurate with their

24 Utvik, *Kva kom inn den opne døra?*, p. 159.

25 See for instance Heba Handoussa, "Crisis and Challenge: Prospects for the 1990s" in Handoussa and Potter (eds), *Employment and Structural Adjustment*, pp. 3–4.

26 After the fall in the oil price in 1985/6 the real value of government and public sector wages and salaries went into steep decline. See Heba Handoussa, "The Role of the State: The Case of Egypt", paper presented at First Annual Conference on Development Economics, Cairo, June 1993, table A7.

qualifications, the only option was to squeeze them into the state apparatus, and the public sector, both already vastly overstaffed. When through the 1980s the problem only grew it was "solved" by delaying more and more the appointment of new graduates, so that by 1987 the average waiting period had become 5–6 years, up from 2–3 years in 1973.[27]

The regime's populist employment policies obviously had a suffocating effect on bureaucratic efficiency and contributed to excessive production costs in public sector companies. The employment guarantee, by making higher theoretical education more attractive, also diverted resources and recruits away from vocational training. Thus it exacerbated the lack of skilled labour for the productive sectors of the economy. There was also a drastic decline in the quality of higher education: universities were overcrowded and although education was in principle free, there was a severe shortage of almost everything; books, library space for study, teachers. And those who finally managed to graduate and find employment would end up with totally inadequate pay. It was estimated in 1991 by the economic weekly *al-Ahrām al-iqtiṣādī* that a family of five needed 280 LE a month to live on as a bare minimum.[28] At the same time the salary of a newly graduated doctor or lawyer in public service was less than half this amount, with the situation even worse further down the educational ladder. This explains why many held two to three jobs and why it was not unusual to find oneself discussing the Egyptian economy with a Cairo cab driver holding a Masters degree in economics. Such moonlighting of course compounded the problem of inefficiency in the public service.

The low salaries came about because increases in the revenue of the state had failed to keep step with either the inflation that followed the *infitāḥ*[29] or the growth of the population—a reflection of low productivity in the economy, but also of a low level of taxation.

There are two important and interrelated aspects of the problems connected to the employment guarantee that contributed to the undermining of social stability. The first has already been touched upon and relates to the class of public servants, the *afandīya*, who in the pre-Nasser era were a self-conscious group enjoying relatively high status and a living standard higher than the working population at large. To a certain extent this situation continued into the Nasser era, when the morale of the group was also boosted by their being seen as the privileged agents of the socialist

[27] Bent Hansen, *The Political Economy of Poverty, Equity and Growth: Egypt and Turkey*, The World Bank/Oxford University Press, 1991, p. 181.

[28] 'Iṣām Rif'at, "Al-ujūr al-khafīya wa takālīf al-ḥayāt", *al-Ahrām al-Iqtiṣādī*, no. 1191, 11 November 1991.

[29] Throughout the 1980s inflation remained on average close to 20 percent per year. See Handoussa, *Egypt's Structural Adjustment Program*, p. 40.

modernisation of Egyptian society. However, entering the period of *infitāḥ*, their feeling of purpose was largely eroded and the group saw itself falling steadily deeper into poverty, while resentment towards the newly-rich and the government that had failed them increased.

Secondly, the demise of the *afandīya* is connected to that of the Third World variant of the welfare state built up under Nasser. Providing a minimum of welfare—cheap food, clothing and housing, free education and health care—was the political cement securing the support, albeit tacit, of the broad masses. The Sadat and Mubarak administrations, though somewhat ideologically removed from Nasser, were nevertheless the direct heirs to the Free Officer revolution of 1952. Apart from Sadat's brief honeymoon with public opinion after the October War of 1973, neither had other major sources of legitimacy to compensate for that of Nasser, not least since their nationalist credentials had been largely eroded by the peace agreement with Israel and the close alliance with the United States.

But in the late-1980s public poverty was day by day undermining what was left of these populist policies. Education deteriorated and to compensate for the lack of learning in overcrowded and understaffed schools and universities, those who could afford it now spent large sums on private tutors for their children. The free health care became an even more morbid joke. The press was full of stories of patients having to bring their own medicine and equipment in order to get any kind of treatment in public hospitals and health stations. The remuneration for work in the public sector and government was exceedingly low. And the subsidies for food, clothes and fuel, though still important, were gradually being eroded under heavy pressure from the IMF, dropping from 12.5 percent of the government budget in 1985 to 6.3 percent in 1988.[30]

An example of the complexity of the problems involved is provided by the issue of landlord-tenant relationships, which remained unsolved throughout the period under study. An important aspect of the land reforms under Nasser was a strict regulation of rents to be paid to landowners by peasant tenants. This was an attempt to ameliorate the conditions of those millions still dependent on renting farmland even after the (rather moderate) redistribution of land that was part of the reforms. A similar reform fixed rents for housing in the cities. Despite protests the system functioned as long as commodity prices were fairly stable. But with the deregulations associated with the *infitāḥ* prices rose rapidly. Since the regulations prohibited raising rents for land and building space, serious imbalances developed. Tenants who had secured a contract in the 1950s were able to sublet for up to a hundred times the rent paid to the

[30] *Ibid.*, p. 58.

owner. The owners of urban houses would in many cases receive totally insignificant sums from the tenants. The results were several; older buildings with tenancy contracts from Nasser's day fell into decay, and the owners of newer buildings tried to keep as many apartments as possible on short-term contracts so they could raise the rents at each turnover. With high-standard apartments in particular, owners aimed at the lucrative market of renting to foreigners. Another solution was to sell the apartments at exorbitant prices. Consequently, for large sections of the population entering the market for new apartments became impossible, increasing the already pressing problems of young people unable to afford marriage costs, a sensitive issue that added much to popular dissatisfaction.

The landlord-tenant impasse in some ways relates to one major question that might be asked about the dismal performance of the Egyptian economy during the first fifteen years of "opening up": To what extent should the problems be blamed on the liberalisation of economic policies, and to what extent should they be blamed on the liberalisation not going far enough?

Throughout the period under discussion many levers for directing economic life remained in the hands of the huge state and public sector apparatus. The dominant parts of industrial concerns were still state-owned, even though some of them, having entered into joint ventures with foreign capital, were exempt from public sector regulations. The reform of the remaining public companies, which were the majority, went very slowly. Just like in similar reform processes elsewhere, there was in Egypt fierce resistance both from trade unions and not least from vested management interests against exposing the public industrial sector to the full force of free market, not to say international, competition. Besides possibly endangering the privileged position of the managerial strata, it was feared that the envisaged market might create a huge unemployment problem, and rock the existing relative, albeit heavily policed, social peace. So both security considerations and pressure from sector interests made the state drag their feet in implementing the reforms foreseen in the *infitāḥ* programme and promised in the "Declarations of intent" signed with the IMF.[31]

Security concerns may have slowed down reform in other ways. Government involvement in and regulation of economic life was seen as facilitating social control in two ways. One was by securing the most rudimentary of people's basic needs, or at least by not allowing a too rapid deterioration of conditions and avoiding direct starvation among the poor.

[31] See Hans Löfgren, "Economic Policy in Egypt: Breakdown in Reform Resistance?", *IJMES*, 25, 1993, pp. 407–21.

The price riots of 1977, that arose when the government had tried to raise prices on some basic items of consumption, were a lasting memory that sent shivers down the spine of the establishment well into the 1980s. Later reduction of subsidies progressed very slowly and were conducted circumspectly, by for instance reducing the size of *righīf al-'aysh*, the round flat bread constituting the central element of the popular diet, instead of increasing the price. Throughout the 1980s consumer subsidies continued to cost the state huge sums, albeit laying claim to a decreasing percentage of the government budget. The government also continued to subsidise publicly-owned industries, though this practice was scaled down in the latter half of the decade. These subsidies were also partly related to the issue of social peace, since bakeries and textile factories, receiving subsidised wheat and cotton respectively, were obliged to produce a certain quantity of cheap goods for popular consumption.

However, there is another side to the social control implicit in state domination of the economy. When the state controls people's livelihood, it is fairly easy to apply heavy sanctions against those seen to represent, by their social or political actions, a threat to state interest. This goes for those directly employed by the state or the public sector, but in Egypt also applies to most of the rural population, since the so-called cooperatives that control the supply of fertiliser, seed and sometimes mechanised equipment are in reality state agencies. Not least important in this regard is the authorities' control of the irrigation system, the *sine qua non* of most of Egyptian agriculture. The opposition media have told stories of villages where the majority in an election have voted against the government candidates and lived to regret it.[32] No doubt considerations of preserving this kind of control may have put a brake on government zeal for economic liberalisation.[33]

Why has Egypt to such a large extent been *allowed* to retain important elements of its old state-directed system without losing favour with Western creditors? No doubt part of the answer is that Egypt is valued as a major strategic ally of the United States and along with Israel the linchpin of its entire Middle Eastern strategy, and has therefore been granted more latitude in this regard than most other countries in the Third World. The threat of losing Egypt to Islamism or a revived Nasserism has caused nervous Washington decision makers to allow Egypt to procrastinate time and again on the implementation of declarations of intent *vis-à-vis* the IMF and the World Bank.

[32] Springborg, *Mubarak's Egypt*, pp. 189–90. See also Hanaa Fikry Singer, *The Socialist Labor Party: A Case Study of a Contemporary Egyptian Opposition Party*, Cairo Papers in Social Science, vol. 16, no. 1, AUC Press, Cairo, 1993, p. 44.

[33] Cf. Waterbury, *The Egypt of Nasser and Sadat*, p. 377.

Furthermore the liberalisation of labour migration combined with other factors enabled Egypt to reap considerable benefits from the oil boom of the late 1970s and early 1980s, which meant the country's financial situation for a period was relatively comfortable, placing the Egyptian government in a strong position *vis-à-vis* external pressure. The fall in the oil price after 1986 created big problems. But in 1990 the country was again able to profit from its strategic position and exact a large debt write-off as a reward for its participation in the US-led anti-Iraq campaign during the Kuwait crisis. Nevertheless, its position was so precarious that there was no escape from agreeing to a more serious commitment to, and foreign control of, carrying out structural adjustment as envisaged by the Bretton-Woods "twins" as preconditions for the actual implementation of a phased write-off.

Retaining state control over the economy also implied retaining the huge bureaucracy meant to supervise and direct economic life. The major reform idea was to place more responsibility with the individual units. The General Organisations hitherto charged with the direction of the productive units had been dissolved in 1975. However, they were not replaced with a real decentralisation, but with a more confused state of responsibility with new struggles emerging between different levels and sections of the public apparatus as to where different decisions should properly be made. This added to the already manifest paralysis of the public sector of the economy.[34] And it was combined with the fact that while the public sector industry had been the dynamic hero of development under Nasser, hailed in songs by the national tenor 'Abd al-Ḥalīm Ḥāfiẓ, its role was now less than clear, something which made long-term planning difficult.

By the 1980s the country's economic development seemed clearly to have reached an impasse. The ruling class created by the Nasserist statist policies, in alliance with remnants of the former capitalist classes, used the *infitāḥ* to enhance the opportunity for turning public capital into private profits. A comprehensive analysis of the pros and cons for the country of thoroughly liberalising the economy was hardly the basis of the change in policy made by the dominant groups. Furthermore there was no clear-cut strategy for how the national economy should be made to develop through the reforms, and those in power never harboured any serious intention of giving up their monopoly of political control.

It might be said that for the country the outcome was the worst of two worlds. From the old socialist system it inherited an inefficient production

[34] Ali E. Hillal Dessouki, "The Public Sector in Egypt: Organisation, Evolution and Strategies of Reform" in Handoussa and Potter (eds), *Employment and Structural Adjustment*, pp. 262 ff.

apparatus and bureaucracy, lacking any capacity for dynamism and initiative and no longer inspired by the Nasserist development strategy. From free-trade capitalism there came a fierce competition from foreign goods and a rapid increase in social tensions. A few grew fabulously rich. A 1983 list of new millionaires typically includes owners of buildings of an area of 1500 m^2 or more, and over thirty apartments, owners of import/export offices, owners of transport companies employing more than ten cars, owners of supermarkets and shoe stores, car dealers, owners of 50 *faddāns*[35] or more of land, representatives of foreign companies in addition to other minor groups like night-club owners, producers of video films and scrap-iron traders.[36] However, the majority remained poor, and received ever less education and health care.

Nasser's vacant throne

However one chooses to view the pros and cons of the Nasserist experiment, for a long time in the 1950s and 1960s Nasser and the group around him seem clearly to have embodied the hope of a brighter future prevalent among large sections of the Egyptian people. To them his policies meant rebuilding national pride; they meant employment, education and better health; they meant independence and economic development.

Through his *infitāḥ* policies, which increased social inequality, and through his peace with Israel and alliance with the United States, President Sadat and his regime lost the position Nasser once held in the public eye. Mubarak has made no effective effort to regain it.

This change in relationship between the regime and the population is connected to the change in the ruling group's social position from the 1950s to the 1980s. The group of young officers taking power in 1952 shared with both their colleagues in the military and the large numbers of other young educated people, the dream of developing a strong Egyptian state. The fulfilment of this dream would secure an outlet for the energies and abilities of their generation and at the very least create vastly expanded opportunities for employment.

Thirty years later the leaders of this generation and their heirs had become entrenched as the governing layer of a greatly-expanded and empowered state bureaucracy and of a huge and dominant state-controlled public sector within the economy. Many of them had amassed considerable private fortunes. Their interests were now geared more towards the

35 1 *faddān* = approx. 4200 m^2 (close to 1 acre).

36 Omar Saad ad-Din, *The Role of State, Private and Foreign Capital in Law 43 of 1974 Projects*, MA thesis in Political Economy, the American University in Cairo, May 1984, p. 35.

profitable investment of the wealth they controlled. For this a liberalisation of the economy was imperative as long as it did not endanger their economic and political leverage.

Having secured privileged access to the income generated by Egypt's present position within the world economy, the top layers of the regime could hardly be expected to produce any new nationalist fervour for independent development. But for the hundreds of thousands of youths passing through universities in the 1970s and 1980s the goals of Nasserism were still highly relevant, primarily because of the prospect of securing themselves the livelihood they and their families had hoped for in seeking an education. However, the persistent structural weakness of the economy adversely affected the finances of the state and the public sector and thus threatened the future employment of the students and reduced their hope of establishing families.

For the frustrated youth and for the radical opposition in general the historical parallels seemed evident. Not only had Nasser's experiment of independent development been crushed by imperialist aggression, like that of the modernising autocrat Muḥammad ʻAlī 130 years earlier, but by the late 1980s there was an ever-worsening debt crisis. Like the Khedive Ismāʻīl in the 1870s, Sadat and Mubarak were mortgaging the country to the foreigners, and the spectre of the *Caisse de la Dette Publique*[37] haunted the country in the form of the IMF's hardening demands for the economic policies to be followed. Furthermore these policies, while making a few immensely rich, were day by day driving the masses deeper into poverty.[38] Where was the force that could take up the banner of independence, development and justice?

The Islamist movement[39] *in Mubarak's "democracy"*

Parallel to Sadat's "opening" of the economy, there was also a certain liberalisation of political life, signified not least in the (albeit heavily cir-

[37] See above, p. 42.

[38] See for instance Muḥammad Ḥilmī Murād, "Raf' al-as'ār aswa' al-ḥulūl li-mu'ālajat azmat al-ḥukūma", *al-Sha'b*, 15 May 1990.

[39] On the Muslim Brothers up to the 1970s we are relatively well informed. On the period up to 1954 in addition to the classic work of Richard Mitchell, *The Society of Muslim Brothers*, there are informative works by: Brynjar Lia, *The Society of the Muslim Brothers in Egypt: The Rise of an Islamic Mass Movement 1928–1942*, Ithaca Press, Reading, 1998; Ṭāriq al-Bishrī, *Al-ḥaraka al-siyāsiyya fī miṣr 1945–1952* [The Political Movement in Egypt 1945–52], Dār al-shurūq, Beirut and Cairo, 1983; and Olivier Carré and Gérard Michaud, *Les Frères Musulmans 1928–82*, Gallimard/Juillard, Paris, 1983. The last of these also covers the activity and writings of Sayyid Quṭb in the 1960s and the revival of the Brothers in the 1970s, as Gilles Kepel does in his *The Prophet and Pharaoh: Muslim Extremism in Egypt*. On Young Egypt the most important source, in

cumscribed) acceptance of party pluralism for the first time since 1953. After a brief hiatus in Sadat's last years the so-called democratisation process returned in the presidency of Mubarak. In the emerging party scene of the 1980s the striking factor was the revival of the pre-1952 forces. When the heavy lid of the Nasserist police state had been partially lifted all four leading political tendencies of the late-1940s made a comeback. The New Wafd was led by Fu'ād Sirāg al-Dīn, general secretary of the Wafd back in 1952. The Socialist Labour Party was dominated by former members of the Young Egypt movement, with Ibrāhīm Shukrī as President. He had been Vice-President of the Socialist Party of Aḥmad Ḥusayn in the early 1950s and represented it in the last pre-1952 Parliament. And the communists were the dominant trend within the *Tajammu'*, although the Communist Party as such remained illegal (and split into a multitude of factions). The Muslim Brothers were also active, but were not accorded legal status as a political party.

The reasons for this shed light on the limitations of the democratic reforms under Mubarak. One is the party system itself, which is regulated by a law leaving the approval of new parties to a commission dominated by government ministers.[40] This commission has refused to accept the Muslim Brothers' application for party status on the grounds that parties based on a religious platform violate the party law, and would threaten national unity.[41] However, a certain ambiguity in the practice of the law is evident in the Socialist Labour Party's continued acceptance as a legal party despite its adoption of a clear-cut Islamist platform in 1989. However, the commission has interfered time and again in the affairs of the Labour Party and of other parties. Throughout the 1980s the Nasserist tendency was refused party status, although several parties led a semi-legal existence under the label "party under formation" (*ḥizb taḥta al-ta'sīs*). Furthermore although parties were allowed to stand for elections,

---

addition to Bishrī's work, is James P. Jankowski, *Egypt's Young Rebels*, Hoover Institution Press, Stanford, 1975. However with regard to the 1980s most writers have tended to concentrate on the more radical groups. There is valuable information on the Muslim Brothers in a number of works, notably Robert Springborg's *Mubarak's Egypt*, several of the listed articles by Saad Eddin Ibrahim, and Hāla Muṣṭafā, *Al-dawla wal-ḥarakāt al-islāmiyya al-mu'āriḍa bayn al-muhādana wal-muwājaha fī 'ahday al-Sādāt wa Mubārak* [The State and the Oppositional Islamist Movements in the Time of Sadat and Mubarak], Markaz al-Maḥrūsa lil-nashr wal-khidmāt al-ṣuḥufiyya, Cairo, 1995. However, there is no major study undertaken of either of the partners in the Islamic Alliance in the 1980s. Hanaa Fikri Singer, *The Socialist Labor Party: A Case Study of a Contemporary Egyptian Opposition Party*, gives some facts and a (one-sided) account of the Islamisation of the party, but is rather shallow.

40 Springborg, *Mubarak's Egypt*, p. 44.

41 Alain Roussillon, "Entre al-Jihâd et al-Rayyân: Phénoménologie de l'islamisme égyptien", *Maghreb-Machrek*, no. 127, Paris, 1990, p. 27.

the governing National Democratic Party (NDP) always received around 70 percent of the votes, securing a commanding majority in Parliament and local assemblies. Nothing indicated that the NDP were willing to let themselves be voted out of government, and suspicions of electoral fraud remained strong.

In any case, although the People's Assembly had legislative power and the right to control the budget of the government, most political power continued to rest with the president. The president was elected by the People's Assembly, even if the people were given the chance through a referendum to vote yes or no to the one chosen by Parliament. And he appointed the government without reference to Parliament.[42] Emergency laws, in place almost without interruption since 1967 and constantly since the murder of Sadat, restricted political life by giving wide powers to the authorities to act preventively against any person believed to threaten national security. The parties were not at liberty to campaign in the streets,[43] and especially the lid was kept tightly on any opposition activity among peasants and workers.[44] As has been pointed out, control of the economic system was an effective tool for controlling the population. In addition of course the state channelled abundant resources into the work of the NDP and the "national" (in reality NDP partisan) daily newspapers, resources the opposition could never hope to match.

By the late 1980s it was clear that the process of democratisation was not really going anywhere. Rather the draconian emergency measures adopted in the campaign against the radical Islamists threatened to abort it altogether. Despite all these obstacles the limited liberalisation of political life in the 1970s and 1980s resulted in a powerful return of the Islamists as the dominant opposition force. In the 1970s Sadat let the Muslim Brothers out of prison, and he seems to have considered their activity, not least in the universities, as a useful counterweight to that of the Marxist and Nasserist left. It seems that for a time in the campuses the *jamā'āt islāmiyya*[45] received some degree of encouragement, possibly including material support from government circles. The Muslim Brothers were allowed to become active, although the legal status of their organisation

[42] For a detailed treatment of the relation between the president and the parliament see 'Amr Hāshim Rabī', *Adā' majlis al-sha'b al-miṣrī* [The Performance of the Egyptian People's Assembly], Markaz al-dirāsāt al-siyāsiyya wal-istrātījiyya bil-Ahrām, Cairo, 1991, p. 16 ff.

[43] See Gehad Auda, "An uncertain response: the Islamic movement in Egypt" in James Piscatori (ed.), *Islamic Fundamentalisms and the Gulf Crisis*, American Academy of Arts and Sciences, Chicago, 1991, pp. 117–18.

[44] Springborg, *Mubarak's Egypt*, p. 187.

[45] "Islamic societies", see the discussion in chapter 5.

remained at best unclear, and intermittently to publish magazines expressing their views.

The new generation of Islamists: between violence and the Ikhwān[46]

From 1954 to the early-1970s Islamist activism was virtually frozen in Egypt—except inside the prison camps. When Islamic student groups (*jama'āt islāmiyya*) emerged in the universities in the 1970s, they were autonomous and influenced as much by *salafī* thought—that is largely apolitical groups focusing on the emulation of the "founding generation" of Islam—as by the Muslim Brothers. Around 1976–7 a group of leaders started to promote the idea of entering into student politics in order to further the cause of Islam, in the process creating a nationwide network of Islamic groups and speeding up the emergence of an organised Islamist student movement at the national level. They met with large success in the student elections and in 1977 Islamists took over leadership over the student bodies in several of the largest universities.

Thus emerged a new generation of Islamist activists. Events during the 1970s and 1980s forced them to take a clear-cut stance regarding the legitimacy of violence as a means for political and social change.

The term *al-Jamā'a al-Islāmiyya* has come to be synonymous with terrorist violence. This is not the place for a serious treatment of the history of the violent Islamist groups in Egypt—an important, but difficult, task that has yet to be undertaken. But in the late 1970s the term was common for the whole of the Egyptian Islamic student movement. Yet towards the very end of the decade there emerged two distinct tendencies within thestudent movement. The most influential leaders chose to enter the old Muslim Brothers movement, which had reemerged (although still technically illegal) into active work under the leadership of 'Umar al-Tilmisāni. They were followed by a majority of members of the student movement, especially in the universities of Cairo and the Delta region. But a minority, concentrated in universities in Upper Egypt and inspired by the prison writings of Sayyid Qutb, considered the Muslim Brothers' moderate line a capitulation *vis-à-vis* reigning authorities whom they charged with having committed apostasy from Islam. For the radical minority it was legitimate, indeed a duty, to launch an all-out jihad against the current regime, including resorting to military struggle. According to these "Neo-Qutbians" a peaceful campaign would lead nowhere. Later this tendency, which was behind the assassination of Sadat, split in two

[46] A lot of information about the new generation of Islamists can be found in Ṭal'at Rumayḥ, *Al-wasaṭ wal-ikhwān* [The Centre and the Brothers], Markaz Yāfā lil-dirāsāt wal-abḥāth, Cairo, 1997.

again with the largest group retaining the name *al-Jamāʿa al-Islāmiyya* and advocating open agitation and activity alongside military operations directed against the security forces (and later politicians, tourists and Copts), while a smaller group, known as *Tanẓīm al-Jihād*, preferred to focus exclusively on secretive conspiratorial work. In some universities the confrontation between the radicals and the mainstream pro-Muslim Brothers tendency at times deteriorated into violent clashes.

Consequently it is important to notice that a principled stance against the use of violence as a means to attain the desired change was integral to the formation of the young generations of Muslim Brothers as a distinct entity; one of its birth marks. Subsequent events seem to have proven to the moderates the wisdom of their choice; notwithstanding harsh setbacks as a result of government oppression, they have been able to keep the organisation functional and not least to maintain their popular base, in contrast to the jihadists who have been militarily destroyed and politically marginalised. Indeed since 1997 the majority of the established leadership of the armed groups have called for a halt to military activity. Two applications for the establishment of legal political parties were filed—apparently in recognition of the futility of the strategy followed thus far. And in the last years a series of books have appeared containing a thorough reappraisal of strategy in favour of peaceful religious and political work. Although for a long time the state refused to acknowledge these initiatives, in October 2003 300 former militants of the *Jamāʿa* were released from prison, including such prominent leaders as Karam Zuhdi.

As for the majority moderate wing of the student movement, its decision to join the Muslim Brothers Organisation under Tilmisani's leadership was of course important in and of itself, in that, for better or for worse, it linked the new generation directly to the legacy of the *Ikhwān*: its interpretation of the faith, its programmes of spiritual and organisational training, its methods of social and political activity, and network of contacts and funding sources inside and outside Egypt. At the ideological level they became heirs to a tradition that was decidedly more modernist in its interpretation of Islam than the early *salafi* influences to which the student activists had been exposed. On the other hand, compared to that of Ḥasan al-Bannā, the thinking of the aged Muslim Brother leaders in the 1970s and 1980s was decidedly more conservative and dogmatic, and less concerned with the burning social issues of the time. There was also a certain timidity *vis-à-vis* the powers that be—born of the traumatic experience of the prison camps. But on the positive side there was a fund of organisational experience to be tapped.

The young students seem rapidly to have developed a very strong sense of loyalty towards the organisation, while distinguishing themselves as more concerned with social reform and not least with a more impatient wish to achieve comprehensive social and political change.

The way through Parliament: the mainstream Muslim Brothers

When the Muslim Brothers were able to start seriously rebuilding their organisation in the early 1970s, a moderate line came to dominate through the leadership of the man who was recognised as the new Supreme Guide after al-Bannā's successor, Ḥasan al-Huḍaybī, had died in 1973, 'Umar al-Tilmisānī.

Although Sadat never agreed to the formal reconstitution of the Society of Muslim Brothers, he gave them permission to publish the magazine *al-Da'wa*, which came out on a monthly basis from 1976 until it was banned in 1981. The *Da'wa* group, which came to be the basis of a formidable resurrection of the Muslim Brothers in the 1980s, was from the start the expression of the least revolutionary, most reformist, wing of the Islamists. Apart from Tilmisānī, a long-time close collaborator of Huḍaybī, many of the leading figures were in fact people who in the 1950s had been expelled from the society by Huḍaybī for their willingness to compromise with Nasser's regime. In the late 1970s *Al-Da'wa* was dominated on the one hand by a call for the application of the *Sharī'a* and the extolling of Islam as a superior religion and the sole solution to the world's problems, and on the other hand by extensive campaigns against what was seen as the four major enemies of Islam in the modern world. The first among these was World Jewry and the reason was of course primarily the existence of Israel, which had been the first case to engage the Brothers deeply outside of Egypt. In the process *al-Da'wa* also drew freely upon the rich reservoir of European anti-Semitic propaganda. Second in the list of enemies was the Crusade. Christians as such were not portrayed as enemies, but the Crusaders had been able to dominate the Christian world and to move it towards an aggressive anti-Muslim stand. Imperialism in the modern sense was merely one avatar of this age-old enemy. Third came communism with its godless materialist propaganda and fourth secularism, which by undermining the link between faith and government, weakened the Islamic world and opened it to the cultural onslaught of the West.[47]

While carrying a high-strung rhetoric when dealing with the "enemies of Islam" at home and abroad, *al-Da'wa* generally used a milder tone towards the government. When in 1977 Sadat's hand-picked Speaker of Parliament, Ṣūfī Abū Ṭālib, called for the application of the *Sharī'a*, the Brothers' hopes were raised high.[48] And Tilmisānī very clearly spelled out

[47] Kepel, *The Prophet and Pharaoh*, pp. 111 ff.

[48] Waterbury, *The Egypt of Nasser and Sadat*, p. 370. Cf. Kepel, *The Prophet and Pharaoh*, p. 126.

that although the goal of a state ruled by God's commandments would never be given up, the road of the Brothers was not violence or even street demonstrations, but education and "proclamation of the truth".[49]

When Sadat allowed the formation of political platforms within the ruling party, later converted into fully-fledged political parties, the Brothers quickly responded by demanding access to the political arena. However, under both Sadat and Mubarak the Brothers were still denied registration as a political party. Yet in 1984, through an electoral alliance with the New Wafd, nine Brothers were elected to Parliament. They used this platform to raise the issue of the promised application of the *Sharī'a*, thereby placing the issue squarely on the public agenda. Incidentally, the unlikely alliance between the Brothers and their old time secularist opponents caused a lot of internal trouble in the Wafd, and a group around the anti-Islamist writer Farag Fawda broke away and formed a party called the Party of the Future (*Ḥizb al-Mustaqbal*).[50]

During Tilmisānī's time as Supreme Guide the dominant faction to emerge within the Muslim Brothers was that which Springborg labels "the Islamic wing of the *infitāḥ* bourgeoisie". A typical case is Muṣṭafā Mashhūr, leader of the faction and later *murshid 'āmm* (Supreme Guide, 1995–2002[51]). From a wealthy landowning family, he did well in business and finance, while other family members won important positions inside the Sadat regime. Mashhūr also developed close connections with Gulf businesses and with the emerging Islamic financial institutions backed by the Gulf countries. As a result of the strong business element in its composition the Tilmisānī-Mashhūr faction possessed material resources superior to those of other factions. The *murshid* from 1986 to 1995, Abū al-Naṣr, was also considered a member of the faction.[52]

Nevertheless, Mashhūr's dominant faction had weak credibility and legitimacy among the youth. With the economic crisis and thereby fading prospects of future material improvement for the generation of students graduating from the mid-1980s onwards, the need for more radical social criticism seemed obvious, as did the need for more radical action for change. Gradually people with leadership ambitions began to emerge from the generation that formed the student *jama'āt* of the 1970s. While sticking to the legalistic line of the Society, they were impatient at the per-

[49] Kepel, *The Prophet and Pharaoh*, pp. 125–6. Cf. Carré et Michaud, *Les Frères Musulmans 1928–82*, pp. 117–18.

[50] Waḥīd 'Abd al-Majīd, *Al-aḥzāb al-miṣriyya min al-dākhil 1907–1992* [Egyptian Parties from Within 1907–92], Markaz al-Maḥrūsa lil-nashr wal-khidmāt al-ṣuḥufiyya, Cairo, 1993, pp. 240–1. Cf. Springborg, *Mubarak's Egypt*, p. 216.

[51] Upon Mashhūr's death in 2002 the leadership went to Ma'mūn al-Huḍaybī.

[52] Springborg, *Mubarak's Egypt*, pp. 233–234.

ceived inaction of the leaders in the *Maktab al-irshād* ("Guidance Office"), and more vigorous in their attack on the lack of democracy and the prevailing inequitable economic situation. Prominent figures were 'Iṣām al-'Iryān and Mukhtār Nūḥ, both elected to the People's Assembly in 1987, 'Abd al-Mun'im Abū al-Futūḥ, and Abū al-'Alā Māḍī, who in 1996 broke with the Muslim Brothers because of the strife provoked by his attempt to set up a new moderate Islamist party, the *Ḥizb al-Wasaṭ* (Centre Party).[53]

Al-'Iryān, Nūḥ, Abū al-Futūḥ and Māḍī were also prominent in the most significant political gains made by the Brothers in the late 1980s and early 1990s, securing dominant positions in one after the other of the professional syndicates. Al-'Iryān became deputy general secretary of the Medical Doctors' Syndicate after the Islamists won a majority on the Syndicate's board in 1986,[54] and Māḍī served in the equivalent position in the Engineers' Syndicate from 1987 to 1995. After Muslim Brothers had come to dominate the syndicates of the doctors, the engineers, the pharmacists and the university professors, the apex of their influence was reached with the takeover of the Lawyers' Syndicate in its elections in the autumn of 1992. Mukhtār Nūḥ and Sayf al-Islām Ḥasan al-Bannā, son of the martyred founder of the Society of Muslim Brothers, emerged as leading figures on the new board. This shocked the intellectual scene because this syndicate, since its formation in 1912, had always been dominated by radical secularist trends of one shade or another.[55]

One aspect of the work of Islamists in the syndicates was their efforts at ameliorating the conditions of the syndicate members and their families. This helped build a reputation for efficiency and caring, and thereby increased their credibility as an alternative to those in power. It was also related to the broader field of Islamic charities, many apolitical, some more or less loosely related to the Islamist movements, which was built around private mosques. The most famous of these is the mosque-hospital complex of the recanted Marxist Dr Muṣṭafā Maḥmūd in Cairo's Muhandisīn suburb, but there are a host of others, organising health clinics, schools, food for the poor etc., stepping in where services of the state appear to be failing.[56] During the Cairo earthquake in the autumn of 1992

53 On this story see Ṭal'at Rumayḥ, *Al-wasaṭ wal-ikhwān* [The Centre and the Brothers], Markaz Yāfā lil-dirāsāt wal-abḥāth, Cairo, 1997, and Rafīq Ḥabīb, *Awrāq ḥizb al-wasaṭ*, [The Centre Party Papers], n.p., Cairo, 1996.

54 Saad Eddin Ibrahim, "Islamic Activism and Political Opposition in Egypt", paper presented to the seminar on Aspects of Egyptian Development, Centre for Development Research, Copenhagen, June 1990, p. 10.

55 Bernard Botiveau, "Egypte: crise de l'Ordre des avocats et normalisation des syndicats professionels", *Maghreb-Machrek*, no. 142, 1993, pp. 5 ff.

56 Ayubi, *Political Islam*, pp. 195 ff.

these Islamic charities showed themselves to be more efficient than the government in organising relief work.[57] However, they were accused by the government of exploiting the disaster for political purposes and had their work restricted. In the same year another incident, involving the *Salsabīl*[58] Research Institute, revealed the government's fear of the growing influence of the Brothers in the middle class, and for the first time in many years made the Muslim Brothers the direct target of anti-Islamist persecution. This institute, run by members of the Society, was accused of using its advanced computer equipment to help organise a subversive international Islamist organisation and, strangely, of being implicated in espionage on behalf of Israel. Fifty members of the Muslim Brothers were arrested in Sharqiyya province.

Later arrests and intimidation have followed. In connection with a manifestation of solidarity with Bosnia, made by six mosques in Cairo and Alexandria in early 1994, arrests for the first time included members of the Cairo leadership of the Brothers. Finally in 1995, in preparation for the parliamentary elections of December of that year, a wave of arrests put a large number of prominent Muslim Brothers of the younger generation behind bars. Many, including 'Iṣām al-'Iryān, were sentenced by military courts to several years imprisonment with hard labour. While the aged leaders of the *Maktab al-irshād* were not imprisoned, the Cairo headquarters of the Society was shut down. Yet, despite the state's massive effort, continuing till today, to link the Muslim Brothers to Islamist violence, no evidence whatsoever has been presented to this effect.

God and the people: the Socialist Labour Party

"*Allāhu akbar wa yaḥya al-sha'b*"—"God is great, long live the people!" This slogan was the rallying call of the Egyptian Labour Party (*Ḥizb al-'Amal*[59]) in the 1980s, as it was of the Young Egypt (*Miṣr al-Fatāt*) movement in the late-1940s and early-1950s. Most academic accounts of the Islamist movement in Egypt[60] do not include the Labour Party as part

[57] Denis J. Sullivan, *Private Voluntary Organizations in Egypt: Islamic Development, Private Initiative, and State Control*, University Press of Florida, Gainesville, FL, 1994, p. xiii.

[58] *Salsabīl* is the name of a spring in Paradise.

[59] The party name is most commonly translated as "the Labour Party" and this translation is used by party members. The word *'amal* may also be rendered as "action". Thus Ibrahim G. Aoude, "From National Bourgeois Development to *Infitah*: Egypt 1952–1992", *Arab Studies Quarterly*, vol. 16, no. 1, winter 1994, speaks of the "Socialist Action Party".

[60] See for instance Saad Eddin Ibrahim, "Egypt's Islamic Activism in the 1980s", *Third World Quarterly*, vol. 10, no. 2, London, April 1988; Alain Roussillon, "Entre al-Jihâd et al-Rayyân"; Ṣāliḥ al-Wardānī, *Al-ḥaraka al-islāmiyya fi miṣr - wāqi' al-thamanīnāt* [The Islamist Movement in Egypt: The Situation in the 1980s], Markaz al- ḥaḍāra al-'arabiyya lil-i'lām wal-nashr, Giza, 1991; and the books and articles of Hāla Muṣṭafā, e.g. *Al-islām*

of this movement. This may be because it only recently adopted a clear-cut Islamist platform (see below). Nevertheless, at least with the establishment of the Islamic Alliance in 1987 the party clearly became a part of this movement, and in fact a central and dynamic factor within it, significantly influencing the wider Islamist movement, in particular the Muslim Brothers.

The Labour Party was founded as the Socialist Labour Party in December 1978. Its president was Ibrāhīm Shukrī, who had been vice-president of the Socialist Party and its only MP in the early 1950s (the Socialist Party being the name taken by the Young Egypt movement in 1949). The party effectively participated in four parliamentary elections. In the 1979 elections, generally acknowledged to be heavily rigged, it won (or was given by Sadat) 29 seats out of a total of 372, becoming the only opposition of any significance within the Parliament. But even its "loyal opposition" became too much for Sadat, who pressured the majority of its MPs into joining the ruling National Democratic Party.[61] In the 1984 elections the Labour Party became the second largest opposition party with 7 percent of the votes, while the New Wafd Party in alliance with the Muslim Brothers received 15 percent. With an 8 percent limit for entrance into parliament, the Labour Party was not represented, although four of its members were among the ten additional deputies appointed by presidential decree. In 1987 the Labour Party, now in an Islamic Alliance with the Muslim Brothers obtained 17 percent, and 56 out of 448 elected[62] representatives (22 of these were from the Labour Party, the rest were Muslim Brothers, independents, or from the small Liberal Party which also joined the alliance).[63] The Wafd, now running on its own, still managed to gather 11 percent of the votes. Ibrāhīm Shukrī became the parliamentary leader of the opposition. The 1990 elections were boycotted by the opposition

---

al-siyāsī fī miṣr [Political Islam in Egypt], Markaz al-dirāsāt al-siyāsiyya wal-istrātījiyya bil-Ahrām, Cairo, 1992. On the other hand the yearly *Arab Strategic Report* published by the *al-Ahrām* Centre for Political and Strategic Studies in Cairo has since 1989 included the Labour Party together with the Muslim Brothers and the radical groups under the heading "The Islamist movement", and the party is also included in the Egyptian "Islamic" movement in Auda, "An Uncertain Response: The Islamic Movement in Egypt".

61 Cf. for example Singer, *The Socialist Labor Party*, p. 14.

62 The President retained the right to appoint ten members bringing the total to 458.

63 The number of 56 representatives for the Alliance is based on information screened from the Minutes of the People's Assembly (see *Maḍābit majlis al-sha'b*, al-faṣl al-tashrī'ī al-rābi', dawr al-in'iqād al-awwal, al-mujallad al-awwal). Rabī', [The Performance of the Egyptian People's Assembly], p. 12 states 58. The difference may be due to his counting of two of those representatives elected outside of party lists as members of the Alliance. The distribution of Alliance MPs between the groups involved was reported by Magdī Ḥusayn in December 1991.

except the small leftist *Tajammu'* Party. In 1995 the Labour party again contested the elections for the People's Assembly along with the rest of the political spectrum. In terms of fraud these elections were generally acknowledged to be the worst under Mubarak. Out of 444 deputies elected, a mere 13 belonged to the opposition. The Labour Party was not represented, while one Muslim Brother was elected as an independent.[64]

Until 2000 the Labour Party published a newspaper, *al-Sha'b* (The People). As a weekly its circulation grew from 45,000 in late 1985 to 170,000 in early 1992,[65] allowing it to compete with *al-Wafd* as the largest opposition paper.

When political parties emerged again under Sadat the leaders of the "new" political groups were often survivors from the pre-Nasser period. The Labour Party was no exception; as mentioned, its President Ibrāhīm Shukrī was a Young Egyptparliamentarian in the early 1950s. Indeed, the early Labour Party membership was dominated by former Young Egypt members and sympathisers. The party newspaper spoke of the charismatic founder and leader of Young Egypt, Aḥmad Ḥusayn, who died in the 1970s, as "the founder of our movement", and the paper's former editor, 'Ādil Ḥusayn, who from 1985 was the party's leading ideologue, said the Labour Party's political line was a continuation of Aḥmad Ḥusayn's ideas in a new period and under different circumstances.[66] Finally it should be noted that the party leadership had some elements of being a family dynasty. 'Ādil Ḥusayn was Aḥmad Ḥusayn's younger brother. He was editor of *al-Sha'b* between 1985 and 1993, and in May 1993 became the general secretary of the party. Muḥammad Ḥilmī Murād, Vice-President of the Labour Party, was the brother-in-law of Aḥmad Ḥusayn, and Magdī Ḥusayn, the leading figure among the younger set of leaders and the foremost MP of the party from 1987 to 1990 besides Ibrāhīm Shukrī, is the son of Aḥmad Ḥusayn. In 1993 Magdī succeeded his uncle 'Ādil as editor of *al-Sha'b*. It should also be noted that other parties, notably the Wafd, had similar dynasties.

Another characteristic of the Labour Party is of course its Islamism. Although it always held Islam and religious values in high esteem, and spoke in favour of the gradual application of the *Sharī'a*,[67] the Labour Party was from the start basically a radical nationalist party. But when

64 Willy Egset, *Conflict or Accommodation: An Analysis of the Transition to Multiparty System in Egypt and the Political Strategies of the Muslim Brotherhood*, University of Oslo, 1998, p. 131.

65 In July 1992 *al-Sha'b* started to publish two issues weekly, Tuesday and Friday.

66 On the Labour Party as a continuation of Young Egypt see also Ibrāhīm Shukrī, *Al-taqrīr al-siyāsī li-ḥizb al-'amal al-ishtirākī*, Cairo, 1987, pp. 40 ff.

67 *Ibid.*, p. 49.

'Ādil Ḥusayn joined the party and took over as editor of *al-Sha'b* in December 1985, he clearly intended to turn the party into an Islamist one. The struggle was hard, but at the party's 5th congress in March 1989 'Ādil Ḥusayn and his supporters were able to have a distinctly Islamist platform voted in and the leading organs filled exclusively with Islamists. This provoked a major split, with many leading members, including half the parliamentary group, refusing to accept the results of the conference.[68]

'Ādil Ḥusayn, though a member of the Young Egypt in his early youth, became a Marxist and an organised communist after 1952. He spent eleven years in prison under Nasser. In the mid-1970s he wrote an article on Islam and Marxism called "The absurd polarisation of contemporary Egyptian politics".[69] Here he argues that Marxists should not challenge the religious feelings of the broad masses, but express their programme of social reform in ways that are in harmony with those feelings. This clearly foreshadows Ḥusayn's later switch to Islamism. Although this change was a matter of faith, Ḥusayn also argued more pragmatically for Islamism as the solution to Egypt's ills (and those of other Islamic countries). He had two main points: one, faith in God is the only solid and lasting basis for a strong public morality, which was necessary to bear the hardships of a fight for truly independent development; two, a civilisation can only progress as long as it is true to its own roots. 'Ādil Ḥusayn spoke of his ideas as "enlightened Islamism". He favoured applying the *Sharī'a*, but emphasised that it must be a *Sharī'a* for the 21st century. Although there are some clear rulings in the Koran and the Sunna, there is still wide scope for human reason to interpret the Law in keeping with changing times and circumstances. Islam is viewed more as a provider of general moral principles, and as an imperative urging action for the common interest (as implied by the slogans mentioned at the start of this section), than as a set of detailed readymade rules and regulations.[70] In this approach Ḥusayn seemed closer to the early Islamic reformers Jamal al-Dīn al-Afghānī and Muḥammad 'Abduh than to the Muslim Brothers.

In the Labour Party's positive programme for reform of Egyptian society democracy was the first goal on the political level. To achieve this required ending one-party rule and lifting the emergency laws that had been in place almost uninterruptedly since 1967 and which severely limited the freedom of political activity.[71] In respect of this 'Ādil Ḥusayn's

[68] Six Members of Parliament formally announced their secession from the party. See Rabī', [The Performance of the Egyptian People's Assembly], pp. 12–13.
[69] 'Ādil Ḥusayn, "Islam and Marxism: The Absurd Polarisation of Contemporary Egyptian Politics", *Review of Middle East Studies*, 2, Ithaca Press, London, 1976.
[70] Interview with the author, Cairo, 10 March 1992.
[71] Ḥizb al-'amal, "Al-barnāmaj al-intikhābī 'alā qā'imat ḥizb al-'amal", part I.

views underwent an interesting development. In the early 1980s, in his book *Naḥwa fikr 'arabī jadīd* (Towards a new Arab thinking)[72] he argued that there should be free elections with several candidates. But he was very sceptical of a multi-party system under Egypt's present conditions. A one-party system, he argued, would probably better serve the purpose of national unity in the struggle for independent development. Yet from 1986 onwards, as revealed in a pamphlet devoted to explaining party doctrine for the broader membership,[73] he unequivocally endorsed a multi-party system as a necessary condition for stable democratic development. And he now stressed party pluralism as indispensable for avoiding the stagnation and sclerosis of political thought. He also linked this stand to Islam. According to Ḥusayn, Islam leaves wide room for interpretation (*ijtihād*) and recognises no priesthood with a monopoly over interpreting the scriptures. Hence the existence of different interpretations is quite legitimate, and these may crystallise into different political programmes and parties. Nevertheless, he added, this freedom must be regulated by respect for the Islamic framework of the state, and for what he called the state's "grand strategy for development". These limitations he equated with respect for the constitutions in Western countries,[74] but it would seem that his formulations are open to quite authoritarian interpretations, at least as long as they remain so vaguely defined.

'Ādil Ḥusayn and the Labour Party were also in the forefront of the struggle against corruption at high levels. And as far as they were concerned replacing the present leadership with Islamists, although an important step, was no real solution if it was not combined with a thoroughgoing reform of the ruling system, away from today's autocratic ruling by decrees. Democracy and consultation (*shūrā*) must become the model at all levels: national, local government, factories, schools and even within the family.

To round off the picture a brief comment on the economic policies of the party is in order, even if this anticipates some of the results of this study. The overall strategic goal for the Labour Party was to build a strong independent Egypt which satisfied the material and spiritual needs of its inhabitants. In this, economic development was central. However, the party stressed this could not mean merely increasing material production at the cost of the environment and of human dignity and security.

[72] 'Ādil Ḥusayn, *Naḥwa fikr 'arabi jadīd - al-nāṣiriyya wal-tanmīya wal-dīmuqrāṭiyya* [Towards a New Arab Thinking: Nasserism, Development and Democracy], Dār al-mustaqbal al-'arabī, Cairo, 1985, p. 240.

[73] 'Ādil Ḥusayn, *Al-islām dīn wa ḥaḍāra* [Islam: Religion and Civilization], Al-manār al-'arabī, Giza, 1990, p. 41.

[74] Interview with the author, Cairo, 10 March 1992.

The Labour Party was very critical of the economic open-door policy initiated under Sadat, and adhered to with some adjustments by Mubarak. This policy, and especially the liberalisation of imports, was conceived as undermining the basis for independent development, and in addition as bearing with it a redistribution of wealth from the poor to the rich.

Nevertheless, the Labour Party stressed that its goal of political and economic independence did not mean isolation. On the contrary it presupposed integration with other Arab states, particularly the Sudan, with its unused agricultural lands seen as a reservoir for future food production and settlement opportunities for Egypt's fast-growing population. But the West, primarily the United States with its local ally Israel, was seen as the major enemy of Egyptian and Arab development. The party was in the forefront of the struggle against the US-led coalition that fought Iraq during the Gulf war of 1991.

Although the Labour Party clearly stated that the highest loyalty should be to the unity and interest of the Islamic *umma* (and supported Iran during its war with Iraq, despite Iraq being an Arab country), it combined Egyptian nationalism, Arab nationalism and Islamism in a similar way to the Young Egypt in the 1930s and '40s.

It also tried to solve the uphill task of achieving unity with the Copts on an Islamic platform. In fact in the 1987 elections the Labour Party-Muslim Brothers alliance was the only party to have a Copt topping a list. This was Gamāl As'ad who was elected in Asyūṭ province, one of the permanent hotbeds of Christian-Muslim sectarian strife, known as *fitna ṭā'ifiyya*.[75] And during the increase in tension in Asyūṭ in 1992 *al-Sha'b* tried to start a "national dialogue" between Copts and Muslims. The party stated the Copts should have equal rights, including political rights, "at all levels", although it was not clear whether a Copt would be acceptable as president or as minister for education with responsibility for the ideological forming of new generations. They often repeated the slogan "*lahum mā lanā wa 'alayhim mā 'alaynā*" which broadly means "they (the local Christians) have the same rights and duties as us".[76] The Labour Party also stressed the need for Muslims and Christians to share in defending faith against "the secularist threat".

Occasionally it was claimed that the Muslim Brothers had taken over the Labour Party.[77] This was clearly not so. Rather the Labour Party kept a

[75] Gamāl As'ad was one of the six "socialist" dissenters within the Labour Party's parliamentary group in 1989. However, by 1994 he had returned as an active member, for instance joining 'Ādil Ḥusayn in a party delegation to Sudan. See *al-Sha'b*, 18 October 1994.

[76] Shukrī, *Al-taqrīr al-siyāsī*, p. 50.

[77] Thus Aoude, "From National Bourgeois Development to *Infitah*", p. 17.

distinct line which on the one hand was influencing the Muslim Brothers and on the other was making them emerge as a competitor to them, especially among the Islamist-oriented students.[78] The Labour Party's boldness in attacking corruption and in opposing the government alliance with the United States was particularly attractive.

The electoral alliance with the Muslim Brothers and the opening of the pages of *al-Sha'b* for the Islamist movement at large were indicative of a central concern of the Labour Party: the establishment of the broadest possible unity both within and without the Islamist movement *vis-à-vis* the government. In particular the party tried to bridge the traditional gap between the Muslim Brothers and the Nasserist tendencies within the opposition. The Muslim Brothers were unwilling to see anything positive in the Nasser period, whilst the Labour Party maintained that although Nasser made major mistakes, in particular with regard to democracy, there was another, positive, aspect of his reign: the serious attempt to achieve national independence both economically and politically.

On the eve of the elections to the People's Assembly in 1987 negotiations took place between all five legally recognised opposition parties and the Muslim Brothers with the aim of running united slates of candidates against the government National Democratic Party. This would provide the opposition with a much greater chance of making significant inroads into the commanding majority of the NDP. Since the election law contained an 8 percent entry limit, and stipulated that all votes for parties not reaching that limit would be given to the biggest party, such an alliance was considered to gain the opposition a far better chance of success. However, the negotiations broke down because the Wafd refused to join the proposed coalition,[79] and in the end there remained an alliance of the Labour Party, the Muslim Brothers and the small Liberal Party, running on an Islamic platform under the slogan "Islam is the solution" (*al-islām huwa al-ḥall*). The Alliance programme called for democratic reforms, an end to Emergency Law and the application of the *Sharī'a*. It also called for a cultural renewal inspired by the Arabic and Islamic roots of Egypt's civilisation. In foreign policy it demanded an end to the special relationship with the United States. Egypt should opt for non-alignment, for Arab integration and a close cooperation with all Islamic countries. Finally the programme demanded an eradication of corruption and a revised economic policy to halt the deterioration of the people's living conditions, and to secure a basis for true independence.[80]

[78] Auda, "An Uncertain Response", p. 114.
[79] The High Commission of the New Wafd Party voted down the proposal by a narrow margin: 11 to 9. Abdel Monem Said Aly, "Democratization in Egypt", *American-Arab Affairs*, no. 29, p. 20.
[80] Ḥizb al-'amal, "Al-barnāmaj al-intikhābī 'alā qā'imat ḥizb al-'amal".

Although the elections of April 1987 resulted in a two thirds majority for the NDP, the alliance emerged as the dominant force within the opposition. Ibrāhīm Shukrī, as leader of the party in whose name the alliance lists had formally been run, became leader of the parliamentary opposition, despite the fact that a majority of the MPs of the Islamic Alliance were in fact Muslim Brothers. This gave both the Labour Party and the Muslim Brothers a new weight in public debate.[81]

An ideology for an aspiring new élite: the Islamists on the socio-political map

In a liberal Western setting advocates of letting religious ethics determine the political course are often spontaneously labelled "religious right-wing activists", a judgment certainly open to debate. Reconciling this label with the line pursued by mainstream Egyptian Islamists on the question of democracy and political reform would seem hard.

From the point of view of economic politics, what criteria should be used to place the Islamists within the broader Egyptian political landscape? In the countries of the formerly colonised South groups working for national independence would probably be considered as somehow left. On this count the Egyptian Islamists would certainly be left as they oppose the policies of the IMF, both because they imply foreign domination of the economy, and because they compromise the state control of important tools for directing development, and especially for protecting local industry.

A more traditional yardstick in Western politics has been to place political tendencies on a left-right scale according to the degree of state, or other collective, intervention in the economy they favour. Those favouring the unencumbered individual enjoyment of the rights of private

[81] Saad Eddin Ibrahim, "Islamic Activism and Political Opposition in Egypt", pp. 9–10. Due to its boycott of the 1990 elections and the general fraud of 1995, the Islamic Alliance no longer became meaningfully represented in the People's Assembly. The three groups involved remain clearly separate entities each with their particular line. While in 1992 the Liberal Party broke away, the Labour Party and the Muslim Brothers still maintained a loose coalition. Their cooperation was renewed by the running of common lists for the local elections in the autumn of 1992, where the Islamic Alliance again emerged as the dominant opposition force. They won in 115 local councils, or just below 20 percent of the total, while the Wafd took 60. (Markaz al-dirāsāt al-siyāsiyya wal-istrātījiyya bil-Ahrām, *Al-taqrīr al-istrātījī al-'arabī 1992*, pp. 319 ff.) In the elections of 2000 the Muslim Brothers, standing as independents, reemerged as the largest opposition group in the People's Assembly (albeit with no more than seventeen representatives). Earlier the same year the Labour Party's activity had been frozen by government order and its newspaper closed down. This remains the situation at the time of writing.

property and a free rein for market forces have generally been considered to be on the right, while those in favour of some kind of collective ownership or at least a right for the collective will of society, usually expressed through the state, to plan and direct economic life would be on the left. Applied here, the Islamists would appear somewhere in the middle, with the Muslim Brothers slightly to the right of centre and the Labour Party to the left. The Muslim Brothers have been energetic defenders of private property and a free market, which should put them on the right. The Labour Party would appear more to the left of centre because of its greater emphasis on the need for planning and an active public sector, albeit within a system dominated by private property. Yet the Muslim Brothers have also underlined the need for investment and production to follow certain priorities dictated by the requirements of justice and development. And the two alliance partners draw in common the conclusion that since humans hold their property in trust from God, society has the right to act as God's overseers, as it were, and interfere against individual owners who use their entrusted wealth in a socially detrimental way. They are also clear that public interest (*maṣlaḥa 'āmma*) takes precedence over private interests.

Finally a basic issue defining "the left" is its defence of the interests of the workers, or of the underprivileged classes in general. In the sense of advocating class struggle and an overthrow of the capitalists the Islamists are clearly not a revolutionary left. In fact probably one of the most consistent features of Islamist discourse on economics is its express will to avoid class conflict. The Islamic ideal is clearly seen as one implying harmony, where the different groups or classes within society have different roles to fill and should do so in a spirit of cooperation and mutual benefit. The idea of "social justice", which is put forth as a salient characteristic of Islamic economics, is understood within this framework, and is not a call for eliminating social differences. This is seen as contrary to human nature because it would kill the incentive for progress and development. The call is rather for inter-class solidarity. Everyone has the right to a livelihood, and this must be guaranteed by the rich sharing their wealth with the poor, the young, the sick, the aged and the disabled. Securing this redistribution at the minimum obligatory level of the *zakāt* is the duty of the Islamic state, although there are questions regarding the role of the state beyond the collection and distribution of the *zakāt*. In their welfare policies the Islamists advocate targeting subsidies or *zakāt* contributions to those in documented need, as opposed to a regime of general benefits to which all citizens are entitled, implemented by for instance the Scandinavian "welfare states" (as well as by Nasser).

The fact that both the Muslim Brothers and the Labour Party favour a concentration of economic activity on the satisfaction of the "basic needs" of the poor could be considered a leftist point of view. However, as long as they have not presented concrete policies to implement such a strategy, the significance of this "leftist talk" should be tempered with the knowledge of the Islamists' liberal views on the market, at least in the case of the Muslim Brothers. Whether the concrete welfare work conducted by the Islamists today should be considered an indication of left leanings is debatable. At least in Europe the left has traditionally argued that social welfare should be a responsibility of the state, not of private charities. Nevertheless, the Islamists clearly campaign for greater freedom for trade union activity, which could be counted as a leftist viewpoint.

Egyptian Islamists clearly make common cause with the left in their defence of national economic autonomy. On internal economic policies they would seem to be a centrist force pretty close to European social democracy, a similarity also noted by Olivier Roy (cf. p. 32 above). While the Labour Party would resemble the social democracy with its classical statist policies of the first post-World War II period, the more pro-market economic policies of the Muslim Brothers place them closer to the modern variety of the 1980s and '90s.

Most probably the mainstay of electoral and other support for the Egyptian Islamists was to be found among the literate groups with a secondary or university education, but with a background outside the economic and political élite. These were the people who filled the ranks of the urban lower middle class, the bulk of whom held or sought jobs in the massive public sector and government bureaucracy. And to a large extent the economic policies of the Islamists reflected the aspirations of these *muwaẓẓafin*, so hard hit by economic recession and public poverty. Hence, the developmentalist emphasis, as well as the stress on national independence, would fit in here, but the character of the Islamists main constituency would probably also account for the marked hesitation in their suggestions for budgetary reform. Removing food subsidies and ending the system of guaranteed state employment would not sit well with the *muwaẓẓafin* and their families.

The reasons for the divergence between the economic views of the Muslim Brothers and those of the Labour Party might be several. Historical events have made the Brothers almost instinctively hostile towards anything connected with the Nasser regime. For instance state manipulation of prices will typically be identified as an integral part of the whole totalitarian system built up at that time. But the difference in social make-up of the leadership and followings of the two parties is also relevant. In contrast to the Labour Party the Muslim Brothers has a considerable following among private entrepreneurs, primarily in small and medium size businesses, but in some cases also quite affluent individuals. This was not the case to any large extent in the "old" Society of Muslim Brothers under Ḥasan al-Bannā, which was probably more akin to the *Jamā'a Islāmiyya* today, being dominated by students, artisans and middle and lower level public servants. But a generation later the Brothers were affected by what often happens to the cadres of popular movements, a strong upward social mobility. Since the prospect of a career in the state and public sector was to a large extent closed to them under Nasser, they used their energies in private business. From early on the Brothers had started economic enterprises in order to create an economic basis for their organisational activities and especially for their social welfare programme. Consequently the cadres gained a lot of experience in the leadership of factories, trade establishments and the like.[82]

By the 1980s a number of Brothers were wealthy businessmen, and they had important connections to a score of others, many of whom had at one time been connected to the Society. Osman Ahmad Osman, the construction tycoon whom the Brothers picked to be leader of the Engineers' Syndicate when they gained dominance there, was the most famous one. The influence of the big business element clearly inclined the Brothers towards a liberal economic line, as did their ideological sympathy for, and sometimes connections to, the "Islamic investment companies" that emerged in the 1980s. The Labour Party, on the other hand, did not contain a dominant group of businessmen within is ranks, which may account for its more pro-statist policies.

The younger generation of Muslim Brothers, those recruited from the student *jamā'āt* of the 1970s, tend to be closer to the Labour Party in their economic views. Some of them, like 'Iṣām al-'Iryān, vice general secretary of the Medical Doctors' Syndicate, and leading MP for the Brothers 1987–90, are clearly critical of the influence that, especially in the early 1980s, was exercised on the economic policies of the Muslim Brothers by Brothers who grew rich during their exile in the Gulf states in the 1950s and '60s.[83]

Filling the vacant throne

The presidencies of Sadat (1970–81) and Mubarak (1981–) saw the return of Islamism as a major articulator of opposition to the regime. The Muslim Brothers were increasingly led by the dynamic of this position and the logic of their ideological discourse towards adopting an economic programme centred on a call for independence, Arab integration, rapid development guided by the state and social justice—the privileged causes

[82] Mitchell, *The Society of Muslim Brothers*, pp. 274 ff.
[83] Interview with the author, 14 May 1994.

of Nasserism. By an inverse logic the dominant trend in the Labour Party gravitated from a radical nationalist position towards Islamism, in search of an ideological autonomy from the West that would buttress the fight for economic independence (and surely also in search of voter support).

On the strength of the evidence presented, the economic policies of the Muslim Brothers and the Labour Party could be said to imply they were picking up the shattered pieces of "the project of the national bourgeoisie" that Nasser once represented, but which was moribund by 1967 and was finally dismantled through Sadat's *infitāḥ* policies.[84] Yet in their economic policies the Islamists of the 1980s and early 1990s differed significantly from the Nasserist programme of the 1960s. The absence of talk of socialism after the demise both of international socialism and of most Third World attempts at "delinking" from the world economy is a case in point. In principle the Islamists supported a privatisation of capital ownership (although Nasser also from the outset, in the early 1950s, intended to rely primarily on the private sector and was more or less led by circumstances into adopting a more "socialist" strategy). Furthermore the Muslim Brothers in particular supported the principle of internal free-trade in opposition to the highly regulated system of Nasser. A general model favourably referred to at times was the success story of South Korea, where capital was left in private hands, but its use directed through state planning, and which exercised only a selective opening to the world market.

Moreover the Islamists could be said to represent a populist variety of the project, as did Nasser, in that securing the welfare of the working classes was put high on their agenda. But they differed from Marxist socialism in that they rejected class struggle and did not envisage any leading role for the working classes.[85] Still both the Brothers and the Labour Party included as part of their programme for Islamic-style democracy the need for *shūrā*[86] to be practised also at the places of work.

84 The term "project of the national bourgeoisie" was coined by Samir Amin to denote the radical developmentalist policies of a number of Third World governments in the period after decolonisation. The aim was a strong local capitalist development, enabling the country in question to take part in the competition on the world market on equal terms. The problem of reviving this project in the 1980s, at least according to Amin, was that the *infitāḥ* in Egypt was not an accidental occurrence, but a first warning of a general defeat for this project of the national bourgeoisie and of the dawning of the age of IMF dictation of the rules. See his "Bandung: Thirty Years Later", paper presented at a conference convened by the Egyptian Diplomatic Institute on the occasion of the Thirtieth Anniversary of the Bandung Conference, Cairo, April 1985. Cf. Aoude, "From National Bourgeois Development to *Infitah*", pp. 5 ff.

85 See 'Ādil Ḥusayn, *Naḥwa fikr 'arabī jadīd*, pp. 229 ff on the leading role of the political élite in an Islamic state.

86 This term literally means "consultation" and refers to the Koranic injunction on the Prophet to seek the advice of the representatives of the people. See Mitchell, *The Society of*

The workers must have the right to air their views on important decisions without fear of reprisal, they stated. Indeed the Islamists distanced themselves more generally from the political authoritarianism of the Nasser era, in that they strongly emphasised the need for democracy, party pluralism and the rotation of power through free elections.

From the point of view of social forces the economic policies of the Islamists could be said to represent the aspirations of a coalition of forces feeling their space for progress hemmed in by the dependent situation of the country and the dominant interests of the present ruling groups. This coalition included parts of the entrepreneurial and commercial private sector bourgeoisie, primarily working with the Muslim Brothers, but the most important social component was (for lack of a better term) the "petty bourgeoisie" of the private and especially the public sectors. This included small shopkeepers and artisans, but primarily students and educated people working as lower and middle level public servants in the state and public sector.[87]

In effect, by drawing on Pierre Bourdieu's analysis of "symbolic power", a bridge may be established between the socio-religious and the cultural impulse behind Islamism, and also to the economic frustration of its adherents, referred to by Ayubi above. For Bourdieu, the struggle for the right to "give names", that is to classify and describe social phenomena, is an integral part of the struggle for dominance between classes and social groups.[88] In the context of the present day Muslim world then, Islamism's attempt to impose a new Islamised language on political debate could well be seen as part of a struggle for upward mobility for educated groups more at home with traditional Islamic references than their more Westernised counterparts now dominating ruling circles. Ayubi sees this point and suggests, with reference to Galāl Amīn, that "the

---

Muslim Brothers, pp. 246–8 and Sami Zubaida, *Islam, the People and the State: Political Ideas and Movements in the Middle East*, I. B. Tauris, London, 1993, pp. 44, 48, for the general application of the *shūrā* principle in Islamist programmes for the political system in an Islamic state.

87 It must therefore be mentioned that the use of the phrase "project of the national bourgeoisie", should be rather freely understood, in that we may talk of a "potential" new state bourgeoisie. This is in line with the analysis of Egypt's development under Nasser presented by Mahmoud Hussein which says that a new state bourgeoisie grew out of the new managerial apparatus recruited from those primarily petty bourgeois groups that gained power in 1952. Cf. Mahmoud Hussein, *Class Conflict in Egypt 1945–70*, Monthly Review Press, New York, 1977, pp. 150 ff. See also Utvik, *Kva kom inn den opne døra?*, pp. 57 ff.

88 See for instance Pierre Bourdieu, *Ce que parler veut dire. L'économie des échanges linguistiques*, Fayard, Paris, 1982, pp. 99–101. Cf. also *Language and Symbolic Power*, Polity Press, Cambridge, 1991, p. 239.

Islamic revival could be seen as a process of "generalisation" of the cultural outlook of the newly urbanised and humble classes".[89]

From this perspective the affinity between Islamism and nationalist mobilisation, which more often than not has centred around a fight for the local majority language to be the privileged means of expression within the state, also becomes clear. A central aspect of this fight has been to increase the chances for nascent local élites rooted in popular culture to gain access to positions in the expanding bureaucracy in competition with more cosmopolitan aristocratic groups.[90] The fact that the educated lower middle classes were among those hardest hit by public retrenchment in Egypt and other Middle Eastern Muslim countries in the 1980s would of course serve to intensify their struggle for a fairer deal and the sense of a need for solidaric community around a shared religious and cultural ideal.

[89] Ayubi, *Political Islam*, p. 228.
[90] Anthony D. Smith, *National Identity*, Penguin Books, London, 1991, pp. 120–1, 128–9.

3

GOD'S STEWARDS ON EARTH

CONSTRUCTING AN ISLAMIST ECONOMIC IDEOLOGY

Early formulations

Among the most prominent early attempts by political Islamists to construct an Islamic economic theory were the writings of the Indo-Pakistani writer and activist Abū al-A'lā Mawdūdī, the Iraqi Shi'a scholar Muḥammad Bāqir al-Ṣadr and the Egyptian Muslim Brothers 'Abd al-Qādir 'Awda and Sayyid Quṭb.[1] These ideologues were active from the 1930s to the 1960s and what prompted their intellectual effort seems to have been the dual pressure of the economic problems experienced by the masses of Muslims and the competition from Marxism. Widespread economic misery created ample reason for discontent and fertile grounds for opposition to incumbent regimes. And competing with the nascent Islamist movement for the leadership of this opposition, for the articulation of the discontent, was an international communist movement claiming to possess a scientific theory explaining the economic malaise and pointing the way to its eradication. The strength of the Islamists in this competition was their ability to tie their message to the enormous and deep-rooted legitimacy of the still dominant system of moral values and the acknowledged source for truth among the broad masses: Islam. Yet to many of the leaders, not least in order to compete for the support of the young impatient intellectuals, Islam had to be shown to be the equal of Marxism in

[1] 'Abd al-Qādir 'Awda, *Al-māl wal-ḥukm fī al-islām* [Wealth and Government in Islam], Al-dār al-su'ūdiyya lil-nashr wal-tawzī', Jidda, 1984; Abū al-A'lā Mawdūdī, *Al-ribā* [Usury], Al-dār al-su'ūdiyya lil-nashr wal-tawzī', Jidda, 1987, *Mafāhīm islāmiyya ḥawla al-dīn wal-dawla* [Islamic Concepts on Religion and State], Al-dār al-su'ūdiyya lil-nashr wal-tawzī', Jidda, 1987 and *Niẓām al-ḥayāt fī al-islām* [The Organisation of Life in Islam], Al-dār al-su'ūdiyya lil-nashr wal-tawzī', Jidda, 1987; Sayyid Quṭb, *Ma'rakat al-islām wal-ra'smāliyya* [The Struggle Between Islam and Capitalism], Dār al-shurūq, Cairo, 1987 and *Al-'adāla al-ijtimā'iyya fī al-islām* [Social Justice in Islam], Dār al-shurūq, Cairo, 1989; and Muḥammad Bāqir al-Ṣadr, *Iqtiṣādunā* [Our Economy], Dār al-ta'āruf, Beirut, 1987.

providing a coherent theory for a harmonious economic life and for social welfare, and superior in its claim for truth and the yielding of results. It also had to be shown to be clearly distinct from capitalism and able to solve the problems created by the domination of that system.

The discourse produced in that situation tends to cut both ways, against communism and against capitalism, with the focus shifting according to the direct political context of the writing in question. Quṭb in the early 1950s was inclined to focus on an anti-capitalist critique, because of his reaction against American society, and because the immediate challenge of the Muslim Brothers was directed against the existing capitalist order. At the same time, while the communists in Egypt were still a force to be reckoned with, they had weakened since the immediate post-war years and did not seriously threaten the Brothers' leading position in the movement of the masses. For a time there was even talk of cooperation between the Brothers and the communists. Quṭb, interestingly, represented the Brothers in the discussions that were held for this purpose.[2] In contrast Ṣadr was writing in a time of intense communist agitation in Iraq and devotes most of his polemic to the fight against Marxism.

Of course the socio-political position of these authors must also be considered. Quṭb came from a poor background, and he was involved with a lay movement advocating radical reform, and challenging both the state and the traditional religious leaders. Ṣadr in contrast was born into an established religious family and at the time of writing was rising rapidly within the religious establishment in Iraq, inclining him towards a more defensive position against the communists. Also in contrast to Egypt the Islamist movement in Iraq was formed as a reaction to the pressure created by the radical take-over of Qāsim and as such was more conservative from the start. For Mawdūdī's part, his rather conservative economic views are probably related both to his aristocratic family background and to a certain doctrinal rigidity springing from his concern to preserve Muslim identity in Hindu majority India.

Despite differing social origins there are a lot of similarities in the discourses of these writers from Egypt and other parts of the Muslim world. The *Sunnī* writers 'Awda, Quṭb and Mawdūdī in principle emphasise private property as the basic form of property in an Islamic economic system. Interestingly Ṣadr does not give one form of property priority even in theory, but states both private, collective and state property have a permanent and essential place in an Islamic system. All agree, though, that private property is bound by certain moral rules and legal regulations, such as those banning *ribā* and monopoly. And all writers point out the

[2] See 'Ādil Ḥamūda, *Sayyid Quṭb—min al-qarya ilā al-mishnaqa* [Sayyid Quṭb: from the village to the gallows], Sinā lil-nashr, Cairo, 1990, p. 118.

solidaric element in Islam, expressed not least in the *zakāt* levied on yearly income as a redistribution of wealth.

Yet there are some marked differences. 'Awda and Quṭb go far in relativising the position of private property, stressing the ultimate ownership belongs to God, and that God has made humanity collectively his vice-regent on earth. All private property is really held on society's behalf and this right lapses if the holder causes harm to society by misuse of the property. And even if he does not, according to the Muslim Brother writers of the 1950s, the state has wide powers to intervene in the case of urgent social need, sequestrating property, directing its use, or levying taxes in excess of the *zakāt*. Ṣadr is close to this view with his heavy emphasis on the positive role of the state in an Islamic economy. Mawdūdī on the other hand tends to make the principle of private economic activity and ownership absolute, leaving very little space for exceptions.

There is a corresponding disagreement concerning the uses of the *zakāt* revenue. 'Awda, Quṭb and Ṣadr all state that society, like individuals, has legitimate needs and therefore has claims on surplus private wealth. Quṭb in particular stresses that *zakāt* and other levies can be used for any useful social purpose including the development effort. Mawdūdī expressly opposes this, in particular saying the *zakāt* must only be spent for the benefit of clearly defined needy groups.

Furthermore, while Quṭb sees equality among human beings as a basic Islamic principle, Mawdūdī attacks this notion and states that distribution in an Islamic system will not be based on the idea of equality, which is against the ways of nature anyway, but on justice.

However, all writers agree in denouncing the tyranny of communism, which they consider leads to the paralysis of creative energy, because it goes against the grain of human nature in not giving scope for the natural inclination to want to control the result of one's own effort and pass it on to one's children. They also agree in criticising capitalism for perverting the principle of individual freedom by refusing to set limits on it. Islam is seen as superior in the economic and in all other fields, because it is the natural religion, in harmony with human nature and because it has a spiritual dimension and is anchored in moral values and ideal goals.

Tyranny at home, tyranny from abroad: the 1980s

In general from the mid-1950s to the mid-1970s there was a relative lull in the development of the Islamist movement, both in Egypt and internationally. This was the golden age of modernising radical nationalist and/or socialist regimes in the Third World, advocating what Samir Amin has called the "project of the national bourgeoisie".[3] To a certain extent there was also a lull in the politically activist Islamists' development of an Islamic economic theory. So the economic theoreticians of the Islamist movements that were revived in the 1970s and started to bloom in the 1980s were in the main building directly on those of the 1950s.

By the 1970s the discussion on Islamic economic precepts was rapidly becoming a growing academic discipline sponsored by Saudi and Pakistani universities. In the 1980s "Islamic economics" became a vast field, yet quite distinct from the discourse of the political Islamist movements.

Centrally placed within the Egyptian political groups being studied here are two writers: Yūsuf Kamāl, an economy professor central in forming the economic policy of the Muslim Brothers in the period in question, and 'Ādil Ḥusayn, the main ideologue of the Labour Party.

The Muslim Brothers: with Islam against capitalism and communism: Yūsuf Kamāl

Yūsuf Kamāl is a professor of economics and has taught at the University of Manṣūra and at the Umm al-Qurā University in Mecca among others. In the 1980s he became central in informing the line followed by the Muslim Brothers in economic questions and he has written widely on Islamic Economics. Two of his works will be considered here. *Islam and Contemporary Schools of Economic Thought*,[4] published in 1986, served in the late 1980s as an important reference in Muslim Brother statements about the alternative economic system of Islam. *The Fiqh of Public Economy*,[5] published in 1990, contains a discussion of the proper role of the state in economic affairs with reference to the *fiqh* traditions of the four *Sunnī* schools of law.

The first work consists of three parts, dealing first with capitalism, then with socialism, before proceeding to a presentation of the ideal Islamic economic system. Though a critique of Marxism is still central, it appears, from the structure of the book, that in the Egyptian situation of the 1980s it would be impossible to present Islam as an alternative without attempting a criticism of the by then dominant capitalist system creating so many problems for the population. However, the book does not proceed from an analysis of the economic problems of Egypt or the wider Muslim world. The discussion is for the most part highly abstract, and the section pre-

3 Samir Amin, "Bandung: Thirty Years Later", p. 8.

4 Yūsuf Kamāl, *Al-islām wal-madhāhib al-iqtiṣādiyya al-mu'āṣira* [Islam and Contemporary Schools of Economic Thought], Dār al-wafā', Manṣūra, 1986.

5 Yūsuf Kamāl, *Fiqh al-iqtiṣād al-'āmm* [The Fiqh of Public Economy], Stābrus lil-ṭibā'a wal-nashr, Cairo, 1990.

senting the Islamic alternative is strewn with quotations from the Koran and the *Ḥadīth*, and in that particular respect resembles the earlier works of ʻAwda and Quṭb.

As with the earlier writers, Kamāl begins his presentation of an Islamic economy by stating that Islam has liberated humankind both through faith and through the *Sharīʻa* (a point he repeats throughout the book). With regard to the economy this translates into securing three features of the ideal happy society (which Kamāl also uses as a plan for his presentation): faith, justice (*qisṭ*) and solidarity (*takāful*).[6] Faith is liberating because it secures good behaviour towards other people. The secret of this lies in the balance it induces between this world and the next. Through the fear of God and awareness of the inevitable Day of Judgment behaviour is shaped by the individual conscience of the believer.[7] However, through the *Sharīʻa* God has also given rules for everyone to follow, and has given the authorities of the Islamic state the right and the duty to see to it that those rules are followed. The *Sharīʻa* secures justice through its protection of the right of individuals to the fruits of their efforts. And it secures solidarity primarily through one of the pillars of the faith: the *zakāt*.[8]

In his exposition of the two central principles of justice and solidarity, Kamāl discusses first the Islamic system of property rights, secondly the Islamic rules concerning business relations (*mushāraka*[9]), and finally the question of differentiation of people's social position, what is spoken of in the Koran as the division of people into *darajāt*. However, the section on "justice" is introduced by a more general treatment of Islam as a system of beliefs. This preamble intends to show how Islam always represents the ideal middle road, the subheadings being: "Matter and Soul", "Worship and Social Life" (*al-ʻibāda wal-muʻāmala*) and finally "The Individual and the Community". Islam is balanced in that while it exhorts individuals to share their wealth for the benefit of the poor, it only takes a minimum, the *zakāt*, as a compulsory tax, leaving further charity to free will, and it demands that before sharing their wealth individuals must secure the needs of their closest dependents.

Islam balances between the demands of the body and those of the soul. In a society where the spiritual has no place there may be rapid technical development and an increase in luxury, but the end result will only be civil

[6] Kamāl, *Al-islām wal-madhāhib al-iqtiṣādiyya al-muʻāṣira*, pp. 117–18.
[7] *Ibid.*, pp. 119–32.
[8] *Ibid.*, pp. 117–18.
[9] Kamāl seems to use this term here in a rather broad sense, since this is the title under which he discusses both the prohibition of *ribā* and that of monopoly. The term also has a more narrow technical meaning in Islamic economics, which will be dealt with in the brief treatment of Islamic banking below (see chapter 5).

strife, wars and a collapse of moral virtues and "women will leave the home in imitation of the men". On the other hand, if the material needs are denied, and the spiritual dominates, as was the case in the Christian world in previous centuries (a well-known theme in Islamist writings, and in Islamic apologetics in general), there will be stagnation and ruin of economic life, leading to a revolt, ending up in moral nihilism. And this is what has happened in Europe. However, Islam, Kamāl says, steers the middle course giving both the body and the spirit their due. It is a religion that is in harmony with human nature. Here he seems to contradict himself, since immediately after it is stressed that human beings cannot know what is right and wrong. Humanity did not know until recently that pork and alcohol are harmful to the body. Only God knows and God's wisdom must set the limits for what goods should be allowed in trade and what sorts of activities should be permitted. So here human nature does not play a positive role and must be curtailed.[10]

In every regard, including the relationship between the individual and the community, the other systems of thought are at fault because, Kamāl says, they are only able to think in terms of a struggle in which they choose one side or the other according to their particular leanings. In contrast Islam's middle course leads to the realisation of cooperation, solidarity and unity. Connected to this relationship between the individual and society, says Kamāl, is the pressing question of the economic debate in the world today: how can a society achieve growth and just distribution at the same time. The indication of growth of Gross National Product per inhabitant is not sufficient because it says nothing about the distribution of the growth. In capitalist countries where the issue of distribution is offered little concern, wealth only circulates among a small group, which leads to violent conflict within society. On the other hand the communist ban on all sorts of income except that of wages, is unnatural, and leads to the removal of every incentive for growth. The result is poverty and illegal returns from perverted capitalist forms.

In reality production is a result of effective demand, says Kamāl, which in turn is a product of the distribution of national income. If the structure of distribution is unbalanced so will be the structure of demand, and therefore of production. The structure of prices must not be discussed simply from the point of view of efficient use of resources, like capitalist economists do, but also from the angle of social justice. On the whole the mistake made in capitalist circles is to think that the question of justice is not an economic one, but primarily one of politics. This is a mistake because the issue of the distribution of national income is the other face of

[10] *Ibid.*, pp. 134–8.

the use of resources. When monopolist exploitation and *ribā* revenue drain income from some groups and place it in the accounts of others, when the poor increase in numbers and decrease in income while the opposite is true for the rich, when therefore the poor lose the ability to effectively place demands in the market even for bare necessities while the rich excel in thinking up new demands for luxuries, then production is inevitably diverted from necessities to luxuries. The result is misery at one end of society and excessive wealth at the other. This illustrates the powerful link between the distribution of resources, the nature of production and the distribution of income.[11]

This at times passionate attack on capitalism and the maldistribution of wealth it causes, might suggest Kamāl was a radical in economic questions on the lines of Sayyid Quṭb. This would be somewhat surprising given the development of the social position of the leading Muslim Brothers from the 1950s to the 1980s outlined in chapter 2. But following his argument further, the picture changes quite a bit.

Kamāl states that although comprehensive studies have been conducted about consumers and their preferences, they have been blind to the effect of income distribution on the purchasing-power of different consumers. The issue of distribution has been touched upon, for instance by Bentham and Keynes, he says, in the sense that the propensity among the poor to consume is higher than that of the rich, and that therefore a redistribution would increase total demand. But these comments have drowned in the ocean of theories on prices and market equilibrium. And behind the studies was always a defence of the freedom of the owner to win income and spend it without regard to the interest of society. The work of economists from Marshall to Friedman have avoided the central problem: just distribution and the purity (*naẓāfa*) of income. They have wasted their efforts in applied studies and mathematical models that have if anything been used to increase exploitation, injustice and social gaps rather than to reduce them.

Modern economic theory, says Kamāl, has imagined the cure for the skewed structure of the economy lay in more state intervention, until the state ended up controlling almost half the national income. And in spite of that, the world has since the 1970s experienced "stagflation", which has become a chronic problem. Even the monetarist solutions tried in the United States and Britain have only been able to limit inflation, while stagnation continues. All these theoretical efforts have failed because they do not grasp the core problem, which lies in the practices of *ribā* and of monopoly. These two cancers must be removed.[12]

[11] *Ibid.*, pp. 144–7.
[12] *Ibid.*, pp. 147–8.

This is the core of the reform that Kamāl favours: the prohibition of interest (*ribā*), and of monopoly and price regulation. His ideal seems to be a free market economy "liberated" from these corrupting practices. His criticism of capitalism concerns exactly these points and not the system of private ownership, competition and free enterprise as such.

On the question of property Yūsuf Kamāl states it is a practical necessity, since owning the result of one's effort is a must. This is what drives production and growth, since it is the reward for exerting more effort than the other person. If there were no link between effort and reward all this would be lost. Humans, says Kamāl, have an instinctive longing for infinity, and since life is limited they must satisfy this instinct by producing children. From here springs the desire to secure the offsprings' future. Therefore Islam confirms the institute of inheritance in harmony with human nature. This would not have any meaning if individual property did not exist. And without inheritance, a powerful mechanism for holding the core of society, the family, together would be lost.

Another deep-seated human instinct is that of wanting to dominate; dominate other humans, and other parts of creation, be they living creatures or dead matter. Here Islam establishes property as an outlet for this instinct, an outlet that does not harm others. For if people are allowed to dominate material things, they might be diverted from seeking domination over other people. However, because of the risk of using property to establish a position of tyranny over others, Islam has provided limits to property and the use of it.

Conversely property also has the function in the Islamic social system of liberating the individual, for by having property a person cannot be exploited and tyrannised by others, since those who have property can control the means of their own livelihood. So property is a protection from exploitation, says Kamāl, not a means of exploitation as the Marxists claim. In connection with this it is interesting of course to consider Kamāl's line of argument in the light of Egypt's repeated experience with despotic governments that have more or less controlled economic life. In modern times examples include Muḥammad 'Alī and of course most recently Nasser's regime. For his part Kamāl cites the example of the Soviet Union as evidence of the reduction of the individual to the status of a dependent slave (*mamlūk*) in regard to the state in a system with state monopoly of property. So private property is a basic prerequisite not only for economic freedom but for political freedom too.

Property therefore liberates individuals from the pressures of necessity and need, since an Islamic society secures property enough to fulfil every individual's needs, by way of the institute of *zakāt*, and if that does not suffice, additional means are deducted from rich people's capital. It is worth noticing here the relative free use of the concept property, which tends to put ownership of means of production on a par with "ownership" of consumer goods needed to fulfil the bare needs from day to day. Furthermore private property instils in people a feeling of responsibility, first towards the small community of the family, but through that also towards the larger community of society.

For all these reasons Islam is very strong in its defence of the right of individuals to own the results of their efforts. However, property must be clean, meaning it must be acquired only in return for the equivalent value, as expressed in work, goods or money. Therefore Islam bans any method of augmenting one's property by means not involving work, and violating the principle of equal exchange, such as *ribā*, monopoly, gambling, deceit, robbery, trade in prohibited goods such as drugs and alcohol etc.

Grasping the nature of property is also necessary, says Kamāl. This leads him to the theme of 'Awda and Quṭb, regarding ownership and God. All people enter this world with nothing. All substances have been created by God and put at the service of mankind. All people do is increase the usefulness of the things they find in nature, by either changing their form, transporting them or storing them till the need to use them arises. Therefore the ownership of nature is God's. And properly understood, what individuals gain the right to through their work is nothing more than the use of what God has made, the privilege of their use before others, the usufruct of the land for instance.[13]

This right to usufruct is strongly guarded in Islam. It follows individuals through their lifetime, after which it will pass to their heirs. It may also be transferred through sale or lease. However, since the ownership is ultimately God's, society has rights over it and may interfere to protect these rights. Hence there is an interesting link between the idea of God and the idea of the human collectivity (though Kamāl emphasises that expropriation is legitimate only in clear cases of rebellion against the legitimate Islamic authority, for instance in the case of refusal to pay the *zakāt*).

Kamāl criticises those who mistakenly interpret the *Ḥadīth* which states that pasture, water and fuel are common property to imply the right to nationalise all projects involving the public interest. The proper understanding, he states, is that the *Ḥadīth* stipulates that resources that are available in nature without prior human effort should not be monopolised by private individuals and used for making profit. On the other hand, anything that is a product of work becomes the property of the one exerting the effort.[14]

[13] *Ibid.*, pp. 150–5.
[14] *Ibid.*, pp. 156–64.

Notwithstanding the space left for public intervention the ideal Islamic economic system in Kamāl's rendering emerges as a free market economy liberated on the one hand from the destructive interest system and capitalist monopolies and on the other from oppressive state monopoly and excessive centralised planning. The basic principle of this economic system is that work is ultimately the only legitimate source of income, or in another formulation "*al-ghunm bil-'azm*", which may be translated here as "gain by determined effort".

Interest, clearly identified by Kamāl as the *ribā* condemned by the Koran, is forbidden precisely because it involves the earning of an income without effort. According to Kamāl, Islam acknowledges that the work which is the source of income may take the form of stored labour as well as direct labour, that is, it may be present in the form of raw materials, tools, buildings or as money capital. (This is a view shared by Ṣadr.) But in the case of interest this work does not really enter the productive process, argues Kamāl, because its owner will receive the same income irrespective of the outcome of production and sales. In the case of a project running at a loss the interest paid to the creditor is really taken from the capital invested in the project, it is consumption of the labour of others with no right. In addition it is harmful because no one will invest if a profit at least as high as the current interest rate is not assured. Many important projects may never see the light of day and unemployment will be rampant. For all these reasons interest is condemned and forbidden in Islam.

In an Islamic system workers have the right to a predetermined fixed income for their work, the same goes for fixed capital which may be rented at fixed rates. This is because in these cases the direct consumption of work is involved. But the general rule for the organisation of the productive process is the system of *mushāraka*, the sharing in profit and loss, which in an Islamic system is also the only legal form for the investment of money capital. This organisation may take different forms and involve the partnership between several owners of capital or between capital and labour, but is based on the principle that the profit or loss accruing from the common venture will be divided between the partners according to a predetermined scheme of partition.[15] In such a system, according to Kamāl, there would be no unemployment, because projects would be implemented as long as they brought a profit no matter how high. Besides, the venturing spirit would be supported by the *zakāt* system which would function as a safety net for the loser from failed ventures.[16]

Alongside the prohibition of interest goes the prohibition of monopoly, both state and private, and of price-fixing. Prices must be the product of

[15] For definitions see p. 221, notes 1–3.
[16] *Ibid.*, pp. 167–79.

the free interaction of supply and demand, if not the consumers will suffer and enterprising initiative will be stifled.[17]

The complete mathematical equality promised by Marxism is impossible to achieve (and were it to be even partially realised the effects would be disastrous), Kamāl claims. Competition belongs to the basic features of life, indeed the desire to achieve distinction from other people is an indispensable motivation for human productive effort. But excessive differences should be avoided. Islam does not condone the existence of social *classes* in the sense of people enjoying privileges inherited and/or protected by law. Therefore Islam speaks rather of the existence of *degrees* among people (*darajāt*). These degrees are open to those willing to exert the necessary effort, and are based merely on individual merit. And as long as the Islamic state secures equal access to education and employment for all the basic spirit of equality in Islam will not be contravened.[18] The obvious critical observation that the principle of inheritance would create differences *not* based on individual merit is discussed by Kamāl, but he avoids the question choosing instead to present a positive defence of inheritance as essential to the upkeep of the family, the moral mainstay of a virtuous society.[19]

In the *zakāt*, one of the five pillars of the Islamic faith, Islam possesses a system of social solidarity superior, for a number of reasons, to any welfare system of the capitalist or socialist states. First, it has a moral basis in the religious faith of the people, while the present tax systems have no legitimate status among the people and no moral scruples stand in the way of evasion. In practice these systems degenerate into a transfer from the poor to the rich.[20] In particular this is the case with the expedient of deficit financing through the printing of money, in reality a hidden tax, amounting to theft on a national scale. This practice by necessity produces inflation, which hits the poorer classes, since the capitalists merely pass the burden on by increasing prices on the goods and services they control. Inflation also hits economic development because it leads to speculative hoarding and weakens export.[21]

In an Islamic system inflation is avoided through the ban on "unjustly consuming the wealth of others", which clearly forbids printing money for financing state expenses.[22] And justice is secured because the *zakāt* is taken only from those who have in excess of their needs and given only to

[17] *Ibid.*, pp. 179–81.
[18] *Ibid.*, pp. 181–8.
[19] *Ibid.*, pp. 188–91.
[20] *Ibid.*, p. 196.
[21] *Ibid.*, pp. 199, 204.
[22] *Ibid.*, pp. 205.

those who have a lack, unlike tax or insurance schemes which may take from and give to both groups. This is linked to the fact that in Islam the satisfaction of the needy is considered a basic right that presupposes no *quid pro quo*. Furthermore the *zakāt* is superior to man-made tax and welfare systems because it incorporates the duty of people to care for their relatives and other dependents. The *zakāt* should only be paid after those duties are taken care of, and then be used precisely for those who do not have relatives able to support them in their need.[23]

Yūsuf Kamāl attacks the idea that the Islamic welfare system is one of charity that merely alleviates a poverty that it presupposes the continued existence of.[24] On the contrary he claims that Islam has imposed economic development as a collective duty on Muslim society, and furthermore that the definition of who is needy includes not only those lacking the most basic necessities for life, but also those lacking a dignified level of existence and those able to work but unable to find gainful employment. The *zakāt* is intended to lift the whole population above the mere survival level and to a minimum of enjoyment of life. The *zakāt* revenue may be used to establish productive or commercial ventures in order to promote economic development, which in turn will secure a stable income for the benefit of the *zakāt*, and provide employment opportunities. The *zakāt* will also provide a safety net for commercial ventures that go bankrupt, in order to relaunch the owners into business, thereby contributing to the feeling of security so vital to encouraging commercial activity.[25]

Kamāl strongly emphasises that the *zakāt* is not a voluntary charitable donation, but a duty that must be enforced by an Islamic state. If this were done properly, he says, no other contributions from the citizens towards the treasury would be needed except in an emergency situation.[26]

Professor Kamāl also takes up the criticism that *zakāt*, which is generally understood to be a 2.5 per cent tax on capital and income, and a 5–10 per cent tax on agricultural production, will not suffice the needs of a modern state. He compares the rate of *zakāt* taxation with that of some leading industrial nations and finds that the higher percentage on capital in the *zakāt* system would compensate for the lower percentage on income, even if fixed capital were exempt from the *zakāt*. Therefore, according to Kamāl, the *zakāt* would collect funds easily comparable to the tax intake of these states, and by implication clearly sufficient.[27]

[23] *Ibid.*, pp. 195, 202, 212.
[24] *Ibid.*, p. 208.
[25] *Ibid.*, pp. 205, 214–16, 222–3.
[26] *Ibid.*, p. 195.
[27] *Ibid.*, pp. 218 ff.

Although his calculations seem to be far off the mark, it is worth noting that in Kamāl's understanding the character of the *zakāt* is a support to those in real need. This may of course reduce the costs compared to those of for instance the Scandinavian social benefits system, which gives general rights to everyone belonging to certain categories: aged, disabled, sick, unemployed and so on. An argument for this system has been to establish certain *rights* and spare people the humiliation of individual scrutiny from society's side to determine the extent of misery.

Kamāl asks, is there a public sector in Islam? He answers in the affirmative, but says that Islam has a distinct understanding of its task. In Kamāl's view Islam opposes state dominance over the ownership of the means of production, and would prefer private property to prevail. But the need for a public sector springs from the three concepts of need, of public interest and of prevention of harm (*man' al-ḍarar*). While Islam guards private property it does not forget the interests of the community. Kamāl sums up the reasons for public intervention in the economy in 6 points:

1. Planning for the future was already recognised in the Koran, as demonstrated by the fifteen-year plan against the drought in Egypt made by the prophet Joseph.
2. Islam has made the development of agriculture and industry, and other useful work, a collective duty (*farḍ kifāya*[28]). And it is the duty of the state as the representative of the community to secure this task in case the individuals do not fulfil it sufficiently.
3. According to Islam the poor have a right to care, therefore the state must collect and distribute the *zakāt*. This is one of the most important tasks of the state.
4. The state must supply workers with the tools of their trade. A part of the *zakāt* must be set aside for reintroducing those that have fallen outside the productive sphere.
5. A precedent for sometimes reserving the income from natural resources in the interests of the community was set by the caliph 'Umar by keeping the black soil lands of Iraq as *kharāj*[29] lands, refusing to distribute it as booty to the Muslim army.
6. The central treasury has from the earliest days had the task of overseeing and satisfying the collective interest of the community.[30]

[28] This refers to a distinction in *fiqh* writings between individual duties (*farḍ 'aynī*), such as prayer, fasting and the like, and collective duties (*farḍ kifāya*) from which the individual is excused as long as society as such is able to fulfil them.

[29] The implication being that this land would remain liable for a tax, the *kharāj*, to be paid to the Caliph as the representative of the community of Muslims. See Joseph Schacht, *An Introduction to Islamic Law*, p. 131.

[30] Kamāl, *Al-islām wal-madhāhib al-iqtiṣādiyya al-mu'āṣira*, pp. 165–7.

The public sector and the more general role of the state as an economic actor is discussed more broadly by Kamāl in *The Fiqh of Public Economy.*[31]

Some observations at the level of methodology and approach are in place. We may for instance notice an interesting mixture of scientism and the belief in the force of ideology. For on the one hand throughout the book mainstream Western economics is referred to implicitly as an "objective, neutral" science of economic life. On the other hand Kamāl emphatically states that the financial system of a country reflects its economic, political and social system, which in turn is directly determined by the ideology to which the society in question is committed. Capitalism implies a night-watchman state, where all values restraining individual freedom are refused and common interests are sacrificed. Under socialism central planning sacrifices the interests of the individual for the sake of the perceived collective good. The merit of Islam is that it balances between the individual and the community. It is as if once the choice of ideology is made then this produces a certain kind of economy working through mechanisms that the universal science of economics may explain.[32]

The choice of Islam as the foundation of society implies the application of the *Sharī'a*, and the science of understanding the *Sharī'a* is *fiqh*. Kamāl emphasises that his book brings nothing new either to *fiqh* or to the modern science of economics. His aim is to connect the two, in a sense to bring the contemporary age in touch with the Holy Text (*waṣl al-'aṣr bil-naṣṣ*). Here Kamāl calls for liberating Islamic writings from vague generalities and slogans. He states that Islam can only show its real potential through an active process of rational reinterpretation and struggle for change (*ijtihād al-'aql wa jihād al-taghyīr*), although he hastens to make clear that he himself does not claim the capability for *ijtihād*, but builds his argument with reference to accomplished *fuqahā'*.[33]

The Fiqh of Public Economy differs from other books on economic questions by Muslim Brother writers in that Kamāl's discussions proceed from the concrete issues affecting the Egyptian economy, as shown by his discussions of the state of the public sector, and in his treatment of the role of the IMF.

He states that the crisis symptoms of the Egyptian economy spring from mistaken financial and monetary policies. Especially critical is the imbalance between production and consumption. As long as Egyptians consume far more than they produce, there will be little saving, little investment and a huge trade deficit. There has to be a thorough reform, he

[31] Kamāl, *Fiqh al-iqtiṣād al-'āmm*.
[32] *Ibid.*, pp. 5–6, 517–19.
[33] *Ibid.*, pp. 10–12.

says. Private capital will not involve itself in the process of development unless it feels security for its investment from dangers of administrative interference and ultimately nationalisation. The pressing question of the age is this: how can the state perform its duty of social leadership without affecting negatively the efficiency of production?[34]

The International Monetary Fund has its solution ready. It suggests reducing consumption by increasing prices, lifting subsidies and floating the currency, while at the same time favouring the reduction of investment by increasing the interest rate. In addition it urges privatisation of the public sector.

The IMF is an important institution, since international creditors demand that debtor nations reach an agreement with the Fund on policy reform before they are willing to renegotiate repayment plans. But the IMF is dominated by rich Western countries that control almost two thirds of the votes on its board. Its policy packages might look good in Western academies, but they do not help the economies of poor countries. They lead to dependence on the rich countries. In fact most countries who have implemented IMF-sponsored so-called "stabilisation" and "structural reform" programs have been plunged into political unrest leading in most cases to dictatorship.

There are several problems for instance with the idea that currency floating and the removal of subsidies will lead to reduced imports and increased exports. In most poor countries import is non-elastic since it consists of necessities and input goods for production, therefore increased prices do not automatically reduce import. Export is also non-elastic, because the surplus available for export is small and because of the intense competition on the world market. Lowering the exchange rate of the local currency also has as an effect in increasing the burden of the foreign debt. Increased interest rates, another favoured IMF measure, would negatively affect investment and development. In the case of Egypt the removal of price regulations and subsidies will hit the poor hard. Subsidies must be reformed, since a lot of them end up in the pockets of the rich, but then there must be an alternative to alleviate the suffering of the poor. With regard to selling off the public sector: this cannot be done indiscriminately. Parts of the sector produce goods that are necessities or that have strategic value. The state must keep control over some branches of production, to exercise economic leadership, even if obviously it should withdraw from others.[35]

An Islamic solution might proceed from the advice given to Pharaoh by the Prophet Joseph in the Koran: tireless production, well-guided con-

[34] *Ibid.*, pp. 52, 520.
[35] *Ibid.*, pp. 415–17, 521.

sumption, utmost saving.[36] A new world system is needed that can secure the optimal allocation of resources, a just distribution and a stable political situation. This system should ideally be so construed that this would come about spontaneously and that political interference in the economy would become exceptional. Islam guarantees the greatness of the community in that it makes the creation of a powerful economy a collective duty, starting from the individuals and only involving the state where individuals fail. Kamāl stresses that initiative and responsibility in the development process should devolve on the localities in order to alleviate the burden of the state, and the pressure on the big cities.

In all this Islam respects human beings and their freedom and safety. It defends private property like it defends life. Nationalisation is prohibited, except when necessity demands it, and then it must be compensated at market prices. Some people mistakenly believe that all natural resources are common property, Kamāl says, but this only applies as long as no human effort has been put into the transformation of these resources. However, Islam does place responsibilities on the property owner, reflecting the fact that all wealth in the last instance belongs to God. The Islamic system establishes a lower limit for a decent life, based on the right (*ḥaqq*) of the poor to a share in the wealth of the rich through the *zakāt*, and an upper limit based on justice (*'adl*) in the form of prohibition of *ribā*, of monopoly and of the exploitation of one person by another more generally. It also respects the right of the members of society to be informed, to know the truth about crises and deficits. Without truthful information the state cannot claim taxes from the citizens.[37]

In connection with this Kamāl refutes the criticism that a market economy is groping in the dark with regard to expectations of future supply and demand. He retorts that if any system is plagued with uncertainty it is central planning, which also tends to be shrouded in secrecy, while the market system gives fast, effective and open information. A central planning system will lead to the suppression of freedom. The market itself tends to produce monopoly and exploitation, but in an Islamic system this will be corrected by the rules of the *Sharī'a* and by the effects of the *zakāt*.[38]

In the West, Kamāl claims, neither the concept of public interest, nor more generally norms or social needs, are allowed to enter into the distribution of resources, it is all left to the "preferences of the consumer", and anything else is frowned upon as representing totalitarian socialism. For this reason the West does not organise its production according to a ladder

[36] *Ibid.*, p. 521.
[37] *Ibid.*, pp. 8, 140, 531–3, 538, 542.
[38] *Ibid.*, p. 153.

— Enforced pricing does not stimulate the producer to improve production, so output remains low and imports soar. This problem weighs especially heavy on the public sector.
— The government imports goods like wheat and sells it at subsidised prices, while locally produced goods of the same kind are sold at market prices, or a fixed price higher than the subsidised one. Thereby the Egyptian economy indirectly pays subsidies to producers abroad while securing for them a market in Egypt.
— This situation leads to a tremendous increase in imports and in the trade deficit. The result is a deepening of the debt crisis, very dangerous for national security.
— The complex web of subsidies makes it hard to set up a realistic account of the national economy, to plan, and to evaluate the real economy of new projects.
— The subsidies create a budget deficit which is resolved by printing money, creating in turn an inflation which hit the poor the hardest.
— The pattern of consumption becomes distorted, for instance even in the countryside people start eating the subsidised imported wheat instead of locally produced corn.
— In some cases producers are able to sell their products at a high price, and then procure the same commodity for themselves at the subsidised price.[46]

For these reasons subsidies ought to be abolished, on the condition of a simultaneous comprehensive and well organised introduction of the *zakāt* system, according to Kamāl.[47] Relating to the more general question of price regulation by the state, he says that this is generally forbidden by Islam, in order to protect the rights of the producer. Yet the state may intervene if the producer is able to set an artificially high price because of a monopolistic position in the market. In this case the state may impose the natural market price to protect the legitimate interests of the consumers.[48]

In Kamāl's view the state is responsible for economic development, but its task consists primarily of planning, and providing the preconditions for private initiative to flourish. The state must take responsibility for things that the market cannot secure. This may include defence, law and order, basic education, health services, infrastructure, and research and development, although Kamāl suggests that in the Egyptian case, health services and education would be better and cheaper if run by private capital,

[46] *Ibid.*, pp. 95 ff.
[47] *Ibid.*, p. 425.
[48] *Ibid.*, p. 507.

with the state subsidising the poor directly to enable them to pay for these services. Still he acknowledges the need also for a public productive sector. But he emphasises that the purpose must be of an economic nature, not a social one. Direct public involvement in production should be in order to fill a gap in the development programmes, break up monopolies, secure self-reliance, and more generally to produce goods that are necessary and would otherwise not be produced. Typical sectors would include railways, military industries, mineral excavation and other strategic industries. The products of the public sector should be sold at their market prices, not at subsidised prices that do not distinguish between rich and poor buyers. The poor will have their purchasing-power supported through the *zakāt*. As for the rich, if they need products produced only by the public sector, like water supply for private houses, they will have to pay the market price (unless the state is wealthy enough to distribute such services freely).

But he is harsh in his criticism of the workings of the public sector in existence in Egypt. It had been expanded far too much. There was no reason why it should venture into businesses like running hotels or light industry, or even shops selling fish or beans. These excesses in state takeovers weighed down the public sector with inefficiently run businesses, while also hampering it with strict rules for the distribution of profit. These rules came to tie up so much of the surplus produced in the industry that the public sector had been forced increasingly to rely on loans. In general it produced low returns and in many cases operated at a loss. From the outset the Nasserist strategy of import substitution industrialisation meant trouble for the balance of trade, since the imports needed to build and work the new industries far exceeded the imports saved and any new exports created.

Even fifteen years of the *infitāḥ* had not succeeded in changing the dominance of the public sector. Kamāl goes on to list a number of negative aspects of the Egyptian public sector:

- Whatever their losses, productive units will continue to operate.
- The dominance of the public sector narrows the scope for private investment. The outlet for accumulated private wealth becomes illegal investments, bribery, smuggling, capital flight abroad, luxury consumption or investments of a non-productive nature in trade, real estate or purely speculative ventures. All this in turn serves to increase the country's indebtedness.
- The class of people who benefit from the rampant corruption connected to the public sector becomes a force against reform, while the masses are exploited for the benefit of a handful of millionaires.

— It possesses experts who can ensure that the payments are correctly meted out among the well-to-do.
— It possesses the ability and the force to move against attempts at evasion.
— The poor have the right to be supported from the *zakāt*, and the state must guarantee this right.
— Some of the purposes for which the *zakāt* should be used, like the *jihād*, can only be organised by the state.[53]

The weakness of the current Egyptian taxation system leads the state into borrowing from private sources inside the country and from public and private sources abroad. This is problematic, says Kamāl, because the state tends to crowd private entrepreneurs out of the market for credit. The state can offer high and secure interest on its loans, since it merely transfers the burden onto the tax payers, something private interests cannot compete with.[54]

In the case of state borrowing from abroad this entails the danger of becoming economically and politically dependent on the West. Before the capitalist powers used to exploit the developing countries directly through their colonial system and their monopolistic companies. Then they used their multinational companies and their trade power, and now it is the turn of exploitation through credit with the IMF as chief executive. But in fact, Kamāl says, even this is nothing new, since there are obvious parallels with what happened in the 1870s. Like the *Caisse de la Dette Publique*, the IMF uses the debt crisis to force the policy wishes of the Western powers on Egypt. It happens under fanfares of "modernisation", but the result is a fall in the GDP and an increase in consumption, leading to increased imports and a spiralling debt crisis.[55]

The increasing reliance of the state on foreign credit, combined with currency remittances from Egyptians working in the Gulf, leads to a drying up of domestic saving. At the same time the debt crisis weakens the Egyptian pound *vis-à-vis* hard currencies, undermining the purchasing power of Egyptian incomes. When this is the foreseeable result of government policies it amounts to unlawful consumption of the wealth of others, *akl al-māl bil-bāṭil*, condemned by the Koran.[56]

In any case, in accordance with the Koranic prohibition of *ribā* the state is not allowed to pay interest on either domestic or foreign loans. But if the state needs external financing for its business ventures an Islamic alter-

[53] *Ibid.*, p. 241.
[54] *Ibid.*, p. 397.
[55] *Ibid.*, pp. 399–403.
[56] *Ibid.*, pp. 395, 404.

native exists in the form of *mushāraka*. This would take the form of government bonds with varying return, that is return according to the success or failure of the government projects the bond holder has contributed to. This has the advantage that the bond holders would take an active interest in the performance of the projects in question, and one might imagine a system where the bonds could be turned into shares on request. Of course other branches of state activities, like defence, do not yield a return. Here the state if needed must primarily rely on voluntary contributions or interest free loans (*qarḍ ḥasan*). If this is not sufficient then the state is allowed to extract compulsory payments from the rich, but only until the need has been satisfied.[57]

The duty to pay a portion of one's income and capital in order to care for the poor is also placed on the *ahl al-dhimma* or "protected people", a classical Islamic term for followers of tolerated religions such as Christians, Jews and Zoroastrians. To Kamāl it is a sign of the justice of Islam that the *dhimmis*' contribution to public finance is not called *zakāt* but *jizya*. This is because *zakāt* is a part of Muslim worship, which non-Muslims should not be forced to take part in. The term *jizya* has to do with compensation, and the *jizya* is normally higher than the *zakāt* in order to compensate for non-Muslims not performing military service. But Kamāl states that if they choose to perform such services, the *dhimmīs* will be exempted from this compensatory payment and will pay a *jizya* which is equal to the *zakāt*.[58]

The Labour Party: with Islam against dependence: 'Ādil Ḥusayn

'Ādil Ḥusayn's political trajectory has been sketched above. His thoughts on economic policy can be found in three books: The first, *The Egyptian Economy from Independence to Dependence 1974–9* (1982),[59] delivers a detailed, well documented and widely lauded critique of the "economic opening" under Sadat. But the focus here will be on the second, *Towards a New Arab Thinking* (1985),[60] and the third, a short pamphlet he wrote for party members *Islam: Religion and Civilisation* (1986),[61] which were

57 *Ibid.*, pp. 422 ff, 533–5.

58 *Ibid.*, pp. 322–34.

59 'Ādil Ḥusayn, *Al-iqtiṣād al-miṣrī min al-istiqlāl ilā al-taba'iyya 1974–1979* [The Egyptian Economy from Independence to Dependence 1974–9], 2 vols, Dār al-mustaqbal al-'arabī, Cairo, 1982.

60 'Ādil Ḥusayn, *Naḥwa fikr 'arabī jadīd—al-nāṣiriyya wal-tanmīya wal-dīmuqrāṭiyya* [Towards a New Arab Thinking: Nasserism, Development and Democracy], Dār al-mustaqbal al-'arabī, Cairo, 1985.

61 'Ādil Ḥusayn, *Al-islām dīn wa ḥaḍāra—mashrū' lil-mustaqbal* [Islam: Religion and Civilisation: A Project for the Future], Al-manār al-'arabī, Giza, 1990.

more equal trade relations are established. The reality is, he states, that any adjustment under present relations of power would just cement the grip of the North on the South. Ḥusayn first of all agrees with what he interprets the Chinese view to be, that the developing countries are best served by conflict between the major powers on the world scene, because this leaves them room for manoeuvre. So any international settlement would not be beneficial at this stage. Secondly he argues that the thought that all Third World countries would stand together in the fight for a new order is unrealistic. The law of unequal development is universal, and this means also that different countries will take different positions at different times. This does not preclude alliances. Indeed alliances with other countries in the Third World are essential, but they cannot be permanently organised and cannot extend over three continents. "We must also reject the idea", says Ḥusayn "that the struggle of the Third World for a new order, could be equated with that of the trade unions in relation to the employers". This is precisely what he opposes, for it implies that what the South is seeking is an improvement of its terms, without a basic change in the roles of the dominant and the dominated. "But what we need is a revolutionary change of order to establish an independent position in international relations", Ḥusayn claims.

The crushing of dependency should not be understood to mean that the dependent state should isolate itself and cut off its relations with the states of the North. Not only would this be harmful, but it is also impossible in the light of the developing countries' inherited position in the international division of labour. The intention is to move towards a position which makes dealing with the North on an equal basis possible. "We must rid ourselves of the power of external powers to siphon off our resources and to shape our economic and social structure in a way that is in harmony with their interests", says Ḥusayn. But this altering of the relationship cannot happen overnight. It will be a drawn-out operation, and by its nature requires planning. It must begin with a reform of the civilisational framework and the political, social and economic regimes, and continue with obliterating the inherited structural distortions, so that Egypt may become capable of dealing with the external world on an equal basis.[67]

3. *"Independence will depend on ourselves"*. Especially among those studying the experience of Latin America there has been a tendency to exaggerate the link between economic backwardness and the issue of dependence, so that the two almost become one in their analysis. But this is both wrong historically and logically and leads to placing the full responsibility with the international order. This again becomes an excuse for the dependent state to wait until there is international change. But how

[67] *Ibid.*, pp. 55–6.

could this international change happen if the dependent states are satisfied with just placing requests and petitions with the big powers and hoping for them to sweeten their ways? This is the method of the so-called "group of 77" and of the "North-South dialogues". But the idea inherent in this approach, that initiative should come from the dominant Northern powers, reveals this is not a project for true liberation, says Ḥusayn.

Conversely, other writers exaggeratedly place the responsibility for both development and backwardness on social structures within the dependent countries and tend to disregard the effects of the world order entirely. This is the case with many of our radical Egyptian economists despite their talk of "world capitalism" and "neocolonialism". But both factors must be kept in mind. Obviously countries may be backward in spite of never being exposed to external hegemony, as was the case with Ethiopia and Yemen. Indeed, says Ḥusayn, colonisation in many cases was not the first cause of a country's weakness, but on the contrary its result, springing from the country's "receptivity for being colonised", as the Algerian thinker Malik Bennabi has it.

Still there are clear cases where a country's attempt at economic development have been crushed by armed force, and a distorted development imposed upon it, and Egypt is an excellent example. In any case, while debating the historical origin of backwardness and development, one needs to recognise the fact that the industrialised centre of the world economy today clearly has the power to plan and to execute on a world scale, and to shape the structure of dependent countries. Both the government apparatus and the civil society in these countries is formed in a way that is amenable to stabilising the dependent situation. Of course the local forces that benefit from the *status quo* carry responsibility for its prolongation, but primarily responsible is the leadership of the international order and its octopus-like network of institutions. "We have to point out the main enemy", says Ḥusayn, who clearly views Western exploitation and domination not only as an "objective process" but as the outcome of willed strategic acts by Western political and economic leaders. Indeed, this is a recurring feature of his thought.

"In the final analysis", says Ḥusayn, "while giving both external and internal forces their due in our understanding of the reasons for the present situation, we must be clear that the dependent model relies primarily on external forces, and on the other hand that the independent model must necessarily rely in the first place on local revolutionary forces". The revolution in China brings evidence to the correctness of this view, he writes, in that it sought to create an alliance of all national forces against foreign powers and the social structures linked to the colonial powers.[68]

[68] *Ibid.*, pp. 56–7.

its investments towards the poorer sectors, for instance in establishing services and securing necessities for the production of artisans and small scale industry. However, this redirecting of state investment remains outside the growth model itself as an appendix.

Ḥusayn states that he has no argument with the warnings against some kinds of redistribution. The problem comes when the proposed model does not include guarantees that a growing part of the economic surplus is not squandered on luxurious consumption by the rich.

If the redistribution in question is to take place without changing the basic traits of the socioeconomic make-up, it may happen in two ways. Either the state could increase taxes, so that it could give more investment to the poorer sectors, without reducing that which it gives as investment to services and infrastructure serving the modern sector. However, the increased taxes would mainly have to come from the owners of the modern sector, which contradicts the original Lewis model, since it will reduce the money available for investment in the modern sector. Or on the other hand the government may decide to keep its tax income stable, but would then have to reduce its investments in the modern sector, to divert it to the poorer sectors. Again this contradicts the model in that it reduces the total investment in the modern sector. The only way to avoid this, would be if the capitalists in the modern sector were willing to pay more taxes, and compensate by reducing their consumption of luxuries, not their investment. Theoretically they would do this on the understanding that in the long run everyone would benefit from the new growth coming from below, somewhat like the poor have until now been expected to wait patiently for growth to trickle down from above. The problem is that at least with the present social make-up of the dependent countries this will not work. It seems highly unlikely that the locally dominant economic classes, which also generally possess the political power, would be willing to involve themselves in such an experiment. They refused increased taxes at a time when these taxes went to support their own sector, and will certainly refuse them when they will be for the benefit of others. These local upper classes are also tightly interwoven with the dominant groups of the industrialised North. Any government who tried to impose the proposed redistribution of state investment would have to do so in the face of fierce local and international opposition, even from the World Bank itself.

The solution is tightly bound up with the question of independence. Marx was right when he said that the relations of distribution was the other face of the relations of production. And in our circumstances, when we are conducting a fight for planned independent development and in the opposition of giant international blocs, the suitable relations of production involves state control over the keys of the national economy.

It may be noted here that in his later writings, as will be seen, 'Ādil Ḥusayn, while still advocating an active role for the state, is much more enthusiastic about private ownership and initiative. The change is discernible for instance in his attitude to the struggle over the Islamic Investment Companies, to be reviewed in a later chapter.

A strong national government holding the keys to the economy would actually be able to implement the revised model of the World Bank, says Ḥusayn. By blocking the flight of capital from the country and limiting the consumption of luxuries, it could increase the investment to the benefit of the poorer sectors of the economy, and even to a certain extent the consumption of the poorest, without reducing investment in the modern sector.[72]

6. *Changing the patterns of consumption.* For the state to control the economic positions that are pivotal in securing independence and development would not be enough, however, to ensure the relations of production had been changed to the necessary depth. With regard to distribution this might only result in a redistribution of the products of the modern sector within the same sector, without benefit to the poorer sectors. The result might well be merely an increase in consumption, reduced levels of growth and increased reliance on foreign countries. As Maḥbūb al-Ḥaqq and Galāl Amīn have shown, a true redistribution must take place at the level of deciding what to produce, since private cars do not turn into buses through a political decision to redistribute income.

Ḥusayn regards the structure of consumption, heavily tilted towards the luxury consumption of the upper and middle classes, as a hindrance to the development of national industry, and when met through import, as a waste of badly needed foreign exchange. He favours an income redistribution and an emphasis on establishing industrial projects that cater to basic needs. In this regard he explicitly gives his support to the "basic needs strategy" school of economic development.[73]

The thought, he says, that production is structured by the consumer sending his signals to the producer through the market is now completely crushed. Especially with the role played by giant corporations the typical situation is now that the producer shapes the tastes and desires which suit his productive capabilities without regard to whether his products serve a real need. And the big corporations are now able to spread the same tastes to the Third World through the same brainwashing methods they have used in their home countries. This can be criticised in itself, but the matter

[72] 'Ādil Ḥusayn, *Naḥwa fikr 'arabī jadīd*, pp. 60–4.

[73] See Hunt, *Economic Theories of Development*, pp. 259 ff. for a discussion of the "basic needs" school.

becomes a real threat to independence when the balance between local productive capacities and the structure of demand is disturbed. This demand must then be met either by importing finished products, or by establishing import substitution industries relying on imported technology and raw materials. The threat from this shaping of consumptive patterns is bigger than that of foreign capital entering into joint ventures with local capital. For the joint ventures only tie a limited number of local companies to the dominant states, while changes in demand link the whole modern sector to the capital of the same dominant states. In fact this is why local capital, whether public or private, is pushed towards seeking joint ventures with multinational corporations. As it happens, Jamāl al-Dīn al-Afghānī pointed to this danger a hundred years ago, says Ḥusayn, stating that those competing to adopt Western habits were in fact undermining local production and opening the way for foreign dominance.

From the Westernised style of consumption there follows by necessity an increasing gap between the income of the modern sector and the income of the poorer sections of the population, and even an increasing gap within the modern sector itself. For with the low level of national income per inhabitant, an equal distribution would not give anyone the purchasing-power to effectively demand the imported luxury goods. Such demand can only be secured as long as distribution remains lopsided. This unequal distribution will not lead to higher rates of saving, since the very culture that goes with it means that the comparatively rich groups will compete in conspicuous consumption. A state takeover of the means of production will not in itself alleviate the situation, since any strategy for independent development will under such circumstances carry within it the seeds of its own defeat.

Clearly, then, the model of independent development is logically linked to the principle of just distribution, which cannot be effected by undertaking a redistribution of income, while the same international and foreign powers remain in control of the relations of production. What is needed, according to the strategy of satisfying basic needs, is a revolution in the style of consumption and a direct attack on the locations of poverty. But in forming the new pattern of consumption, one must not merely consider the current productive capacities of the local forces of production. Likewise the long term goal should not be the maximum achievement of the same consumption the West has today. This would mean carrying a dependent attitude of thinking. On the contrary it must be understood that Egyptian society should evolve according to its own standards of evaluation, and that the resulting society may well be quite different from those of the West.[74]

[74] 'Ādil Ḥusayn, *Naḥwa fikr 'arabī jadīd*, pp. 64–7.

7. *Self renewal, not Westernisation.* The concept of modernisation (*taḥdīth*) usually proposed as a goal for development is not good since its general connotation is that of "becoming like the West", or "a part of Europe" as it was expressed by the Khedive Ismā'īl. The essential element for mobilising the energy of the masses in the fight for independent development lies above all in self confidence in confronting the dominant powers. Therefore the goal should rather be termed "self renewal" (*tajaddud dhātī*), since it is an effort for progress springing from the heart of the *umma*. This does not mean neglecting what happens in the world around, says Ḥusayn. It means being critical, and relating to, and interacting with, others on one's own terms. The resultant situation will be one of several distinct civilisational centres.[75]

8. *Civilisational independence.* The aim must be civilisational independence (*istiqlāl ḥaḍārī*), not to become a part of the West, says Ḥusayn, interpreting civilisation as the sum total of the development of means to secure material, intellectual and spiritual needs taking place among a certain people. Because of the differences in natural, social and religious environment this civilisation as a fabric of productive and social practices will be distinct from one people to another, and this is the basis for the existence of nations. The fabric must certainly develop or else the Arab nation will stagnate and deteriorate and end up dependent on stronger nations, Ḥusayn says. But the development must be self-centred. It must not be dictated from the outside, or give in to attempts to tear it apart.[76]

9. *The failure of Marxism.* Marx criticised Western civilisation from the inside. He considered that the emerging capitalism was breaking down all noble values that had existed in society. However, the hope was that it would promote an economic growth that in the future would lay the grounds for the first truly humane society, communism, where noble values would reemerge and reign. But history since Marx has proven him wrong, says Ḥusayn. The leading society in material progress, far beyond what Marx considered a prerequisite for communism, is the United States, which is very far removed from a communist social and economic system. However, the communist Soviet Union has not developed the humane society where new communist values would reign either. Rather, as it has progressed materially its people have moved closer to embracing Western values, which has continued their fall towards the worshipping of material goods.

[75] *Ibid.*, pp. 67–8.
[76] *Ibid.*, pp. 68–70.

Marx was also confused in thinking that an industrial revolution would necessarily have to happen in every country of the world in the same fashion that it did in Europe.[77]

10. *Against determinism*. We do not believe in the necessary correspondence between a certain degree of growth and the required and desired changes in society, says Ḥusayn. "We must seek our own way to a rebirth of Arab society". If they succeed, the Arabs will also have helped the West and others by way of inspiration, but the process must be their own, building on their inherited civilisation based on the balance between the material and the moral aspects of life. There must be a link between independent economic development and civilisational independence, for without this link both will be a sham.

One aspect of achieving this double independence requires creating a suitable pattern of consumption. This will be patterned in the interest of the poorest sectors of the population. "We do not aim at equality in income and property", says Ḥusayn. But the higher income groups will be affected in several ways:

— The general concentration on satisfying the basic needs and attacking directly the locations of greatest poverty will lead to a certain equalising of levels and kinds of consumption. This means the rich will have to reduce their consumptive ambitions somewhat.
— Consumption will have to be adjusted to fit with the local productive capacities, although these will be growing. This will also create a relatively low ceiling of consumption for an extended period of time.

This reshaping of the consumptive pattern for the purpose of buttressing independence will clash with the culture of the present generations among high income groups. "But this is only part of a general process of liberating our thoughts", says Ḥusayn. The present consumptive pattern is a symptom of disease. People have exchanged the *galabiyya* for the suit, in spite of Egypt's hot climate, in fear of being seen as backward by the West. The disease is the idea that people here are incapable of achieving anything by themselves, incapable of achieving economic development on an independent basis. "We must rid ourselves of this mental dependence, cultivate pride in our heritage", he says. Then maybe the sacrifices in consumption that some will have to make for a time will be bearable. As the Koran says "God does not change a people's lot unless they change what is in their hearts".[78]

[77] *Ibid.*, pp. 70–3.
[78] *Ibid.*, pp. 73–5.

11. *The Chinese example.* Ḥusayn goes on to cite Japan and China as examples of what he means by civilisational independence. Here he chooses to discuss only China. He considers that despite all Marxist rhetoric, what Mao Zedong was striving for was the rebirth of China as an independent civilisational centre. He came into conflict not only with the West, but also with the Soviet Union because of his insistence that Chinese development should build on Chinese values for human behaviour. Ḥusayn sees things such as the emphasis on regular manual work for intellectuals, sessions of self-criticism and even the cultural revolution as signs of this emphasis on cultivating specific Chinese values. He claims that when the Chinese were talking of a revolution in the "superstructure" this was just Marxist lingo for what he calls the civilisational model or framework.

There is no doubt, says Ḥusayn, that the cultural or civilisational emphasis of the revolution contributed to the success of economic development, to the development of an independent consumptive pattern, to the satisfaction of basic needs, and through all this to the realisation of the most equal distribution of income known to a human society.

Their experience also showed that the creation of what they called the communist man, that is a balanced person, who is moved not only by material incentives, but also, and even more, by moral ones, does not have to wait until production has reached a level securing an abundance of goods. That is, it shows a role for the intellectual or moral factor far above that recognised by orthodox Marxism. Mao Zedong, more than being a Marxist, was a thinker who based his ideas on Chinese intellectual and moral traditions. China has set a model of independent civilisational development, from which the Arab world must learn, although its development will necessarily be different from that of China in many respects, since it springs from different roots, says Ḥusayn.[79]

12. *GDP per capita is not the measure of development.* Economic development is a basic indispensable factor in the quest for the long term main goal of civilisational independence. But here one needs to look critically at the blind use of GDP per capita as a basic indicator of progress. Ḥusayn refuses this. The basic indicator must be the question of independence or dependence on the civilisational, political and economic level, even if this cannot be measured so neatly in numbers, he says. Here the main factor regarding economic development will be: does the country have an independent national direction of the economy or not? One must ask, how is the GDP composed, does it fit the goal of independence?

[79] *Ibid.*, pp. 75–7. Cf. p. 33.

Of course if such independence is established, then the indicators of the level of growth and of GDP per capita gains importance. For as long as one is proceeding along a path of securing basic needs through production, and increasing local independent technological capacity, then these indicators will be helpful as measures of progress. Then the emphasis on the exact figure of GDP per capita should not be exaggerated, but one should attach importance to the gap between Egypt and the developed Western nations. For this implies something about economic strength, which is important for independence in the long run. It is certainly necessary to acquire the most up-to-date scientific and technological knowledge, and the capacity to use it, says Ḥusayn. Also, if the "basic needs strategy" implies certain sacrifices from the richer classes, it becomes important that the process should not take more than at most a generation to produce marked improvement in living standards. For Marx and Engels were right in stating that it is a law that poor societies tend to develop sharp class divisions. And even if this is not an iron law, and Eastern societies do not have to wait for abundant production in order to implement a redistribution of wealth and a building of noble values, the present poverty creates a pressure for achieving fast results. The point is then that growth rates and GDP per capita have their place as indicators, but one should not strive to achieve high scores on these accounts at any cost, or to the detriment of the main goals. One may even accept that the strategy may for a certain time, or under certain conditions, lead to falling growth rates, says Ḥusayn. Here he again points to China, which achieved outstanding growth rates from 1950–75 compared with other densely populated countries. But they were prepared to put growth in second place for a period if major battles of independence were at hand, as during the Cultural Revolution. Even if countries like Taiwan and South Korea achieved higher growth rates, this was a kind of growth that was dependent and distorted.[80]

It is worth noting here that later in the 1980s Ḥusayn more than once mentioned South Korea as a positive example of development. The question of whether this was the result of closer study or of a certain change in ideological priorities or both will be considered later.

13. *Not an easy task.* Finally Ḥusayn stresses that the struggle for independent civilisational development will not be an easy task. There will be massive resistance on the political, economic and cultural, even possibly military, level from the West and from its local allies. Even so this is just the minor *jihād*, and it can be accomplished by national mobilisation.

[80] *Ibid.*, pp. 77–81.

"But the greater *jihād* will the struggle within ourselves", says Ḥusayn. In particular the middle classes have been inculcated with Western standards of consumption, but if these attitudes cannot be changed, if a thorough reform of the people themselves is impossible, then the envisioned model of independence and satisfying basic needs is not feasible. However, the energies that can be released by a cultural, civilisational awakening are enormous and in such a situation, Ḥusayn believes, the necessary changes in human attitudes may be brought about. But to be sustained and channelled into the struggle against the enemy the released energies must be organised by a strong and able leadership exercised by a well organised party. He doubts whether the most intense phases of the struggle for the long term goal of civilisational independence are compatible with the multi-party system, since the odds against the nation's struggle are so massive that they require the utmost unity, and in many cases secrecy on the part of the struggling nation.[81]

To his thirteen points Ḥusayn adds a discussion on the necessity of Arab solidarity in the economic field. He considers a dominant public sector and the use of central planning as indispensable to the development effort in view of the forces opposed to the independent development of Third World countries. But he makes it clear that this is no solution in itself, and may also lead to just switching dependence from the West to the Eastern Bloc. To be really independent and sustainable development must have a wider scope than the individual Arab state. In line with Samir Amin, Ḥusayn states that the goal of independent development, a "self-centred" development, seems unattainable for any Arab country in isolation. This calls for a "collective reliance on oneself", and regional integration in the economic as well as in other fields. But he warns against the current trend of relying on projects of economic integration in lieu of a political will to achieve Arab unity. This is an instance of exaggeration of the role of the economy in development. Any concrete step, such as increased exchange of commodities, joint ventures, improved trans-Arab communications etc., must be welcomed and one must support their implementation and fight for their continued existence. But it must be realised that real Arab unity, especially one including the oil countries, is not a matter to be taken easily by the powers dominating the world today, Ḥusayn warns. This is not any regional cooperation but the historical unification of a nation, and it will create a new super power in the midst of a highly strategically sensitive area, because of its control of a strategic resource. It implies disentangling the oil producers from their incorporation into Western economy and in general Arab economies from their

[81] *Ibid.*, pp. 81–3.

being shaped by Western economic power. Therefore the opposition to it will be great, and therefore it demands before anything else the existence of an independent will on the part of the Arabs. This means that comprehensive economic integration can only come as the *result* of political unity, and cannot *produce* it. And it means there must be a firm belief in a sacred doctrine (*'aqīda muqaddasa*) so that the nation will be willing to accept the necessary sacrifices and even martyrdom.[82]

Two central issues that must be tackled on the road to Arab unity and economic integration, are the food gap and the role of oil in the Arab economy. The lack of self reliance in the production of food, and in particular cereals, is a pressing issue, says Ḥusayn. In particular this is so, because the trade in cereals on the world market is almost monopolised by a handful of Western countries, the United States alone controlling half the market. With the prospect of a future shortage of cereals on the world market, this situation seriously threatens the possibility for independent action on behalf of the Arab nation. But pooling Arab resources it would be possible to double the cultivable area in the Arab world, in particular through the better exploitation of the irrigation potential in Iraq, Egypt and Sudan, and to increase the yield of the acreage currently sown with cereals. However this would also involve a struggle against vested interests in the dispersed Arab nation, interests centring on each capital. One must also expect resistance to the transfer of large populations that would be required for an optimal utilisation of the economic potential.[83]

As for the question of oil and the money earned from its extraction and sale, its current use has many negative effects, says Ḥusayn, but perhaps the most damaging is that it breaks down people's esteem for work. The immense wealth that the sale of oil has made available to the Arab world, in particular since the mid-1970s, is not the result of a comprehensive development of the forces of production. So on one level the fact that some of the least developed areas of the Arab world have become vastly richer than their neighbours with a long history of economic modernisation is not an incentive for taking seriously the effort to modernise and industrialise. On the individual level the availability of easy wealth, not just for the inhabitants of the countries rich in oil, but for millions of people migrating to the Gulf and Libya in search of work from countries such as Egypt, Yemen, Jordan and Syria, breaks down the idea of work as a social value, while it tends at the same time to also break down the very cement of society. The gifted people no longer stay at home and contribute to a collective development effort, but go abroad as unconnected individuals in search of their personal piece of the oil wealth.

[82] *Ibid.*, pp. 85–8.
[83] *Ibid.*, pp. 89–90.

Along with the wealth come Western habits of consumption further eroding the individual's feeling of belonging to his community and its history. Also important, there is no real link here between production and consumption. It is interesting to note that Ḥusayn stresses that whatever criticism can be levied against Western society, it must be kept in mind that in the West standards of consumption are indeed linked to the productive effort. In the West work and the purposeful use of time is held in high esteem, he says.[84]

Islam: Religion and Civilisation is a pamphlet of seventy-five small pages explaining the ideology of the Labour Party and its proposed solutions to the problems of Egyptian society. It was first written in 1986, when 'Ādil Ḥusayn had only relatively recently joined the party, and is a statement of the Islamist course which finally triumphed in the party as a whole in 1989, albeit against fierce resistance.

In the perennial debate of the relationship between the individual and society Ḥusayn clearly stresses the rights of society more than for instance Yūsuf Kamāl. He uses expressions such as "the worship (*'ubūdiyya*) of God is expressed in work for the good of the group, and nearness to God is in the service of the people"[85] and "an individual human being is nothing, with the others he is everything".[86] And he states that the main focus of all religions, while not neglecting the individual, has been the life of the community.[87]

In the chapter on "independent development", which takes up almost half the pamphlet, Ḥusayn starts by emphasising the radical difference between Islam and Western economic and social theories and models like Marxism and capitalism. In the West the economy has been given first rank, and the measure of its success is the maximum fulfilment of the sensual and beastly desires of the individuals. Islam does not deny the importance of the economy and of production. "What we deny is that the number of tons of steel or the number of cars or refrigerators produced should in itself be the main measure of the human progress of a society", Ḥusayn says.[88]

The problem of economic dependency is obvious when considering the large import component in Egypt's food consumption. This situation gives the food exporting countries the power to starve Egypt if they do not like its political course, Ḥusayn writes. But true independence in our time

[84] *Ibid.*, pp. 91–8.

[85] 'Ādil Ḥusayn, *Al-islām dīn wa ḥaḍāra*, p. 5. Here we see how Ḥusayn echoes the old slogan of the Young Egypt: "God is great and long live the people!".

[86] *Ibid.*, p. 3.

[87] *Ibid.*, pp. 3–4.

[88] *Ibid.*, pp. 29–31.

also demands technological independence. Though he rejects increased production as a goal in itself, with disregard for values, it is obvious, Ḥusayn says, that a country like Egypt must seek to achieve high rates of economic growth. But Egyptians must rid themselves of the current technological dependency, he says. One needs to be on the alert when dealing with the major international corporations that more or less monopolise the technology market today. The decision of what to buy must reside with Egypt, and the best possible terms must be sought regarding quality and price, Ḥusayn writes. But in the long run the only solution is to develop one's own capacity for technical innovation. In this field independence is also imperative, since although the natural sciences may be universal, technical solutions are specific to the natural environment and to the social values of the society in which they are applied. For example one cannot allow the use of a technique that destroys the fertility of the soil even if in the short run it is the most efficient and economic. This might work in the secular West, where the interests of later generations do not enter the question, Ḥusayn says, but in an Islamic society the people have, as God's deputies on earth, a responsibility to those who come after. To use such a technique would constitute "mischief on the earth" (*ifsād fī al-arḍ*) fiercely condemned in the Koran.[89]

Furthermore the sources of wealth and income must be in national hands. The thought that all the capital of the country should be state property must be rejected, yet it must remain the property of Egyptians, and not held jointly with Westerners, though there may be exceptional cases. Then there should be a division of roles between the national private and public sectors. Since 1974 Egypt has strayed from this principle.

Especially dangerous is the foreign influence in the field of banks and foreign trade, Ḥusayn says. Foreign investment in this sector should be banned, and the Egyptian banks should be tightly controlled in their foreign relations, so that the country's limited financial resources could be mobilised for the development effort, and possibly one could retrieve that which has been smuggled abroad. An end must be put to dealings in *ribā*.[90]

As for the private sector Islam recognises the right of individuals to a legitimate return on their efforts or investment. It warns against the creation of monopolies, but this does not mean that private interests are banned from developing large business undertakings. What is important is that the private sector must operate within the framework of the grand strategy of the state. As it holds its property in trust from God it is bound by God's limits (*ḥudūd*) and by the interests of the nation. But state planning does not mean the state should own most means of production.

[89] *Ibid.*, pp. 44–7. Cf. Koran 11:116.
[90] *Ibid.*, pp. 48–9.

On the question of distribution of the national product, Ḥusayn claims that the *zakāt* is not the only way to achieve this.[91] Not least important is the fact that the distribution is already implicit in the decision of what to produce. If a lot of the productive apparatus is put into the production of luxury goods, then this cannot afterwards be turned into goods satisfying the needs of the poor: a private car cannot be converted into a bus. In an Islamic system the priority in production will be put on necessities in line with Islamic principles and with the development strategy of satisfying basic needs.[92]

Finally Ḥusayn argues that what is most threatening to national independence is the growth of classes who are dependent for their livelihood on foreigners, like workers in foreign owned businesses, rich business men profiting from dealings with multinational enterprises and people employed in projects sponsored by the American government, or Western agencies more generally.[93]

Guided freedom and the quest for independence

Emerging from these texts produced in the 1980s is obviously neither a coherent theoretical blueprint for a new economic system nor a detailed programme for reform. What we find is a collection of general principles which according to the Islamists ought to guide economic life in an Islamic state-principles mostly of a moral nature.

A fundamental idea common to the Islamist writers on economic questions is that of humanity as "God's steward [*khalīfa*] on earth". Every individual has the right to private property, but it is limited by fundamentally being God's property. The individual is seen as holding property in trust from God and (most explicitly with Yūsuf Kamāl) from society as God's deputy, as it were. Therefore, private property involves a social responsibility. It should be made to bear fruit in the service of society, and it should be preserved and developed for future generations. Others have claims on the property: the return it brings, or even parts of the property itself, may be needed to satisfy urgent needs of the wider community. If this social responsibility is not taken seriously, then society has the right to intervene in the management of the property, or in some cases take it away from the owner.

[91] *Ibid.*, pp. 49–54.

[92] *Ibid.*, pp. 55–8.

[93] *Ibid.*, pp. 54–5. In passing we may note here that Ḥusayn uses the word *ifranj* for foreigners, at the same time a word of more popular than academic usage, and a word that calls forth the image of the aggressive "Frankish" invaders from the Crusades to Napoleon Bonaparte.

However, there is some ambiguity among these Islamists with regard to the question of equality among the members of society. Above it was noted how Sayyid Quṭb had presented this as a basic Islamic principle. However, while ʻĀdil Ḥusayn wrote of the positive effects of equal distribution, praising the Chinese experience in this regard, Yūsuf Kamāl was more reserved. He stressed that the human desire for distinction was a necessary driving force in a sound economy. So in an Islamic state people would have differing economic situations. The essential thing to Kamāl was that the state must secure equal access to education and employment, so that the emerging distinctions between people would be based solely on individual merit.

Kamāl can at times be seen delivering vehement attacks on capitalism for allowing the rich to wallow in luxury while the poor struggle to make ends meet. However, this does not lead to a desire to set up an egalitarian system, but to a call for the abolition of interest, after which the economy should ideally spontaneously work to secure the required basic needs.

There is common agreement among the writers surveyed that private property is the basic principle in Islam and that this is necessary for stimulating individuals to exert their best efforts to develop and preserve wealth. It is emphasised that the only legitimate way to acquire income and wealth is through work, but inheritance and the investment of accumulated capital is made to fit into this framework, in the sense that the capital involved is considered the result of previous work by the owner or his or her family. However, the right to private property is seen as limited in two ways, in accordance with the works of the previous generation of Islamist writers. First there are prohibitions on immoral practices, most important of which are monopoly (*iḥtikār*) and "usury" (*ribā*), considered by these writers as synonymous with the interest system practised by modern financial institutions. Secondly, private property is limited by the call for social solidarity expressed through the duty to pay the *zakāt*, and in case of need even more.

The divergence starts when the elements of individual freedom and state responsibility on behalf of the community are weighed against each other. The Muslim Brother Kamāl strongly emphasises that private property must be defended like life itself, and should be guaranteed against expropriation except in the case of absolute necessity. The reform he envisions of the present state of the economy is narrowed to the prohibition of *ribā* and of monopoly, by which term he more often than not refers to the domination of the state in the economy. In contrast, ʻĀdil Ḥusayn states that in a country like Egypt seeking to break out of backwardness and dependency, the state must play a dominant role, controlling the keys to the economy and exercising leadership through centralised planning.

However, the differences can easily be overstated. A closer examination reveals on the one hand that Kamāl acknowledges the need for a public productive sector as part of the development effort and more generally for the state to exercise planning for development, which is also implicit in his call for Islamic priorities to guide investment and production. It is true that he emphasises that the state must only step into productive ventures where private initiative fails, and that he warns that the *Ḥadīth*-based Islamic principle of "common ownership to firewood, water and pasture" provides no *carte blanche* for nationalisations of economic resources of public interest. But on the other hand ʿĀdil Ḥusayn stresses that although the sources for wealth should be kept in national hands, they need not all be state property, and private entrepreneurs have a legitimate place even in large scale business. The essential thing for Ḥusayn is that private capital should operate in accordance with state strategy, it should be "bound by God's limits and the interests of the nation".

The writers agree that public interest takes priority over private interests.

The duty to develop

Economic development emerges as a central concern for the Islamists. For ʿĀdil Ḥusayn this is an integral part of the quest for independence which remains at the heart of his political and intellectual efforts, and Islam primarily enters the picture as a mobilising force towards this end.[94] Kamāl, for his part, states that the *Sharīʿa* aims at comprehensive development in order to achieve strength and glory for the Muslim nation. He claims that economic development is a *farḍ kifāya*, a collective duty, to be secured by the state if individuals fail to promote it with sufficient force. The whole development effort is likened to a *jihād*, ironically reminding one of the decidedly non-Islamist former Tunisian leader Habib Bourguiba who in the 1960s tried to exempt his people from the fast during *Ramaḍān* on the grounds that they were engaged in a *jihād* for development. Kamāl emphasises the centrality of the development effort in an Islamic system through stating that *zakāt* revenue can be used for productive investment. Another central economic writer of the Brothers, Ḥusayn Shaḥḥāta (see below, p. 176), states that work is to be considered an *ʿibāda*, part of the worship of God, reminding us of the Protestant idea of work as a calling, considered by Weber and others essential to the success of capitalist development in Northwestern Europe.

The Islamists draw on an old principle in *fiqh* of adopting a ladder of priority where consideration of public interest (*maṣlaḥa*) is involved. In

[94] This is not to suggest that Ḥusayn is insincere in his Islamism, merely that the goal of independent development is taken for granted and not deduced from Islamic teachings.

questions of investment and production one should proceed first to secure necessities, then needs, then improvements. Emphasis is placed on the production of basic needs. For ʻĀdil Ḥusayn this gives Islamic legitimation to adopting the basic-needs-strategy for economic development. As will be shown later, the same connection was sometimes drawn by Muslim Brothers.

The third road to balance and harmony: an Islamic welfare state

The writers surveyed consider it the task of an Islamic state to secure a minimum of welfare for all members of society. This is to be realised through concentrating investment and production on the provision of basic necessities and, centrally for Kamāl, through the *zakāt*. The Muslim Brother writer emphasises that the *zakāt* should provide more than what is necessary for mere survival, every member of society should have the right to a certain degree of enjoyment of life.

The ideal of the just Islamic society was not one of radical egalitarianism, but rather of balance, of Islam as a moderate, third way avoiding the excesses of capitalism and communism. This implied that the ideal was to seek a harmonious balance between different social groups and between generations. Class conflict was seen as an evil which it was an imperative to avoid lest its divisive cancer split society into warring factions.

The Islamic ideal also involved a balance between the concerns of this world and the next. While Islam values the spiritual aspects of life and abhors materialism, the Muslims should be actively engaged in the affairs of this world and strive to make this life as good as possible. They rejected asceticism on the one hand and hedonism on the other, in contrast to Christianity, which they considered guilty of a one-sided preoccupation with the next world and of denying the needs of the flesh, and to the different materialist trends making the opposite mistake.

Faith works wonders

Over and above the general principles enunciated as guiding an Islamic economy, the Islamist writers emphasise the liberating force of faith in itself. Faith induces good behaviour towards others and thereby creates a solid framework for social solidarity, says Kamāl. Ḥusayn stresses belief in a sacred doctrine as an indispensable prerequisite for the will to sacrifice without which any serious development effort is doomed to failure.

In opposition to what they see as the materialist determinism of Marxism, the Islamists propose an idealist, even voluntarist, view of social history. While growth is necessary and desirable, it does not by itself lead to the desired changes in society. And it is the ideology to which a society is committed that is the basis for its political, social and economic system and not vice versa.

Differing styles and approaches

It might be said that in their divergent approaches the writers surveyed demonstrate the elasticity and flexibility of the Islamist discourse. Kamāl, as the representative of an organisation that by the 1980s included within its ranks quite a number of wealthy businessmen and high ranking 'ulamā', presents an economic ideology that is conservative both in its style and approach and in its content. It is full of Koranic and *Ḥadīth* quotations, and proceeds from the Koran to society. This is not to deny that his is a *selective* reading of the canonical sources, but the *form* in which he chooses to present his argument calls forth the image of the Islamic economy as a timeless recipe readily available in the holy texts. It stresses the almost sacred character of private property, and it advocates solving the country's economic problems through enlarging the scope of the free enterprise of the private sector. The introduction of the *zakāt* and the prohibition of *ribā* will take care of reducing existing social gaps without further state interference. Ḥusayn on the other hand, with his communist background and as a representative of a party with a weak, but overwhelmingly pettybourgeois, social basis, writes in a quite distinct style. He is on the one hand steeped in the concepts of "modern" social science and on the other, especially when he writes for a broader public, very conscious of using a language at once simple and clear, and interspersed with references to Islamic history and Islamic concepts. But Islam is seen primarily as the bond between humanity and God and between humans themselves that gives strength and guidance for the struggle. The emphasis is not so much on isolated Koranic rulings, although Ḥusayn also concludes with a call for basing the economy on the principles of Islam. While agreeing with the view of humanity as God's steward on earth, he does not construct his ideas primarily around particular *Sharī'a* concepts, such as the prohibition of *ribā* and the duty of paying *zakāt* (in fact he scarcely mentions them, and he does not favour making the *zakāt* a publicly enforced tax). In content his economic prescriptions lean much more in the direction of state interference and direction of the economy.

Ḥusayn starts from an analysis of the concrete situation of the country, and from the wish for independence, a theme curiously rarely mentioned as a central issue by other writers, with the exception of Kamāl's discussion of foreign debt. Most likely this reflects their approach from the text, not from society and its real problems. Ḥusayn's three main themes are (1) the need for a planned strategy of self-centred development, relying on one's own human and material resources, (2) the need for this strategy to put "satisfying the basic needs of the poor" at the top of the agenda, and (3) that what is needed is self renewal, not Westernisation. In *Towards a New Arab Thinking* he calls for civilisational independence, somehow forwarding a culturalist version of Samir Amin's call for a "polycentric world" in the more purely economic sense.[95] However, in his booklet *Islam: Religion and Civilisation*, written later and directed at a wider audience, this relativist idea is largely gone, and more emphasis is put on Islam as a superior civilisation fighting the infidel Franks of the North.

Comparing the writings on economic principles by Kamāl and Ḥusayn with those of the previous generation briefly discussed above, the most striking thing is perhaps the strong element of continuity from the pioneers, with the partial exception of Ḥusayn, who comes from outside the Islamist tradition and writes in a distinct style. Recognizable elements include the principle of man as God's steward on earth, and society as the overseer of what is ultimately God's property. Likewise there is the principle of private property as basic, but moderated by the ban on interest and monopoly and the duty to pay the *zakāt* as a major means to achieve a just distribution. The general idea of Islam as the moderate third road is also common to the writers of the 1950s and the 1980s alike.

Some of the divergences evident among the pioneers of Islamist economic thought are also present. While 'Ādil Ḥusayn seems to favour a rather egalitarian regime of distribution close to the views of Sayyid Quṭb, the Muslim Brothers of the 1980s emerge as more "Mawdudian", in particular this goes for Kamāl who stresses the human urge for distinction as a necessary driving force in the economy. A similar division can be discerned on the question of the role of the state in the economy. Again Kamāl comes out as closer to Mawdūdī with his near-sacralisation of private property and call for minimisation of the public sector and state intervention, while Ḥusayn who advocates a leading role for the state seems to be more in tune with Sayyid Quṭb and in particular Muḥammad Bāqir al-Ṣadr. However, as discussed above, it must be noted that beyond his anti-state rhetoric Kamāl both implicitly and at times explicitly acknowledges the need for positive state involvement in the development process.

The emphasis on development as a duty for an Islamic state and society is otherwise something setting the writers of the 1980s off from those of the 1950s. The exception here in the older generation would be al-Ṣadr, who can interestingly be seen to foreshadow also the idea of Islamic priorities for development and on the whole the quasi-consensus which will later be seen developing among the Egyptian Islamists towards 1990 on a mixed economy guided by state planning.

[95] Samir Amin, *Delinking: Towards a Polycentric World*, Zed Books, London, 1990, p. xii.

Finally the question of economic independence, always central in Islamist politics, makes its first appearance in the theoretical Islamist discourse on the economy in the 1980s through the newcomer ʻĀdil Ḥusayn and, although as a minor question, in one of the works by Yūsuf Kamāl.

4

INDEPENDENCE, STRENGTH AND JUSTICE
ISLAMISTS ON EGYPT'S ECONOMIC PROBLEMS

To what extent have the theoretical formulations discussed in chapter 3 informed the policies of the Islamists on current economic issues? With the partial exception of the work of 'Ādil Ḥusayn, it might be tempting to say: Not very much. Not that the general actions of the Islamists have contradicted the theoretical lines laid out for an Islamic economy in the books of their leaders. Rather these books have been largely irrelevant to the formulation of policies on most questions of the hour, except in a very general sense. However, the interpretation of this will be taken up in the conclusion of the work.

Of course measuring the principles of economic policy proclaimed by the Egyptian Islamists directly against their practice is impossible, since the parties in question in the period under study (and until the time of writing) did not possess the political power to implement their ideas. Nor can we take the experiences of Iran and the Sudan under Islamist rule as evidence, partly because of the differences in the ideologies of the ruling groups of these countries compared with that of their Egyptian counterparts, but also because of the differences in the respective socio-economic situations. Nevertheless, the experience of economic development in these Islamist-ruled countries will be briefly considered later, as will the kind of economic practice somewhat related to Islamism that *does* exist in Egypt, namely that of Islamic banking and finance.

Although a study of the Egyptian Islamists' economic ideas put into practice is out of the question, there still exists an abundance of material for studying how their general ideological statements on economic reform translate into positions on concrete issues. This material appears in the form of running comments of the Muslim Brothers and the Labour Party on economic issues in the period from 1984 to 1990 as expressed through the Islamist press and through their representatives in the People's

Assembly, and the existing corpus of programmatic documents from the two groups.[1]

Most of what was written in the Egyptian debate on economic policy during the 1980s reflected more or less one of two basic positions. On the one side were those, already alluded to, who wanted to open the economy further, eliminating as far as possible all constraints on the free movement of market forces. Constantly suggesting new measures to be carried through in implementing liberalising reform, it was definitely the wing on the offensive. Pressurised by international agencies the government officially leaned in this direction, but the most vocal argument for liberalisation came from certain local business circles, not least the relatively newly founded Businessmen's Association. Politically the New Wafd Party and parts of the government National Democratic Party represented this attitude. At the other end of the spectrum were those who warned of the possibly disastrous consequences of liberalisation for social conditions and independent manoeuvring. The proponents of this line, whether Marxists, radical nationalists or Islamists tended to be defensive, arguing against measures proposed by the liberalisers in government or the IMF. The Socialist Labour Party and the leftist National Progressive Unionist Rally Party (*Tajammu'*) were the primary political upholders of this line of thinking.

Early in Mubarak's period as president he convened a national conference on the economy, to which the opposition and the academic community were invited to present their views on economic reform. This created some optimism. The conference seems to have been dominated by a rather critical attitude at least towards some aspects of the *infitāḥ*. And for a period thereafter Mubarak emphasised the need for turning the *infitāḥ* productive, in stead of the flourishing of mere commercial and financial ventures that had been its result so far. Despite both this and the somewhat more restrictive import policies implemented at certain times in the mid-1980s, the government course did not basically change. The cautious attitude towards the *infitāḥ* policies in Mubarak's early years should probably be seen mainly as a reflection of the new president's need for stabilising the social and political climate in order to secure his position. The invitation to a broad dialogue on economic policies in order to build a national consensus has until the time of writing not been effectively repeated.

Although it has already been indicated that the Labour Party were situated in the anti-*infitāḥ* camp, interesting developments in their views in the course of the latter half of the 1980s will be noticed. It will also be

[1] See pp. 17–18 above for a presentation of the sources utilised.

seen how the staunch anti-Nasserists of the Muslim Brothers were induced by the dynamic of the political role they came to play as leaders of the opposition to move towards a position on economic policy very close to that of their Labour Party allies.

In very broad terms three main positive themes underlying the discourse of Muslim Brothers and Labour Party representatives on economic issues may be identified. The quest is for *independence, strength*, and *justice*.

First and last: independence

The most prominent theme uniting the Islamists from the Brothers and the Labour Party is the quest for independence not only in the economic but also all other spheres of life. It is the single most frequently occurring theme in their discourse on economic questions.

However, in the literature surveyed in chapter 3 this theme hardly surfaced. In his book *The Struggle between Islam and Capitalism* Sayyid Quṭb does raise the issue of the need to build an Islamic bloc that can operate in world politics independent of the capitalist and communist blocs, but he does not specifically discuss the question of economic independence.[2] The main exception to the lack of discussion of economic independence is represented by the works of ʻĀdil Ḥusayn, who explicitly stated time and again both in his books and in his newspaper writings that dependence or independence was the major question, but rarely does he link this claim to Islam.

As is discussed below, economic independence is taken for granted as a goal, and rarely ever provided with any specifically Islamic legitimation. To the extent that implicit arguments for this target may be inferred, it is primarily that economic independence is a *sine qua non* of the possibility to choose one's own course of action in the political field. But this desired freedom of action does not seem to be in need of supporting argument. The threat against Egyptian and Arabo-Muslim independence is perceived as twofold, springing from the structures of the world economy into which Egypt is being ever-faster woven, and more directly and immediately from conscious Israeli-US efforts to make Egypt in particular a pliant pawn in their plot to dominate the Middle East.

For the Islamists the aim is not to break off relations with the world economy, but to be able to participate in it from a position of strength. Although they consider a complete delinking both unrealistic and unde-

[2] Cf. Quṭb, *Ma'rakat al-islām wal-ra' smāliyya* [The Struggle between Islam and Capitalism], p. 54.

sirable, they do consider it necessary to reach a situation where Egypt is basically self-reliant in the procurement of food and other necessities. Likewise local industry must be developed in order to break the total dependence on the West for technology. In this regard the Islamists consider it both legitimate and necessary to reserve the right to shield the national economy from the full force of outside competition by restricting imports and currency trade.

The Islamists' concern for independence therefore caused them to launch passionate attacks against the influence exercised on the Egyptian government by the International Monetary Fund, who called for liberalising Egypt's external trade regime to an extent the Islamists feared would undermine the possibilities of building a local industrial base. The Labour Party took the lead in attacking the Bretton Woods institutions as agents of the United States, stating that their policy intended to break down the local price structure in Egypt, thereby endangering the preservation of a national independent economic structure. The West used Egypt's foreign debt as a weapon in forcing their policies on the country. The government in Cairo kept insisting that the IMF was just an institution for technical expertise, and not at all like the *Caisse de la Dette Publique* of the 1870s. For the Islamists the realities were otherwise; the Fund was primarily a tool for US-Israeli schemes to dominate Egypt and thereby the region as a whole. The Muslim Brothers supported the rejection of the IMF guidelines for economic policy, and in particular warned against the detrimental impact the IMF's call for increased interest rates would have on the "national private sector" of small scale entrepreneurs.

The strong nationalist content of Islamist economic policies was reflected in a very restrictive view of direct foreign investment. Gradually the parties seem to have united in the view that the only foreigners allowed to hold capital assets in Egypt ought to be Arabs, or in some formulations Muslims in general. They were also sceptical of the foreign influence embedded in loans and grants for development projects, and wanted to reduce this kind of finance drastically. However, they did acknowledge that the country would remain dependent on flows of finance from abroad for the foreseeable future. In this situation the Islamists wanted to lessen dependence on the United States and the old colonial powers by letting countries like Japan, Canada and Sweden provide an increasing share of the loan portfolio. But above all they wanted the huge financial sums controlled by the Arab oil states to be made available for Egyptian development purposes, even if the Gulf states were at times accused of imposing conditions on their loans that were no better than those imposed by the major Western powers.

The need for Arab integration was in fact a consistent theme in the economic discourse of the Islamists. Interestingly, also when the talk was of the need for general *Muslim* cooperation and solidarity, a discussion of the potential benefits always focused on forging stronger economic links between Egypt and other *Arab* countries. This observation might put into question the clarity of the dichotomy between Islamists and Arab nationalists, a matter returned to below.

Fighting dependence on the United States and Israel

Two interrelated perils to economic independence were identified by the Islamists. One was the general danger of further incorporation into the world economy in a dependent position, as expressed through indebtedness, unbalanced trade relations etc. The other was the particular and immediate danger of being brought increasingly under the economic and political dominance of the US-Israeli alliance.

The question of normalisation of relations with Israel remained a hot issue. Since Camp David Egypt had been at peace with Israel, had exchanged diplomatic representatives, and tourists were allowed to travel between the two countries. However, the Egyptian government, anxious not to further alienate Arab and internal opinion, more or less froze relations with Israel at a low level, especially after the Israeli invasion of Lebanon in 1982. But pressure from the United States on the Mubarak administration to develop economic links with Israel remained strong. Time and again the opposition press carried stories revealing government or private enterprises doing business with the Zionist enemy, and usually the authorities at least officially stopped the activity in question.

At the centre of the Islamists' concerns was the influence of the IMF and the World Bank. The Bretton Woods institutions were seen by the Islamists as a mere tool for the United States. In particular the IMF was seen to undermine Egyptian economic independence both by the detrimental effects of the policies it suggested, and directly by more or less replacing the Egyptian government as the real decision maker. Egyptian economic policies were guided by principles laid down in the recurrent "declarations of intent" *vis-à-vis* the IMF. The Fund's approval of these declarations remained the key to the coffers of Western creditors.[3]

In April 1985 ʻĀdil Ḥusayn wrote that the United States, in reality controlling the Egyptian economy since May 1977, had seen too it that public sector units were closed down, because of competition from imported goods, or from joint ventures inside the country enjoying special privileges. Foreign capital controlled joint ventures through token capital participation and control over technology or foreign markets. The efficiency

[3] Muḥammad Ḥilmī Murād, "Lā takhdaʻūnā: azmatunā lan yuḥilliha ta'jīl al-qurūḍ al-ajnabiyya", *al-Shaʻb*, 4 October 1988. Cf. his article "Istimrār duwwāmat al-qurūḍ al-ajnabiyya wa tijārat al-ʻumla", *al-Shaʻb*, 26 May 1987.

of production was measured in what was termed "world prices" by the World Bank and the IMF, in close collusion with the United States. But these prices were merely a reflection of the present world division of labour, and forcing Egypt to use them was just a way of reproducing its place within that order.

In agriculture crop structure was being changed so that foreigners, including Israel, would control central input factors, and leading farmers would be linked to the outside world. This was also achieved by liberating prices and directing more money into private hands in the countryside, money that was used for conspicuous consumption of imported luxury goods, emulating what was going on among the newly rich in the cities.

The sources of foreign currency listed above could all be cut off by the will of the United States, for instance if there should be talk of war against Israel on the part of Egypt. The same obviously went for US aid.

US aid to Israel and to Egypt could not really be compared. Israel was given to with no conditions, and had been able to use the aid to build a self-centred economy. For instance they were allowed to exercise a strict price control. Egypt on the other hand was given aid only by meeting a host of conditions that aimed at making its economy dependent and opening the way to integration with Israel, said Ḥusayn.[4]

Apart from Israel, some Arab regimes were also seen as pawns in the American effort to secure its hegemony over the region. It is interesting to note the comments of 'Abd al-Ḥamīd al-Ghazālī, a leading Muslim Brother economist,[5] in connection with the situation after Iraq's invasion of Kuwait in 1990. The Muslim Brothers have long, and with some justification, been considered close to Saudi Arabia. Nevertheless Ghazālī emphasised that though tears were cried ostensibly for the *Sharī'a* and international law, the issue was really an economic one, the intent of the West to secure stable deliveries of oil at the lowest possible price. What the mobilisation against Iraq amounted to, wrote Ghazālī, was the West defending its interest against Arab interests for Arab money, since the Gulf countries were going to pay. This was part of a larger picture, where most of the money earned by Arab countries on the sale of oil were left in

[4] 'Ādil Ḥusayn, "Kayfa ḥawwala al-infitāḥ iqtiṣād miṣr ilā haykal hashsh?", *al-Sha'b*, 23 April 1985 and "Al-taṭbī' mas'ā lil-haymana al-isrā'īliyya min al-dākhil", *al-Sha'b*, 30 April 1985.

[5] 'Abd al-Ḥamīd al-Ghazālī was Professor of Economics at Cairo University. In 1995 he was sentenced to jail for being an active member of the Muslim Brothers, something he denied under oath in front of the military court that sentenced him, although he declared that had the charges been true it would have made him proud. Whatever may be the case, al-Ghazālī is one of a small group of economists who since the 1980s have been leading spokesmen of an Islamic economic alternative for Egypt and the wider Muslim world, and who have been approvingly quoted by representatives of the Muslim Brothers.

Western banks to finance economic investments and activities there. Arab assets in the West amounted to four times the aggregate Arab debt. Still the oil-rich countries remained underdeveloped while other Arab countries were starved of finance.[6]

Loans, grants, aid: the spectre of the Caisse de la Dette

The question of aid, grants and loans was a constant bone of contention in the People's Assembly between the government and the opposition from the Labour Party and the Muslim Brothers throughout the period in question.

The debates on foreign loan packages kept arising in the People's Assembly because one of its functions was to ratify agreements on loans and aid with foreign countries. Although on a handful of occasions the Koranic ban on *ribā* was invoked in the debate on foreign loans,[7] the overwhelming concern of both Labour Party and Muslim Brother MPs was the reliance on foreign finance as a threat to Egypt's independence. Real independence required relying on one's own resources to secure welfare and development. The lesson from history was that indebtedness had opened the gates to Egypt for imperialism.[8] Government investments were no source of pride, wrote 'Ādil Ḥusayn, as long as they were all based on loans that Egypt never would be able to pay back. Drowned in debt, the country had no option but to follow the dictate of the creditors. He warned that Mubarak was repeating the disastrous policies of the Khedive Ismā'īl in the 1870s and of Sadat in the late 1970s.[9]

Besides this general criticism of the amount of borrowing, the concrete arguments against each loan or grant agreement would generally be of three sorts. In some cases the loan or grant was considered unnecessary, either because the proposed project was not of a high priority, or because it was thought that mobilising local resources was preferable.[10] In particular it was thought that in many cases loans were contracted to pay for foreign expertise when Egyptian experts not only possessed the necessary skills but also knew the terrain better.[11]

6 'Abd al-Ḥamīd Al-Ghazālī, "Al-bu'd al-iqtiṣādī al-duwalī lil-kāritha wal-wāqi' al-siyāsī", *al-Nūr*, 3 October 1990. Cf. Magdī Muṣṭafā, "Kayfa tajid tharwāt al-muslimīn ṭarīqahā lil-istithmār fi bilādihim", *Liwā' al-islām*, 20 October 1990.

7 See for instance Sayf al-Islām al-Bannā, MB Cairo, People's Assembly, 1 November 1987, *MMS*, F5, 1–31, pp. 3170–2 and 'Abd al-'Azīz Ghubārī, LP Fayyum, 12 February 1990, *MMS*, F5, 3–31, ṭm, pp. 2–28.

8 Ibrāhīm Shukrī, People's Assembly, 23 April 1985, *MMS*, F4, 1–73, pp. 4816–24.

9 'Ādil Ḥusayn, "Al-islāmiyyūn wal-ittifāq ma'a ṣandūq al-naqd", *al-Sha'b*, 12 May 1987.

10 See Shukrī's argument in Parliament on 27 April 1987 against a loan from the World Bank for the development of small and medium sized industrial projects in *MMS*, F5, 1–4, pp. 136–42.

11 See for instance Basyūnī Basyūnī, MB Alexandria, 9 June 1987, *MMS*, F5, 1–10,

Secondly, some government loans were opposed because they were considered to impose conditions that constituted violations of Egyptian sovereignty because they involved certain changes in the government's economic policies. Especially this was linked to US loans for buying foodstuffs from the United States, where the US preconditions stipulated a deregulation of internal Egyptian trade in agricultural goods: the reduction of subsidies, opening for private traders and the like.[12] The 1987 election platform of the Islamic Alliance stated that any foreign aid entailing conditions should be rejected.[13]

Thirdly, a recurring criticism concerned the internal conditions of some of the loan or grant agreements. These conditions were felt as an affront to Egyptian sovereignty and dignity because they gave the foreign partner the upper hand in control and supervision over the projects. Examples included stipulating that the director of the project must be from the donor country, that the law of the donor country should rule in the case of disputes, that disbursement would be conditional on the satisfaction of the donor with reports.[14]

More especially the agreements regularly tied the project to purchasing goods from the donor or creditor country or in some cases even from particular companies, thereby making it impossible to search for the best and cheapest option, and at the same time creating a lasting dependence for instance on spare parts. An example is provided by the intervention of the deputy from Gharbiyya province, Maḥfūẓ Ḥilmī from the Muslim Brothers, in the People's Assembly on 27 April 1987. Ḥilmī criticised an agreement on a grant from Britain for developing the supply of electricity on the Northwest coast. This grant is really a cover for a marketing campaign for British producers in Egypt, Ḥilmī said. A grant seems harmless, since it is not to be paid back, but the agreement, in line with most grants and loans "received", would bind Egypt to the purchase of British products for the 1.3 million pounds sterling involved. This, he said, would rule out a search for the cheapest alternatives.[15]

According to Magdī Ḥusayn, in the case of deals with the United States 93 percent of the money granted or lent went straight back to the United States in the form of purchases or salaries and fees.[16]

---

pp. 1004–6. Cf. Gamāl As'ad, LP Asyūṭ, 26 March 1990, *MMS*, F5, 3–45, ṭm, pp. 11–13.

12 See Gamāl As'ad, LP Asyūṭ, 1 November 1987, *MMS*, F5, 1–31, pp. 3160–8. Cf. Sayyid Rustam, LP, 7 May 1985, *MMS*, F4, 1–78, pp. 5116–20.

13 Ḥizb al-'amal, "Al-barnāmaj al-intikhābī 'alā qā'imat ḥizb al-'amal", part VII.

14 For examples of this kind of criticism see Magdī Ḥusayn, People's Assembly, 8 June 1987, *MMS*, F5, 1–9, pp. 827–32. Cf. Muḥammad Ḥusayn, MB Alexandria, 9 June 1987, *MMS*, F5, 1–10, pp. 991–7.

15 *MMS*, F5, 1–4, pp. 144–5.

16 Magdī Aḥmad Ḥusayn, "Al-tawassu' fī al-minaḥ al-ajnabiyya ni'ma am naqma", *al-*

There might also be stipulations that the transport of goods purchased or granted should be left to ships from the donor country. In January 1988 Ma'mūn al-Huḍaybī claimed that in the case of American wheat for PL 480 loans the transport was done by US ships for 47 dollars a ton at a time when the market rate was between 13 and 17 dollars.[17]

In June 1987 Magdī Ḥusayn wrote that the USAID was becoming a state within the Egyptian state, financed by US grants and *de facto* directing the work of a large group of public employees all the way down to the village level. Aside from the inherent loss of sovereignty this involved, a whole social layer was created with its loyalty where the money came from, the United States. Thus Egypt's state of dependency was deepened.[18]

Even if the Islamists wanted to reduce the reliance on foreign finance, they did not oppose any foreign loans. In his speech in the People's Assembly on 9 July 1984 Shukrī enthusiastically supported the ratification of a 22 million ECU loan agreement with the European Investment Bank, to build a gypsum factory in Sadat City, one of the new industrial cities in the desert outside Cairo, and a brick work in Minya. In particular the latter was important, said Shukrī, since it would alleviate the present illegal use of the fertile alluvial soils of the Nile valley in making red brick for building purposes.[19] Shukrī's positive attitude towards this loan exemplified a certain tendency among the Islamists to favour diversification of the sources of finance. Although there were examples where they would welcome individual deals with the United States,[20] in general they would be more positive towards deals with Japan and with smaller countries like Canada and Finland, no doubt because these were seen as less of a political and military threat.[21]

As might be expected the Islamists also favoured deals with Arab countries in the name of Arab and Islamic unity. Some deals with Kuwait and

---

Sha'b, 23 June 1987. Three years later Yūsuf Kamāl puts the same ratio at two thirds, see Magdī Muṣṭafā, "Al-isqāṭ al-juz'ī li-madyūniyyat miṣr al-khārijiyya hal yakūn furṣa li-murāja'a shāmila wa iṣlāḥ haykal al-iqtiṣād al-miṣrī", *Liwā' al-islām*, 19 November 1990.

[17] Ma'mūn al-Huḍaybī, People's Assembly, 24 January 1988, *MMS*, F5, 1–61, pp. 4773–7.

[18] Magdī Aḥmad Ḥusayn, "Al-tawassu' fī al-minaḥ al-ajnabiyya ni'ma am naqma", *al-Sha'b*, 23 June 1987. Cf. Gamāl As'ad LP Asyut, People's Assembly, 5 July 1987, *MMS*, F5, 1–24, pp. 2563–6, where he describes how there are two classes of employees within the provincial development banks, those privileged working on the "American project" and the miserable others.

[19] *MMS*, F4, 1–6, pp. 437–40.

[20] See Fu'ād 'Abd al-Magīd, MB Kafr al-Shaykh, 18 December 1989, *MMS*, F5, 3–12, pp. 34–43 and Shukrī, June 1987, *MMS*, F5, 1–10, pp. 1006–8.

[21] 'Iṣām al-'Iryān, People's Assembly 12 January 1988, *MMS*, F5, 1–56, pp. 4596–9, Basyūnī Basyūnī, MB Alexandria, 1 November 1987, *MMS*, F5, 1–31, pp. 3170–2 and Shukrī 15 November 1987, F5, 1–34, pp. 3375–8.

the United Arab Emirates were hailed as positive examples in this regard, merging Gulf capital with Egyptian labour power and know-how and creating the potential for developing production with an Arab export market.[22]

But by no means was there an uncritical acceptance of the deals with the Gulf countries. They were often criticised for having the same kind of conditions as the US loans. On one occasion Ma'mūn al-Huḍaybī characterised a deal with Abu Dhabi as constituting an interference worse than that of the *Caisse de la Dette Publique*, since every step of the project would be subject to the control of the creditor country, from drawings to purchases and consultancy contracts.[23]

On 10 January 1988 in the People's Assembly Maḥmūd Nāfi', a Muslim Brother representing Daqahliyya province, referred to a rumour that the Arab countries (presumably here indicating the Gulf countries) had offered to pay off 20 billion dollars of Egypt's debt, if the country would join in the war against Iran, which was still going on at the time. As Muslims Egyptians must never accept such a proposition, said Nāfi',[24] thereby giving a glimpse of an important fact, that was to reveal itself again during the Second Gulf War. Many observers for long considered the Muslim Brothers a staunch ally of the Gulf states, and above all Saudi Arabia and Kuwait, because of the many existing economic links, and the alleged financial support afforded them by the Gulf regimes. But though there was internal strife around this, the Gulf War would show again that the Brothers were certainly an independent movement following their own line. Notwithstanding the potential negative economic cost for their own organisation and potentially for Egypt, while they consistently condemned the Iraqi invasion of Kuwait, they denounced the Western-led coalition, in which Saudi Arabia as well as Egypt took part, as an alliance of infidels led by the United States and Zionism.[25]

Protecting the home market

The Islamists viewed the development of exports as an essential part of a long term solution to the balance of payments deficit. And on a few occasions mention was made of the need to remove bureaucratic obstacles to export and to create viable institutions with the task of export promotion.[26] But during the period under investigation their focus was clearly

[22] Shukrī, 14 January 1990, *MMS*, F5, 3–19, ṭm, pp. 14–15. Cf. his speech on 14 December 1987, *MMS*, F5, 1–44, pp. 3985–90.
[23] Ma'mūn al-Huḍaybī, 25 February 1990, *MMS*, F5, 3–36, ṭm, pp. 26–8. Cf. Shukrī, 18 December 1989, *MMS*, F5, 3–12, ṭm, pp. 6–15.
[24] *MMS*, F5, 1–53, pp. 4504–31.
[25] Auda, "An Uncertain Response: The Islamic Movement in Egypt", pp. 118–19.
[26] 'Ādil Ḥusayn, "Al-ithnayn al-aswad wa mu'tamar al-intāj", *al-Sha'b*, 10 November 1987.

on protecting local industry from devastating foreign competition on the home market. They criticised government policies for going too far in allowing the import of goods that were also being produced in Egypt or where locally produced alternatives existed. These policies led to the stock-piling of unsold local produce, and in turn to financial problems for local industry and to under-utilisation of productive capacity.[27] The Islamists pointed out that in some areas the system of customs tariffs was tilted against the promotion of local production. For instance they claimed that for some sorts of machinery customs dues on an imported machine were less than 15 percent of the dues on the parts needed to assemble the same machine inside Egypt. In their mind the reverse ought to be the case so that customs dues would be higher on finished goods. At the very least there ought to be parity.[28]

The Islamists also seemed to favour tight state control of the trade in foreign currency. Hard currency was looked upon as a scarce resource, which ought to be channelled into high priority imports like food and input goods for basic industries. ʻĀdil Ḥusayn complained that while procuring currency for the import of Mercedeses, Italian marble and caviar seemed to be easy, there was a shortage of it for importing wheat and machines for Egyptian factories.[29] To remedy this the government must strike against the black market. It must also abolish the own-exchange import system.[30] Not least it must stop Egyptian producers selling their products for dollars on the local market. For instance the Alexandria Cement Company was selling its produce only for dollars. This practice was forcing people to resort to the black market. The buyers of cement would not get foreign exchange from the banking system, since they were usually not registered importers.[31]

Cf. Ibrāhīm Shukrī, 30 December 1984, *MMS*, F4, 1–39, pp. 2717–34, and see Ṣalaḥ ʻAbdallāh, LP Cairo, 24 June 1987, *MMS*, F5, 1–19, ṭm, pp. 3–37, where he complains that lucrative markets have been lost to Egyptian medicines in West Africa because, due to lack of control, outdated medicines had been exported to that area.

[27] Mamdūḥ Qināwī, LP, 8 June 1985, *MMS*, F4, 1–84, pp. 6544–62. Cf. Ḥanafī Fahīm ʻUthmān, MB Cairo, 28 January 1988, *MMS*, F5, 1–62, pp. 4820–55.

[28] Maḥfūẓ Ḥilmī, MB Gharbiyya, 24 March 1990, *MMS*, F5, 3–42, ṭm, pp. 16–21. Cf. Ibrāhīm Shukrī, *ibid.*

[29] ʻĀdil Ḥusayn, "Miḥnat al-muwaẓẓafīn wa ḥukm al-aghbiyā'", *al-Shaʻb*, 6 September 1988.

[30] This was a facility whereby private sector importers were not required to acquire or convert foreign exchange through public sector banks. Cf. Waterbury, *The Egypt of Nasser and Sadat*, p. 170.

[31] Maḥfūẓ Ḥilmī, MB Gharbiyya, 11 February 1990, *MMS*, F5, 3–28, ṭm, pp. 2–27. Cf. Ḥizb al-ʻamal al-ishtirākī: "Taqrīr ḥizb al-ʻamal al-ishtirākī ilā al-mu'tamar al-iqtiṣādī ʻan al-mashākil al-iqtiṣādiyya wa ṭarīqat ḥalliha", *Al-ʻamal al-ishtirākī*, no. 19, Cairo, 1981, pp. 44–5, although here it is stated that the own-exchange system should be

The Labour Party was not always consistent in taking the side of those wanting to protect the local market. In early 1985 a heated debate broke out around a series of measures introduced by the then Minister of Economy Muṣṭafā al-Sa'īd. The measures included a tightening of import restrictions, increasing the list of products barred from import, and a crackdown on black market currency dealers. A massive attack against al-Sa'īd was launched from the business community apparently with strong support inside the government itself.

However, the debate was confused, in a manner typical of public debate in Egypt in the 1980s, by not remaining confined to the question of to what extent the measures introduced by Sa'īd were beneficial or not. The personal integrity of Sa'īd was questioned in relation to dealings made by companies where he or his family members had been directly involved, an issue that had already been raised in the press before January 1985. Questions were also raised about his attitude to the money dealers, and it was insinuated that the crackdown had been made not in the general interest, but as part of an internal competition among different interests in the currency dealing community. In any case, Sa'īd had to resign and the measures were scaled down or withdrawn. *Al-Sha'b* makes interesting reading with regard to this incident. The Labour Party seems to have been caught in a dilemma, not knowing which leg to stand on. On the one hand it had always defended a strict control on imports and called for a clamp-down on speculative currency dealings, as part of its fight for the protection of national industry. On the other hand the party was also very eager to reveal cases of corruption in government circles. At least since the autumn of 1984 *al-Sha'b* had been involved in a campaign against Muṣṭafā al-Sa'īd for alleged participation in shady stock dealings that also concerned close members of his family.

The Labour Party and increasingly the Muslim Brothers were fervent critics of the policies proposed for Egypt by the International Monetary Fund.[32] There are two main strains to this criticism that are often hard to disentangle, but the distinction is important to keep in mind since at least the Labour Party reacted quite positively to IMF-like measures when these were seen to be initiated by a firmly independent-minded government in Sudan.[33] The Islamists first of all react to the fact that a foreign

operated "until better solutions could be found" for drawing the savings of migrant workers into the national economy.

[32] See for instance their common platform for the 1987 elections, Ḥizb al-'amal, "Al-barnāmaj al-intikhābī 'alā qā'imat ḥizb al-'amal", part V.

[33] 'Ādil Ḥusayn, "Al-thawra al-islāmiyya fī al-sūdān: ḥurriyya kāmila lil-sūq wal-as'ār ma'a takāful yaḥmī al-mustaḍ'afīn wa tanmīyat al-i'timād 'alā al-nafs", *al-Sha'b*, 10 March 1992 and "Durūs fī al-iqtiṣād al-siyāsī nata'allamhā min al-sūdān al-islāmī", *al-Sha'b*, 17 March 1992.

institution, controlled by the main Western powers should be in a position to heavily influence, if not dictate, the economic policies of the Egyptian state. Secondly they argue that most, if not all, the concrete policies promoted by the Fund and its Bretton Woods "brother", the World Bank, would actually be detrimental to the local economy. The IMF wanted to promote a liberalisation of Egypt's trade regime, both externally and internally, that collided with the Islamists' insistence on the necessity to exercise state control over foreign trade.

In a similar vein the Muslim Brother economist 'Abd al-Ḥamīd al-Ghazālī was quite positive in principle to some of the IMF-proposed measures, but he warned against the dangers of the Fund gaining a control over the Egyptian economy equivalent to that exercised by the *Caisse* in the years leading up to the 'Urābī revolt and the British occupation in 1882.[34]

At the political level the fear was that the IMF, as a tool for the West and primarily the United States, would use economic pressure to force Egypt into cooperation with Israel. On the more purely economic level the IMF's goal was seen as being to enable Egypt to serve its debts as far as possible while remaining in a state of dependency. Therefore the Fund might help ease the burdens for a while through helping negotiate a rescheduling of debt repayment, but what was needed was a thoroughgoing economic reform, while the IMF measures remained on a purely financial level.[35]

In the more concrete argument against the measures proposed by the IMF there is generally an implicit or explicit, especially from the Muslim Brothers, acceptance of the benefits of a free market economy. However the line is taken that in a Third World country generally, and in Egypt particularly, removing all fences against the advanced industrial economies and abandoning all state control would be very detrimental.[36] A central issue here was IMF insistence that all kinds of subsidies be removed, and prices brought to their international level. Egyptian "declarations of intent", like that of 1987, typically involved promises to raise the prices of petroleum products and electricity to bring them closer to world prices, adjusting the prices of the products from the public sector, and letting the private sector set prices freely. This would affect the prices of basic necessities like foodstuffs, clothes, medicine and electrical appliances.[37] The IMF insistence on deregulation of prices was out to break down the local price structure in Egypt, and any national independent economic structure

[34] Maḥmūd Bakrī and Muḥammad Gamāl 'Arafa, "Al-ittifāq ma'a ṣandūq al-naqd", *al-Sha'b*, 12 May 1987.

[35] See 'Abd al-Ḥamīd al-Ghazālī in Maḥmūd Bakrī and Muḥammad Gamāl 'Arafa, "Al-ittifāq ma'a ṣandūq al-naqd", *al-Sha'b*, 12 May 1987. Cf. Muḥammad Ḥilmī Murād, "Raf' al-as'ār aswa' al-ḥulūl li-mu'ālajat azmat al-ḥukūma", *al-Sha'b*, 15 May 1990.

[36] Muḥammad Ḥilmī Murād, "Lā takhda'ūnā: azmatunā lan yuḥilliha ta'jīl al-qurūḍ al-ajnabiyya", *al-Sha'b*, 4 October 1988.

[37] Magdī Aḥmad Ḥusayn, "Wa ishta'alat nīrān al-as'ār!", *al-Sha'b*, 19 January 1988.

at large, Magdī Ḥusayn wrote.[38] The concept of "indirect subsidies", meaning the difference between local prices and prices for the same goods in international trade, was vehemently criticised by Muḥammad Ḥilmī Murād, among others. It is quite normal that a state distributes important locally produced goods, like petroleum products, at cost prices, he wrote, adding rhetorically that if people were supposed to pay world prices they should be paid world wages.[39] 'Ādil Ḥusayn stated that the world prices in question had not been formed through the free effects of supply and demand, rather they were effects of the international power structure. Nor was there any natural law that forced Egypt to copy the price structure of the advanced industrial countries. The editor of *al-Sha'b* discussed the particular issue of the "under-pricing" of oil and related products on the local Egyptian market. If the Western powers used their world power to keep oil prices low during their reconstruction and development after World War II, he argued, why was it a sin for a developing country like Egypt to make the same considerations and sell oil at cost price in the local market? He emphasised that there might be a danger of waste of resources and a lack of incentives for improved productivity involved in the current pricing of these products, but these could be remedied. The core of the issue, as he would reiterate time and again, lay in the crucial independence of decision-making, which must never be compromised if real development was to be achieved.[40]

Another important issue at stake was the exchange rate of the Egyptian pound against hard currencies and in particular the US dollar. The IMF consistently argued for floating the pound, which would involve removing the system of multiple exchange rates for different purposes, and a marked devaluation of the pound at the new unified rate. The Islamists were in favour of rather strict currency control. In early 1988 Magdī Ḥusayn argued that already the decreasing value of the pound was an important factor behind a new violent wave of price increases, more than consuming the current increases in wages and salaries. To float the Egyptian pound in relation to the dollar and other foreign currencies, he argued, would surely mean drowning it. For the Egyptian economy was not in a position to take up this so-called free competition.

38 Magdī Aḥmad Ḥusayn, "Matā nuwaqqif ṣandūq al-naqd al-amrīkī—'inda ḥaddihi?", *al-Sha'b*, 25 November 1986.

39 Muḥammad Ḥilmī Murād, "Raf' al-as'ār aswa' al-ḥulūl li-mu'ālajat azmat al-ḥukūma", *al-Sha'b*, 15 May 1990.

40 'Ādil Ḥusayn, "I'linū al-ittifāqiyyāt al-sirriyya ma'a ṣandūq al-naqd", *al-Sha'b*, 4 July 1989. Cf. Muḥammad Ḥilmī Murād, "Raf' al-as'ār aswa' al-ḥulūl li-mu'ālajat azmat al-ḥukūma", *al-Sha'b*, 15 May 1990. We may note, however, that when arguing against the economic feasibility of a new oil refinery in Asyūṭ, Murād himself calculates the value of the crude oil at international prices, and the refined products at local prices! See "Faḍīḥat ma'mal takrīr al-bitrūl bi-Asyūṭ", *al-Sha'b*, 27 October 1987.

The problem was that floating the pound was exactly what the government had solemnly promised in a "declaration of intent" *vis-à-vis* the International Monetary Fund, a declaration that was kept a secret to the People's Assembly, but which was well known in international economic agencies.

Floating the pound would mean dissolving the whole system of incentives constructed by the local price structure *vis-à-vis* the international one. It would surely not benefit the incomes of the great majority of Egyptian citizens, Ḥusayn wrote.[41] When the issue was debated in the spring of the previous year 'Abd al-Ḥamīd al-Ghazālī of the Muslim Brothers, otherwise quite in favour of a liberal economic policy, stressed the need for government control over currency transactions. A unified exchange rate could have positive effects, he said, but since Egypt was a Third World country with a constant large need for hard currency, the state needed to control the demand for foreign currency and foreign goods. It must regulate private and public spending and keep a reserve of at least 2 to 3 billion US dollars to ward off speculation against the pound, instead of the present 500 million. Ghazālī warned that as long as the general policies of the government continued, implementation of the IMF advice would merely lead to increased inflation.[42] This fear was echoed two weeks later by Muḥammad Ḥilmī Murād. In relation to the partial currency reform introduced in May 1987, he complained that the resultant devaluation of the pound from an official rate of LE 1.35 to one of LE 2.16 to the dollar would primarily lead to increased prices on imported goods, leading to increased costs both for consumers and producers. He also complained that the proposed system would not do away with the black market, since the official "free market" would only sell foreign currency for certain purposes. Legal activities such as the *ḥajj*, tourism, import of non-essential goods or the need to pay Egyptian producers who demanded dollars were excluded and would still resort to the black market. Finally Murād stated that the system where a council would decide on the rate in relation to the dollar price at the London Stock Exchange, would mean officially tying the pound to the dollar, thus making dependency explicit.[43]

Aside from liberalised trade and currency policies, the other leg of the "economic opening", indeed its supposed main pillar, was of course the opening for foreign investment. Law No. 43 of 1974, later amended by Law No. 32 of 1977, was seen to herald the new age of *infitāḥ*. In keeping

[41] Magdī Aḥmad Ḥusayn, "Wa ishta'alat nīrān al-as'ār!", *al-Sha'b*, 19 January 1988.

[42] Maḥmūd Bakrī and Muḥammad Gamāl 'Arafa, "Al-ittifāq ma'a ṣandūq al-naqd", *al-Sha'b*, 12 May 1987.

[43] Muḥammad Ḥilmī Murād, "Istimrār duwwāmat al-qurūḍ al-ajnabiyya wa tijārat al-'umla", *al-Sha'b*, 26 May 1987.

with pan-Arab sentiment (never so dead in reality as in the Western press) and more pragmatically, as a bid for petrodollars from the Gulf, it was named the Law on Foreign and Arab investment. The implication was that Arabs constituted a category somewhere in between Egyptian and foreign, and in some fields they were given more extended investment privileges than other foreigners.

To a certain extent this same view is reflected in the electoral platform of the Islamic Alliance for the 1987 elections. The programme states that investment must be made easier for national and Arab capital in accordance with the priorities of production. Tax and customs exemptions must be strengthened. All the work force must be utilised. The *infitāḥ* must be reformed so that it does not impose dependence but contributes to independence, and becomes productive, not consumptive. The opening must be to all the world, not only to the West. Foreigners, and especially the United States, must be prevented from controlling Egypt's economy, since they are the enemies of the national Islamic renaissance.[44]

In the programmatic document from the Muslim Brothers from 1990 it is stated that investment must be made easier in licit fields according to the priorities of production and consumption. Especially obstacles to Arab investment must be removed. New means of investment must be developed to correspond with the situation of different groups of the public. And incentives like tax and tariff exemptions must be strengthened.[45]

The most important field where foreign capital was active was in fact the oil business which was ruled by a separate law outside the scope of Law 43. It seems that Ibrāhīm Shukrī and other Alliance MPs were generally in favour of the deals governing the foreign involvement here, which stipulated that the foreign companies did the exploration with no cost to Egypt, and were then paid back from the sales revenue if oil was struck and production started. Above that they would receive 20 to 50 percent of the income from oil sales. Similar schemes worked for other minerals like sulphur or phosphates. In particular the Islamists praised the cooperation treaties in this field because they clearly stated that in the case of a legal dispute the Arabic version of the treaty text would be valid and that Egyptian courts would settle the disputes. They argued that similar clauses ought to be included in fields like manufacturing industry, trade and finance.[46] Nevertheless some were critical of this policy for being too favourable towards foreign oil companies. The foremost younger politician of

[44] Ḥizb al-'amal, "Al-barnāmaj al-intikhābī 'alā qā'imat ḥizb al-'amal".

[45] Shaḥḥāta, *Al-minhaj al-islāmī lil-iṣlāḥ al-iqtiṣādī*, p. 15.

[46] Ibrāhīm Shukrī, People's Assembly, 22 June 1987, *MMS*, F5, 1–14, ṭm, pp. 25–9. Cf. Ḥanafī Fahīm 'Uthmān, MB Cairo, *ibid.* and 'Abd al-'Aẓīm al-Maghribī, MB Banī Suwayf, *ibid.*, pp. 29–33.

the Labour Party, Magdī Ḥusayn was always more critical than Shukrī, and in the same meeting where Shukrī in 1987 praised the oil deals, Ḥusayn argued that paying the foreign companies even as little as 20 percent of the sales revenue was a waste of national resources.[47]

On 4 July 1989 the People's Assembly started its discussion of a proposal for a new investment law, No. 230 of 1989, to substitute the old *infitāḥ* investment law, No. 43 of 1974. For once Ma'mūn al-Huḍaybī of the Muslim Brothers gave the opening statement on behalf of the Islamic Alliance, instead of Ibrāhīm Shukrī, which might be taken to indicate that his views on this occasion reflected the common view of the Labour Party and the Muslim Brothers. However, throughout his speech he never takes a clear position on whether to adopt the new law or not, or makes any proposal to change certain paragraphs in it. None of the Alliance deputies used the opportunity for suggesting an alternative law regulating foreign investment. Their critique remained somewhat ambiguous in that they argued for the need to narrow the freedom of foreign capital, while at the same time criticising the meagre amount of capital that had come and the bureaucratic obstacles in the way of foreign investment.

Despite the somewhat vague character of the Islamist discourse on foreign investment, it seems that gradually during the latter half of the 1980s an at least partial consensus was developing around the following view: Internally the regulations governing private investment should be liberalised. Arab investment should also be further encouraged, although criticism is quite often levelled at the behaviour of, and priorities of, Gulf capital. On the other hand a need is felt to limit somewhat the influence of foreign non-Arab capital. Eventually this would crystallise into a firm stance against foreign direct ownership of Egyptian capital. Finally while wanting to give freer room for local private interests, both the Labour Party and the Muslim Brothers have started by the late 1980s to talk about priorities both of consumption and production which must guide investment. Taken together with the increasing enthusiasm for the Korean success story this point becomes significant, and shall be returned to later.

Arab and Muslim integration

While the Islamists argued consistently for the reduction of Western influence over the national economy, they held up economic integration with other Muslim countries as a panacea for current shortcomings. A typical statement is that of the Muslim Brothers' Economic Committee from 1990, which stated that it was of utmost importance to develop the coordination and integration with the other Islamic countries. From the

[47] *MMS*, F5, 1–14, ṭm, pp. 21–5.

economic point of view the Islamic world consisted of three types of countries:

— Those with abundant natural resources, like Sudan, Iraq and Yemen.
— Those with abundant financial resources, like the oil states.
— Those with abundant human resources, like Egypt, Syria and Jordan.

From this, and from God's words that the Muslims are one nation (*umma*), sprang the necessity for the creation of an economic union between these countries to liberate them from dependence on the outside world. In this regard an end must be put to the obstacles facing investment and trade between the Islamic countries.[48] It is worth noting here that though the reference is to integration among *Islamic* countries, the concrete examples are all taken from the *Arab* world. This holds true with few exceptions when the Islamists discuss this issue, and is an indication of the strong affinity of Arab Islamism with Arab nationalism.

The fall in the oil price, and later the collapse of the Eastern bloc, which increased the world market power of the major Western powers, while diverting European development funds into Russia and Eastern Europe, served to intensify the call for the pooling of Arab and Muslim resources for development. In the People's Assembly there was call for an Arab common market and for Arab and Islamic integration in the fields of agriculture and arms production in order to secure independence and rectify the balance of power *vis-à-vis* Israel.[49] And in *Liwā' al-islām* Yūsuf Kamāl called for an integrated Islamic monetary policy, including a unified currency and an Islamic Monetary Fund, in order to further intra-Muslim trade and the development of Muslim economies. The use of Muslim funds for Muslim development was a duty for the faithful, he said. Muslims should not wait for the foreign *khawāgas* to distribute the roles in the world economic play.[50]

However, it was clear to the Islamists that the integration they hoped for was in reality not taking place. They lamented the fact that the huge financial surpluses commanded by the oil-producing Arab countries during the boom years had above all benefited the Western industrial countries. In 1990 'Abd al-Ḥamīd al-Ghazālī estimated the Arab assets in the West at 800 billion dollars, four times the aggregate Arab debt with

48 Shaḥḥāta, *Al-minhaj al-islāmī lil-iṣlāḥ al-iqtiṣādī*, p. 16.

49 Maḥmūd Nāfi', MB Daqahliyya, 11 February 1990, *MMS*, F5, 3–29, ṭm, pp. 3–12, and Muṣṭafā al-Wardānī, MB Giza, 25 February 1990, *MMS*, F5, 3–36, ṭm, pp. 31–44. Cf. Ḥizb al-'amal al-ishtirākī, "Taqrīr ḥizb al-'amal al-ishtirākī ilā al-mu'tamar al-iqtiṣādī", p. 59.

50 Magdī Muṣṭafā, "Kayfa tajid tharwāt al-muslimīn ṭarīqahā lil-istithmār fi bilādihim", *Liwā' al-islām*, 20 October 1990.

Western creditors. At the same time, he said, the oil countries remain economically underdeveloped, and other Arab countries are starved of capital and fall prey to Western creditors.[51]

In fact the most concrete translation of the grand idea of Arab and Islamic integration for the Egyptian Islamists of the late 1980s was the desirability of Arab oil money being invested for productive purposes within the Egyptian economy.[52] This need was especially felt after the fall in the oil prices since 1986 had reduced Egypt's income from worker remittances, oil export and the Suez canal.[53] The Islamists were eager to promote Arab investment in Egypt. They argued that Egypt itself was partly to blame for the lack of funding from the Gulf and Libya, since it failed to convince potential Arab investors of the safety and effective use of their capital.[54] In general the contracting of loans from Gulf institutions of development finance for productive purposes in Egypt was welcomed.[55] But Islamist MPs on more than one occasion also complained that the conditions for these loans constituted an interference in internal Egyptian affairs through rigid control of the use of the invested funds,[56] and even rejected outright some loans for such reasons. The Labour Party in particular criticised the Gulf countries for tying the use of their funds to the policies of the IMF, and thereby to the United States. The keys to the Gulf money were kept in Washington, according to 'Ādil Ḥusayn.[57]

An issue which in the mid-1980s gave cause for grave concern, was the situation regarding the flow of water in the Nile river. Although it had many other aspects, this problem touched in a very concrete manner the question of national independence. For several years in a row the water level in the Nile remained disturbingly low. The situation would have been catastrophic without the High Dam at Aswān, but even so there were heated debates as to what the government intended to do in case the Nile continued to run low. In later parliamentary debates and in the press the strategic aspects of the issue and its importance for Egyptian national

[51] 'Abd al-Ḥamīd Al-Ghazālī, "Al-bu'd al-iqtiṣādī al-duwalī lil-kāritha wal-wāqi' al-siyāsī", *al-Nūr*, 3 October 1990. Cf. Anwar al-Hawārī, "Al-gharb yanhab 'awā'id nafṭ al-muslimīn", *Liwā' al-islām*, 17 May 1988.

[52] The Labour Party document on economic reform from 1982 mentions this along with the promotion of Arab tourism to Egypt as the two first points where the strengthening of Arab economic cooperation was concerned. Cf. Ḥizb al-'amal al-ishtirākī, "Taqrīr ḥizb al-'amal al-ishtirākī ilā al-mu'tamar al-iqtiṣādī", p. 59.

[53] 'Ādil Ḥusayn, "Kārithat al-mūdi'īn fī sharikāt al-tawẓīf", *al-Sha'b*, 1 November 1988.

[54] 'Ādil Ḥusayn, "Al-ithnayn al-aswad wa mu'tamar al-intāj", *al-Sha'b*, 10 November 1987.

[55] See for one instance Ibrāhīm Shukrī, *MMS*, F5, 3–19, ṭm, pp. 14–15.

[56] Gamāl As'ad, LP Asyūṭ and Ibrāhīm Shukrī, People's Assembly, 14 January 1990, *MMS*, F5, 3–19, ṭm, pp. 18–20.

[57] 'Ādil Ḥusayn, "Kayfa yaḥkumūnanā wa kayfa tuṣdar al-qarārāt", *al-Sha'b*, 17 March 1987.

security were more strongly emphasised. The Islamists warned against the role played by Israeli connections to the regime in Ethiopia where the sources for the Blue Nile are located. Especially there was concern at the role of Israeli experts helping to build hydroelectric dams, albeit not on the Nile, and the existence of plans to build dams across the Blue Nile. The whole issue was seen as part of an Israeli strategy to establish a stranglehold on Egypt's lifeblood in order to prevent Egypt from resuming its rightful role as leader of the Arab world and of resistance to Zionism. Possibly the Israelis even hoped to gain Egyptian acceptance of plans for pipelining Nile water into Israel.[58]

Strength: from Islamic socialism to South Korea: policies for economic development

The earliest writings and programmes of Egyptian Islamists on economic matters were produced under the impression of the crisis of the old regime of the king and the Wafd prior to 1952, a regime that was built on a very unequal distribution of wealth. And they came about in a period when socialism stood perhaps at its peak of popularity in the Third World. The victory of the Soviet Union in the Second World War and the revolution in China had made a powerful impression, and was seen by many as showing the way to a possible alternative course to development, independent of the old colonial powers. In this situation the Egyptian Islamists, both the Muslim Brothers and the Young Egypt, if we count them,[59] adopted programmes of a radical land reform, a state-led drive for industrialisation and the development of social and educational services for the poor. The more theoretical discussions on Islamic economic principles by the Muslim Brother Sayyid Quṭb were flavoured with an emphasis on society as collectively responsible for the powers and duties with which God had entrusted humanity. Therefore to Quṭb the state as society's representative possessed wide prerogatives of interfering with the property rights of individuals either by directing the use of their property or by outright sequestration, if this was deemed necessary from the point of view of the interests of society.

Compared to this the Islamist discourse on economic questions in the late 1980s, while sharing some basic tenets, and certainly the desire for economic independence, with that of the 1950s, had moved to a decidedly more liberal position. Three historical developments can probably be

[58] See the speeches by Muslim Brother MPs 'Iṣām al-'Iryān, Basyūnī Basyūnī and Muḥammad al-Shitānī, as well as that of Shukrī, in the People's Assembly on 26 March 1990, *MMS*, F5, 3–44, ṭm, pp. 18–25.

[59] On the relationship of Young Egypt to Islamism cf. pp. 92, 256.

singled out as having seriously influenced the economic thinking of the Muslim Brothers and the Labour Party, albeit somewhat differently. The first is the experience of Nasserism, the second the *infitāḥ* policies that followed under Sadat, and the third is the crisis and ultimate demise of socialism in the Eastern bloc, and concomitantly of the attractive force of socialist ideology.

Islamist attitudes towards Nasser, Nasserism and Sadat's infitāḥ *policies*

In the Egyptian context of the 1980s the policies of the Nasser regime (1952–70) were in the collective memory the antithesis of the IMF-inspired liberalising economic policies of President Mubarak and his team. Therefore anyone criticising government economic policies was immediately faced with having to take up a stand towards the Nasserist experience. The response to this challenge differed substantially between the two allies under discussion.

The Free Officer take-over in 1952 was at the time widely looked upon as the revolution of the Muslim Brothers. This was natural in view of the close links between the Brothers and leading members of the officer group, added to the fact that the Brothers were the leading political mass organisation in the country and played an important role in the early days in mobilising support for the revolution. Furthermore the economic programme implemented by the officers was close to that which had been propagated by the Brothers for quite some time. Only gradually did the rift between the regime and the Brothers become clear, culminating by 1954 in their brutal repression.[60]

When in the 1970s the Muslim Brothers reemerged from the prisons and detention camps, they understandably came to emphasise the link they saw between the political despotism of Nasser's one-party regime and the state's domination of the economy. This double control was seen as giving the state an unprecedented domination over the livelihood of individuals, which it did not hesitate to use to quell any attempt at organising independent political movements in opposition to its policies. And the fact that it was the promoter of economic liberalisation, Anwar al-Sadat, who let the Brothers out of prison and gave them a chance to rebuild their shattered organisation, helped incline them towards a rather positive attitude to the *infitāḥ*, at least for a time. But it is also important to note that several leading Brothers were by the time of Mubarak's pres-

[60] See for instance Carré et Michaud, *Les Frères Musulmans*, pp. 49 ff. Cf. Ḥasan Ḥanafī, *Al-dīn wal-tanmīya al-qawmiyya* [Religion and National Development], Maktabat Madbūlī, Cairo, 1989, p. 11.

idency either wealthy business men themselves, or had close contact with business circles at home and in the Gulf. In this sense there was also immediate economic interest influencing the attitude of the organisation.

In the late 1970s the Brothers are seen to talk little about economic matters, and when they do so, they are primarily concerned with criticism of the remains of state control.[61] But in the 1980s the Muslim Brothers began to play a more open political role, especially after they entered the People's Assembly in some force in 1987 and gained dominance over several professional syndicates from 1986 onwards. This prompted both a more active discourse on economic issues, and a move slightly to the left. But they remained stark critics of Nasser, laying the blame for the present misery on the Nasser era.

Leading Muslim Brother economic spokesmen like 'Abd al-Ḥamīd al-Ghazālī tended to blame Nasser's socialist policies for all that was wrong, and did not clearly distinguish between the policies of Nasser, Sadat and Mubarak.[62] For them the dominance of the public sector with its low productivity, its waste of resources and its corruption of consciences, its bureaucratic central planning and its unstable priorities and policies, was the cause of the excessive dependence on the outside world. And in spite of the slogans of *infitāḥ*, Egyptian society was still shackled by the chains of the 1960s. Privatisation and liberalisation was needed to remedy the situation. Yūsuf Kamāl even went so far as to suggest that the Egyptian people would be better served if both health services and education were run by private interests.

On this point there is a clear difference between the Labour Party and the Muslim Brothers in economic thinking, at least on the ideological plane. For in contrast to al-Ghazālī the Labour Party ideologue 'Ādil Ḥusayn in his writings clearly identified the *infitāḥ* as the cause of Egypt's dependent position, as indicated by the title of his book from 1982, *The Egyptian Economy from Independence to Dependency 1974–1979*. While for al-Ghazālī the problem was that the Nasserist policies still dominated to too large an extent, Ḥusayn tended to blame Sadat's break with them for the crises of the 1980s.

It is also interesting to notice that al-Ghazālī includes Nasser's economic policies as an integral part of his despotism, in line with the linkage between political and economic "liberty" dominating international politics in the aftermath of the Cold War. The same linking of economic and political freedom is expressed when the same writer in 1988 described the

[61] See for instance 'Umar al-Tilmisānī, "Idhā jā'a al-muslimūn fa-lā māl li-aḥad", *al-Da'wa*, 383, February 1977, and Yūsuf Kamāl, "Qaḍīyat al-da'm min khilāl naẓara islāmiyya", *al-Da'wa*, 394, January 1978.

[62] See below pp. 161–2.

new law restricting the activity of the "Islamic investment companies" as an "Emergency Law for the economy". A basic defence of the right to individual property, and the view that it represented a guarantee for political freedom and a protection against exploitation, had always been part of the Islamist discourse. But in the 1980s it came to the forefront.

Nevertheless, in spite of their general dislike for state ownership and centralised planning, in their critique of government policies and in their positive suggestions for reform, the Brothers time and again seemed to take for granted the positive need for a state possessing both the capacity for and the will to intervene in the run of the economy. Especially after 1987 they often talked of the need to direct investment into the production of basic necessities, and to adjust consumptive patterns according to local productive capacity.

The Labour Party's attitude towards the legacy of Nasser was somewhat different, as already indicated. Apparently Sadat had urged Ibrāhīm Shukrī to form the party in late 1978 in order to cover his flank against the leftist-Nasserist tendency organised through the *Tajammu'* party.[63] In any case the party rapidly posited itself as a defender of national control of the economy and of what remained of the welfare systems established under Nasser—schools, health care, subsidised basic necessities. And the thrust of its criticism was directed against liberalising moves seen to threaten these concerns, though the party acknowledged the need for reform of the Nasserist system.[64]

'Ādil Ḥusayn, who became the leading ideologue of the Labour Party from the mid-1980s onwards, had spent eleven years in prison under Nasser as a communist. Other members of the party had also suffered from the political oppression of Nasser's reign. Nevertheless it is possible to see some of the reason for the difference in attitude towards Nasser between the Labour Party and the Muslim Brothers in the fact that whereas the break remained nearly total between the regime and the Brothers throughout the whole presidency of Nasser, some earlier members of the Young Egypt and later Labour Party leaders had at times worked with the regime, albeit not without contradictions arising. We might mention the case of Muḥammad Ḥilmī Murād, Vice President of the Labour Party, who had been Minister for Education in the late 1960s.

In the People's Assembly the Labour Party stressed that economic planning was indispensable both for industrial development and in order to secure a just redistribution of wealth. A consistent theme of the party was that development and justice hinged on the decision on what to produce, implying that this was a political, not merely an economic,

[63] Waterbury, *The Egypt of Nasser and Sadat*, p. 370.
[64] See for instance Shukrī, *Al-taqrīr al-siyāsī*, p. 55.

question. In clear contrast to the rhetoric of the Muslim Brothers the Labour Party tended to blame the lack of central planning for all that was bad—inflation, unemployment, debt, dependency and declining standards of living.

As with the attitude *vis-à-vis* Nasserism in general, the stance towards the nationalisations of the Nasser era ranged from outright condemnation to praise. At one end of the spectrum the massive state take-over of economic property in the 1950s and '60s was described by Muslim Brothers like Ḥusayn Shaḥḥāta as a theft of what people legitimately owned.[65] 'Ādil Ḥusayn emphasised that the gains from the past should be defended, but mentioned concretely only the nationalisation of the Suez Canal and of foreign assets after the Suez War of 1956,[66] about which every Islamist would probably agree. Finally there were the socialist dissidents Gamāl As'ad and 'Ādil Wālī who, *after leaving* the Labour Party in protest against its Islamisation, spoke aggressively of anyone wanting to sell the public sector as people who did not love Egypt, and called for defending the fruits of the July Revolution.[67] There was from an early date a close link between attitudes towards Nasserism and towards the new economic policy of Sadat. With regard to the Labour Party their criticism of *infitāḥ* policies was only strengthened when 'Ādil Ḥusayn became editor of the party newspaper in late 1985. Despite shortcomings in its political system linked to a refusal to accept democratic participation, and to an excessive public take-over of economic assets,[68] Nasserism was for Ḥusayn basically a positive experience. It had been a serious attempt to build the economic basis for an independent Egypt. The *infitāḥ* represented a surrender of this attempt in the face of Western and Israeli military, political and economic pressure. 1974 for him represented the official abandonment of an independent policy. In his work from 1986 on "a new Arab thinking" the model that emerges for regaining independence may well be described as a kind of reformed Nasserism.

Ḥusayn criticised the *infitāḥ* policies for having dismantled all tools for planning by opening the doors wide to import, and letting the public sector and government apparatus decay while élite experts switched to the new sector of joint ventures with foreign capital or migrated to the Gulf or

[65] Ḥusayn Shaḥḥāta, "Al-ḍawābiṭ al-islāmiyya li-tarshīd al-qiṭā' al-'āmm", *Liwā' al-islām*, 25 May 1990.

[66] For instance 'Ādil Ḥusayn, "Bay' miṣr fī al-mazād wa qaḍīyat al-qiṭā' al-'āmm", *al-Sha'b*, 12 December 1989.

[67] See their interventions in the People's Assembly: Gamāl As'ad, 27 January 1990, *MMS*, F5, 3–21, ṭm, pp. 6–26 and 'Ādil Wālī, 10 February 1990, *MMS*, F5, 3–27, ṭm, pp. 5–32. See also the speech by 'Abd al-Ḥalīm 'Alam al-Dīn, LP, Giza, 29 January 1990, *MMS*, F5, 3–25, ṭm, pp. 6–33.

[68] 'Ādil Ḥusayn, *Naḥwa fikr 'arabī jadīd*, pp. 241–53.

the United States. The IMF's insistence on using "world prices" in measuring economic performance would merely add to the malaise and fix Egypt in its current position within the international division of labour.[69]

The apparent rapid growth of the GDP was solely due to oil-related income from oil exports, tourism, the Suez Canal and workers abroad. All four sources were dependent on the price of oil, something not controlled by Egypt, and worse: they could be cut off by US decision. Ḥusayn went far in suggesting that the whole *infitāḥ* policies were a US scheme to make Egypt economically dependent and forcing it to integrate economically with Israel.

Although Ḥusayn towards the end of the 1980s had developed a generally positive attitude towards what he termed the "national private sector", his negative view of the *infitāḥ* was intact.

In contrast the Muslim Brothers from an early date actively supported the *infitāḥ*.[70] And they consistently demanded a greater "opening" in terms of liberalising prices and providing more room for "Islamic capital", whether this was in the form of local Egyptian Islamic banks and investment companies, or the diverse Islamic financial institutions of the Gulf countries.[71]

The Brothers had of course fallen out with Sadat by the time of his assassination, and gradually throughout the 1980s their emphasis on defending Egyptian independence led them to criticise at least certain aspects of the *infitāḥ* policies leading to dependence on food imports and to problems for local industry. But the ideological bias against Nasser remained very strong, and the Brothers never talked in terms of the *infitāḥ* being a break with an earlier policy more favourable to independence. Rather they would fuse their criticism of Nasser, Sadat and Mubarak into one both in the political and the economic field, the economic argument

[69] Though Labour Party members might on occasion be seen to use world prices as a legitimate accounting tool when it fitted their argument, as in Ḥilmī Murād's opposition to the construction of an oil refinery in Asyūṭ (see p. 190 below).

[70] See 'Umar al-Tilmisānī, "Idhā jā'a al muslimūn fa-lā māl li-aḥad", *al-Da'wa*, 383, February 1977. Some writers cite this article to the opposite effect, as expressing opposition to the *infitāḥ*, notably Saad Eddin Ibrahim, "An Islamic Alternative in Egypt: The Muslim Brotherhood and Sadat", *Arab Studies Quarterly*, vol. 4, no. 1/2, spring 1982, p. 82. But Tilmisānī clearly says that the Muslim Brothers support the *infitāḥ*. It is true that he denounces the huge gaps developing between rich and poor, and that he deplores the *infitāḥ* turning "consumptive" rather than "productive". But he does not propose to solve this by returning to more state control. And when Ibrahim goes on to claim that the Brothers in the late 1970s had a socioeconomic policy close to that of the secular left, he quotes evidence from the 1950s and does not seem to perceive the shift that has taken place.

[71] By the late 1980s this last point was shared by the Labour Party, at least with regard to the Egyptian Islamic financial institutions (see the discussion on pp. 222 ff.).

being that Nasser's policies had stifled initiative and weakened the economy, leading to the indebtedness of the *infitāḥ* period.

A prime example of Muslim Brother anti-Nasser rhetoric appears in two articles by 'Abd al-Ḥamīd al-Ghazālī, written as late as January 1990, interesting in light of the fact that the policies of the Brothers by this time had otherwise moved slightly "to the left". "Our society suffers from a dualism", he says. For one thing is what the people believe in, another thing is what is practised. Since the early 1960s the structure of Egyptian society has economically, politically, socially and culturally come to resemble that of the Eastern bloc. On the economic front this has meant the dominance of the public sector with its low productivity, its waste of resources and corruption of consciences, its bureaucratic central planning and its unstable priorities and policies. One result has been that the agricultural sector is starved of investments, and inhibited by mistaken centralised policies in pricing, marketing and the cooperative field. This has meant a squandering of agricultural resources and diminishing opportunities for development in this field. The outcome is increasing dependence on the outside world through heavy reliance on the import of wheat, in its turn leading to an increasing indebtedness. All these evils are linked to a primitive political structure, which is in form based on party pluralism but in reality on totalitarian dictatorship. Justice is preached, but the ordinary person experiences all sorts of exploitation, and people with limited incomes lose day by day what remains of their livelihood. The comedy of the subsidies is an example of what happens, for most of them go to those who exploit them, not to those who need them.

So, al-Ghazālī claims, in spite of the slogans of *infitāḥ*, whether consumptive or productive, Egyptian society remains shackled by the chains of the 1960s, to which the recent catastrophe of the investment companies (see below, pp. 203 ff.) brings fresh evidence. "Now that the Eastern bloc itself is breaking those chains", he writes, "I hope to God that we will too". The "mother problem" of political oppression must be solved first.[72]

In November of the same year Yusuf Kamāl, reiterating al-Ghazālī's argument, blames the Egyptian debt crisis squarely on the "corrupt centralised planning practices" initiated under Nasser, which created insoluble problems in the vast public sector, leading in turn to improvisation, carelessness, flight of capital abroad, currency speculation etc.[73]

[72] 'Abd al-Ḥamīd al-Ghazālī, "Sanat al-taghyīr wa irādat al-binā' amama ma'āwil al-hadm wa quwā al-jumūd" (1) and (2), *al-Nūr*, 24 and 31 January 1990.

[73] Yusuf Kamāl, cited in Magdī Muṣṭafā, "Al-isqāṭ al-juz'ī li-madyūniyyat miṣr al-khārijiyya hal yakūn furṣa li-murāja'a shāmila wa iṣlāḥ haykal al-iqtiṣād al-miṣrī?", *Liwā' al-islām*, 19 Nov 1990.

The supposed main pillar of the *infitāḥ* was the opening for foreign investment. From early on the Islamists criticised the lack of positive results in the form of technology transfer and export improvement. They were also highly critical towards the way Law No. 43 favoured foreign investors to the detriment of local Egyptian capital. Calls were raised for a "reunification" of the national economy in the sense that tax and other privileges should be offered to all investors irrespective of nationality. Gradually, however, the Islamists came to focus on the need to make investment more attractive and easy to Arabs and Egyptians, while the scope for non-Arab foreign direct ownership of Egyptian assets should be restricted. All along they called for increased state involvement in directing investment into the productive sectors that were pivotal to economic development.

When the Law on Foreign and Arab investment came up for revision in 1989 the Islamists raised a number of critical questions. They suggested that tax incentives for non-Arab capital might be cut, and that generally a more efficient and incorrupt system of directing the investment into productive sectors be found. They did not, however, propose to alter the basic framework.

Muḥtasib *or entrepreneur: the role of the state*

What then did the Islamists have to say about the positive alternative, the way to solve the problems and get Egypt out of the economic quagmire depicted in their critique of the government?

In an article on the need for economic reform in April 1985 the President of the Labour Party, Ibrāhīm Shukrī, stated that the issue is not socialism or capitalism, but that any economy, whatever the system, cannot be left totally without regulation. We need a grand strategy for development, implemented by the state, but no such strategy exists in Egypt today, he wrote.[74]

It is worth noticing here Shukrī's use of the concept "grand strategy of the state", which is central to 'Ādil Ḥusayn's ideas presented in *Towards a New Arab Thinking*,[75] published in the same year. This may well point to Ḥusayn's influence on the leadership of the Labour Party at a time when he had as yet no formal position in the party.

Especially from 1987 onwards this call for a state strategy for development was often repeated by Islamists. It was typically linked to the claim that Egypt needed to define its identity, and build its economic strategy on this identity. We must find our own way which is neither capi-

[74] Ibrāhīm Shukrī, "Al-siyasāt al-iqtiṣādiyya taḍ'afunā fī muwājahat amrīkā wa-isrā'īl wa tushī' al-maẓālim al-ijtimā'īyya", *al-Sha'b*, 23 April 1985.

[75] See 'Ādil Ḥusayn, *Naḥwa fikr 'arabī jadīd* [Towards a New Arab Thinking], p. 240.

talism nor socialism, but is suited to our concrete conditions, said ʻĀdil Wālī, a Labour Party deputy from Cairo, who later left the party as a result of the split in 1989.[76] In the wake of the international economic problems following the stock market crisis of 1987, ʻIṣām al-ʻIryān said that Egypt needed to define an economic line based on its own identity in order not always just to be affected by the world economy, but to contribute something to solving its problems.[77] And in 1990 he talked of the need for "a moral and political project for national reconstruction" in order to ensure a peaceful controlled process of change and avoid an explosion like those taking place in Eastern Europe (this was said only a few weeks after the bloody revolt against Ceausescu in Rumania).[78]

There was a consistent call, echoing the earlier discussion about the emphasis on independence, for the strategy to be based on self-reliance. But this self-reliance should be extended to include tight coordination with the rest of the Arab world.

It was claimed that people would be willing to carry the burden of economic reform if only they saw that the state possessed a clear strategy for development.[79] But the Islamists also emphasised that the indispensable mutual trust between the state's leadership and its citizens required the establishment of a democratic system and putting an end to corruption.

While the degree to which the state should play a role in directing the economic life is a matter of debate among Islamists, it seems that the two parties under study agreed in refusing the reduction of the state to the liberal idea of a state merely responsible for security and for infrastructure. An article in *Liwā' al-islām* outlines a view of the role of the state in the economy which in general seems to be pretty close to the common view within the Islamic Alliance partners.[80] The basis for state intervention is seen as threefold:

— First of all while the Islamic economy is based on private ownership and a market economy, the market must be regulated by the state, in order to secure "just prices". It seems that this latter term primarily refers to a price established when no interest is involved, nor monopoly or speculation in hoarding. Monopoly is abhorred since it creates inflation, unemployment and undue concentration of wealth. So the state should break up

[76] See ʻĀdil Wālī's speech in Parliament on 22 June 1987, *MMS*, F5, 1–15, ṭm, pp. 3–21.
[77] See his speech in parliament on 12 January 1988, *MMS*, F5, 1–57, pp. 4644–68.
[78] ʻIryān in the People's Assembly, 28 January 1990, *MMS*, F5, 3–24, ṭm, pp. 2–30.
[79] See for instance the speech by Gamāl Asʻad, Labour Party deputy for Asyūṭ, in the People's Assembly on 27 January 1990, *MMS*, F5, 3–21, ṭm, pp. 6–26.
[80] See the review in *Liwā' al-islām* of a study by Muḥammad Fatḥī Ṣaqr on state intervention in the economic life under an Islamic economic system, "Tadakhkhul al-dawla fī al-nishāṭ al-iqtiṣādī", *Liwā' al-islām*, 23 June 1990.

monopolies, forbid price agreements between companies as well as unfair competition in the form of dumping.[81]

Still the concept of "a just price" would seem to allow for other forms of state intervention as well. For instance it is established as a legitimate concern to protect local industry, although not to the point where local producers can comfortably "exploit the consumers" behind a protective tariff shield.[82] For the state to directly fix prices may be necessary but should always be an exception, according to the cited article in *Liwā' al-islām*. In case this expedient is used, it is imperative to secure that it does not generate a black market where goods are more expensive than they were in the first place.[83]

— The protection of local industry is connected to another basis for state intervention, namely that it is a task entrusted to the state by God to secure economic development. First of all this means to create conditions for the spiritual and bodily development of the most important productive factor, the human one. In addition it is a responsibility of the state to establish a sound infrastructure and preserve a sound environment, it should establish basic industries and it should control foreign trade.

The state must also secure the use of farmable land. It should help those wanting to reclaim fallow lands, and secure a just distribution of land by following the old Islamic principle, that land left fallow for more than three years is forfeited.[84]

— Finally the state must intervene in the economy in order to secure everyone a basic level of welfare. Consonant with the views of the writers surveyed in chapter 3, this is considered to go beyond bare survival to mean everyone has the right to enjoy life and should feel safe about food, clothing, housing, education and to be able to afford a minimum of recreational leisure. For this reason the state must secure employment for all those able to work, and sustenance for all others. The right of the individual Muslim to a certain level of welfare also forms the basis of the right and duty of the state to direct the use of productive resources according to Islamic economic priorities.[85]

[81] On this point see also 'Ādil Ḥusayn, "Al-ghalā' wal-amn al-markazī wal-qamar al-isrā'īlī", *al-Sha'b*, 27 September 1988, and 'Abd al-Ḥamīd al-Ghazāli in Maḥmūd Bakrī and Muḥammad Gamāl 'Arafa, "Al-ittifāq ma'a ṣandūq al-naqd", *al-Sha'b*, 12 May 1987. Cf. Fatḥī 'Abd al-Wāḥid, LP Minya, People's Assembly, 5 March 1990, *MMS*, F5, 3–38, ṭm, pp. 16–19.

[82] Cf. 'Ādil Ḥusayn, "Qānūn al-istithmār al-jadīd", *al-Sha'b*, 20 June 1989.

[83] On the question of pricing regulations cf. Ḥizb al-'amal al-ishtirākī, "Taqrīr ḥizb al-'amal al-ishtirākī ilā al-mu'tamar al-iqtiṣādī", pp. 55–6.

[84] "Tadakhkhul al-dawla fī al-nishāṭ al-iqtiṣādī", *Liwā' al-islām*, 23 June 1990.

[85] *Ibid.*

The issue of the role of planning versus market forces in the running of the economy is one where there appears, at least on the ideological level to be a sharp difference of opinion between the Labour Party and the Muslim Brothers. This might well be a reflection of the historically determined aversion of the Brothers to the Nasser regime, which is synonymous with centralised planning in Egypt. However, the difference tends to melt away somewhat when more concrete suggestions for reform are considered.

Time and again, in their critique of government policies and in their positive suggestions for reform, the Brothers in practice presuppose a government possessing a quite comprehensive capacity for and will to intervene in the running of the economy. In the Islamic Alliance election platform from 1987 the need for the state to define goals and priorities in a twenty year perspective is held forth. This long term strategy should be followed up through running medium term plans for three to five years.[86] In the same document the Muslim Brothers also support the need for a national council to control prices and wages. This council should have trade union representation and the power if necessary to regulate prices on certain goods.[87] This was not merely a tactical concession to the Labour Party. In Parliament in late 1987 the Muslim Brother Cairo MP Sayf al-Islām al-Bannā castigated the government for not having fulfilled its promise to install a supervisory authority for prices and wages that would ensure that wages were raised in keeping with inflation in order to secure the welfare of the people of modest income.[88]

More important, from 1987 on the Muslim Brothers often emphasise that development and justice hinges on the decision on what to produce, implying that this is a political, not merely an economic, question. They call for the direction of investment into productive sectors that supply basic necessities like food and clothing for the population, and even of directing consumption towards that which can be produced locally.[89] And by 1991 we find explicit references to the need for "a balanced plan for economic development, taking in all sectors of economic activity", as a prerequisite for escaping from Egypt's current position of dependency towards the West.[90]

According to the common electoral programme between the Labour Party and the Muslim Brothers from 1987, the Islamic priorities of production starts with necessities end everyday needs and demand that the

[86] Ḥizb al-'amal, "Al-barnāmaj al-intikhābī 'alā qā'imat ḥizb al-'amal", part VI.
[87] *Ibid.*, part V.
[88] Sayf al-Islām al-Bannā in the People's Assembly on 28 December 1987, *MMS*, F5, 1–47, pp. 4259–85.
[89] Shaḥḥāta, *Al-minhaj al-islāmī lil-iṣlāḥ al-iqtiṣādī*, p. 14.
[90] *Ibid.*, pp. 23–4.

government does not approve of projects outside these priorities, but concentrates on production of food, housing, popular clothing, defence equipment, communications and the necessities of production. Consumption must be reformed: conspicuous consumption must be limited, and consumptive patterns steered away from copying the West and in a direction that is in harmony with production.[91]

With the Labour Party the reform of consumptive patterns is a consistent theme.[92] More generally the party's positive attitude towards planning (and towards Nasser) is evident already in the document they produced on economic reform in 1982, although it is stressed that the planners should take market laws into consideration and leave freedom of action for the private sector.[93] The pro-planning stand is reflected in the interventions from Labour Party MPs in the People's Assembly. They support planning as a method in order to secure the development of local industry, and to secure the people necessities at reasonable prices.[94] They argue that private investment should be directed to projects foreseen in the government's five-year plans.[95] And they blame lack of central planning for all that is bad—inflation, unemployment, debt, dependency and declining standards of living.[96]

The lack of local savings and investment was seen as an important obstacle for the development effort. Besides inviting in Arab capital, the solution that was always held forth was to attract home the funds held by Egyptians abroad, a great part of which was generated by the millions working in the oil producing countries of the Gulf. These funds were generally held to exceed by far the foreign debt, which by 1990 had reached 50 billion dollars. Ma'mūn al-Huḍaybī seemed to be calculating from a sum of 120 billion dollars in funds held abroad by Egyptians when he suggested that creating the right climate for investment could attract 12 billion dollars each year for 10 years, and do away with any need for other sources of external finance.[97] When funds were instead still leaving the country, he said, it was because of the erratic economic policies which

[91] Ḥizb al-'amal, "Al-barnāmaj al-intikhābī 'alā qā'imat ḥizb al-'amal". Cf. Shaḥḥāta, *Al-minhaj al-islāmī lil-iṣlāḥ al-iqtiṣādī*, p. 19.

[92] See for instance 'Ādil Ḥusayn, "Al-ithnayn al-aswad wa mu'tamar al-intāj", *al-Sha'b*, 10 November 1987.

[93] Ḥizb al-'amal al-ishtirākī, "Taqrīr ḥizb al-'amal al-ishtirākī ilā al-mu'tamar al-iqtiṣādī", p. 37.

[94] For instance Mamdūḥ al-Qināwī, 8 June 1985, *MMS*, F4, 1–84, pp. 6544–62 and Ṣalāḥ 'Abdallāh from Cairo, 29 December 1987, *MMS*, F5, 1–49, pp. 4320–41, where he particularly discusses the situation of the local pharmaceutical industry.

[95] Gamāl As'ad, LP Asyūṭ, 4 July 1989, *MMS*, F5, 2–92, pp. 6707–46.

[96] 'Abd al-'Azīz al-Ghubārī, LP Fayyūm, 12 February 1990, *MMS*, F5, 3–31, ṭm, pp. 2–28.

[97] Huḍaybī in the People's Assembly 15 January 1990, *MMS*, F5, 3–20, ṭm, pp. 5–25.

destroyed investor confidence, the most extreme case being the government's destruction of the Islamic investment companies from 1988 onwards. Earlier the Islamists had argued that the investment companies ought to be stimulated to invest in the productive sectors of the economy, precisely as a way of channelling the savings of Egyptian migrant workers into positive economic development efforts, rather than having them hoarded abroad or wasted on inflation-fuelling consumption at home.[98]

The same argument we find in the Muslim Brothers' programmatic statement from 1991, which calls for encouraging saving by all methods, in the spirit of concern for future generations. Channels for saving must be increased and made more accessible and there must be support for small projects based on the Islamic principle of *mushāraka* (see p. 201, n. 43).[99] Gradually the improvement of the climate for private saving and investment also becomes a theme in Labour Party writings. Aḥmad Ḥirik, a Labour Party MP for Cairo, called for greater freedom for the banks to take risks. Under the present system of controls, he said, credit evaporated from the market. A liberalisation here was needed, especially in order to strengthen the small industrial enterprises, so important in job creation.[100]

Regarding the investments that were in fact taking place, the Islamists complained about the lack of proper priorities.[101] In an article from January 1989 Ḥusayn Shaḥḥāta spelled out what he saw as the proper rules for truly Islamic investment according to the *Sharī'a*. Apart from avoiding the use of interest and the production of illicit goods like alcohol, Shaḥḥāta stressed the following points:

— Investments should be directed to production of first "necessities" (*ḍarūriyyāt*), second "needs" (*ḥājiyyāt*) and third "improvements" (*taḥsīniyyāt*) (cf. p. 94).

— Investment projects should be chosen with an eye to the balance between present and coming generations. Long and medium term projects should have priority.

— The preferred projects must be those which provide a proper income for the largest possible number of poor people, raise the general standard of living, increase food security for the Islamic world, and reduce Muslim dependence on hostile powers.

98 Muḥammad Ḥilmī Murād, "Al-ḍajja al-khādi'a ḥawla ittifāqiyyāt al-baḥth 'an al-bitrūl", *al-Sha'b* 17 November 1987. Cf. Ḥizb al-'amal al-ishtirākī, "Taqrīr ḥizb al-'amal al-ishtirākī ilā al-mu'tamar al-iqtiṣādī", pp. 33–6, 45.

99 Shaḥḥāta, *Al-minhaj al-islāmī lil-iṣlāḥ al-iqtiṣādī*, p. 14.

100 28 January 1990, *MMS*, F5, 3–23, ṭm, pp. 2–31.

101 Magdī Muṣṭafā, "Al-isqāṭ al-juz'ī li-madyūniyyat miṣr al-khārijiyya hal yakūn furṣa li-murāja'a shāmila wa iṣlāḥ haykal al-iqtiṣād al-miṣrī?", *Liwā' al-islām*, 19 Nov 1990.

— One should avoid the production of luxuries as long as there are Muslims dying of starvation, disease and ignorance.
— The wealth of the Muslims should be preserved and developed, not hoarded or thrown away on speculative ventures.[102]

A debate that gathered momentum towards the end of the decade was the question of privatisation of public sector enterprises. The opposition to this remained strong, sometimes couched in rather Nasserist terms. But as the crisis of international socialism changed the ideological climate, a slightly different line of argument became dominant. The question was asked: who in Egypt can afford to buy the mainly large scale public enterprises, if they shall not be given away? The implied answer was "no one", the indication being that the proposed privatisation would really end up being a de-Egyptianisation of the economy, selling the means of production off to foreigners.

The issue also prompted a more general debate on the correct relation between public and private sectors and public and private ownership according to Islamic standards. Both the Muslim Brothers and the Labour Party seemed to agree that both sectors had their place, and that in Egypt the public sector had become too dominant. However, there were differences in emphasis.

Yūsuf Kamāl and Ḥusayn Shaḥḥāta of the Brothers both emphasised that the private sector must be the basis in an Islamic economy. A public sector may exist if there are products that are needed by society, but which private interests for one reason or another cannot or will not produce. This might be because the production of these goods demands too high an investment or yields too low a profit in the initial period, for national security reasons etc.. Kamāl gives concrete examples from Egypt including the High Dam at Aswān, military industry, iron and steel-production and heavy industry in general.[103] But both Shaḥḥāta and Kamāl emphasise strongly that this should not be confused with the state's responsibility for satisfying the needs of the poor. What they are out to attack here is

[102] Ḥusayn Shaḥḥāta, "Al-ḥaqā'iq al-tā'iha wal-awrāq al-mukhtalaṭa fī qaḍiyat sharikāt tawẓīf al-amwāl", *Liwā' al-islām*, 9 January 1989. A similar view is presented by 'Abd al-Ḥamīd al-Ghazālī at about the same time. Ghazālī adds that there should be an emphasis on small projects technologically suited to Egyptian conditions and which contribute to the integration of economic sectors. A million small projects was better than a few projects worth millions, he wrote. See Ḥamdī al-Baṣīr, "Al-insān wal-minhaj al-islāmī fī al-tanmīya al-iqtiṣādiyya", *al-Nūr*, 7 December 1988.

[103] Al-Sayyid Abū Dāwud, "Al-qiṭā' al-'āmm min wijhat naẓar islāmiyya fī ḥiwār ma'a Yūsuf Kamāl khabīr al-iqtiṣād al-islāmī", *al-Nūr*, 16 May 1990. Cf. also Ḥusayn Shaḥḥāta, "Al-ḍawābiṭ al-islāmiyya li-tarshīd al-qiṭā' al-'āmm", *Liwā' al-islām*, 25 May 1990.

basically the state's practice of manipulating prices both of raw materials, energy and finished products, with the argument of providing affordable products for the poor. They strongly claim that caring for the poor must remain a separate sphere, as it were, of the state's activity, ideally served by the *zakāt*. Islam abhors the manipulation of prices, says Kamāl,[104] and subsidies must be direct in the sense of the state buying goods at market prices and supplying them directly to the needy at a lower price.

'Ādil Ḥusayn has a slightly different approach. First he seeks a basis in the international debate on the preconditions for development. Everybody, he says, now agrees that the state has a role as a direct investor in order to speed up development and to direct it. And the more backward a country's economy is to start with, the more this is the case.

Then he gives two *raisons d'être* for the public sector in an Islamic state: independence and social justice. The first point he links to the fact that no country in our time can avoid a substantial degree of transactions on the world market. But there Egypt would face the giant multinational corporations and the governments backing them, who have tremendous resources and not least broad access to information about Third World countries. To be able to do business with them on something like an equal basis, the only solution is that the state takes care of external trade. In addition Egypt, with Israel as a neighbour, is forced to have a high military expenditure. To place the military effort on a secure financial footing, the state needs to establish production which can generate income directly for the treasury.

The same goes for social justice. The *zakāt*[105] and charitable contributions from the rich will cover some of the expenses needed to secure the living standards of those with a limited income. But the state must supplement this through subsidised basic commodities and services. The financing will be partly through taxes, but also partly through the income from state-owned production.

Egypt needs a fairly large public sector, Ḥusayn said, although not nearly as large as it is today. The goal must be an economy with thriving private and public sectors, he wrote, but they should both submit to a national strategy for development. Decisions must be taken in Cairo, not in Washington.[106]

104 Cited in Magdī Muṣṭafā, "Al-qiṭā' al-'āmm 'alā al-ṭarīqa al-miṣriyya", *Liwā' al-islām*, 5 July 1989.

105 In an interview with the author on 10 May 1994 Ḥusayn said he thought the *zakāt* ought to remain a voluntary contribution in the hands of non-governmental committees even in a future Islamic state.

106 'Ādil Ḥusayn, "Bay' miṣr fī al-mazād wa qaḍīyat al-qiṭā' al-'āmm", *al-Sha'b*, 12 December 1989. Cf. Gamāl As'ad, LP Asyūṭ, People's Assembly, 4 July 1989, *MMS*, F5, 2–92, pp. 6706–46.

The question of independence is not absent from the concerns of the Brothers in their argument for a public sector. Yūsuf Kamāl explicitly says that the public sector is there to ensure that the society is strong enough to defend itself against its enemies.[107] But when Ḥusayn places the establishment of social justice as one of the tasks of the public sector, the Muslim Brothers clearly disagree. This is linked to the question of state manipulation of prices. Ḥusayn clearly sees this as a legitimate tool of state direction, both for social and for developmental purposes. He cites Japan and not least South Korea as models of the third road between a free-wheeling capitalism and a bureaucratic state-dominated economy. And he praises the use of import tariffs and quotas, subsidies, credit control and price regulations in order to create the desired balanced development and to aid the export to foreign markets.[108] While the Muslim Brothers would agree with this to quite an extent, they distinctly oppose price regulations.

The question of privatising the public sector remained a permanent demand from the Bretton Woods institutions, and when the government in 1990 indicated a new seriousness in obliging, a heated debate followed. In April 1990 ʻĀdil Ḥusayn wrote an article in *al-Shaʻb* bearing the title "The public sector is being sold to foreigners, move to stop the crime!". While strongly opposing the idea of foreign ownership of Egyptian industry, the article also indicates the shift in Labour Party attitude to the private sector since the early 1980s. The party is in favour of a privatisation programme within a national framework, Ḥusayn says, but in order to succeed this will need time for a gradual transformation of the whole socioeconomic regime.

The first step would be to encourage those possessing capital and expertise to expand their private activities to the utmost degree possible, and to create new private projects. It is a mistake to believe that the local private sector is still too weak to undertake capital intensive and technologically complicated projects, or that it cannot sustain projects that need a long time in gestation before they can start production and reap profits. For in Egypt there are now people with large savings, and gifted entrepreneurs capable of realising huge private projects. The fact that these possibilities are not realised at present is a huge loss to the development of the national economy. It seems that it is the fear of state interference that scares prospective investors away.[109] If the Labour Party were to gain

107 Al-Sayyid Abū Dāwud, "Al-qiṭāʻ al-ʻāmm min wijhat naẓar islāmiyya fī ḥiwār maʻa Yūsuf Kamāl khabīr al-iqtiṣād al-islāmī", *al-Nūr*, 16 May 1990.

108 ʻĀdil Ḥusayn, "Tasā'ulāt ʻan al-qiṭāʻ al-ʻāmm baʻda khiṭāb awwal māyū", *al-Shaʻb*, 8 May 1990.

109 For a similar argument from the Muslim Brothers see Sayf al-Islām al-Bannā, MB Cairo, People's Assembly, 11 February 1990, *MMS*, F5, 3–28, ṭm, pp. 2–27.

power, it would implement policies that would allay those fears and release the potential energies of private investors in line with a national strategy for development.

With regard to the existing publicly owned assets, while Ḥusayn opposes the plans of the United States and the international institutions, he proposes another concept for the privatisation of public sector companies. The first condition would be that the buyers, whether persons, companies or institutions, be Egyptian or Arab. Secondly it must be clear that privatisation is not in the first place a means of cutting losses, but must spring from an integrated understanding of what are the suitable forms of ownership in an Islamic economy, and in harmony with human nature. Here we may possibly discern the influence on Ḥusayn of his intensified readings of Islamist writers and in particular Muḥammad Bāqir al-Ṣadr, whom he admires much. An Islamic economy, says Ḥusayn, means creating a balance where the state does not strangle people's initiative on the one hand, and on the other individuals are not left to act without the direction of a central planning apparatus.

It is clear that the state should only sell off a company after it has been reformed and is not making losses. For if not the company would be sold at a loss, and this would mean losing the public capital invested in it. The state acting as the trustee of society does not have the right to do this, but must secure that the sale recovers the original public investment. On the other hand this of course does not mean that the state should sell off every company making a profit. The state must hold on to projects that can finance development, social services and the needs of the defence of the country.

As for companies to be privatised, this may happen through a sale of all assets, or partly, through inviting private shareholders into *mushāraka*, thereby providing an outlet for those billions of pounds of savings that exist, while at the same time securing the companies badly needed liquid means both in Egyptian and foreign currency. This is the national alternative to "debt for equity" in that in this scheme foreign debts would be exchanged for the savings of Egyptians in foreign currency.[110]

Some weeks later Ḥusayn set up three conditions for accepting the sale of public sector assets: (1) They should as a rule only be sold to Egyptians or other Arabs, (2) the price should be correct, and not a cheap way for a handful of people to get their hands on public capital and (3) there must be some guarantee that the transfer to the private sector will lead to real increases in productivity (and not merely higher profits as a result of artificially high prices on products, or the lay-off of workers).[111]

[110] 'Ādil Ḥusayn, "Al-qiṭā' al-'āmm yubā' lil-ajānib, taḥarrakū li-man' al-jarīma", *al-Sha'b*, 10 April 1990.

[111] 'Ādil Ḥusayn, "Tasā'ulāt 'an al-qiṭā' al-'āmm ba'da khiṭāb awwal māyū", *al-Sha'b*, 8 May 1990.

One thing to notice here is the shift in emphasis from Ḥusayn's writings in 1985. While in both cases foreign interference in the economy is held forth as the big threat, in 1985 the US pressure to strengthen the role of the private sector *vis-à-vis* the public sector is cited as, in and of itself, a conscious attempt to weaken the Egyptian economy. In 1990, however, the principle of privatisation is accepted as something desirable as long as foreign ownership or other control can be blocked.

For the Muslim Brothers in principle there was all along a more unmitigated positive attitude towards the private sector. Nevertheless in political practice they were not spokesmen for an all-out liquidation of the public sector, to put it mildly, although they were clearly spokesmen for a greater space for private business.

In the programmatic document from 1991 Ḥusayn Shaḥḥāta advocates the need for a thorough review of the public sector. Some of its companies operate in fields which are not suitable for public ownership, and should be sold to the employees. On the other hand projects which are of strategic importance should be kept and improved in order to safeguard the capital invested in them.[112] This view is mirrored in the election platform of the Islamic Alliance from 1987 where it is stated that the public sector must move out of sectors where it does not belong, but the remainder of the sector must be strengthened "since it is the central nerve of Egyptian industry".[113]

In 1987 al-Bannā suggested to the People's Assembly the sale of up until 50 percent of the shares in some public sector companies: 20 percent to the employees and 30 percent to private interests. This, he said, would liberate capital for new investment without the need for loans, while preserving a dominant public ownership.[114]

However, in January 1990, 'Iṣām al-'Iryān, always close to the line of 'Ādil Ḥusayn, argued against the hurried sale of the public sector, since no one in Egypt could afford to buy. We cannot again have the cancer of foreign privilege in a weak Egyptian economy, he said, also warning against the rash sale of the assets of the Islamic Investment Companies taken over by the government, with the same argument.[115]

Ḥusayn Shaḥḥāta in May 1990 discussed the Islamic principles for the public sector, and gave his version of the correct conditions for a sale, which in most respects were quite similar to those of 'Ādil Ḥusayn cited above. On the question of who should be allowed to buy he widens the category to include all Muslims, not only Arabs as with Ḥusayn. He takes

[112] Shaḥḥāta, *Al-minhaj al-islāmī lil-iṣlāḥ al-iqtiṣādī*, p. 16.
[113] Ḥizb al-'amal, "Al-barnāmaj al-intikhābī 'alā qā'imat ḥizb al-'amal".
[114] 24 June 1987, *MMS*, F5, 1–18, ṭm, pp. 2–31.
[115] The People's Assembly, 28 January 1990, *MMS*, F5, 3–24, ṭm, pp. 2–30.

up a persistent theme of the Muslim Brothers saying that the preferred thing is to sell to the employees. This will increase efficiency since they will then feel that they are working for themselves. Ḥusayn warned against this as a plot to sugar the pill and gain acceptance for the idea of privatisation, in order for the foreigners to step in in the next round. Shaḥḥāta also suggests that the value of the firm be divided into small shares so that there will be an opportunity for small savers to enter. He agrees with Ḥusayn that the assets must be sold at a good price, and through a proper sale, not given away cheaply behind closed doors. He also agrees that the aim of the sale must be increased productivity, but is more elaborate than Ḥusayn regarding what should happen in connection with the sale. While all honest, skilled and hard-working employees must be guaranteed work, he said, those whose employment has been forced on the company for political reasons must be laid off, and in general the staff must be cleansed of unqualified and corrupt personnel.[116]

In the same article Shaḥḥāta also discusses what should be done with the parts of the public sector that should remain in public ownership. These companies, he wrote, must be reformed according to the following principles:

The leadership must be reformed. God-fearing and well qualified people must take the place of those who are corrupt and have only got their positions because of family, connections or party loyalty. There must be a better balance between self-financing and external finance to ease the debt burden. Accumulated *ribā* interest must be written off, the expenses covered by the state, and no more *ribā* loans must be contracted. Instead private interests must be invited in as partners in a *mushāraka* arrangement with up to 49 percent of the shares. Accounting practices should be improved and the wasting of funds on representation, dinner parties and "political advertising"[117] brought to an end. State intervention in prices must be ended. National production, private as well as public, would need to be shielded from the full force of international competition, but this should be achieved through customs tariffs. Shaḥḥāta finishes off on a high note: "we need honest, fighting men who fear neither Jews, Christians, nor Americans [*sic!*], but who will act like the first Muslims did when they turned the arid Arabian peninsula into green orchards".

[116] Ḥusayn Shaḥḥāta, "Al-ḍawābiṭ al-islāmiyya li-tarshīd al-qiṭā' al-'āmm", *Liwā' al-islām*, 25 May 1990.

[117] Egyptian newspapers are full of costly advertisements in which companies, private and public, greet a prominent political personality, in particular the President, on occasions like his returning from a trip abroad, presumably entered to maintain a good relationship with the authorities.

Defending muwaẓẓafīn, *workers and farmers*

The rising unemployment figures, especially among educated youth, were discussed in the People's Assembly time and again, and connected to it the problems created by the employment guarantee operated by the government for everyone with secondary or higher education.

In 1988 Gamāl As'ad complained in the People's Assembly that productivity could hardly be expected to increase while companies remained weighed down by compulsory overstaffing. For the state to provide people with jobs was all right, but it must happen according to a plan for real development, not by assigning to companies needing ten employees a hundred new staff members in addition to the hundred forced on them already, As'ad said.[118]

Yet, while complaining about the problems connected to the running of the system of guaranteed employment for graduates, Islamic Alliance deputies seemed to favour its reform, rather than its abolishment. Obviously such an abolishment would have been vastly unpopular among the lower and lower middle class families who probably made up the bulk of the Alliance's constituency.

Several speakers in the People's Assembly raised the issue of the bad fit between education and the needs of the economy. It is a waste, said Magdī Ḥusayn, that society spends 5000 LE to educate a student, who then proceeds to work as a tailor or a *kabābgī*. Education must be reformed so as to produce those skills in demand in our economy, he said.[119] The same point had been taken up by Mamdūḥ Qināwī back in 1985.[120] Especially the need for expanded technical education was held forth as a necessity in order to alleviate the lack of skilled labour due to migration to the Gulf countries. It is indicative of pervasive negative attitudes in Egyptian society towards anything smacking of manual labour, that it was felt necessary to suggest that as a "carrot" the road to higher education should be opened to the brightest among those choosing a technical secondary education.[121] To relieve the pressure of creating artificial jobs in the public and government sectors it was suggested that graduates be given 5 *faddān* each of reclaimed agricultural land,[122] and that credit facilities be made

[118] 9 January 1988, *MMS*, F5, 1–51, pp. 4447–72.

[119] The People's Assembly, 23 January 1988, *MMS*, F5, 1–59, pp. 4712–37. Cf. Ibrāhīm Shukrī, 11 June 1985, *MMS*, F4, 1–89, pp. 6655–62.

[120] The People's Assembly, 8 June 1985, *MMS*, F4, 1–84, pp. 6544–62.

[121] 'Umar al-Zīr, LP Giza, People's Assembly, 23 June 1987, *MMS*, F5, 1–17, ṭm, pp. 2–23. Cf. Ḥizb al-'amal al-ishtirākī, "Taqrīr ḥizb al-'amal al-ishtirākī ilā al-mu'tamar al-iqtiṣādī", pp. 33, 36–7, and Ḥizb al-'amal, "Al-barnāmaj al-intikhābī 'alā qā'imat ḥizb al-'amal", part V.

[122] Aḥmad al-Fiqī, LP Daqahliyya, People's Assembly, 10 January 1988, *MMS*, F5, 1–53, pp. 4504–31.

available for those establishing small workshops in the new cities in the desert, or small restaurants and shops in new tourist areas like the Sinai and the Red Sea.[123] It was also proposed that government and public sector employees be given the opportunity to retire at the age of 55 with full pension rights, in order to make room for new graduates.[124] On one occasion the Labour Party deputy Aḥmad al-Fiqī suggested a scheme whereby women employed in the public sector would be offered to return home for half pay, with the option of going back to their jobs after three years. This he thought would both open new job opportunities for fresh graduates (presumably men), and improve the standard of children's up-bringing. However, despite the ambiguous attitude of the party to women's employment,[125] this proposal seems not to have been an expression of party line, and is not followed up.[126]

In some contrast, perhaps, to the reserve expressed above by Gamāl As'ad, in general representatives of both the groups argued consistently for the need for wages and salaries in the government and public sectors to be raised to compensate for inflation.[127] Interestingly they also argued for the establishment of a High Council for prices and wages, where representatives of employees, capitalists and the state would meet every six months to adjust the wage level.[128] In their 1991 programmatic document the Brothers suggested that wage levels should be tied to productivity.[129]

The Labour Party and the Brothers intervened in the People's Assembly on many occasions for the improvement of workers' conditions,[130] and for the greater freedom and independence of trade unions.[131] Increasing worker

[123] Aḥmad Ḥirik, LP Cairo, People's Assembly, 28 January 1990, *MMS*, F5, 3–23, ṭm, pp. 2–31.

[124] Ṣalāḥ 'Abdallāh, LP Cairo, People's Assembly 24 June 1987, *MMS*, F5, 1–19, ṭm, pp. 3–37.

[125] See for instance 'Ādil Ḥusayn, *Al-islām dīn wa ḥaḍāra*, pp. 34–5. As for the Muslim Brothers their stated view was that the employment of women should be regulated in order to ensure they were put in positions that were in harmony with their nature. See Shaḥḥāta, *Al-minhaj al-islāmī lil-iṣlāḥ al-iqtiṣādī*, p. 16.

[126] Aḥmad al-Fiqī, LP Daqahliyya, People's Assembly, 10 January 1988, *MMS*, F5, 1–53, pp. 4504–31.

[127] From Sayyid Rustam of the Labour Party, 2 December 1984, *MMS*, F4, 1–27, pp. 2264–85 to Muṣṭafā al-Wardānī of the Brothers, 25 February 1990, *MMS*, F5, 3–36, ṭm, pp. 31–44. Cf. Ḥizb al-'amal, "Al-barnāmaj al-intikhābī 'alā qā'imat ḥizb al-'amal", part V, where a raise of the official minimum wage is also demanded.

[128] See both Shukrī and al-Bannā in the People's Assembly, 6 July 1987, *MMS*, F5, 1–25, pp. 2667–77.

[129] Shaḥḥāta, *Al-minhaj al-islāmī lil-iṣlāḥ al-iqtiṣādī*, p. 15.

[130] For two instances see Sayyid Rustam, LP, 6 July 1984, *MMS*, F4, 1–6, pp. 433–7 and 'Abd al-Raḥmān al-Raṣd, MB, Sharqiyya, 25 January 1988, *MMS*, F5, 1–62, pp. 4820–55. See also Shaḥḥāta, *Al-minhaj al-islāmī lil-iṣlāḥ al-iqtiṣādī*, p. 12.

[131] 'Iṣām al-'Iryān, 7 July 1987, *MMS*, F5, 1–27, pp. 2801–14 and again 12 January 1988, *MMS*, F5, 1–57, pp. 4644–68.

welfare was even given a central role in moving the wheel of development. The Muslim Brothers declared that the "closed circuit of poverty" was a major obstacle to progress. Low average income led to a low level of saving and investment, which in turn led to shrinking economic activity, unemployment and again to a low level of income. This circle must be broken by increasing production through a better use of resources, better conditions for the workers and better direction of investment.[132] The Brothers argued strongly the need for fostering a positive spirit among workers. The workers must be educated in the Islamic work ethic, and in their rights and duties. The principle of *shūrā* must be implemented in the productive units and the workers given appropriate representation on the boards. They must be encouraged to develop their knowledge and skills through a combination of material and moral incentives.[133]

But the ideology of social harmony and the aversion for class struggle, embedded both in the Nasserist heritage of many Labour Party members, and in the vision of the Muslim Brothers, makes them hesitate in accepting a full autonomy for workers' organisations. It is no accident, of course, that it is an MP for the Labour Party with a central position in the state-controlled Egyptian Federation of Trade Unions, Aḥmad Ḥirik, who on principle opposes the right to strike "in a country like Egypt where the state protects the workers".[134] In fact the newspaper *al-Sha'b* on numerous occasions supported strikes, but the question of the right to strike in a future Islamic state remained moot.

Finally we may take note that while the Islamists moved to reduce the working hours for children in the cotton fields (as a step towards the total eradication of child labour),[135] they urged more liberal opening hours for artisans and shopkeepers in the cities,[136] in line with their general concern for increasing the economic viability of this section of "national capitalism". It was sometimes argued that while the prescribed closing at 6 pm might save some electric power, it reduced trade and pushed idle youth into drugs and alcohol, since after 8 pm only cafes and bars were open. Furthermore these restrictions were contrary to the *Sharī'a*, according to which trading hours run from dawn to the evening prayer.[137]

[132] Shaḥḥāta, *Al-minhaj al-islāmī lil-iṣlāḥ al-iqtiṣādī*, p. 12–13.
[133] *Ibid.*, pp. 16, 21.
[134] People's Assembly, 28 January 1990, *MMS*, F5, 3–23, ṭm, pp. 2–31.
[135] Yāsīn 'Abd al-'Alīm, LP, Bani Suwayf, People's Assembly, 24 February 1990, *MMS*, F5, 3–34, ṭm, pp. 2–25.
[136] Sayyid Rustam, People's Assembly, 2 December 1984, *MMS*, F4, 1–27, pp. 2264–85.
[137] Ḥasan Gawda, MB, Banī Suwayf, 5 May 1985, *MMS*, F4, 1–75, pp. 4891–912 and Ibrāhīm Shukrī, 27 December 1987, *MMS*, F5, 1–46, pp. 4237–56.

With regard to agricultural policies the most consistent plead of the Islamists was for self-sufficiency in the production of food, seen as a prerequisite for real political independence. At the top of the agenda was the issue of wheat production, since import by the late 1980s provided the lion's share of Egyptian consumption of this cereal, the basis for the subsidised loaves of bread that was the staple menu of the popular classes.

Magdī Ḥusayn argued that usual profit accounting should not apply to the question of wheat growing any more than it did when Israel spent fortunes on nuclear missiles. Both were issues of strategic security and it would be better to bear a high cost in Egyptian pounds for locally produced wheat, than to accumulate lesser amounts in foreign debts in dollars for imported wheat. Besides, he said, was not Egypt once the granary of the world? The climatic conditions had not changed drastically, he said, implying that Egypt could once more become an effective grain producing country.[138]

In June 1987 the People's Assembly debated agricultural policies, in connection with an interpellation from the Wafd MP 'Alawī Ḥāfiẓ about the crisis in food supply, especially the situation with regard to wheat. Forced deliveries of wheat from Egyptian farmers were introduced during the Second World War, and lasted till 1976, Shukrī said. He had himself been Sadat's Minister of Agriculture at the time, and had opposed ending the forced delivery system. The result of the discussions in 1976 was a compromise: the deliveries were made voluntary. The result was a decline in wheat growing, leading to reliance on imported cheap wheat from the United States. In addition to filling the high demand for wheat in Egypt, this imported wheat had also increasingly been used as animal fodder, because of its low price. The same happened to subsidised bread made from this wheat. The solution lay in a policy that would give priority to local wheat production. Shukrī said. Prices to farmers must be heightened and every *faddān* must be grown with wheat. New varieties of wheat with high yields and a short growing period should be introduced so that wheat could be combined with cotton or other crops in the same year, he said. An end should be put to the use of wheat and bread as animal fodder. Those who practised this should not be considered true Egyptian farmers. A limit should be put on animal husbandry by tying it to the amount of land held by the farmer, for instance holding 5 *faddān* could give the right to keep 7 animals etc.. Large cow farms of several thousand animals should only be allowed in desert regions, Shukrī said.[139]

On wheat policies there seems to have been total agreement between the Labour Party and the Muslim Brothers. MPs from the Brothers emphas-

[138] Magdī Ḥusayn, "Al-ra'īs wal-qamḥ wal-sūfyat", *al-Sha'b*, 1 September 1987.
[139] 7 June 1987, *MMS*, F5, 1–7, pp. 591–618.

ised that increased wheat production was a question of securing independence.[140] They suggested a yearly increase of 120,000 *faddān* of wheat growing area during the 1990s,[141] and complained that the World Bank resistance to finance wheat expansion in Egypt was due to US protection of their own producers' interests.[142]

In line with the priority put on wheat growing there was also a general idea that basic necessities like grain, beans, and lentils should have priority over the commercial crops advised by USAID and the IMF like strawberries and other fruits and vegetables. Priority should also be given to cotton, a traditional export crop, but also the basis for the textile industry, along with food processing the dominant local industry, and producer of cheap subsidised cloth for the popular masses.[143] Muḥammad Ḥilmī Murād described the experience of strawberry production as a rather dismal one, the export plans in particular having been a failure. And he criticised the idea of introducing greenhouse farming. Egypt in its present circumstances was not in need of winter crops in summer and vice versa. It needed instead a food policy that would ensure that the basic food crops were available in sufficient quantities and at prices affordable for the common citizen.[144]

One important source of healthy nourishment which was being very poorly exploited according to the Islamists was fish.[145] Murād complained that the potential wealth of fish resources was going untapped. "At the moment the Qārūn lake which used to fill the markets of Fayyūm and Cairo with fish, gives only 300 kg a day", he wrote. And while lakes were being polluted, or being filled for agricultural and building purposes, reclaimable land was being dug out to create ponds for industrial fish production. There was a catastrophic lack of planning, he said.[146] The

140 Basyūnī Basyūnī, MB, Alexandria, People's Assembly, 29 January 1990, *MMS*, F5, 1–26, ṭm, pp. 2–29.

141 'Abd al-Jābir 'Uthmān, MB, Minya, People's Assembly, 24 February 1990, *MMS*, F5, 1–33, ṭm, pp. 4–30.

142 Lāshīn Shanab, MB, Gharbiyya, 25 February 1990, *MMS*, F5, 1–36, ṭm, pp. 31–44.

143 See for instance Al-Sa'īd Sha'bān Rakhā, LP Daqahliyya, People's Assembly, 11 January 1988, *MMS*, F5, 1–55, pp. 4562–91 and 'Abd al-Jābir 'Uthmān, MB, Minya, 24 February 1990, *MMS*, F5, 1–33, ṭm, pp. 4–30. Cf. Shaḥḥāta, *Al-minhaj al-islāmī lil-iṣlāḥ al-iqtiṣādī*, p. 22.

144 Muḥammad Ḥilmī Murād, "Li-mādha yabqā Wālī wazīran lil-zirā'a wal-amn al-ghadhā'ī raghma fashlihi?", *al-Sha'b*, 30 September 1986 and "Raf' al-as'ār aswa' al-ḥulūl li-mu'ālajat azmat al-ḥukūma", *al-Sha'b*, 15 May 1990.

145 See for instance 'Abd al-'Azīz al-Ghubārī, People's Assembly, 13 January 1988, *MMS*, F5, 1–58, pp. 4670–702, where he complains that Egypt's 13 million *faddān* of water surface in rivers, lakes and sea only produce 5 grams of fish per *faddān* yearly, while in the United States there are fish farms that produce a ton per *faddān*.

146 Muḥammad Ḥilmī Murād, "Li-mādha yabqā Wālī wazīran lil-zirā'a wal-amn al-ghadhā'ī raghma fashlihi?", *al-Sha'b*, 30 September 1986.

Muslim Brother Basyūnī from Alexandria led a vigorous campaign to save the fisheries in the Maryūt lake. And in May 1990 both he and Gamāl As'ad of the Labour Party raised the issue of the falling production of the fisheries in Lake Naṣr, the artificial lake created by the High Dam at Aswān. In stead of growing as planned, the production by 1988 had dropped to less than half of what it was in 1981. The number of fishermen there was falling, because what the state paid them for the fish was less than cost price.[147]

An issue causing heated debate what was came to be known as the chicken scandal. From 1978 onwards local production of chicken and eggs greatly expanded. But while price controls on the products of the industry remained in effect, the subsidies on maize, the most important chicken feed, were gradually removed from 1984 on. The result was a deep recession.[148]

Murād took up the issue in *al-Sha'b*. Investment in the local poultry industry was encouraged by the state, he wrote, and local production had managed in recent years to cover local needs for chicken and eggs. But then the prices of fodder suddenly rose, and farms with an aggregate investment of 1 billion LE were closed down, and the country was back to importing chicken. This had been a tremendous waste of resources, Murād wrote. It was an example of bad planning, and would not increase the trust of the private sector in dealing with the government.[149]

'Abd al-Jābir 'Uthmān, MP for the Muslim Brothers from Minya raised the issue in the People's Assembly in January 1988. He claimed that 4 billion LE had been invested in poultry farms. Now 80 percent of these farms had closed down. The reason was that the price for maize, the preferred fodder, had risen from 200 LE to 500 LE per ton, while the price of slaughtered chicken had fallen from 1.90 LE per kilogram to only 1.40 LE, the cost now being 2 LE per kilogram. Since the state had encouraged this industry, he said, it must now take responsibility. He urged a ban on the import of frozen chicken. It was wrong to import when the country could by itself produce sufficient amounts of a commodity, he claimed. Besides, going back to importing would mean that consumers would once more have to wait in line for rationed chicken, and this would adversely affect nutritional standards, 'Uthmān claimed.[150]

The situation for the traditionally central crop of cotton, important both as a currency earner and as raw material for the leading local industry,

[147] Basyūnī Basyūnī, MB Alexandria and Gamāl As'ad, LP, Asyūṭ, People's Assembly, 26 March 1990, *MMS*, F5, 3–45, ṭm, pp. 9–13.

[148] Springborg, *Mubarak's Egypt*, pp. 268, 290.

[149] Muḥammad Ḥilmī Murād, "Li-mādha yabqā Wālī wazīran lil-zirā'a wal-amn al-ghadhā'ī raghma fashlihi?", *al-Sha'b*, 30 September 1986.

[150] People's Assembly, 23 January 1988, *MMS*, F5, 1–59, pp. 4712–37. Cf. Basyūnī Basyūnī, *MMS*, F5, 3–26, ṭm, pp. 2–29.

became an issue of grave concern in the 1980s as the area grown with cotton shrank and production fell.[151]

In particular Basyūnī of the Brothers was a harsh critic of the cotton policy (or lack of such) pursued by the government. True to the liberal tone of the Brothers he declared that the problem went back to the nationalisation of the cotton trade by Nasser. The cotton exchange should be re-opened and the cooperative monopoly of marketing should be ended, he repeatedly claimed. But it was clear, he said, that the problems had turned markedly worse since 1985. The farmers turned away from the cotton crop because of a price system that gave them in 1989 only 200 LE per *qinṭār*,[152] while the state exported for the equivalent of 574 LE per *qinṭār*.[153] Prices to farmers should therefore be increased, since the present low cotton yield led to the impossible choice between supplying local industry or exporting. In order to keep up the foreign markets for this important source of hard currency, he urged as a stop-gap measure in 1988 immediate import of cheap American cotton for local industry, so that the high quality, long-fibre Egyptian cotton could be exported. Anyway, he said, it is a waste to put our finest qualities into the production of cheap cloth for popular consumption in Egypt.[154]

The call for higher prices for farmers was in fact a general one. The issue was raised with regard to all crops where the state was the only or main purchaser, like wheat, sugar and other basic foodstuffs, and crops which were important as input to local industry. It was emphasised that prices must be announced *before* planting time in order to have the effect of an incentive.[155]

This was another instance where the Muslim Brothers pragmatically relaxed their principled resistance to state interference with the free play of supply and demand. On the other hand both they and occasionally Labour Party MPs argued for a relaxation of forced deliveries to the state and of the cooperative monopoly of marketing for many products.[156]

[151] See Alan Richards, "Agricultural Employment, Wages and Government Policy in Egypt during and after the Oil Boom" in Handoussa and Potter (eds), *Employment and Structural Adjustment*, pp. 60–2.

[152] 1 Egyptian *qinṭār* = 44.93 kg.

[153] Basyūnī Basyūnī, MB Alexandria, People's Assembly, 29 January 1990, *MMS*, F5, 3–26, ṭm, pp. 2–29. Cf. also Basyūnī, 25 June 1987, *MMS*, F5, 1–21, ṭm, pp. 40–62.

[154] Basyūnī, People's Assembly, 13 January 1988, *MMS*, F5, 1–58, pp. 4670–702.

[155] See for instance Aḥmad al-Fiqī, LP Daqahliyya, People's Assembly, 11 February 1990, *MMS*, F5, 3–29, ṭm, pp. 20–30 and Muṣṭafā al-Wardānī, MB Giza, 25 February 1990, *MMS*, F5, 3–36, ṭm, pp. 31–44. Cf. also Magdī Ḥusayn, People's Assembly, 15 November 1987, *MMS*, F5, 1–34, pp. 3370–5.

[156] See Basyūnī, *ibid.*, and Khālid Ḥamād, LP Daqahliyya, 23 June 1987, *MMS*, F5, 1–17, ṭm, pp. 2–23.

Towards a common platform

In general Muslim Brothers throughout the period tended to be somewhat more liberal in their economic views than the Labour Party. One particular case in point is the question of price policies, or whether the state should intervene to manipulate the price structure in the market. Muslim Brother writers like Ḥusayn Shaḥḥāta were adamant that prices should find their own level through the mechanisms of supply and demand and that state intervention could only do harm, whereas the Labour Party on several occasions argued for continuing the subsidies, even if reforming them. Not least ʻĀdil Ḥusayn consistently argued against the principle of accepting "world prices", stating that the tool of manipulating the price structure was indispensable if the state were to direct the economy according to a strategic plan. "World prices", he argued, represented a price structure reflecting the present international division of labour, and to look on them as sacred would only mean cementing existing conditions. He pointed to South Korea where the state had actively used manipulation of relative prices in order to guide economic activity in desired directions.

Despite this difference, and despite the vague character of much of Islamist discourse on economic questions, certain elements of a common thinking about the proper strategy for economic development emerging by the late 1980s may be identified. There was a rapprochement, in particular in the period after 1987, on a line for building a strong and independent market economy, with the private sector as the main economic actor, but guided by state-formulated strategy within a framework of "cooperative competition", to use one of ʻAbd al-Ḥamīd al-Ghazālī's expressions.

This meant that the Muslim Brothers and gradually also the Labour Party came to put great emphasis on the need to stimulate private investment, and not least to create a climate where investors would feel secure about their investments. This was essential if Egyptian capital abroad were to be drawn into the country. The Islamists also supported the privatisation of large parts of the public sector, but called for a "national privatisation", where foreigners, except for Arabs and perhaps other Muslims, were to be excluded from holding capital assets in Egypt. But even the Muslim Brothers stressed the need for the retention of public ownership over industries of strategic importance. And they stressed that the private sector would have to act according to a national strategy for development.

Central to this strategy would be to strengthen in both absolute and relative terms the productive sectors of industry and agriculture, and to seek the building of an independent base for technological development. Investment and production must be made to follow Islamic priorities among which the first place was accorded to the provision of basic necessities.

In order to secure that development would proceed in line with these priorities the state must have a strong guiding role *vis-à-vis* the private sector. The government should reduce its interference in pricing policies, but direct investment through a mixture of regulations and incentives. It should use tariffs to create the necessary protection of emerging national industries *vis-à-vis* the world market. The public productive sector must be reduced, but the state must keep control of certain industrial enterprises indispensable for defence and development purposes. The remaining public sector must be given more liberty to run its affairs according to sound business principles.

Although the Egyptian Islamists in this period never presented a comprehensive strategy for development for instance on the question of import substitution versus an export led strategy, it is interesting to see how they increasingly came to refer to the example of South Korea as a positive case of a Third World country being able to industrialise. The Koreans had not followed the prescription of the IMF. Their export drive had been initiated and led by the state. Their opening for foreign capital and foreign goods was very selectivc. They had protected their industries against foreign competition in the crucial early stages of development. They had kept ownership in the main private, but they had formed a national strategy for development which the private enterprises were led to follow both by positive incentives and by the threat of losing credit and state contracts. This was the road for Egypt to follow.

The rapprochement between the two parties was made possible by important developments in the parties and their environment during the 1980s.

On the one hand the Labour Party moved away from some of its "socialist" positions towards a more favourable attitude to the market system and private enterprise. In the early 1980s the Labour Party was still talking socialism and state direction of the economy. Indeed socialism was a part of its name, although it was always clear, as it had been for the Socialist Party of the charismatic Young Egypt leader Aḥmad Ḥusayn in the 1940s and '50s, that theirs was a socialism alien to Marxism and to the idea of class struggle. A reason for the pro-statist inclination might be found in the more purely middle and lower middle class dominance among the members of the Labour Party when compared with the Brothers, with no dominant group in the party having its interest tied up with the continuance of the liberal *infitāḥ* policies.[157] But with the international wave of new conservatism during the 1980s, as Thatcherism, Reaganism and Friedmanism went on the offensive, and with the final collapse of the Eastern bloc by the end of the decade, socialism as a positive word more or less

[157] For a discussion of the social make-up of the two groups, see above pp. 86–7.

disappeared from the party's discourse and from its name. Now there was a general acceptance of the market system as the preferable means of distribution, and the principle of the dominance of private ownership.

Apart from the international ideological climate another thing preconditioning this move was the party's Islamisation. The intensified search for a distinct Islamic view of economic questions contributed to changing the party line in the direction of a more positive attitude towards private ownership. In particular 'Ādil Ḥusayn from 1987 onwards engaged in a passionate defence of the non-*ribā* "Islamic investment companies", surpassing in this regard the Muslim Brothers, who remained somewhat more critical in their comments on the companies. During this debate Ḥusayn, somewhat in contrast to his earlier ideas, stressed the positive aspect of the emergence of powerful private financial centres that might break the government monopoly.

On the other hand we see the Muslim Brothers becoming somewhat sharper in their criticism of the *infitāḥ* policies,[158] but especially of the government's willingness to toe the IMF and US line. They held forth independence as a central issue, especially through their activities in the People's Assembly, and they criticised the "lack of a positive identity" as the major problem of Egyptian economic strategy. Muslim Brothers began using concepts such as economic "dependency" (*taba'iyya*)[159] taken from radical development theory, an indication of a move especially among the younger leaders towards a more radical stance on questions of development strategy.

Probably this development was partly a result of the alliance with the Labour Party. For one thing compared with the Brothers the Labour Party had a relatively developed economic policy, since it had always put considerable emphasis on this aspect of politics. In a way it was filling a partial vacuum in the policies of the Brothers, especially through the influential character of 'Ādil Ḥusayn, who was consciously seeking to cultivate links with the Brothers. A large number, especially of the younger generation of Muslim Brothers, seemed to adopt many of the analyses and policies of the Labour Party. The document from the Brothers' Economic Commission from 1991 contained long paragraphs that were almost an exact replica of the Alliance programme from 1987. 'Ādil Ḥusayn's criticism of pure redistributive reform also found its way into the Brothers' arsenal of economic critique, so that there was a consensus in saying that reform

[158] In an interview with the author on 14 May 1994 'Iṣām al-'Iryān, one of the leading younger members of the Brothers, declared outright that the *infitāḥ* had been a negative experience for the country.

[159] See for instance Shaḥḥāta, *Al-minhaj al-islāmī lil-iṣlāḥ al-iqtiṣādī.*, p. 16.

should start with the decisions on what to produce. In perfect harmony with Ḥusayn the Muslim Brothers adopted the satisfying of basic needs as the "first Islamic priority" for production and investment.

'Ādil Ḥusayn was eager to bridge the gap between the Brothers and the Nasserists as a link in his strategy for a united front against the government and the United States. And formulating an economic programme that was acceptable to both was a central element in such a strategy. But whatever the possible influence from the Labour Party, there were other factors at work. Throughout the 1980s the Muslim Brothers increasingly became directly involved in the national political debate, and from 1987 they emerged as the leading opposition group. This situation combined with their strong emphasis on the need for an all-comprehensive cultural, political and economic independence guided by Islamic principles, to produce a dynamic that forced them to take up the cause of independent economic development.

In increasingly forwarding themselves as an alternative to the present regime, the Muslim Brothers needed to be seen to possess an answer to the grave problems of poverty and of the dependence of the economy. As a pressure group for Islamisation in the early 1980s they contented themselves mostly with the call for liberalisation on all fronts, for the prohibition of *ribā*, and for widening the sphere of activity of Islamic credit institutions. This would not suffice any more if the Brothers were credibly to present themselves as leaders of the national opposition to Mubarak's rule, and the partial and cautious leftward adjustment of the Brothers' economic agenda in the late 1980s should be seen in this light.

Clearly the influences went both ways between the Alliance partners. The Alliance programme from 1987 was a product of discussion and compromise and contained elements from the thinking of the Muslim Brothers as well as that of the Labour Party. In particular with regard to the issue of a better investment climate for private Egyptian and Arab capital, the fact that the Labour Party put greater emphasis than before on the need for a dynamic national private sector was most likely at least partly due to the influence of the Brothers.

Justice: a prerequisite for social peace

The Egyptian Islamists saw themselves as the vanguard of a moral revolution that would root out the deep-seated evil of corruption from their society. In their programmes and political agitation a central place was accorded this task: they worked hard at exposing illicit dealings in high places, and kept hammering against age-old practices of favouritism, nepotism and patron-client relations. This, they considered, had to be the first point on the agenda for social justice to be achieved (and indeed for real development to take place).

The second point was a narrowing of the income gap through a redistribution of wealth in favour of the poor. This was claimed to be a prerequisite if the market system was to operate in favour of real economic development. However, it is perhaps significant that though the rhetoric on this point was often highly pitched, and though it could be seen to fit in well with their idea of a concentration of the development effort on satisfying basic needs, the Islamists were seldom concrete on the ways in which the desired redistribution was to be effected. Representatives of the Muslim Brothers on many occasions seemed to suggest that if interest and the monopolistic dominance of the state were removed, the market system would spontaneously work to establish social justice.

The Islamists criticised the government for placing the toughest burdens of economic reforms on the poor, and in particular wanted to change the main emphasis of the tax system from indirect taxes, always hitting the poor the hardest, to direct taxes levied on the wealthy. They also wanted more effort and money put into the public health system, into alleviating the housing shortage for the poor, and into rural development in order to bring a fairer deal to a long neglected countryside. But there was no mention of any more drastic measures in the direction of social equality. Part of the problem was that some of the old Nasserist ways of tackling such issues ran up against the Islamists' call for a general liberalisation of economic life. The Muslim Brothers wanted, for instance, to see a removal of consumer subsidies, albeit gradually and timed to coincide with the establishment of the *zakāt* system, which would then make the subsidies superfluous. Also, both the Brothers and the Labour Party were extremely reluctant to take sides in the debate over a reform of the system of regulation of farm and housing rents.

In any case, the call for social justice was never a call for social revolution or radical equality, merely for a certain amelioration of the most glaring misery suffered by low income groups. The Muslim ideal was portrayed as harmonious cooperation among the various classes making up society. Class struggle was abhorred, and the rich were not condemned for being so, but urged to use their riches to care for the poor and to contribute to development. It would even appear that justice was often not seen primarily as a goal in and of itself, but rather as a prerequisite for the social harmony that would secure a stable environment in which the development effort could become effective. Indeed the question of justice became subordinate to the call for national unity, and the "civilisation struggle" (*ṣirā' al-ḥaḍārāt*), in which all true Egyptians would stand together against Western encroachment, replaced the divisive class struggle (*ṣirā' al-ṭabaqāt*) propagated by the leftists. It is a striking fact that this strong emphasis on unity to the detriment of internal struggle and indeed often of political pluralism has under different ideological labels been emblematic of modernising regimes around the globe in areas left out of the first wave of European and Japanese industrialisation in the 19th century. This is even true of the avowedly Marxist communist regimes except during episodes like the Cultural Revolution in China. And besides the real need for unity in late modernising nations, it perhaps reflects the social character of the leading strata, with their middle and lower middle class background and their fear of working class and peasant unrest undermining their position.

In the spring of 1990 the Muslim Brother economic expert Ḥusayn Shaḥḥāta discussed "the Islamic concept of development" in an article in *al-Nūr.* The basic precondition of development, he said, is that both capital and workers are safe and free of fear. Fear leads to backwardness, since the productivity of the workers will be reduced, and the capital will flee to a safer haven. Then the main problem is the emergency laws which instil fear: workers may be fired or arrested, and capital may be confiscated if an owner is seen to be "a threat to national security". In a true Islamic system, Shaḥḥāta says, the right balance is struck between the interests of the workers and those of the capital. Private property is preserved as an incentive for work, while the system prevents parasitic practices and excessive amassing of wealth. The worker has safety for his work and the right to speak his mind, but must conscientiously fulfil his duties to his employer.[160] In fact Islam puts the worker on a par with the *mujāhid* and considers work to be part of the worship of God (*'ibāda*). It is the duty of the state to guarantee suitable work to its subjects. Shaḥḥāta cites the industrial enterprises run by the Muslim Brothers in the 1940s as examples of the positive effects on economic performance if the Islamic system is implemented.[161]

We see again that justice does not mean the elimination of classes. In that respect it is interesting how some of the more Nasserist leaning Labour Party MPs from time to time use a Nasserist idiom to present a similar view of social relations. Thus they would say that true democracy was contingent on the "melting away of class distinctions", but hasten to add that this did not mean the elimination of classes.[162] The implication is that the "melting" should be a gradual, peaceful process controlled by the state

[160] Ḥusayn Shaḥḥāta, "Hākadhā takūn al-tanmīya", *al-Nūr*, 12 February 1990.
[161] Ḥusayn Shaḥḥāta, "Asās al-tanmīya fī al-mujtama'", *al-Nūr*, 25 April 1990.
[162] 'Abd al-Ḥalīm 'Alam al-Dīn, LP Giza, People's Assembly, 11 January 1988, *MMS*, F5, 1–55, pp. 4562–91.

where everybody grew rich, rather than a violent autonomous action by the oppressed classes.[163]

Against corruption and mismanagement

The third of seven chapters in the common programme of the Islamic Alliance for the 1987 elections was entitled "Establishing virtue and closing the gates of corruption". Besides a call for religious values to be spread, especially through education and culture, the chapter spells out the need for rooting out possibilities for illegal gain. Especially it worries about public servants, and demands that everyone holding high public office should be forbidden to receive gifts or material and immaterial services. The awarding of contracts should be practiced in a clean way, on the basis of the best offer, without the influences of middle men, and without the interference of direct orders from above.[164]

The fight against corruption and related malpractice in political and economic life was indeed a central part of the political campaigns led by the Egyptian Islamists in the 1980s. It was concentrated on corruption in high places, but the Islamists also fought against the generalised practices of favouritism, nepotism and patron-client relationships in private and public economic activities in Egypt. "We must strike with an iron fist against these degenerate practices if we want to release the productive energy of the people", said Sayf al-Islām al-Bannā in the People's Assembly.[165]

The issue of corruption relates to an important feature of the general ideological climate in the Egypt of the 1980s: the increasing tendency to see problems as moral questions. There is no conscience to be found in our society, complained the Muslim Brother al-Marāghī to the People's Assembly.[166]

Time and again corruption was revealed in the opposition press. Each example was used to hammer home the idea that the Egyptian society was in the grips of an all-encompassing moral decay that had set in with the *infitāḥ*. Increased criminality (albeit still at very low levels compared to for instance the United States), youngsters cheating at exams, and traders demanding exorbitant prices, all were joined together in the popular mind and in the pages of the leftist *al-Ahālī* and of *al-Sha'b*, as an indication of

[163] Waterbury, *The Egypt of Nasser and Sadat*, p. 315.

[164] Ḥizb al-'amal al-ishtirākī, "Al-barnāmaj al-intikhābī 'alā qā'imat ḥizb al-'amal", part III.

[165] 28 December 1987, *MMS*, F5, 1–47, pp. 4259–85. Cf. Ḥizb al-'amal al-ishtirākī, "Taqrīr ḥizb al-'amal al-ishtirākī ilā al-mu'tamar al-iqtiṣādī", p. 10, where the elimination of corruption is presented as the first precondition for creating a proper climate for economic reform. See also Shaḥḥāta, *Al-minhaj al-islāmī lil-iṣlāḥ al-iqtiṣādī*, p. 12 for a description of the problems facing workers as a result of the current state of affairs.

[166] 7 May 1985, *MMS*, F4, 1–77, pp. 5053–62.

where the country was heading when capitalism was allowed to erode traditional norms for collective behaviour. This line of argument was dominant whether the traditional norms were understood in religious terms or otherwise. Increasingly, with the general ideological backlash for all ideas connected to socialism and communism, what remained as the ideological platform for opposition was varying mixtures of nationalist and moralist criticism. The government was castigated for spreading corruption, or at least allowing it to spread, and for selling out the country to the West. On the other hand criticism of capitalism as such, as a system, was less easy to come by than it had been in the first years of the *infitāḥ* in the 1970s.

The corruption hunter *par excellence* was Muḥammad Ḥilmī Murād, Vice-President of the Labour Party. His weekly column in *al-Sha'b* was largely devoted to this task. A long-time target of Murād's campaign against corruption in high places was the Minister of Oil in the late 1980s, 'Abd al-Hādī Qandīl. In 1985 Murād criticised him for holding the double position of Minister and President of the Oil Authority, the central institution supervising all public companies working in the oil business and conducting the negotiations with foreign oil companies. This led to over-centralisation of power and to lack of checks and balances in this important sector, Murād wrote. He also criticised the system of selling oil through agents, since some agents were allowed to exercise undue influence on decisions as to the distribution of quotas between them. Some of them were moreover mere profiteering ventures without any real economic activity of their own, and should be barred from the business.[167] Two years later Murād reiterated his call for a reduction of the centralised power of the Minister over the oil industry, and criticised Qandīl for undemocratic treatment of employees. Furthermore he questioned the awarding in 1982 of several construction contracts for a petrochemical complex in al-'Āmiriyya near Alexandria to the Italian company Technipetrol. This company had shown itself unwilling and unable to follow the specifications concerning construction materials and the like. It should have been black-listed. The problem was that it had a friend in a high place, the later Minister, at the time President of the Committee for Investment Purchases, who campaigned hard *vis-à-vis* the local Egyptian firm in charge of the project for awarding the construction contract to Technipetrol even if its bid was not the lowest.[168]

[167] Muḥammad Ḥilmī Murād, "Idārat qiṭā' al-bitrūl fī ḥāja ilā murāja'a", *al-Sha'b*, 23 April 1985.

[168] Muḥammad Ḥilmī Murād, "'Innā uttahim wazīr al-bitrūl shakhṣiyyan", *al-Sha'b*, 6 October 1987. Cf. two other articles by Murād, "Wa mādhā 'an al-tasattur 'alā al-inḥirāf fī

Several other dubious dealings involving Qandīl were reported. In 1978 a law regulating a concession for an Italian oil company stipulated that the right to retrieve outlays through a part of the oil produced did not concern equipment bought before the start of the concession or not actually used in prospecting or drilling. But in 1982 this clause was set aside by agreement with the company in contravention of the law and without the consent of the People's Assembly. When the issue was raised some years later Qandīl as Minister appointed an investigative committee without qualifications and including two members who had signed the suspect agreement of 1982. It was no wonder, said Murād, that this committee accepted what had happened in spite of its costing the country millions of dollars in crude oil.[169] Qandīl was also accused of securing for Elf Aquitaine the payment of 80 million dollars not warranted by Egypt's agreement with this French oil company.[170] In 1990 Murād complained that Shell Oil was getting more than their lawful share of Egyptian oil (80 percent instead of 75 percent) extracted from the Western Desert with the support of the Minister, and at the same time was given permission to open petrol stations in Egypt. "The Ministry should rather cut down on expenses for luxurious offices and nice cars, and use the money to improve the standards of the Egyptian run petrol stations, instead of letting the foreigners take a part of the distribution profits in addition to what they get from extraction", Murād wrote. Moreover he clearly hinted that Shell was getting preferential treatment because Ṭāriq Ḥajjī, the local Shell representative was a close friend of Qandīl.[171]

The Islamists were also defending the interests of people threatened with losing their jobs because of criticising management, especially in the public sector.[172] Muḥammad Ḥilmī Murād time and again castigated Qandīl for destroying the intellectual and scientific standards of the top employees within the oil sector by sacking or moving anyone who dared to open his mouth in critique of mismanagement and corrupt practices.[173]

---

qiṭā' al-bitrūl", *al-Sha'b*, 29 September 1987, and "I'tirāfāt kādhiba bi-irtikāb jināya lam yuḥāsab al-mas'ūlūn 'an ṣudūrihā", *al-Sha'b*, 22 December 1987.

169 Muḥammad Ḥilmī Murād, "Qiṭā' al-bitrūl fī ḥāja ilā ṣaḥwa qawmiyya", *al-Sha'b*, 13 October 1987.

170 Muḥammad Ḥilmī Murād, "'I'tirāfāt kādhiba bi-irtikāb jināya lam yuḥāsab al-mas'ūlūn 'an ṣudūrihā", *al-Sha'b*, 22 December 1987.

171 Muḥammad Ḥilmī Murād, "'Alā al-ra'īs Mubārak an yuwaqqif nahb bitrūlna li-ṣāliḥ sharikat shil", *al-Sha'b*, June 1990.

172 For instance Mamdūḥ Qināwī, People's Assembly, 6 May 1985, *MMS*, F4, 1–76, pp. 4956–62.

173 See for instance the following articles: "Idārat qiṭā' al-bitrūl fī ḥāja ilā murāja'a", *al-Sha'b*, 23 April 1985, "Man alladhī yatasattar 'alā al-inḥirāfāt fī hay'at al-bitrūl", *al-*

Besides the direct accusations of corrupt practices, there was also a more general critique of mismanagement of the country's resources by the people in charge. With regard to the oil business Murād was very critical towards the huge investments made to build a petrochemical complex in 'Āmiriyya, and a refinery in Asyūṭ in Upper Egypt, which he thought were not based on sound economic calculations. Especially he attacked the Asyūṭ refinery. Murād claimed that the local market was already saturated with the produce of the six refineries already in existence, and that export of refined products was no option because of the prevailing protectionism in this field. Any need for increased future consumption could have been easily met, and in a much cheaper way, by expanding existing facilities. He dismissed any argument that the refinery would bring employment to a region starved of industry and that it would remove the need for road transport of petroleum products to the South. Employment should be created by building industry that produced things the country really needed. As for transport, the prospected pipeline intended to bring crude oil to the refinery from Shuqayr on the Red Sea could just as well be used to bring refined products to the South from the Suez refinery, where partially implemented expansion schemes were now frozen because of the Asyūṭ refinery. Murād argued that it would be better to export the crude oil than to create an overcapacity for refined products.[174]

The difficult redistribution: dilemmas of taxation and subsidies

While corruption was one basic obstacle to development and social harmony in Egypt, according to the Labour Party and the Muslim Brothers, another was the unjust distribution of resources. "Our people are being split in two", Sayyid Rustam complained to the People's Assembly, "the haves and the have-nots".[175]

In the budgetary debate in the People's Assembly in June 1985 Ibrāhīm Shukrī, on behalf of the Socialist Labour Party (as the party still called itself at the time), demanded a comprehensive economic redistribution in favour of the poorer classes. He pointed to a World Bank report showing that over the last years the richest 5 percent had increased their share of national income from 17 to 28 percent, while the share of the poorest 50 percent had declined from 45 to 38 percent. Similarly the distribution

---

Sha'b, 4 June 1985, and "Qiṭā' al-bitrūl fī ḥāja ilā ṣaḥwa qawmiyya", *al-Sha'b*, 13 October 1987.

174 Muḥammad Ḥilmī Murād, "Qiṭā' al-bitrūl fī ḥāja ilā ṣaḥwa qawmiyya", *al-Sha'b*, 13 October 1987, and "Faḍīḥat ma'mal takrīr al-bitrūl bi-Asyuṭ", *al-Sha'b*, 27 October 1987.

175 2 December 1984, *MMS*, F4, 1–27, pp. 2264–85.

between wage earners and capital owners had shifted 7 percentage points in favour of the latter. "In this situation", he complained, "the government continues to place the hardest burdens on the poor". He demanded wage increases that would compensate for inflation at the very least, and warned against the increase in indirect taxes and lifting of subsidies in ways that would hit the poor the hardest.[176] In 1989 the Islamists rejected the proposed budget because of the excessive burdens it would place on low income groups.[177]

The Muslim Brothers time and again repeated their view that in the Islamic scheme of things it was the state's duty to secure everyone not only the bare necessities, but a "minimum level of wealth and access to leisure". It must secure work for all able hands, and support those unable to work. And it must reduce the gap in living standards. The Koran had clearly stated that the wealth produced in society must not be allowed to circulate only among the rich.[178] There must be guarantees that the income from production be justly distributed on the different factors of production, in order to stop the hoarding and squandering of wealth. Every citizen should be obliged to explain how his wealth had been acquired.[179]

In the People's Assembly Sayf al-Islām al-Bannā called for securing equal opportunities and equal treatment for all irrespective of class. Everybody must receive a fair reward for their work. If the workers see that the surplus from production is monopolised by a tiny rich upper class, they will not be willing to exert any serious effort, he said.[180]

'Ādil Ḥusayn also warned of the detrimental moral effects of a situation where the honest public servant (*muwaẓẓaf*) had been reduced to a pauper while the nouveau-riches led a provocative luxurious life in fancy clubs.[181] And a Labour Party deputy argued in the People's Assembly that while social justice entailed protecting legitimate earnings, it was a mere provocation to the struggling *muwaẓẓafīn* when two rich artisans were rumoured to be competing for the purchase of ex-Queen Narimān's house to the tune of 2 million LE.[182] Action was urgently needed to alleviate the

176 People's Assembly, 11 June 1985, *MMS*, F4, 1–89, pp. 6655–62.
177 'Ādil Ḥusayn, "I'linū al-ittifāqiyyāt al-sirriyya ma'a ṣandūq al-naqd", *al-Sha'b*, 4 July 1989.
178 See for instance "Taḍakhkhul al-dawla fī al-nishāṭ al-iqtiṣādī", *Liwā' al-islām*, 23 June 1990.
179 Shaḥḥāta, *Al-minhaj al-islāmī lil-iṣlāḥ al-iqtiṣādī*, p. 15.
180 Sayf al-Islām al-Bannā, People's Assembly, 11 February 1990, *MMS*, F5, 3–28, ṭm, pp. 2–27.
181 'Ādil Ḥusayn, "Miḥnat al-muwaẓẓafīn wa ḥukm al-aghbiyā'", *al-Sha'b*, 6 September 1988. The term *muwaẓẓaf*, literally meaning "employee", is also used more generally of white-collar workers, including those in the private sector.
182 'Abd al-Rāziq Manṣūr 'Uthmān, LP Dumyāṭ, 24 January 1988, *MMS*, F5, 1–60, pp. 4740–63.

situation of those with limited incomes, a situation that was constantly worsening with inflation and growing unemployment. "If belt-tightening is needed in our country, as they say, why do they not focus on those who waste hundreds of millions of dollars on luxuries?", Ḥusayn asked.[183]

The aspect of the "permanent economic crisis" that was most immediately socially explosive was that of the rapid increase in the cost of living. In October 1984 Mamdūḥ Qināwī got into a heated exchange with the Speaker of the People's Assembly Rif'at al-Maḥjūb, in the wake of violent clashes between workers and security forces in the industrial centre of Kafr al-Dawār in the Delta. "Why does the Minister of Planning deny that there is a price increase taking place, then we hear on foreign radio that there are riots taking place in Kafr al-Dawār because of price increases? How can we have a serious, informed debate on the problem of the subsidies under these circumstances?", Qināwī asked. Infuriated, Maḥjūb interrupted, stating that if the government said that prices had not risen, then they had not done so, and that the Assembly was not the place to talk about non-existing things.[184]

Whatever the truth of the matter at that exact moment, price increases on basic goods and services certainly did take place across the board in the period under study.[185] And the Islamists complained that since wages and pensions were not adjusted accordingly this meant an increasing burden on the poor majority of the population. Especially the situation was bad for those in government employment, where adjustment of wage levels was slow.[186] Muḥammad Fawzī of the Labour Party pointed in 1988 to the fact that an extra yearly allowance for state employees had been fixed at 2 LE since 1978, which meant it was now of no significance whatsoever.[187] Two years later Maḥfūẓ Ḥilmī from the Muslim Brothers asked how a fresh graduate in government employment would have any chance of establishing a family when his whole wage would be used just buying the daily meals.[188]

183 'Ādil Ḥusayn, "Al-mushīr Abū Ghazāla wa kuttāb al-ḥukūma wal-ḥamla ḍidda sharikāt tawẓīf al-amwāl", *al-Sha'b*, 17 May 1988.

184 3 October 1984, *MMS*, F4, 1–18, pp. 1363–87.

185 See Aḥmad Al-Ṣādiq and Muḥammad 'Alā' al-Dīn, "Al-as'ār tashta'il wal-badhakh al-ḥukūmī mustamirr", *al-Nūr*, 16 May 1990, for a list of increases on everything from train tickets to flour during the last year of the period, ranging from 15 to 180 percent.

186 Basyūnī Basyūnī, MB Alexandria, People's Assembly, 13 January 1988, *MMS*, F5, 1–58, pp. 4670–702. Cf. Aḥmad al-Fiqī, LP Daqahliyya, 11 February 1990, *MMS*, F5, 3–29, ṭm, pp. 20–30.

187 Muḥammad Fawzī, LP Alexandria, People's Assembly, 25 January 1988, *MMS*, F5, 1–62, pp. 4820–55. In January 1988 a bottle of cooking oil cost 3 LE. See Basyūnī Basyūnī, MB Alexandria, *MMS*, F5, 1–58, pp. 4670–702.

188 Mahfūẓ Ḥilmī, MB Gharbiyya, 11 February 1990, *MMS*, F5, 3–28, ṭm, pp. 2–27.

As for inflation, the policies promoted by the IMF of removing direct and indirect subsidies were seen as important factors,[189] a matter discussed below. But the main focus of criticism was directed against the government. It was argued that if the legitimate demand for wage compensations for price hikes was met by just printing money, this could only lead to more inflation.[190] In fact both ʻĀdil Ḥusayn and Ḥusayn Shaḥḥāta of the Muslim Brothers saw one basic cause of inflation: in order to cover its increasing expenses the state printed money, issued bonds and contracted loans. Thereby it increased the quantity of money without a corresponding increase in production taking place. The result was rampant inflation.[191]

The practice of deficit financing by printing money was singled out for particularly harsh criticism by the Muslim Brother economists Ḥusayn Shaḥḥāta and Yūsuf Kamāl. According to Kamāl it was equal to official robbery on a nationwide scale. It was an act of political cowardice by a weak government, an undeclared tax on the population. And this was an anti-social tax in that businessmen could shift the burden onto the poor through raising prices, while the poor who used their whole income for buying necessities had no escape. Furthermore it worked to stifle economic development. Among the poor many were forced to look for extra jobs, and the resultant increase in moonlighting was sure to hurt productivity. Among the capital owners money would be invested in fixed property or in commodity speculation, rather than in production. The result was an evil circle of "stagflation".[192] The common election platform of the Labour Party and the Muslim Brothers from 1987 demanded an end to this method of covering the budget deficit.[193]

Closely related to the problem of inflation was the question of consumer subsidies. By the 1980s these subsidies on bread and other foodstuffs, fuel and clothing had become a heavy burden on the government budget. In December 1984 in connection with the third general conference of the party, the Labour Party issued a 20 page special report on the question of

[189] See for instance Muḥammad Ḥilmī Murād, "Rafʻ al-asʻār aswa' al-ḥulūl li-muʻālajat azmat al-ḥukūma", *al-Shaʻb*, 15 May 1990.

[190] *Ibid.* Cf. Gamāl Asʻad, LP Asyūt, *MMS*, F5, 1–15, ṭm, pp. 3–21.

[191] ʻĀdil Ḥusayn, "Al-ghalā' wal-amn al-markazī wal-qamar al-isrā'īlī", *al-Shaʻb*, 27 September 1988 and Ḥusayn Shaḥḥāta, "Al-fā'ida al-ribawiyya wuqūd al-taḍakhkhum al-naqdī wa laysat taʻwīḍan ʻanhu", *al-Nūr*, 23 August 1989.

[192] Magdī Muṣṭafā, "Laʻbat al-iṣdār al-naqdī taʻnī mazīdan min al-taḍakhkhum wa ghalā' al-asʻār", *Liwā' al-islām*, 1 November 1989. Cf. Ḥizb al-ʻamal al-ishtirākī, "Taqrīr ḥizb al-ʻamal al-ishtirākī ilā al-mu'tamar al-iqtiṣādī", p. 55, where increased taxing of the rich is suggested as a measure against inflation.

[193] Ḥizb al-ʻamal, "Al-barnāmaj al-intikhābī ʻalā qā'imat ḥizb al-ʻamal", part V. Cf. Shaḥḥāta, *Al-minhaj al-islāmī lil-iṣlāḥ al-iqtiṣādī*, p. 20.

subsidies.[194] The document envisaged a reform of the subsidies through the following measures:

— Subsidies must be removed from certain objects considered "luxurious", like private cars and air conditioners.

— The subsidy should apply only to the final stage in the marketing of the commodities in question. Subsidies on input goods like fertiliser for farmers and raw material for industry, should be taken away and as compensation producers should be left to set output prices according to the market, instead of low prices being enforced by the government.

— Only those in real need should enjoy the subsidy. This would be secured through extensive use of rationing cards.[195] (It must be noted here that almost all public employees and pensioners were considered worthy of the subsidy, along with all those farmers holding less than 10 *faddān*. With families this would add up to a large majority of the Egyptian population.)[196]

The Muslim Brothers never published any similar review of the question of subsidies. Generally speaking they tended to be more fiercely critical of the system of subsidies, stating that in its present shape it merely benefited the speculators. But their criticism was mainly directed at indirect subsidies in the shape of state manipulation of prices. The Muslim Brothers acknowledged the need for aiding the poor in securing basic means of livelihood. But as long as subsidies were necessary for this purpose they favoured a system where the state would buy goods at the market price and supply them directly to those in need at a lower price.[197]

Throughout the 1980s the Islamists criticised the reduction of subsidies, because this hurt the poor, who were not given sufficient compen-

[194] Ḥizb al-'amal al-ishtirākī, *Al-da'm bayna al-ilghā' wal-tarshīd* [The Subsidies between Abolishment and Adjustment], Cairo, 1984.

[195] Rationing cards were not limited to the poor (although there were different types depending on income). The point was that if the goods were sold outside the rationing card system, many poor people risked not getting anything at all, especially since the accessibility of shops selling rationed goods varied greatly from one area to another. In January 1988 the Islamists complained in the People's Assembly that several items like flour and cooking oil had been taken off the rationing cards, and for others the amount had been severely reduced. This would only lead to the total domination of the black market, they said. See for instance Aḥmad al-Fiqī, LP Daqahliyya, People's Assembly, 10 January 1988, *MMS*, F5, 1–53, pp. 4504–31, and Bashīr 'Uthmān, MB Buhayra, *MMS*, F5, 1–60, pp. 4740–63, who also criticised that the rule limiting the time spent in one district by inspectors from the Ministry of Supply to six years was not being upheld.

[196] Ḥizb al-'amal al-ishtirākī, *Al-da'm bayna al-ilghā' wal-tarshīd*, pp. 14–20. Cf. Ḥizb al-'amal al-ishtirākī, "Taqrīr ḥizb al-'amal al-ishtirākī ilā al-mu'tamar al-iqtiṣādī", p. 48.

[197] Yūsuf Kamāl cited in Magdī Muṣṭafā, "Al-qiṭā' al-'āmm 'alā al-ṭarīqa al-miṣriyya", *Liwā' al-islām*, 5 July 1989. The concern for better targeting was also behind the suggestion by Fu'ād Shawshān, LP Buḥayra, in the People's Assembly that the distribution of subsidised bread be separated from production. See *MMS*, F5, 3–29, ṭm, pp. 3–12.

sation. And it was emphasised that the subsidies should not be given the blame for every budgetary problem. In principal they were a way of compensating structural imbalances in the economy, Shukrī said, by redistributing some of the wealth from the rich to the poor.[198] But both the Labour Party and the Muslim Brothers acknowledged the problems posed by the tremendous cost of the subsidies and while opposing their abolition, argued positively for a reform that would secure a better "targeting" of the subsidies to those really in need.[199]

In debates on taxation, a hot issue in a country struggling to reduce the deficit in the government budget, the main concern of the Islamists was the socially unjust effects of the increasing domination of indirect taxes as the main source of government income. They demanded that this tendency be reversed and that direct taxes be made the main provider of funds for the Treasury. Indirect taxes should be concentrated on luxury goods.[200] When the government in the summer of 1987 proposed drastic increases in the stamp duty, in order to remedy some of the deficit, it met with vigorous opposition from the Alliance MPs.[201] In 1990 Magdī Muṣṭafā wrote in *Liwā' al-islām* that indirect taxes now accounted for 75 percent of the tax revenues of the government. The bulk of these taxes would be paid by the poor, and there was no way of getting around them, while the direct taxes, supposed to be the contribution of the rich, were the object of massive evasion.[202] In fact those who mostly paid the direct taxes were ordinary people, since the upper limit of a tax-free income was as low as 960 LE a year for an individual and 2000 LE for families with children. Several Islamist MPs urged these limits be raised to at least 1500 LE and 3000 LE respectively.[203]

[198] See for instance Ibrāhīm Shukrī, People's Assembly, 11 June 1985, *MMS*, F4, 1–89, pp. 6655–62. Cf. Muḥammad Ḥilmī Murād, "Raf' al-as'ār aswa' al-ḥulūl li-mu'ālajat azmat al-ḥukūma", *al-Sha'b*, 15 May 1990.

[199] Ḥizb al-'amal, "Al-barnāmaj al-intikhābī 'alā qā'imat ḥizb al-'amal", part V.

[200] For instance Ibrāhīm Shukrī, People's Assembly, 11 June 1985, *MMS*, F4, 1–89, pp. 6655–62. Cf. Ḥizb al-'amal al ishtirākī, "Taqrīr ḥizb al-'amal al-ishtirākī ilā al-mu'tamar al-iqtiṣādī", pp. 45–7, and Ḥizb al-'amal, "Al-barnāmaj al-intikhābī 'alā qā'imat ḥizb al-'amal", part V.

[201] See Ibrāhīm Shukrī and Gamāl As'ad, People's Assembly, 8 July 1987, *MMS*, F5, 1–28, pp. 2900–13. However, the Islamic Alliance was willing to condone the imposition of a small duty on certain kinds of printed matter for the benefit of pensions for journalists. For instance 'Ādil Wālī and 'Iṣām al-'Iryān, 15 November 1987, *MMS*, F5, 1–35, pp. 3617–33.

[202] Magdī Muṣṭafā, "Al-tahrīb al-ḍarībī wa al-'ab' alladhī yataḥammaluhu al-fuqarā' wa maḥdūdī al-dakhl", *Liwā' al-islām*, 23 July 1990. Cf. "Al-zakāt rakīza iqtiṣādiyya ḥaḍāriyya tanammuwiyya yajib al-akhdh bi-hā fī al-tawajjuh al-iqtiṣādi", *Liwā' al-islām*, 5 June 1989, and 'Ādil Wālī, LP Cairo, People's Assembly, 8 July 1987, *MMS*, F5, 1–28, pp. 2900–13.

[203] Muḥammad al-Shitānī, MB Gharbiyya, People's Assembly, 24 January 1988, *MMS*, F5,

Yūsuf Kamāl complains that things have been turned on their head. "The state now takes from the poor and gives to the rich", he said. The rich had a larger influence on the use of the tax revenues. And if they paid any taxes they would immediately shift the burden onto the poor through increasing the prices of their products.[204]

Ḥusayn Shaḥḥāta in 1990 summed up what he saw as the reasons for the massive tax evasions—13 billion LE according to official figures. First of all there was a moral decay that undermined the tax system from two sides: the taxpayers did not feel the tax to be a moral obligation, and among the tax collecting officials there were corrupt individuals who would easily be bribed to turn a blind eye to evasions. Secondly the bureaucracy was inefficient and the tax laws complicated, which increased the opportunities for evasion. Finally taxes were too heavy on small entrepreneurs and artisans.[205] This last concern had been raised two years before by Muḥammad al-Shitānī, a Muslim Brother MP from Gharbiyya. Small shopkeepers, barbers and owners of workshops did not operate sophisticated book-keeping procedures, he said. Often they were forced to pay thousands, sometimes tens of thousands, of pounds in tax based on an arbitrary estimate of their income. This drove scores of them to bankruptcy and their employees to unemployment, he complained.[206] There was also concern for over-taxing of Egyptians working abroad. Ma'mūn al-Huḍaybī argued against levying income tax on these people. They were playing a very positive role in the economy in that they brought essential hard currency to the country, while at the same time, through their migration, easing the pressure on housing and employment inside the country. Many of those working abroad were already in crisis because of the demise of the Islamic investment companies through which they had invested

---

1–61, pp. 4767–73, Ṣalāḥ 'Abdallāh, LP Cairo, 27 January 1990, *MMS*, F5, 3–22, ṭm, pp. 2–28 and Ḥasan al-Gamal, MB Cairo, 12 February 1990, *MMS*, F5, 3–30, ṭm, pp. 4–33. Cf. Magdī Muṣṭafā, "Da'wa 'ilmiyya li-iḥyā' farīḍat al-zakāt", *Liwā' al-islām*, 18 December 1990. On one occasion in 1985 Shukrī opposed such a lifting of the tax floor out of concern for the budgetary balance, *MMS*, F4, 1–73, pp. 4816–24.

[204] See Magdī Muṣṭafā, "Al-tahrīb al-ḍarībī wa al-'ab' alladhī yataḥammaluhu al-fuqarā' wa maḥdūdī al-dakhl", *Liwā' al-islām*, 23 July 1990. Cf. Gamāl As'ad, LP Asyūṭ, People's Assembly, 22 June 1987, *MMS*, F5, 1–15, ṭm, pp. 3–21.

[205] Magdī Muṣṭafā, "Al-tahrīb al-ḍarībī wa al-'ab' alladhī yataḥammaluhu al-fuqarā' wa maḥdūdī al-dakhl", *Liwā' al-islām*, 23 July 1990. Cf. Aḥmad al-Fiqī, LP Daqahliyya, People's Assembly, 10 January 1988, *MMS*, F5, 1–53, pp. 4504–31, and Ḥanafī Fahīm 'Uthmān, MB Cairo, 25 January 1988, *MMS*, F5, 1–62, pp. 4820–55.

[206] People's Assembly, 24 January 1988, *MMS*, F5, 1–61, pp. 4767–73. Cf. Ḥanafī Fahīm 'Uthmān, MB Cairo, 25 January 1988, *MMS*, F5, 1–62, pp. 4820–55, and Sayf al-Islām al-Bannā, 11 February 1990, *MMS*, F5, 1–28, ṭm, pp. 2–27. Similar concerns with regard to farmers were raised by Aḥmad al-Fiqī, LP Daqahliyya, People's Assembly, 25 June 1987, *MMS*, F5, 1–20, ṭm, pp. 3–42.

their savings, Huḍaybī claimed. Imposing more taxes would make them feel that the state was only out to grab their earnings while giving nothing in return.[207]

The Muslim Brothers held forth the introduction of the Islamic tax of *zakāt* as the positive solution to the ills of the taxation system, and claimed it would secure a just redistribution from the rich to the poor. The document from the Brothers' Economic Commission from 1991 demands that the *zakāt* must be implemented in stead of the present "man-made" taxes. This must be prepared through a process where one concentrates on direct taxation, and tax levels must conform to the various levels of income without killing the spirit of seeking economic gain. The minimum income needed to provide basic necessities must be exempted from taxes. The moral spirit of those working in the tax collecting apparatus must be strengthened.[208]

Landlords and tenants in the countryside

The problematic relationship between landlords and tenants in agriculture (see p. 51) was particularly conspicuous for the *lack* of Islamist interest in discussing it and especially in taking up a clear position. This relationship had been embittered under the *infitāḥ* by the regulations inherited from the Nasser period when rents were frozen as a measure to secure social equality, and the eviction of tenants was made well nigh impossible.

Even if the rents had been increased in 1975–6, they remained by 1985 less than LE 80 a year per *faddān*, while the market value of the land had increased to 20,000 LE per *faddān* and more, and an annual return of several thousand pounds per *faddān* was common.[209] When the NDP's Agriculture Committee in 1985 fielded proposals for a reform that would double rents and facilitate the termination of rental contracts and the sale of land, it was taken by the leftists in the *Tajammu'* as a rolling back of Nasser's agrarian reform, and giving in to greedy landowners who wanted to squeeze more out of poor peasant tenants. The NDP countered by claiming that the issue also involved quite a number of the smallest landowners. Owing to Islamic inheritance laws, the number of families owning small plots had increased dramatically. The plots being too small to earn them a

[207] People's Assembly, 5 July 1989, *MMS*, F5, 2–94, pp. 6817–38.

[208] Shaḥḥāta, *Al-minhaj al-islāmī lil-iṣlāḥ al-iqtiṣādī*, p. 15. Cf. "Al-zakāt rakīza iqtiṣādiyya ḥaḍāriyya tanammuwiyya yajib al-akhdh bi-hā fī al-tawajjuh al-iqtiṣādi", *Liwā' al-islām*, 5 June 1989, and Magdī Muṣṭafā, "Da'wa 'ilmiyya li-iḥyā' farīḍat al-zakāt", *Liwā' al-islām*, 18 December 1990.

[209] Robert Springborg, "State-Society Relations in Egypt: The Debate over Owner-Tenant Relations", *Middle East Journal*, vol. 45, no. 2, spring 1991, pp. 235–6.

living, this group had the choice of either renting more land or of renting out their plots to others, which many did, then seeking employment elsewhere. According to the NDP these poor people were left with next to nothing in income from their land, while the tenants profited from the increase in the value of the agricultural crops.

Although both presentations certainly grasped a part of the truth, solid statistics were never presented underpinning the view that poor landowners constituted a significant part of those letting their land for rent.[210] However John Waterbury presents statistics showing that in 1961 owners of plots of less than 5 *faddān* were renting out a quarter of their land, amounting to 800,000 *faddān*, about 13 percent of the country's total cultivated surface. And the indications are that the number of the smallest owners had grown from 1961 to the mid-1980s.[211]

By 1985 in excess of 1.5 million *faddān*, about 25 per cent of Egypt's agricultural land, was cultivated by tenants. This means first of all that the issue of tenancy relations was a crucial question affecting rural social relations, and secondly that, from the information given by Waterbury, small owners were in fact most probably a not insignificant part of those renting out land, and therefore benefiting from the proposed reforms. In any case the picture of who would benefit and who would lose by a reform was a complicated one, and certainly the reform might threaten rural unrest,[212] a central reason for the fact that the government dragged their feet on the reform well into the 1990s.

As stated above the Islamists spoke little of these questions. In their press they were merely reporting the progress, or lack of such, of government initiatives. In the People's Assembly they sometimes took up the issue, but typically they would only be calling for "something to be done" without specifying what.[213] Sometimes the issue was presented in terms indicating a sympathy for the owners,[214] at other times in more neutral terms stating that to calm the countryside a decision was needed.[215]

[210] *Ibid.*, p. 241.

[211] Waterbury, *The Egypt of Nasser and Sadat*, pp. 269–70.

[212] When a reformed law along the lines of the 1985 proposals was finally implemented in the autumn of 1997 it did result in widespread rioting and confrontations between landlords and tenants. However, the unrest remained mostly localised and died down after a while.

[213] For instance Basyūnī Basyūnī, MB Alexandria, People's Assembly, 13 January 1988, *MMS*, F5, 1–58, pp. 4670–702, and Fatḥī 'Abd al-Wāḥid, LP Minya, 10 February 1990, *MMS*, F5, 3–27, ṭm, pp. 5–32.

[214] Fatḥī 'Abd al-Wāḥid, LP Minya, People's Assembly, 13 January 1988, *MMS*, F5, 1–58, pp. 4670–702, and Maḥmūd Nāfi', MB Daqahliyya, 11 February 1990, *MMS*, F5, 3–29, ṭm, pp. 3–12, who called for ridding the country of "these imported communist laws". Cf. Muṣṭafā al-Wardānī, MB Giza, *MMS*, F5, 3–36, ṭm, pp. 31–44.

[215] 'Iṣām al-'Iryān, 28 January 1990, *MMS*, F5, 3–24, ṭm, pp. 2–30.

The sole exception to this rule was Khālid Ḥamād, a Labour Party MP from Daqahliyya, who in 1988 vigorously opposed any changes that would make the tenants lose out, despite the effort they had put into cultivating the land and raising its value, to absentee landowners returning from abroad to reap the profits.[216] And Fatḥi ʻAbd al-Wāḥid, LP Minya, two years later suggested that changes in the law must only affect future contracts, leaving the existing ones as they were, a suggestion pretty close to avoiding tackling the real issues involved.[217]

Robert Springborg explains the general "abstention" of the Islamists from the debate in two ways. One, the Labour Party, he says, was largely disinterested because of its mainly urban implantation. And two, the Muslim Brothers were sympathetic towards the owners because of the dominant capitalist element within the organisation. This may also have influenced the Labour Party because of their alliance from 1987.[218] But even if the Islamists had been inclined to sympathise with the proposed reforms, they were reluctant to come out in open agreement with their main opponent the NDP.[219]

This analysis may be true to a certain extent. But it would seem that Springborg too easily refuses the argument that the social content of the problem was complicated, and that this may have contributed to the difficulty in taking up a clear position. Later the Labour Party proposed that the present contracts be transformed according to the system of *mushāraka*, so that instead of a fixed money rent the tenant would pay the landlord a pre-agreed share of the income from the marketed crops. This way the landlord would not be deprived of his share of the increased money value of the crops. Critics argued that this would make the tenants less interested in increasing the productivity of the soil since the profit from this would have to be shared.

"*Always talking about* Asyūṭ": *bringing local grievances to the ear of the* sulṭān

"I now pass the floor to the Honourable Member Gamāl Asʻad", said the speaker of the People's Assembly, "and I sincerely hope he will stick to the subject on the agenda, and not start talking about Asyūṭ". "All right, I'll speak about Asyūṭ, but call it Aswān", Asʻad retorted.[220] (The agenda was the discussion of a report on the progress of development projects in Qinā and Aswān.)

216 11 January 1989, *MMS*, F5, 1–54, pp. 4535–59.

217 Fatḥī ʻAbd al-Wāḥid, LP Minya, 10 February 1990, *MMS*, F5, 3–27, ṭm, pp. 5–32.

218 During the unrest in 1997 the Labour Party sided squarely with the tenants who opposed being forced off their land as a result of the implementation of the reformed law. The Muslim Brothers, a victim of severe repression at the time, remained more aloof.

219 Springborg, "State-Society Relations in Egypt", p. 242.

220 26 March 1990, *MMS*, F5, 3–45, ṭm, pp. 11–13.

Since As'ad represented Asyūṭ province, this exchange illustrates a salient feature of Egyptian parliamentary life: the fact that most MPs were at least as active in furthering the local causes of their constituencies, as in debating national issues.

The local grievances raised by MPs of the Muslim Brothers and the Labour Party were of all kinds: the need for more public buses in Alexandria during the summer season,[221] a demand for reinstating laid-off workers in al-Maḥalla al-Kubrā[222] or a complaint against a sugar mill in Minya cheating the farmers on the weight of their sugar cane.[223] However, if we look for recurring issues one thing that stands out is the need for rural development, bringing electricity, telephone, sewage systems, drinking water and health services to Egypt's fast growing villages.[224] In this sense the content of the local complaints brought to government attention by the Islamists can be seen to be in harmony with a picture of the Islamists as agents of economic modernisation.

However, it is striking that the sources covered do not indicate that the glaring North-South division of the country was ever systematically raised by the Islamists of the Alliance.[225] *Al-Ṣa'īd*, the area south of Cairo, harbouring close to 30 percent of Egypt's population, is the poorest and least developed region of the country, and largely neglected by the government. Perhaps the apparent lack of interest in the problems of the South was a reflection of the fact that the parties in question, and certainly their parliamentary group, were dominated by people from Cairo and the Delta. It is interesting to note that of the 115 local councils carried by the Islamic Alliance in the 1992 elections only four were in the South, where the *Jamā'a Islāmiyya* was at the apex of its strength and had called for a boycott.[226] It was the few Alliance MPs from the South who from time to time championed the cause of the deprived region stretching from Banī Suwayf to Aswān, complaining that *al-Ṣa'īd* always came last when resources were being allocated.[227]

221 Muḥammad Fawzī, LP Alexandria, 25 January 1988, *MMS*, F5, 1–62, pp. 4820–55.
222 Maḥfuẓ Ḥilmī, MB Gharbiyya, 11 February 1990, *MMS*, F5, 3–28, ṭm, pp. 2–27.
223 'Abd al-Jābir 'Uthmān, MB Minya, 24 February 1990, *MMS*, F5, 3–33, ṭm, pp. 4–30.
224 See for instance Aḥmad al-Fiqī, LP Daqahliyya, People's Assembly, 10 January 1988, *MMS*, F5, 1–53, pp. 4504–31, and 'Abd al-Raḥmān al-Raṣd, MB Sharqiyya, 25 January 1988, *MMS*, F5, 1–62, pp. 4820–55.
225 Perhaps an exception could be made for the 1991 Muslim Brothers document on economic reform, which states that the imbalance between different geographical regions within the country leads to increasing gaps between rich and poor. See Shaḥḥāta, *Al-minhaj al-islāmī lil-iṣlāḥ al-iqtiṣādī*, p. 13.
226 Markaz al-dirāsāt al-siyāsiyya wal-istrātījiyya bil-Ahrām, *Al-taqrīr al-istrātījī al-'arabī 1992*, p. 320.
227 For two instances see Muṣṭafā Maḥgūb, MB Qinā, People's Assembly, 24 January 1988, *MMS*, F5, 1–61, pp. 4779–855 and Fahmī Bakhīt Dīb, LP Suhāg, 25 January 1988, *MMS*, F5, 1–62, pp. 4820–55.

5

THE "ISLAMICNESS" OF THE SOLUTION

In the sphere of economic policies the slogan "*al-islām huwa al-ḥall*" translated into a fight for an independent, strong and just society in Egypt. The *language* and *symbolism* the Islamists adopted in this fight differed markedly from that of other radical, nationalist and populist movements in the global South. But to what extent did the *content* of their project possess features that could be construed as specifically Islamic, serving to distinguish the economic ideas of the Islamists from those of others striving towards such an ideal society?

What is special about the Islamic solution?

In two articles in *al-Nūr* on 24 and 31 January 1990, 'Abd al-Ḥamīd al-Ghazālī summarises his views on the economic and political situation of Egypt. His point of departure is that the world is rapidly becoming a village in the sense that modern communication technology brings all kinds of influence upon people and this cannot be stopped. This technology in itself is neutral. It can be used for good or for bad. In the present-day world it aggravates the competition between cultures and civilisations, a competition which ought to be for good. This happens in a situation were the old order in the East is breaking down under *perestroika* and in the West under Thatcherism and its privatisation programme. To face this situation, Ghazālī writes, we possess in Islam a comprehensive integrated civilisational project. And he goes on to list the main features of the ideal Islamic economic system. This system is based on freedom and justice. It makes work an integral part of the service of God, and man the caretaker of God on earth. It does away with exploitation and is based on making the different sectors of society work in harmony, not in conflict.[1]

Two years earlier he had spelled out in some detail what in his mind distinguished the Islamic economic system from the "man-made" (*waḍ'ī*)

[1] 'Abd al-Ḥamīd, Al-Ghazālī, "Sanat al-taghyīr wa irādat al-binā' amama ma'āwil al-hadm wa quwā al-jumūd", *al-Nūr*, 24 and 31 January 1990.

systems. No system is value neutral, he wrote, whatever its pretensions. But Islam openly states that it bases its economy on moral values and norms, and furthermore these norms are an integrated part of the system itself. Islam is open-minded in its economic thinking, since it is an Islamic imperative to utilize all useful human discoveries and ideas. He states in this regard that the ground rule is that what is not forbidden is legal and goes far towards identifying the public interest with God's will ("*ḥay-thumā wujidat al-maṣlaḥa fa-thamma shar' allāh*"). Islam declares war on poverty, Ghazālī says. It has made work a part of serving God and economic development a duty until Judgment Day. The human being is the dynamic factor in the economy. And since we are God's caretakers on earth, and since all wealth ultimately belongs to Him, collective self-reliance is an Islamic principle. Investments must proceed according to priorities putting the provision of basic necessities first. There should be an emphasis upon small scale projects, and economic operations should be free of interest, this would ensure that the individual's economic return will depend on effort. Finally the system should in general be one of a market economy built on "cooperative competition", free from the stifling shackles of total state control yet far from the cannibalistic competition of capitalism.[2]

In a similar statement Ḥusayn Shaḥḥāta is basically in agreement, but adds the need to establish the security of both workers and capital and a harmonious cooperation between them, the need for *zakāt* to replace the "man-made" tax system, and the need for economic integration between Islamic countries.[3]

Faith and development

To 'Ādil Ḥusayn the role of Islam in solving Egypt's problems was mainly linked to the need for faith in God as a uniting and energising factor within the population. Ḥusayn rarely referred to classical Islamic sources of learning, but often to modern economic theory and concrete economic problems. *Ribā*, or the charging of interest, was clearly prohibited by the Koran and should be done away with. But as Ḥusayn saw it, such a move in isolation would be of rather limited value. It had to be part of a comprehensive reform of the economy, where the major goal must be achieving independence from the West.[4] This line of thinking is in considerable

[2] Ḥamdī al-Baṣīr, "Al-insān wal-minhaj al-islāmī fī al-tanmīya al-iqtiṣādiyya", *al-Nūr*, 7 December 1988.

[3] 'Imād Al-Shīwī, "Wal-sanadāt al-dūlāriyya ayḍan ghayr shar'iyya", *al-Nūr*, 27 December 1989.

[4] 'Ādil Ḥusayn, "Al-islāmiyyūn wal-ittifāq ma'a ṣandūq al-naqd", *al-Sha'b*, 12 May 1987.

contrast to the more general works on Islamic economy by Muslim Brother writers both in the 1950s and in the 1980s discussed in chapter 3, which are characterised by a tendency towards abstract discussion of Islamic principles rather than an analysis of the concrete problems of the existing economy.

In the debate on current economic issues it was Ḥusayn's line that was pursued in practice by both Labour and Muslim Brother writers and speakers. With the particular exception of the ban on *ribā* (see below), the substantial issues were very rarely discussed with reference to particular *Sharī'a* rulings. Instead the goals of independence, strength and justice were taken for granted and the issues were then discussed in a concrete way that does not differ much from the discourse of any modern politician.

Judging by the articles written and speeches given by the Egyptian Islamists of the late 1980s, the road to a true Islamic economy would seem to consist of "faith + modernisation". Typically it is emphasised that the import of technology and "material sciences" is a must, while in the case of "human sciences" the Muslims ought to be the exporters. The West has lost its faith and should not be emulated in this regard, a theme going all the way back to the early Islamic reformers Afghānī and 'Abduh.[5] There can be no moral standards without religion, the Islamists claim.[6] The religion in question should be Islam, but this seems mainly to be argued from the fact that this is after all the faith of the Muslim majority, and the only reliable source for legitimising the development effort as a collective duty in pursuit of a better future. When focus is on unity with the Copts the moral reference is often "the heavenly religions".

In the success story of the East Asian "tigers" a central role was played by Confucian social norms, 'Ādil Ḥusayn wrote. In the same way Egyptians had to reject the idea that they should become "like the West", and choose a road based on respect for their own values, which meant reintroducing the *Sharī'a*.[7]

In an article in *Liwā' al-islām* from mid-1982 'Abd al Ḥamīd al-Ghazālī is quoted as saying that the Islamic countries are backward because they have prevaricated between the various imported systems of capitalism and socialism. These systems were able to succeed in their homelands because they were in harmony with the ideological make-up of the populations, but not in Muslim countries where they conflicted with people's beliefs. "People are told in the mosque that interest is prohibited,

[5] See the speech in the People's Assembly given by 'Abd al-'Azīz al-Ghubārī, LP Fayyūm, 13 January 1988, *MMS*, F5, 1–58, pp. 4670–702.

[6] Ḥizb al-'amal, "Al-barnāmaj al-intikhābī 'alā qā'imat ḥizb al-'amal", part III.

[7] 'Ādil Ḥusayn, "'An al-iqtiṣād wa al-sharī'a wa al-ḥiwār al-qawmī", *al-Sha'b*, 6 June 1989.

but when they enter the street they are compelled to deal with an interest-dominated economic system", Ghazālī said. The solution lay in a return to Islam. But Ḥusayn Shaḥḥāta, interviewed in the same article, emphasised that while Islam is a religion containing fixed rules, these rules must be flexibly applied and hence there is a need for *ijtihād* taking the circumstances of time and place into consideration.[8]

In late January 1986 'Ādil Ḥusayn commented on the fall in oil prices that was causing economic crisis.[9] Ibrāhīm Nāfi', the editor-in-chief of the leading government daily *al-Ahrām*, had called for all forces, opposition and government, to work together to meet this crisis that had been brought on by fate. Ḥusayn disputed this view. There had been clear warnings since 1984 that the price of oil would eventually fall. But, he wrote, when the government took some positive measures in early 1985 to remedy Egypt's persistent trade deficit, they quickly backtracked. Here we see a clear-cut positive estimation of the Sa'īd reforms.

The problem, said Ḥusayn, was that while Egypt had received enormous incomes in foreign currency, which in a period in the late 1970s and early '80s contributed to a GDP growth of 9 percent a year, nothing of this was used in a productive way. The lesson was that material possibilities are not in themselves a magic key to progress. Progress and development require belief in God, and the fighting spirit and intellectual effort that spring from such belief. When in spite of ten affluent years foreign debt had spiralled to 33 billion US dollars, it was no excuse to say that this happened to all developing countries, for Egypt had enjoyed the good fortune of extraordinary streams of income from abroad. But easy come easy go, and now the lean cows had come to eat the fat ones, Ḥusayn wrote, with a reference to the Koranic (and Bible) story of Joseph interpreting Pharaoh's dream.[10] What other factor, Ḥusayn asked later, besides religious legitimation (*tabrīr min al-dīn*) and love of the motherland would be able to mobilise Egyptians for the sacrifices needed for development?[11] The country needed a national project for development built on faith in God, and on the values that are based on such faith, especially the view of work as an integral part of the service of God. Thus the energy of *jihād* could be mobilised for development. But the project must combine

[8] Aḥmad al-Suyūfī, "Al-islām huwa al-ḥall, kayfa? Qaḍīyat al-iqtiṣād al-islāmī—al-iṭār wal-huwīya", *Liwā' al-islām*, July–August 1982..

[9] 'Ādil Ḥusayn, "Al-azma al-iqtiṣādiyya: la'allahu khayr la'allanā nufīq", *al-Sha'b*, 28 January 1986.

[10] Koran, 12:43.

[11] 'Ādil Ḥusayn, "'An al-iqtiṣād wa al-sharī'a wa al-ḥiwār al-qawmī", *al-Sha'b*, 6 June 1989.

the Islamic faith with a thorough analysis of the current situation of Egypt and the wider Arab and Muslim world. This was a task yet to be accomplished by the Islamist movement, Ḥusayn thought.[12]

Apart from the question of people's identification with the faith, the actual Islamic character of the required faith may not after all have been so decisive, for the Labour Party at least. This is indicated in a speech given in the People's Assembly in early 1988 by 'Abd al-Ḥalīm 'Alam al-Dīn, Labour Party deputy for Giza. The Egyptian people are quite willing to work hard, he says, because of their love for their country (*waṭan*). But a positive model of sound and committed leadership is lacking, he says, citing the caliph 'Umar ibn al-Khaṭṭāb and Mao Zedong as ideal examples in this regard.[13]

Time and again it is emphasised that real development cannot be achieved by focusing narrowly on increasing the volume of production. Faith, piety and strong morality will boost development because it will create unity, a spirit of sacrifice, and it will lead the youth in particular away from waste and corruption, gambling and alcohol.[14] The efficacy of the trade unions of the free professions, dominated by Islamists, is held forth as proof.[15]

The spirit of the never-tiring *mujāhid* is praised,[16] and it is even asserted that the struggle for development should properly be considered a form of *jihād fī sabīl allāh*.[17] In the same vein it is stated that development is a collective duty on the Muslim society, a *farḍ kifāya*, like the *jihād*,[18] and that the effort for "making the earth flourish" is an integral part of the worship of God, the *'ibāda*.[19] Even the later "socialist" dissident from the Labour

12 See 'Ādil Ḥusayn, "Qānūn al-istithmār al-jadīd", *al-Sha'b*, 20 June 1989 and an earlier interview with Ḥusayn in Sayyid Zahrān, "Miṣr ilā ayn", *Ṣawt al-'arab*, 29 May 1988. Cf. 'Ādil Ḥusayn, "Kārithat al-ittifāq al-sirrī ma'a amrīkā wa ṣandūq al-naqd", *al-Sha'b*, 26 May 1987.

13 *MMS*, F5, 1–55, pp. 4562–91. In the Labour Party document from 1982, before the party's Islamisation, the same concern for moral values (*akhlāq*) is exhibited, but here these values were tied to nationalism and socialism. See Ḥizb al-'amal al-ishtirākī, "Taqrīr ḥizb al-'amal al-ishtirākī ilā al-mu'tamar al-iqtiṣādī", p. 58.

14 See for instance the speeches in the People's Assembly given by Lāshīn Shanab, Muslim Brother MP from Gharbiyya province, 22 June 1987, *MMS*, F5, 1–15, ṭm, pp. 3–21, and Sayf al-Islām al-Bannā, 28 December 1987, *MMS*, F5, 1–47, pp. 4259–85.

15 Sayyid Khalīl, "Mawākib al-isrāf al-ḥukūmī mustamirra", *Liwā' al-islām*, 1 November 1990.

16 Zaynab Al-Ghazalī al-Jubaylī, "Hal yakill al-mujāhid?", *al-Nūr*, 16 May 1990.

17 See the speech in the People's Assembly given by 'Iṣām al-'Iryān, 12 January 1988, *MMS*, F5, 1–57, pp. 4644–68.

18 Yūsuf Kamāl in Magdī Muṣṭafā, "La'bat al-iṣdār al-naqdī ta'nī mazīdan min al-taḍakhkhum wa ghalā' al-as'ār", *Liwā' al-islām*, 1 November 1989.

19 'Abd al-Ḥamīd al-Ghazālī in "Al-zakāt rakīza iqtiṣādiyya ḥaḍāriyya tanammuwiyya yajib al-akhdh bi-hā fī al-tawajjuh al-iqtiṣādi", *Liwā' al-islām*, 5 June 1989.

Party Aḥmad Migāhid came close to this rhetoric when he stated in the People's Assembly already before the occurrence of the Islamic alliance that "work for the Egyptian people is equivalent to working for God".[20]

There is a modernising aspect to this sacralisation of work both by the Labour Party and the Muslim Brothers, eminently typified by an article of the engineer Ṣubḥī 'Abd al-Mun'im Fawda published in *Liwā' al-islām* in September 1990. Part of a series named "Towards an Islamic economy", his article discusses the problem of organising one's time properly. Apparently directed primarily at people in leading positions in businesses and organisations, the article is light-years removed from any idea of the immanent meditative Oriental. Stating briefly that God has ordered us not to waste time, Fawda delivers a lesson in time organisation that might have been taken directly from Western literature of the 1980s directed at business executives.[21]

Bring back the Sharī'a*!*

The Islamists called time and again for the application of the *Sharī'a* and saw its absence as the cause of current problems.[22] The Egyptian constitution had since 1971 stated that the *Sharī'a* was the basic source of legislation in the country. In 1978 the Assembly had approved in principle the general revision of Egyptian laws to secure their accordance with the *Sharī'a*. However, the government's procrastination ensured that no concrete proposal for such revision ever came to the vote. In the early days of the 1987–90 assembly Ḥasan al-Gamal complained that the Muslim Brothers had fielded thirteen proposals for *Sharī'a*-harmonised laws in the parliamentary period 1984–7, but that these proposals were still stuck in the bureaucracy.[23]

[20] See his speech in the Assembly on 11 November 1986, *MMS*, F4, 3–1, ṭm, p. 5.

[21] Ṣubḥī 'Abd al-Mun'im Fawda, "Idārat wa tanẓīm al-waqt ḍarūra li-taḥqīq al-iqtiṣād al-nājiḥ", *Liwā' al-islām*, 21 September 1990.

[22] There were nevertheless some nuances between the Labour Party and the Muslim Brothers. The Brothers tended (in some contrast to the legacy of Ḥasan al-Banna) to underline the need for legislating in accordance with the interpretations of the great classical *fiqh* authorities of the past. With regard to the proposal for a new Law for Maritime Trade, Huḍaybī complained that neither a single *faqīh*, nor any verse from the Koran were mentioned. The Labour Party on the other hand tended towards a more modernistic stand, emphasising more the need for integrated social and political reform to bring the country in accordance with Islamic ideals, than details of *Sharī'a* legislation. This was true for the party as a whole, though most markedly so with those who in 1989 left the party in opposition to the dominant Islamist trend. See Aḥmad Migāhīd in the People's Assembly 4 May 1985, *MMS*, F4, 1–74, pp. 4852–83.

[23] Ḥasan al-Gamal, MB Cairo, 25 June 1987, *MMS*, F5, 1–20, ṭm, pp. 3–42. Cf. his speech on 12 February 1990, *MMS*, F5, 3–30, ṭm, pp. 4–33.

In April 1990 the Law for Maritime Trade, introduced by the British in 1883, was revised. The Labour-Muslim Brother alliance complained bitterly over what they saw as their virtual exclusion from the preparation of the proposal, but most of all over the fact that no serious attempt had been made to bring the law into accordance with the *Sharī'a*, merely a general OK-message had been extracted from the Muftī.[24]

On the whole the discussion of the *Sharī'a* with regard to economic questions was conducted in very general terms, with few concrete explanations of how economic legislation would substantially change. In the case of the Maritime Trade Law, the only thing mentioned was that some *'ulamā'* held that the commercial insurance which the law regulated was un-Islamic and should be replaced by the system of mutual insurance.[25]

From time to time the government was called upon to adhere to the *Sharī'a* by ordering the state-owned Gianaclis wineries to switch to the production of non-alcoholic beverages and raisins,[26] by stopping the sale of alcohol on the flights of Egypt Air,[27] by banning gambling in tourist hotels,[28] and even by lengthening legal working hours.[29]

MPs from the Muslim Brothers repeatedly called for *awqāf* lands to be returned to the Ministry of *Awqāf*, after at least 150,000 *faddān* had been transferred to the Ministry of Agriculture as part of the land reform, in violation of the *Sharī'a*. The ministry needed the income from this land to fulfil its task of supervising the mosques and securing qualified personnel for the tasks of preaching and leading the prayers. *Awqāf* lands were set aside for the purposes of the faith in the first place and should not be used for other things. Failure to correct this would be punished on the Day of Judgment, said Ḥasan al-Gamal.[30]

Of primary importance to Muslim Brother writers is the call for applying the *zakāt* system instead of the present system of taxation. However, it

[24] Ma'mūn al-Huḍaybī, MB Giza, 10 April 1990, *MMS*, F5, 3–47, ṭm, pp. 15–20, and Sayf al-Islām al-Bannā, MB Cairo, *ibid.*, pp. 24–6.

[25] Mukhtār Nūḥ, MB Cairo, *ibid.*, pp. 21–2. See also Ḥusayn Shaḥḥāta, "Al ta'mīn al-ta'āwunī badīl lil-ta'mīn al tijārī", *al-Nūr*, 27 December 1989, for an argument in favour of mutual insurance as a non-*ribā* Islamic alternative.

[26] Ḥasan Gawda, MB Banī Suwayf, People's Assembly, 11 June 1985, F4, 1–90, pp. 6722–32, and Ibrāhīm Shukrī, 27 December 1987, *MMS*, F5, 1–46, pp. 4237–56.

[27] Ibrāhīm Shukrī, People's Assembly, 27 December 1987, *MMS*, F5, 1–46, pp. 4237–56, and Basyūnī Basyūnī, MB Alexandria, 13 January 1988, *MMS*, F5, 1–58, pp. 4670–702.

[28] Ḥasan Gawda, MB Banī Suwayf, People's Assembly, 11 June 1985, *MMS*, F4, 1–90, pp. 6722–32.

[29] Ḥasan Gawda, MB Banī Suwayf, People's Assembly, 5 May 1985, *MMS*, F4, 1–75, pp. 4891–912, cf. Ibrāhīm Shukrī, 27 December 1987, *MMS*, F5, 1–46, pp. 4237–56.

[30] People's Assembly, 25 June 1987, *MMS*, F5, 1–20, ṭm, pp. 3–42 and 12 February 1990, *MMS*, F5, 3–30, ṭm, pp. 4–33. Cf. also Basyūnī Basyūnī, MB Alexandria, 13 January 1988, *MMS*, F5, 1–58, pp. 4670–702.

is hard to see what is so unique to the *zakāt* except for its name and its religious legitimation (which might of course turn out to be of importance), especially since it is argued that the state may claim taxes over and above the fixed rates of the *zakāt* if the need should arise.

Consequently, with regards to the question raised above, about the possible distinguishing traits of an Islamic economic solution, the answer primarily revolves around the Islamic prohibition of usury, *ribā*, and the Islamic financial institutions that claimed to offer non-*ribā* services.

"God has laid His curse on usury ...": Islamic financial institutions

The debate over the question of usury, or *ribā*, centred on the issue of whether the interest paid by banks to their depositors and claimed from their debtors should be identified with the *ribā* condemned and forbidden by God in the Koran. The debate gained its heat from the struggle over the exponential growth of the so-called "Islamic investment companies" in the 1980s. And this was interwoven with a power struggle between the government and the "Islamic" private sector of the economy. But before looking at that in greater depth, it is worth considering the more theoretical argument over the *ribā*.

In substance the current comments of the Islamists on this question do not differ markedly from the general ideas presented in chapter 3 above: interest is equivalent to *ribā* which is clearly forbidden by God, it contradicts the Islamic principle that work is the source of legitimate income, it is a parasite that stifles the productive dynamism of the society and increases the gap between rich and poor. On one occasion Ḥusayn Shaḥḥāta even stated that interest was *ribā* and as such one of seven mortal sins, that it was worse than a man marrying his own mother, and that anyone who declared it legal (*ḥalāl*) was an infidel (*kāfir*).[31]

Of some interest here are the arguments used in the polemics that broke out after first a former Minister of *Awqāf*, 'Abd al-Mun'im Nimr, and then the Muftī of Egypt, Ṭanṭāwī, had issued fatwās in the summer of 1989 in favour of bank interest and interest-yielding so-called "investment certificates" (*shahādāt istithmāriyya*), stating that no *ribā* was involved.

Writers from both the Muslim Brothers and the Labour Party complained that these *fatwās* were a retrograde step, reopening a debate that had been concluded long ago. At the introduction of modern banking to Egypt, the Muftī Bakrī al-Ṣadafī had pronounced that interest was for-

[31] Ḥusayn Shaḥḥāta, "Al-tandīd bil-muta'āmilīn bil-ribā fī ḍaw' al-qur'ān wal-sunna", *al-Nūr*, 27 May 1987.

bidden, which since that time had been supported nearly unanimously by *'ulamā*, both individually and in big conferences convened to discuss the issue.[32] The Islamists reiterated the view, which they considered that of an overwhelming consensus of *fuqahā'*, that the *ribā* forbidden in the Koran designates any risk-free return on the lending of money. 'Abd al-Ḥamīd al-Ghazālī emphasised that when the capital itself is guaranteed, no profit is allowed in Islam. Properly speaking the only loan acceptable in Islam is the "good loan" (*qarḍ ḥasan*[33]), which is interest-free. What Islam encourages is partnerships involving the sharing of loss or profit.[34]

The debate brought to light the evolving contradiction between the increasingly independent-minded al-Azhar under Gād al-Ḥaqq 'Ālī Gād al-Ḥaqq's leadership, which sided with the Islamists on the *ribā* issue, and the "government Islam" of the *Awqāf* ministry and the *Dār al-iftā'* of the Muftī. The latter was accused by the Islamists of tailoring its *fatwās* according to the wishes of the rulers. As the Islamists saw it, when the government issued investment certificates and the so-called "dollar bonds" in order to attract the savings of Egyptians working abroad, the Muftī willingly said what the government needed to convince the people that these were legitimate ways of investing.

The argument that interest really represents the profit made by the investment that the funds are used for, and is therefore in line with Islam, was ruled out by the Islamists. For it was known, said Ḥusayn Shaḥḥāta, that the general rate of return on investment in the public sector hovered around 1 percent, while the interest rate on the dollar bonds was 16 percent. In reality, he said, the money gathered through these mechanisms did not go to investment but to service the enormous foreign debt.[35]

When the Minister of Economy decided to change the name of the profit on the investment certificates from "interest" (*fā'ida*) to "return" (*'ā'id*) in order to avoid the debate, the Islamists declared this was just a scam and that these investment mechanisms were as *ḥarām* as ever.[36]

However, apart from drawing on Scripture the Islamists also argued against interest based on its social and economic effects. Ḥusayn Shaḥḥāta

[32] 'Abd al-Ḥamīd Al-Ghazālī, "Ḥawla al-fawā'id al-maṣrafiyya: min al-aghlabiyya al-ṣāmita ilā jumhūr al-iqtiṣādiyyīn", *al-Ahrām al-iqtiṣādī*, 9 October 1989.

[33] A benevolent loan free of interest, the repayment of which is not imperative. See Muhammad Abdul Mannan, *Islamic Economics: Theory and Practice*, Hodder and Stoughton, Cambridge, 1986, p. 132.

[34] "'Ulamā' al-sharī'a wa asātidhat al-iqtiṣād al-islāmī yunāqishūn al-fawā'id al-maṣrafiyya bayna al-ibāḥa wal-taḥrīm", *al-Qabas*, 25 August 1989.

[35] See 'Imād al-Shīwī, "Wal-sanadāt al-dūlāriyya ayḍan ghayr shar'iyya", *al-Nūr*, 27 December 1989.

[36] Ḥamdī al-Baṣīr, Muḥammad Fatḥallāh and Muḥammad Sālimān, "Mashrū' wazīr al-iqtiṣād khuḍ'a i'lāmiyya", *al-Nūr*, 31 January 1990.

stated that rather than being a compensation for inflation, a claim some made to justify it, interest was a central factor in producing inflation. Basically inflation, he said, was caused by the government's printing of money to cover the increasing gap between its revenues and its ever-increasing expenses, a gap that was not least a result of the servicing of accumulated external and internal debt. This way the money supply increased more than the production of goods and services. The government then reacted by increasing the interest rate in order to draw money away from the market. But this caused a new bout of inflation, since producers and traders passed the cost of the interest on to consumers through price increases. As a result government expenses increased further, the negative spiral movement of inflation was in motion, and the government debt and its dependence on foreign finance increased. Setting the rate of interest was clearly based on other considerations than compensating for the rate of inflation, since for instance in Egypt the rate was 12 per cent while inflation ran at 35 per cent.[37]

Here, 'Ādil Ḥusayn seems to imply, at least in one of his articles during this debate, that the interest received on bank deposits is not really *ribā* as long as the interest rate remains below that of inflation, since *ribā* means the guaranteed increase of capital without work, and the capital of the depositors actually *decreases* in real terms in the present Egyptian situation.[38]

It was further argued that interest was socially unjust, most basically because it represented a sort of parasitic tax exacted from the rest of society by those with accumulated money wealth,[39] but also because if the interest rate is lower than the average rate of profit, this would be unjust to the depositor/creditor, and if it was the other way around it would be unjust to debtors.[40]

If interest is unjust it is also uneconomic, the Islamists maintained. It skews the distribution of investment capital in favour of less efficient and less productive big capital, while strangling small scale ventures that involve more risk but are also in general more dynamic and efficient. This is precisely because the interest system is based on the guaranteed security of the initially invested (lent) capital plus a guaranteed and fixed

[37] Ḥusayn Shaḥḥāta, "Al-fā'ida al-ribawiyya wuqūd al-taḍakhkhum al-naqdī wa laysat ta'wīḍan 'anhu", *al-Nūr*, 23 August 1989. See also Shaḥḥāta's comments in 'Imād al-Shīwī, "Wal-sanadāt al-dūlāriyya ayḍan ghayr shar'iyya", *al-Nūr*, 27 December 1989.

[38] 'Ādil Ḥusayn, "Awqifū munāqashat al-fawā'id fa-hunāka su'āl akhṭar", *al-Sha'b*, 17 October 1989.

[39] Ḥusayn Shaḥḥāta, "Al-fā'ida al-ribawiyya wuqūd al-taḍakhkhum al-naqdī wa laysat ta'wīḍan 'anhu", *al-Nūr*, 23 August 1989.

[40] 'Abd al-Ḥamīd al-Ghazālī, "Ḥawla al-fawā'id al-maṣrafiyya: min al-aghlabiyya al-ṣāmita ilā jumhūr al-iqtiṣādiyyīn", *al-Ahrām al-iqtiṣādī*, 9 October 1989.

rate of profit (interest). Therefore under this system creditors will look above all for security, and since large businesses are more likely to be able to service their debt, whatever the success or failure of individual projects, they have the easiest access to credit. More generally the interest system also leads to a diminishing portion of capital being invested in risk-taking ventures, according to Ghazālī a major factor in the stagnation observed in the West since the early 1970s.[41] This highlights once again the concern of the Muslim Brothers for small and medium-scale entrepreneurs.

The Islamists are eager to dispel the fear that the banning of interest would mean denying the right of capital to a profitable return on its investment. In connection with the *ribā* debate the economist Sa'īd al-Naggār had written in defence of interest in *al-Ahrām*. He stated there are four factors of production: land, labour, capital and entrepreneur, all of which must have remuneration for their contribution. In this picture, he said, profit is the remuneration for the entrepreneur, while interest is that of capital, and dropping it would mean leaving capital without return. This again would lead to its maldistribution according not to profitability but to the political or social influence of various groups.

In their arguments against him both 'Ādil Ḥusayn and 'Abd al-Ḥamīd al-Ghazālī accepted that this was the common view among Western-trained economists. But the Islamic world needed independent thinking, wrote 'Ādil Ḥusayn. Both he and al-Ghazālī stressed that in Islam the distinction between capital and entrepreneur would perish, since credit would take the form of partnership and the sharing of profit and loss. So profit (*ribḥ*) would take the place of interest as the remuneration for capital, which would in this setting be an active risk-taking partner rather than a passive parasitic creditor.[42] Therefore there was no need for interest-carrying financial transactions since there were a number of alternatives conforming to Islamic standards and having to some extent been put to the test by Islamic banks and investment companies. These most importantly included *mushāraka*,[43] *muḍāraba*[44] and

[41] *Ibid.*

[42] 'Ādil Ḥusayn, "'An al-fawā'id al-maṣrafiyya marra ukhrā", *al-Sha'b*, 19 September 1989, and 'Abd al-Ḥamīd al-Ghazālī, "Ḥawla al-fawā'id al-maṣrafiyya: min al-aghlabiyya al-ṣāmita ilā jumhūr al-iqtiṣādiyyīn", *al-Ahrām al-iqtiṣādī*, 9 October 1989.

[43] Applied to banking this is a system whereby the bank enters into partnership with the client for a limited period on a certain project. The bank and the client each contribute a part of the capital for the project, and in the case of a profit they will share it according to prior agreement, primarily based on the relative weight of their capital contribution. See Mannan, *Islamic Economics*, p. 201. *Mushāraka* is also often used as a more general term encompassing all three forms mentioned here and some others.

[44] In this case the bank/creditor provides the capital and the client the entrepreneurial skills, and they agree in advance on the distribution of profits. Any loss is born by the creditor. Mannan, *Islamic Economics*, p. 201.

murābaḥa.[45] The Islamists urged the government to encourage those forms of finance,[46] and to allow banks to form trading and industrial companies after the model of the famous "national capitalist" of the inter-war years, Ṭal'at Ḥarb, and his Bank Miṣr.[47]

Typically for the concern of mainstream Islamists to present an image of moderation and responsibility, however, they emphasised that reform would have to be gradual and that a total elimination of *ribā* transactions could only be effected after a transition period that would take years. Regarding dealings with foreign countries, relations involving interest payment might be upheld as a matter of necessity, but a conscious effort should be made to develop non-*ribā* financial relations with other Muslim countries.[48] In this connection it was stated that the *ribā*-system caused the rich states to dominate the poor, and that its use represented a continuation of colonialism within the economic culture. Full emancipation required its abolition.[49]

'Ādil Ḥusayn took special care to emphasise that his party did not condemn those Egyptians who were forced to deal with the *ribā*-infested institutions out of a lack of alternatives. Had the Muftī in his *fatwā* restricted himself to condoning the involvement in interest-carrying dealings on the basis of the Islamic principle that necessity makes legal what is otherwise forbidden, there would have been no discussion, he said.[50]

Finally two aspects of the Islamists' intervention in the *ribā* debate might be worthy of notice. On the one hand there was a conservative streak that claimed such a question as the legality of interest should preferably be solved by *fiqh* experts, and not by politicians. (Although this

45 Here the bank purchases commodities for its client and sells them back at an agreed mark-up with payment deferred. This is a form of credit accepted as legal by Islamists, but not favoured, and Islamic banks are criticised for concentrating too much of their business in the form of *murābaḥa* contracts. Mannan, *Islamic Economics*, pp. 201–2. This is one of the age-old *ḥiyal* (ruses) developed by the jurists to circumvent the *Sharī'a* interest ban. It is also known as *bay' al-ajl*.

46 'Imād al-Shīwī, "Wal-sanadāt al-dūlāriyya aydan ghayr shar'iyya", *al-Nūr*, 27 December 1989.

47 Sayf al-Islām al-Bannā in the People's Assembly, 24 June 1987, *MMS*, F5, 1–18, ṭm, pp. 2–31.

48 'Ādil Ḥusayn, "'An al-fawā'id al-maṣrafiyya marra ukhrā", *al-Sha'b*, 19 September 1989, Yūsuf al-Badrī, Liberal Party, The National Assembly, 23 June 1987, *MMS*, F5, 1–16, ṭm, pp. 2–19, and 'Izz al-'Arab Fu'ād Ḥāfiẓ, MB Qalyūbiyya, 25 February 1990, *MMS*, F5, 3–36, ṭm, pp. 3–26.

49 Ḥusayn Shaḥḥāta, "Al-tandīd bil-muta'āmilīn bil-ribā fī ḍaw' al-qur'ān wal-sunna", *al-Nūr*, 27 May 1987, and "Al-ḥaqā'iq al-tā'iha wal-awrāq al-mukhtaliṭa fī qaḍīyat sharikāt tawẓīf al-amwāl", *Liwā' al-islām*, 9 January 1989.

50 'Ādil Ḥusayn, "Awqifū munāqashat al-fawā'id fa-hunāka su'āl akhṭar", *al-Sha'b*, 17 October 1989.

could of course be said to be contradicted by the eager participation of non-*'ālim* Islamists in the debate.)[51] On the other hand, while the debate on *ribā* was for the Islamists an opportunity to show the unique character of the Islamic alternative, they nevertheless time and again called Western thinkers to the witness stand in defence of their cause. A prime example was the Muslim Brother MP 'Izz al-'Arab Fu'ād Ḥāfiẓ who in his speech on the issue to the People's Assembly on 25 February 1990 cited Keynes, Veblen, Roosevelt and Karl Marx in support of his argument against interest.[52]

The "Islamic investment companies"

No doubt the most celebrated instance, at least internally in Egypt, of "re-Islamisation from below" in the economic field was the case of the meteoric rise and expansion of the so-called "Islamic investment companies" (IICs), and their subsequent conflict with the authorities and downfall, the reverberations of which were still being felt in the late 1990s.

In his 1989 book *The Great Financial Deception: The Political Economy of the Investment Companies*,[53] Maḥmūd 'Abd al-Faḍīl, Professor of Economics at the University of Cairo, and a leftist, links the emergence of the companies to the vast number of Egyptians who since the liberalisation of work migration under the *infitāḥ* came to work in the oil countries of the Gulf and Libya. Between them these workers earned enormous sums of money by Egyptian standards, and then faced the problem of how to transfer it back to their families. Here the question of the exchange rate arose. While the state still in the 1970s and 1980s kept an "artificially" high exchange rate for the Egyptian pound, a host of currency dealers were ready to step into the breach. Offering a rate well above the official one, they ensured most of the remittances went outside the official banking system. From the outset it was common that the transaction involved a time lag: the client would hand over his dollars to the dealer, but would only receive his due in local Egyptian currency at an agreed later date. Gradually this evolved into an informal banking system, where the currency dealers set themselves up as middle-men between the migrant

[51] See Yūsuf Kamāl's comments in Ḥamdī al-Baṣīr, "Wa-khubarā' al-iqtiṣād al-islāmī yu'āriḍūn al-muftī", *al-Nūr*, 27 September 1989, and 'Ādil Ḥusayn, "Awqifū munāqashat al-fawā'id fa-hunāka su'āl akhṭar", *al-Sha'b* 17 October 1989.

[52] *MMS*, F5, 3–36, ṭm, pp. 3–26.

[53] Maḥmūd 'Abd al-Faḍīl, *Al-khadī'a al-māliyya al-kubrā. Al-iqtiṣād al-siyāsī li-sharikāt tawẓīf al-amwāl* [The Great Financial Deception: The Political Economy of the Investment Companies], Dār al-mustaqbal al-'arabī, Cairo, 1989. For an interesting treatment of the Islamic investment companies see also Alain Roussillon, *Societés islamiques de placements de fonds et "ouverture économique"*, CEDEJ, Cairo, 1988.

workers, their families, and local credit-hungry businesses in Egypt. Many of them established firms known as "companies for the placement of funds" (*sharikāt tawẓīf al-amwāl*).[54]

Most of the migrants, who now possessed significant sums of money, had no experience in dealing with the ordinary banks. They also shared the scepticism, widespread outside the urban élite, towards what was seen as their un-Islamic *ribā* practices. This situation, combined with the general Islamic revival of the time, lead many of the *sharikāt* to proclaim themselves Islamic. These "Islamic investment companies" dispensed with a lot of bureaucracy, simply giving the depositors a paper stating that the money would be invested according to Islamic principles. 'Abd al-Faḍīl gives us examples of these contracts from some of the largest companies. In al-Sharīf the contract pertained to the category of *mushāraka* discussed above, and stipulates that the depositor will be considered a partner in whatever commercial or industrial activity the company ventures into, and will receive his or her share of the resulting profit or loss in proportion to the deposit or investment made. In al-Rayyān, perhaps the most famous case, the contract was one of *wikāla*: the company acted as the trusted agent of the depositor in the investment of the capital, and profit or loss was shared fifty-fifty between the two (somewhat like the system of *muḍāraba* outlined above). However, the depositor had virtually no rights except the right to receive his share. The full right to estimate the correct return due to the depositor in both the examples above lay with the manager of the company, "relying on his conscience" as the text put it. And the depositors also had no right to interfere in the running of the company.[55]

Despite so little guarantee for their money the depositors flocked to the companies to the detriment of the public sector banks. No doubt the companies' guarantees to follow Islamic precepts played a role. But so did the companies' offer of high returns, in the range of 24 per cent a year or 2 per cent a month, a figure pretty close to the inflation rate, which meant depositors were protected from the decimation of the purchasing-power of their savings. The richest depositors are said to have received even higher rates of up to 40 per cent a year.

'Abd al-Faḍīl divides the depositors into three groups. The first consisted of small savers, pensioners, widows and unskilled workers, whose average saving did not exceed five thousand Egyptian pounds. For this group the monthly return from their investment in the IICs was an indispensable addition to their income needed to secure the necessities of life.

[54] *Ibid.*, p. 11.
[55] *Ibid.*, pp. 28–30.

For group two, somewhat wealthier artisans, shopkeepers, officers and skilled workers, with savings from ten to a hundred thousand LE, the returns enabled them to add some luxury to life. Group three were the really wealthy people who put some of their capital ranging from 250,000 to 2 million pounds into the IICs in order to reap high returns and spread their capital for security. All these groups were important. No statistics had as yet been revealed regarding their relative weight, 'Abd al-Faḍīl wrote, but the total number of depositors was in the hundreds of thousands.[56]

With regard to the investment of the deposits 'Abd al-Faḍīl presents figures from 1984 showing that 49 per cent of IIC investments under Law 43 went into tourism. 24 per cent went into housing and was concentrated in tending to the wants of the more affluent classes. In comparison only 4 per cent went to industry and 9 per cent to agriculture. If this distribution continued it would mean that even if the companies were in a sense modernizing, by encouraging the investment of savings generally kept outside the credit system, they did not, judging by their investment choices, make any great contribution to the development effort.[57]

Some, says 'Abd al-Faḍīl, have seen in the growth of the "Islamic investment companies" a strengthening of civil society *vis-à-vis* the state, because here was a powerful group of private entrepreneurs independent of the state who were able to instigate economic activity that, in the expression of 'Ādil Ḥusayn, would make the sugar monopoly of 'Abbūd in the 1950s and the empire of Osman Ahmad Osman under the *infitāḥ* look like dwarfs. Because the companies designed themselves as Islamic and used this in competing for the means of the savers, the struggle around these companies turned into more than a question of the regulation of financial activities. It became a test of strength in a struggle where what was at stake was the future of the whole political and economic system. Only in this sense, says 'Abd al-Faḍīl, can we understand the heated defence of the companies by a newspaper like *al-Sha'b* (and also for a time *al-Wafd*). The main reason for this defence, he states, was neither the protection of the interests of the depositors and the livelihood of their families, nor an admiration for the investment performance of the companies. Rather the forces supporting the companies saw in them an indomitable power that would help to splinter the dominance of the state over the society.[58]

This became clear, he says, during the first crisis of the Rayyān company in November 1986. At the time the Wafd newspaper wrote in

[56] *Ibid.*, pp. 25–6.
[57] *Ibid.*, p. 36.
[58] *Ibid.*, p. 66.

criticism of what they saw as a government campaign to spread rumours against Rayyān. It is easy, *al-Wafd* wrote, to bring down a financial institution by spreading the idea that the company in question will not be able to meet its obligations. By doing precisely that, the government had caused a run from depositors wanting to withdraw their money. This had a domino effect. It caused a crisis of liquidity in the banks, who had to cash the cheques given by the company to depositors withdrawing their deposits. The banks then had to postpone the payment of these cheques. According to *al-Wafd* on 13 November 1986, depositors had withdrawn 150 million Egyptian pounds of a total of 1 billion LE that the company had deposited with the banks. This led to the extraordinary event of the Federation of the Banks of Egypt issuing a public declaration denying that there was any problem with serving the depositors of the investment companies, and stating that the bank deposits of the investment companies constituted only a "tiny share" of the capital controlled by the Egyptian banking system. In ʻAbd al-Faḍīl's estimate this incident merely demonstrated that despite their short time in existence the investment companies already carried an impressive weight within the Egyptian economy and, if they were to collapse, were capable of rocking the economic boat considerably.[59]

To demonstrate their Islamic character the companies were eager to establish connections to leading Islamic personalities and preachers, who could be used in advertising as guarantors of the religious piety of the venture. Among those personalities was the famous preacher Mitwallī al-Shaʻrāwī who time and again appeared in the ads of the Al-Hudā Miṣr company and kept close contacts with its chairman of the board Ṭāriq Abū Ḥusayn. Another was Dr. ʻAbd al-Ṣabūr Shāhīn, a former professor of the Faculty of *Uṣūl al-Dīn* at al-Azhar and a member of the Shūrā Council, the upper (and powerless) house of the Egyptian Parliament. Shāhīn was elected (without prior knowledge according to himself) to the board of al-Rayyān where he had a dollar deposit (a tiny—*zahīd*—one, in his own words), but later had to withdraw in conformance with the regulations for members of the *Shūrā* Council. A third was *shaykh* Ṣalāḥ Abū Ismāʻīl, a leading independent Islamist in the 1984–7 People's Assembly, who at one time had deposited with the Hilāl company 200,000 LE, which he claimed to have acquired through work for "Arab and Islamic media". Al-Hilāl subsequently went bankrupt and its owner Muḥammad Kamāl ʻAbd al-Ḥādī fled to America "never to return". The company was taken over by al-Rayyān, whom Abū Ismāʻīl felt had a style of business, including expensive advertising, that he did not like. He therefore demanded from

[59] *Ibid.*, pp. 66–7.

the director of investment the return of his remaining hundred thousand pounds without loss or profit.[60]

The companies also ventured into important sectors like publishing and private kindergartens and hospitals. This is seen by 'Abd al-Faḍīl as a conscious policy for tying important groups and interests to the companies in anticipation of future battles with the state.[61]

And the battle did come. On 7 June 1988 the People's Assembly voted in Law No. 146 on Reception of Funds for Investment (*qānūn talaqqī al-amwāl li-istithmārihī*), which imposed strict government control over the companies and ultimately led to the closure of all the major companies, their assets being placed under public administration. The writing had been on the wall for some time, and the Islamists had defended the companies against the coming storm, while criticising some of their practices and stressing the need for regulation by the state.

It must be emphasised that the Islamists always eagerly denied any direct connection between the Islamic investment companies and the Islamist political organisations.[62] "There is an analysis", wrote 'Abd al-Ḥamīd al-Ghazālī, "that is current, which says that the Islamic investment companies were established on the basis of currency trading. Then they supposedly grew as a part of the Islamic revival and in their turn supported the Islamic political tendency, representing its 'material' wing. This analysis is utterly false and is not worthy of comment".[63] However, on one occasion Muḥammad Ḥilmī Murād of the Labour Party suggested the government had a real fear of such a connection. He stated that this fear had prevented the government from developing a constructive relationship with the serious IICs, and referred to an incident where a contract between an IIC and the Cairo provincial authorities for setting up a minibus network had been cancelled because the government feared the minibuses might be used to transport Islamist demonstrators.[64]

While denying direct links to the IICs, the Islamists were acutely aware that the fate of the companies would influence that of their own movement.[65] If the IICs met with success this would reflect positively on the

[60] *Ibid.*, pp. 74–6.
[61] *Ibid.*, pp. 76–7.
[62] This is not to say there were no personal connections. For instance Ḥusayn Shaḥḥāta had worked as an auditor and consultant for several IICs.
[63] 'Abd al-Ḥamīd al-Ghazālī, "Sharikāt tawẓīf al-amwāl bayna islāmiyyat al-tawajjuh wa khaṭa' al-mumārasa (1)", *al-Nūr*, 25 January 1989. Cf. 'Ādil Ḥusayn, "9 ittihāmāt ḍidda sharikāt tawẓīf al-amwāl", *al-Sha'b*, 15 September 1987.
[64] Muḥammad Ḥilmī Murād, "Al-niẓām al-ḥākim yuqarrir iḥtikār al-majālis al-maḥalliyya wa khanq sharikāt tawẓīf al-amwāl", *al-Sha'b*, 14 June 1988.
[65] 'Ādil Ḥusayn, "Fī sharikāt al-amwāl: kayfa bada'a al-musalsal wa kayfa sa-yantahī?", *al-Sha'b*, 22 November 1988.

trend for Islamic revival in the broad sense. On the other hand they claimed the government was using the real and imagined faults of the companies as a weapon to strike at anything calling itself Islamic.[66]

Both before and after the introduction of Law No. 146 the Islamists presented a critical view of the practice of the Islamic investment companies on several counts. Most of this critique centred around two broad issues: the lack of security for the depositors' money, and the use of the funds collected by the companies in ways incompatible with the development needs of the country.

On the first point it was stated that the accounting practices of the companies had not evolved in keeping with the explosive growth in the sums of money they had come to control. Therefore there had been a clear need for regulation, not least securing the separation of the dealings of the companies from the personal economy of their owners.[67] The reform must also establish rules securing a flow of information to the depositors about the financial status of the companies and the use of their funds.[68]

The typical Islamist critique of the investment practices of the IICs is exemplified in an article Ḥusayn Shaḥḥāta wrote in early January 1989. Shaḥḥāta stated there was no doubt that there were negative sides to the activity of some of the investment companies "operating under the banner of Islam". Some of them were caused by ignorance, and some by people who were not serious and only out to exploit Islam for private gains. In any case true Islamic economic theory was innocent of these negative features, which included in Shaḥḥāta's view:

— The preference for investing in projects producing luxury goods and services, to the detriment of basic necessities.
— Investment of capital in such a way that it strengthened rich states or states hostile to Islam. The capital of Muslims was meant for the service of Muslims.
— Investment of capital in currency trade and speculation (*muḍāraba*) in international markets. Even if some *fuqahā'* may have accepted this practice it does not, from the point of view of Islamic economics, contribute to the comprehensive development of society.

66 See for instance Ḥasan al-Gamal, MB Cairo, in the People's Assembly, 25 June 1990, *MMS*, F5, 3–20, ṭm, pp. 3–42.

67 See Muḥammad Ḥilmī Murād, "Al-niẓām al-ḥākim yuqarrir iḥtikār al-majālis al-maḥalliyya wa khanq sharikāt tawẓīf al-amwāl", *al-Sha'b*, 14 June 1988, and 'Ādil Ḥusayn, "Fī sharikāt al-amwāl: kayfa bada'a al-musalsal wa kayfa sa-yantahī?", *al-Sha'b*, 22 November 1988.

68 See the comments by 'Alī Sulaymān of the Labour Party in Aḥmad Al-Suyūfī, "Al-sharikāt mushkila tuhimm kull bayt", *al-Sha'b*, 16 February 1988. Cf. Ḥamdī Al-Baṣīr, "Akbar tajammu' iqtiṣādī miṣrī yuṭālib bi-ilghā' al-ribā", *al-Nūr*, 15 June 1988.

On this point there are two things to be considered. One is the double meaning of the word *muḍāraba*. Here it is used pejoratively by Shaḥḥāta in the sense of speculation, but it is also a technical term in Islamic economics for one of the legal and recommended ways for investing capital. So Shaḥḥāta, like other Islamist writers, in their "symbolic revolution" are not absolute, but continue to mix the "new-old" Islamic vocabulary with the entrenched Western-inspired "modern" vocabulary. More importantly here is an instance of a Muslim Brother writer actually giving his holistic concept of what the development of an Islamic society requires priority over the rulings of the *fuqahā'* of old. There was a marked tendency among the Muslim Brothers after their resurrection to slide into an Azhar-style reliance on traditional *fiqh*. But Shaḥḥāta plays down the *fiqh* tradition here by stating that it is merely "some *fuqahā'*" who have accepted speculation. More significant, the argument for ignoring them is not that other *fuqahā'* think otherwise, but that the ultimate Islamic goal is the "comprehensive development of society".

— The haughty spending of capital on expensive advertising campaigns. This represented intemperateness and conceit and did not conform with Islamic principles.[69]

In a similar critical vein 'Ādil Ḥusayn as early as September 1987 stated that for the Labour Party the most important thing was not whether a company wrote Koranic verses on its banner, but whether its activity furthered the goal of an Islamic economy. Moving towards this goal necessitated above all a strengthening of independence, justice and development. Therefore the companies should reform their investment policies, move away from real estate speculation and trade in luxury articles and move into agricultural and industrial production. A little later in the year he criticised them for not choosing labour intensive technology suited for Egypt's conditions when they did invest in industry, and for investing in luxurious tourist accommodation instead of cheap housing for the poor. The Islamic investment companies should take Ṭal'at Ḥarb—the nationalist entrepreneur of the 1920s and '30s who created the Miṣr group—as a model in seeking to further national development. In this they should work *with* the public sector, but this would require a positive change in government attitudes towards the IICs as well. As was common among the Islamists Ḥusayn held up the al-Sharīf Islamic investment company as a positive example.[70]

[69] Ḥusayn Shaḥḥāta, "Al-ḥaqā'iq al-tā'iha wal-awrāq al-mukhtaliṭa fī qaḍīyat sharikāt tawẓīf al-amwāl", *Liwā' al-islām*, 9 January 1989.

[70] 'Ādil Ḥusayn, "Sharikāt tawẓīf al-amwāl al-mushkila wal-ḥall", *al-Sha'b*, 22 September 1987 and Al-baṭāla wal-siyāḥa wa sharikāt tawẓīf al-amwāl, *al-Sha'b*, 8 December 1987.

A strict view of the need for IICs to toe the line of national priorities for investment and development is also presented by the Muslim Brother economist 'Abd al-Ḥamīd al-Ghazālī. Writing in 1989 he claimed the position of the Islamic movement had been crystal clear all along. They fully supported companies who would collect the capital of the small saver, Muslim and non-Muslim alike, and invest them in economic projects for the best of the community in line with the priorities decided by the society and in conformity with the current laws. But the Islamists, Ghazālī claimed, were the first to condemn their conduct if they used the collected capital to deal in currency, speculate in precious stones or in stocks in the international markets, or even if they invested them in local projects that had a low priority for the development of the country, or if they sought to gain and exploit a monopoly of trade in some basic commodities. In that case, he said, "we call for them to be held responsible and corrected if possible, in defence of the capital of the depositors and the interest of society". He was also critical of the IICs' forging of special links with influential personalities, although here the blame was also placed with the government, whose practices made corruption the order of the day.[71]

In line with their critique of the investment companies, the Islamists criticised what they saw as a lack of appropriate government intervention towards the companies from the outset. Until the introduction of the new law in June 1988 there had been a lack of constructive action, and when action did come it was destructive.

Just three weeks before the government rushed the bill through Parliament, after a single day of debate, 'Ādil Ḥusayn discussed the issue in *al-Sha'b*. "The government has promised a new law regulating the work of these companies, but it has not fulfilled this promise", he said. More than two months before, wrote Ḥusayn, the Labour Party had called for the government to act quietly in order to rectify some apparent imbalances in the structure of several of the companies. Any responsible government in a situation with problems for important banks or companies would act to limit the damage to the economy at large. All governments but that of Egypt.[72]

In the view of the Islamists the government had been doubly wrong. Firstly, when the Islamic investment companies started to emerge in the late 1970s and early 1980s it failed to introduce legislation to safeguard

[71] 'Abd al-Ḥamīd al-Ghazālī, "Sharikāt tawẓīf al-amwāl bayna islāmiyyat al-tawajjuh wa khaṭa' al-mumārasa (1)", *al-Nūr*, 25 January 1989.

[72] 'Ādil Ḥusayn, "Al-mushīr Abū Ghazāla wa kuttāb al-ḥukūma wal-ḥamla ḍidda sharikāt tawẓīf al-amwāl", *al-Sha'b*, 17 May 1988.

the interests of the depositors. Secondly when the phenomenon grew to encompass over a hundred companies controlling more then ten billion LE, the government failed to constructively involve the serious ones among them in positive development projects. Instead bureaucratic obstacles were put in their way, inducing corrupt practices in order to curry favour with high-ranking officials.[73]

However, the government at the same time had in some ways been responsible for building public trust in the IICs, negatively by avoiding any action to regulate their activity and positively by seeking their assistance in certain situations. For instance on television Rayyān and the Prime Minister had been shown shaking hands when the government asked Rayyān for help in supplying it with foreign currency in a hurry.[74]

Fundamentally, however, the Islamists saw the government as hostile to the Islamic investment companies. Most basically this was not in their view caused by a fear of their alleged links to the Islamist movement, but was a question of money and power. Increasingly as the 1980s progressed, the government saw the companies as a dangerous competitor for the vast sums of foreign currency repatriated each year by Egyptians working abroad, especially in the Gulf and Libya.[75] This weakened the four large publicly owned banks, and thereby the government's hold on the economy. And despite the official commitment since 1974 to a market system with the private sector in the leading role, the governing circles did not seem prepared to accept the existence of powerful independent private actors in the economy.[76]

However, the government delayed its action, fearing a crisis for the IICs would translate into a crisis for the banks themselves, since vast sums of the companies' funds were at any time held in the banks. It chose to bide its time preparing the ground for the final onslaught.[77] By 1988 it was ready and launched what the Islamists saw as a campaign of black rumours spread by "government pens" against the companies, causing the depositors to panic and demand immediate recovery of their deposited funds.

73 Muḥammad Ḥilmī Murād, "Al-niẓām al-ḥākim yuqarrir iḥtikār al-majālis al-maḥalliyya wa khanq sharikāt tawẓīf al-amwāl", *al-Sha'b*, 14 June 1988 and 'Abd al-Ḥamīd al-Ghazālī, "Sharikāt tawẓīf al-amwāl bayna al-maraḍ al-hūlandī wal-maraḍ al-miṣrī wal-maraḍ al-bākistānī", *al-Sha'b*, 13 December 1988.

74 Muḥammad Ḥilmī Murād, "Min i'ṣār sharikāt al-Rayyān ilā mufāja'at tamāthīl al-ḥukkām", *al-Sha'b*, 22 November 1988.

75 Muḥammad Ḥilmī Murād, "Al-niẓām al-ḥākim yuqarrir iḥtikār al-majālis al-maḥalliyya wa khanq sharikāt tawẓīf al-amwāl", *al-Sha'b*, 14 June 1988.

76 'Ādil Ḥusayn, "Sharikāt tawẓīf al-amwāl al-mushkila wal-ḥall", *al-Sha'b*, 22 September 1987.

77 Muḥammad Ḥilmī Murād, "Al-niẓām al-ḥākim yuqarrir iḥtikār al-majālis al-maḥalliyya wa khanq sharikāt tawẓīf al-amwāl", *al-Sha'b*, 14 June 1988.

At first, wrote 'Ādil Ḥusayn in May 1988, he had thought the campaign merely heralded the season of the return of workers from abroad for their annual holidays, and that the government wanted to persuade them to put their savings into the banks instead of into the Islamic investment companies. But now it seemed the aim was much wider, and the campaign had reached a level where it affected all the IICs. "Why do they push some of the companies to close their activities and move their capital abroad?" he asked. "Do they imagine that the depositors will move their money to the public banks? We know that the IMF and the United States have been pushing the government to do something about the growth of the Islamic investment companies. But does the government not know that those circles don't care for our welfare?"[78]

According to the Islamists, the government campaign against the companies was a mixture of two kinds of accusation. First there were the blatant and conscious lies. These included allegations that the IICs were trafficking in drugs, and that they were financing terrorist actions planned outside the country. The Islamists also branded a lie the idea that the companies were financing moderate Islamists, i.e. the Muslim Brothers and the Labour Party. Rather, said 'Ādil Ḥusayn, the companies kept a distance from the Islamist movement, and to the extent that they did nurture relations with politicians, these would rather be linked to the government. Ḥusayn also placed in the category of "lies" the press claims that when some companies paid returns to their depositors of a yearly rate of 20 per cent, while reaping a similar profit for themselves, this could not possibly stem from a return on investment, but must be proceedings from criminal activity or, as bad, the paying of returns on older deposits from fresh deposits coming in. Those who make this claim, said Ḥusayn, carefully "forget" that the Islamic investment companies do not borrow money at interest. Other investors, who finance their projects through the banking system at 20 percent interest, are in many cases able to retain a profit of 20 per cent. So why not the IICs?[79]

Secondly the government campaign against the Islamic investment companies contained accusations that were partly true, but presented with a great deal of exaggeration and with ulterior motives. For instance this concerned allegations that some IICs were known to have paid bribes in dealing with the government. But, said Ḥusayn, everybody dealing with the government has to pay bribes. In particular he aimed to deny the idea that the activities of the IICs were one giant fraud. Opinions might vary as

[78] 'Ādil Ḥusayn, "Al-mushīr Abū Ghazāla wa kuttāb al-ḥukūma wal-ḥamla ḍidda sharikāt tawẓīf al-amwāl", *al-Sha'b*, 17 May 1988.

[79] 'Ādil Ḥusayn, "9 ittihāmāt ḍidda sharikāt tawẓīf al-amwāl", *al-Sha'b*, 15 September 1987.

to how beneficial they were from a socioeconomic point of view, but that was another question. Even if like everyone else IICs paid bribes to government officials, there was real business involved, and goods were actually produced and delivered. Even when the fact that leading IIC executives like Rayyān had been involved in the black market for foreign currency in the early 1980s was used to prove the fraudulent character of the IICs, Ḥusayn protested. Rather this experience was a qualification for the business and a reason for the confidence people had in the IICs, he said. These were not petty money dealers, but people running a system controlling billions of dollars. Formally it had been illegal, but it had to arise in a situation where there was a huge offer of dollars from people having worked abroad and in need of local currency for their families, and on the other hand a huge demand because of bureaucratic obstacles hindering people's access to foreign currency. And there was not a single Egyptian, Ḥusayn claimed, from the top of society to the bottom, including the government, who had not at one time or another done business with these money dealers.[80]

The allegations that were partly true also included the fact that the companies invested a lot of their capital abroad and did not sufficiently contribute to productive projects in accordance with national priorities. The Islamists shared this criticism. But, 'Ādil Ḥusayn wrote, these were general phenomena, and the accusations were also true of the rest of the private sector and even of the public sector banks, which kept huge sums abroad. In fact the net effect of the activity of the IICs was to take home 9 billion LE which would otherwise have remained abroad—the difference between their estimated accumulated capital and deposits of 10 billion LE and the 1 billion LE they had placed abroad. The problem of capital flight was caused not least by the bad climate for investment in Egypt. In Ḥusayn's view there was no reason why the Islamic investment companies should be singled out for attack on these counts.

As to the charges that there was no supervision of the IICs from the Central Bank, he agreed that this was a problem, but here the culprit was government incfficiency. Effective control could well be established based on existing regulations. As for the problem of insufficient safeguards for the capital of the depositors something should be done, but Ḥusayn questioned the motives of the government on this count. Could anyone trust the government's sincerity, when it watched the people being squeezed by exorbitant prices for food, housing and health services without moving a finger, he asked.[81]

80 'Ādil Ḥusayn, "Kānat hunāka nawāqiṣ wa-inḥirāfāt wa-lākin lam takun al-mas'ala mujarrad 'amaliyyat naṣṣāb", *al-Sha'b*, 29 February 1988 and "Ittaqi allāh yā Bahā'", *al-Sha'b*, 6 December 1988.

81 'Ādil Ḥusayn, "9 ittihāmāt ḍidda sharikāt tawẓīf al-amwāl", *al-Sha'b*, 15 September

In the view of the Islamists, not only were most of the accusations against the Islamic investment companies either simply untrue or else grossly exaggerated, but most important, the serious IICs constituted a positive innovation and had made many positive contributions. The late 1970s and early 1980s had seen an unprecedented flow of foreign currency into the country. Millions of Egyptians had found well-paid jobs in the major Arab oil producing countries, and this for the first time created a situation in which several million Egyptian families had a surplus to save. Here the Islamic investment companies stepped in and for several reasons became the preferred medium for the savings of the expatriates. First, unlike the state banks they operated without interest, making this way of investing seem more *ḥalāl* to people raised in a traditional Islamic environment and cherishing Islamic values. Secondly, their procedures were simple and based on personal trust. And thirdly, by paying regular monthly returns to their depositors, they provided a secure income for those many families that were hard hit by the deteriorating real value of the wages of family members working in the government or public sector.[82]

In early 1989 Ḥusayn Shaḥḥāta summed up his view of the IICs' positive contributions:

— They had provided an Islamic model of investment based on the principle of *mushāraka*, as an alternative to the *ribā* system that basically meant gaining by the loss of others. International financial institutions had lauded this experiment and many international *ribawī* banks had started to practice it.
— They had thereby provided an outlet for the many that were not happy dealing with the *ribā* system, an invention of the Jews.
— They had started numerous projects in industry, agriculture and the services, which, Shaḥḥāta emphasised, had been controlled and found in order by people from the Central Auditing Agency.
— They had created employment for a lot of people, thereby easing the burden on the state in this field.
— They had contributed to increasing the revenues of the state through their payment of tax, customs duties and different kinds of fees. This amounted to many billions in addition to what they spend as *zakāt* for the poor.

1987 and "Fī sharikāt al-amwāl: kayfa bada'a al-musalsal wa kayfa sa-yantahī", *al-Sha'b*, 22 November 1988.

[82] See Muḥammad Ḥilmī Murād in "Qānūn tawẓīf al-amwāl yadkhul dā'irat al-khilāf al-ḥizbī", *al-Ḥawādith*, 19 August 1988, where he is even joined by Ismā'īl Ṣabrī 'Abdallāh of the *Tajammu'* party in a positive view of the IICs. Cf. 'Abd al-Ḥamīd al-Ghazālī, "Sharikāt tawẓīf al-amwāl bayna al-maraḍ al-hūlandī wal-maraḍ al-miṣrī wal-maraḍ al-bākistānī", *al-Sha'b*, 13 December 1988.

— They had trained many people who were now capable of working and exercising leadership according to the Islamic model.

Both the state and Muslims in general should support the serious Islamic investment companies and neither believe nor spread any rumour about them without investigating, Shaḥḥāta wrote. Those making mistakes should be corrected, and those only exploiting the label "Islamic" should be exposed and either set right or stopped from using this name. The state should also establish Islamic economics as a subject in the universities in order to produce the knowledgeable experts needed to develop the field of Islamic investment.[83]

'Ādil Ḥusayn, while not disagreeing with any of Shaḥḥāta's points, put the stress on the positive *potential* of the IICs in two senses. For one thing they were creating a powerful economic centre outside the government with possible positive repercussions both for the economic dynamism of the society and for the chances for future political pluralism. The government must realise that the state no longer possessed a monopoly over financial resources and their allocation, he wrote.[84] Why should the private sector be limited to breeding chickens, he asked, why should they not build steel factories and reclaim wasteland?[85] Secondly he stated that for a large part the activity of the IICs constituted a national (*waṭanī*) effort to employ some of the vast sums of foreign currency available to the country in building local economic activity.[86] Ḥusayn was not uncritical, though. He clearly wanted the IICs to develop a stronger sense of national responsibility for the use of resources, and hoped to see them as a sort of "patriotic bourgeoisie", as can be seen in his frequent admonitions to them to take Ṭal'at Ḥarb as a model.[87]

Since the Islamists acknowledged the existence of grave problems in the way the IICs were run, they remained committed to the need for reform and regulations. But they were adamant these reforms must be made so as to provide an environment in which the IICs could grow and prosper, while increasing the security for the depositors and channelling the resources more into productive investment. In this they differed from the government, which was especially noticeable when the latter launched the new law regulating the investment companies in June 1988.

[83] Ḥusayn Shaḥḥāta, "Al-ḥaqā'iq al-tā'iha wal-awrāq al-mukhtaliṭa fī qaḍīyat sharikāt tawẓīf al-amwāl", *Liwā' al-islām*, 9 January 1989.

[84] 'Ādil Ḥusayn, "Al-mushīr Abū Ghazāla wa kuttāb al-ḥukūma wal-ḥamla ḍidda sharikāt tawẓīf al-amwāl", *al-Sha'b*, 17 May 1988.

[85] 'Ādil Ḥusayn, "Mādhā yaqūl al-qānūn al-ghādir al-ẓālim", *al-Sha'b*, 7 June 1988.

[86] 'Ādil Ḥusayn, "Bal tuṣaffūn al-sharikāt wa li-maṣlaḥat al-ajānib", *al-Sha'b*, 28 June 1988.

[87] 'Ādil Ḥusayn, "Sharikāt tawẓīf al-amwāl al-mushkila wal-ḥall", *al-Sha'b*, 22 September 1987.

Writing in May 1988 'Ādil Ḥusayn commented upon statements by the then powerful Minister of Defence Abū Ghazāla. The Minister had recently said that the savings held outside the banks were between 23 and 30 billion dollars and that they must be encouraged to enter the field of investment. He had suggested that an amnesty be announced so that everybody could invest without being asked where their capital came from. This would be a dangerous move, said Ḥusayn, that needed a lot of consideration because it could open the road for drug traffickers, embezzlers and organised crime in general. What was urgently needed was to guarantee the safety of the capital of those millions of honest people who had worked in the Arab countries and deposited their hard-earned savings with the Islamic investment companies. Here legislation was needed to ensure the depositors had insight into the accounts and the budgets of the companies upon which the distribution of returns was based. The major companies had long since outgrown the phase where merely personal trust was sufficient. But security would not be created by making decisions overnight in obscure ways. No rash government decrees would bring the money of the IICs into the government's coffers. Any reform measures should be undertaken in a spirit of cooperation between the government and the companies, Ḥusayn warned.[88]

When the government finally decided to act they consulted neither with the companies nor with the opposition. The proposal for what came to be Law No. 146 of 1988 on the Reception of Funds for Investment was rushed through the People's Assembly in two sessions on 7 June 1988 with little time for the opposition even to read the final proposals properly. As official spokesman for the Islamic Alliance Ibrāhīm Shukrī at the outset of the debate complained bitterly at having received the final text of the proposal only the same morning.[89] In a seminar held the following week to discuss the new law, Ḥanafī Fahīm 'Uthmān, Muslim Brother MP from Cairo, added that there had not been enough copies to go round and that the first fifteen articles of the law were voted in after just fifteen minutes of discussion.[90]

The Islamists rejected the new law and quickly branded it the "Emergency Law for the Economy", in reference to the Emergency Law that had governed Egyptian political life since 1981.

88 'Ādil Ḥusayn, "Al-mushīr Abū Ghazāla wa kuttāb al-ḥukūma wal-ḥamla ḍidda sharikāt tawẓīf al-amwāl", *al-Sha'b*, 17 May 1988. Cf. also 'Ādil Ḥusayn, "Sharikāt tawẓīf al-amwāl al-mushkila wal-ḥall", *al-Sha'b*, 22 September 1987.

89 *MMS*, F5, 1–104, pp. 8482–516.

90 Aḥmad al-Suyūfī, "Innahū qānūn lil-ṭawāri' fī majāl al-iqtiṣād", *al-Sha'b*, 14 June 1988. Cf. Ḥamdī al-Baṣīr, "Thalāthūna khabīran iqtiṣādiyyan yunāqishūn ḥāḍir al-sharikāt wa mustaqbalaha", *al-Nūr*, 15 June 1988.

A number of objections were listed:

— In limiting the right to collect capital to joint stock companies, the law neglected the plethora of small cooperative *muḍāraba* projects, especially in the countryside, often concluded between individuals on a basis of personal trust, a typical case being that a farmer agrees to feed and look after animals owned by another in return for a share of the eventual profit in accordance with a prior agreement.[91]

— Even if the investment companies should according to Law 146 take the form of joint stock companies, Law 159 of 1981 on joint stock companies would not apply. Strict limits were set on the capital: a minimum of 5 million LE for the founding capital—ten times as much as for other joint stock companies—and the shareholders' capital would not be allowed to grow beyond 50 million LE. These limits would exclude small projects and also hit the largest existing companies which were already far above the ceiling of 50 million LE. Furthermore the founders would not be allowed to sell their shares till five years after the founding of the company, also an undue restriction of the flexibility of the companies and something that might scare potential investors away.

— The right to hold stocks would be limited to Egyptians. This might in itself seem good, but in view of the fact that foreigners were allowed to operate in the field of traditional banking, this clause was meant to exclude Arabs, perhaps fearing the support they might mobilise from their governments in case the state threatened the interests of the investment companies.

— The companies would no more be allowed to pay monthly dividends to their depositors, but must do so only on a yearly basis.

— The law gave far too wide powers to the Capital Market Authority (*hay'at sūq al-māl*) and the Central Auditing Agency (*al-jihāz al-markazī lil-muḥāsabāt*) to interfere in the running of the companies. In particular the Authority was given the right to refuse licensing a new company, or to withdraw license from an existing company on the basis of a report from the Ministry of the Interior indicating that its activity was harmful to "national security" or to the "public (*'āmm*) economic interest". These were elastic expressions that would give freedom of interpretation to the Authority and the Ministry for the Interior.

The Authority and the Agency were also given the right to appoint special auditors and board members when this was deemed necessary

[91] This criticism seems to have been accepted, and the law in its final shape exempted these kind of projects from its regulations. Cf. Ḥanafī Fahīm 'Uthmān in Ḥamdī al-Baṣīr, "Thalāthūna khabīran iqtiṣādiyyan yunāqishūn ḥāḍir al-sharikāt wa mustaqbalaha", *al-Nūr*, 15 June 1988.

and to regulate the distribution of investments between fields of economic activity. All this would amount to setting aside the companies' own leading organs and to make the business highly insecure and therefore unattractive.

— The provisions for a transition period in which the existing companies would be given a chance to bring their affairs into conformity with the new law were highly unfavourable for the companies. For instance they would have to freeze their operations and not receive any new deposits for three months while waiting for the government to issue the detailed provisions for how the law should be put into effect, something that would damage their operations and cause capital to flee from the country.

— The provisions for possible exemptions for individual companies after an application to the government would create an additional breeding ground for corrupt back-door practices, especially in view of the harsh provisions of the law itself.[92]

While the Islamists rejected the new law, during the debate in the People's Assembly they suggested several minor changes in order to ameliorate the ensuing crisis for the IICs and their depositors: lowering the minimum limit for founding capital of a company from 5 million LE to 1 million LE[93] or even to 500,000 LE;[94] removing the rule preventing founders from selling their shares during the initial five years of the company's existence, or reducing it to two years, which was the rule for ordinary joint stock companies;[95] reducing the right of interference for the Capital Market Authority and other government agencies;[96] and dropping the reference to "national security" as a reason for refusing or withdrawing the license of a company.[97]

The Islamists considered the law and its results a national catastrophe. They stated that its obvious intent had been to kill off the investment companies and that its effect would be to drive them to liquidation. According

92 'Ādil Ḥusayn, "Mādhā yaqūl al-qānūn al-ghādir al-ẓālim", *al-Sha'b*, 7 June 1988, Ibrāhīm Shukrī, People's Assembly, 7 June 1988, *MMS*, F5, 1–104, pp. 8482–516, and Muḥammad Ḥilmī Murād, "Al-niẓām al-ḥākim yuqarrir iḥtikār al-majālis al-maḥalliyya wa khanq sharikāt tawẓīf al-amwāl", *al-Sha'b*, 14 June 1988.

93 Ibrāhīm Shukrī, People's Assembly, 7 June 1988, *MMS*, F5, 1–104, pp. 8482–516.

94 Maḥfūẓ Ḥilmī, MB Gharbiyya, People's Assembly, 7 June 1988, *MMS*, F5, 1–104, pp. 8482–516.

95 Ibrāhīm Shukrī, People's Assembly, 7 June 1988, *MMS*, F5, 1–105, pp. 8539–74.

96 See the interventions by Ibrāhīm Shukrī, Sayf al-Islām al-Bannā, MB Cairo, Maḥfūẓ Ḥilmī, MB Gharbiyya, Ma'mūn al-Huḍaybī, MB Giza and 'Iṣām al-'Iryān, MB Giza, People's Assembly, 7 June 1988, *MMS*, F5, 1–105, pp. 8539–74.

97 See the interventions of Muḥy al-Dīn 'Isā, MB Minya, and Ibrahīm Shukrī, People's Assembly, 7 June 1988, *MMS*, F5, 1–104, pp. 8482–516.

to 'Ādil Ḥusayn the law stipulated compulsory placements in reserve funds and the like, that would leave the owners with a return of merely 4 to 5 per cent if the overall return on the capital was 15 per cent. If this did not drive the companies out of business, then the requirement that the equity capital be at least 10 per cent of the total funds held by the companies would. Since these were estimated at 10 billion LE, the companies would have to raise 1 billion in shareholders' equity in order to be allowed to continue their activity. This seemed near impossible. Furthermore the law stipulated that those companies that could not meet this and the other requirements in the new law would then have one year to liquidate their assets and reimburse depositors. This situation would almost certainly arise for all or most of the companies. But how could assets worth 10 billion LE be sold off in a year? The result would be that the assets would be auctioned off at far below their real value, ruining owners and depositors alike. Especially hard hit would be the small and medium-size depositors. Meanwhile, the company owners could profit from the contact network they had taken care to build within government circles. They would be able to strike deals where they would secure the repayment of the deposits of high-placed officials in return for the chance to export themselves and their money. A huge flight of capital was the likely outcome.[98] Ḥusayn Shaḥḥāta estimated that at least 40 per cent of the value would be lost this way.[99] The destruction of the IICs would also negatively effect the national economy at large, since it would destroy the climate for private investment for a long time to come.[100] And there was no reason to believe that the savings of labour migrants would instead fill the state-owned banks, rather they would be spent in consumption or kept abroad.[101]

The predictions proved right in so far as all the major companies were unable to meet the requirements, and were one after the other put under administration by the General Prosecutor's office in order to be sold off. And the depositors got little or none of their deposits back.

In December 1989 'Ādil Ḥusayn commented that the current plans of selling off 3 billion LE of the companies' assets in 6 months was sheer

98 'Ādil Ḥusayn, "Bal tuṣaffūn al-sharikāt wa li-maṣlaḥat al-ajānib", *al-Sha'b*, 28 June 1988 and "Kārithat al-mūdi'īn fī sharikāt al-tawẓīf", *al-Sha'b*, 1 November 1988. See also "Fī sharikāt al-amwāl: kayfa bada'a al-musalsal wa kayfa sa-yantahī", *al-Sha'b*, 22 November 1988.

99 Aḥmad al-Suyūfī, "Al-qānūn al-jadīd yaḥmī ḥuqūq al-mūdi'īn am yuhdir amwālahum", *al-Sha'b*, 5 July 1988.

100 'Ādil Ḥusayn, "Kārithat al-mūdi'īn fī sharikāt al-tawẓīf", *al-Sha'b*, 1 November 1988. Cf. 'Abd al-Ḥamīd al-Ghazālī, "Sharikāt tawẓīf al-amwāl bayna al-maraḍ al-hūlandī wal-maraḍ al-miṣrī wal-maraḍ al-bākistānī", *al-Sha'b*, 13 December 1988.

101 Muḥammad Ḥilmī Murād in Aḥmad al-Suyūfī, "Al-qānūn al-jadīd yaḥmī ḥuqūq al-mūdi'īn am yuhdir amwālahum", *al-Sha'b*, 5 July 1988.

madness from a national point of view. It meant auctioning off Egypt. Prices would drop to below 50 per cent of real values, and the only ones in a position to buy were foreigners, including the Zionists, albeit via middlemen. The Westerners and the Israelis were the only ones who would not be afraid to buy, since they had a grip on the Egyptian government and would not fear for the future confiscation of their investment.[102]

The Islamists advanced several proposals for how the government should deal with the disastrous situation it had created. Some of these concerned revisions in Law 146.

In July 1988 Ḥusayn Shaḥḥāta had already argued that the companies must be allowed to finish projects under construction that had been ordered shut down with reference to the law. These projects must be finished, he argued, to rescue the funds invested in them and to secure the interests of the workers.[103] In December 1988 'Abd al-Ḥamīd al-Ghazālī demanded a whole new law regulating the IICs together with the Islamic banks, considering them a new type of business and investment bank based on short term deposits and operating according to the principle of *mushāraka*.[104] The Islamists also called for the government to contribute money to cover the depositors' losses, since it had created the crisis in the first place.[105]

Gradually, as the demise of the companies seemed irreversible, the suggestions became more concerned with easing the terms for liquidation. In January 1990 'Iṣām al-'Iryān suggested in the People's Assembly that the companies be given 2 years to liquidate their assets after a final court decision, instead of 6 months, in order to reduce the risk of having to sell at low prices. In the same vein he suggested the companies be allowed to return the investment to the depositors in kind. A lot of the assets, he argued, were in land holdings, which foreigners were not allowed to buy, and for which there were no buyers in Egypt. Or, he asked, did the government intend to let the foreigners in the back door?.[106]

Although the above points of view were generally shared between the Labour Party and its Muslim Brother allies, there were some nuances to the picture. For one thing, and unsurprisingly, at the time of the introduction of Law 146 the later "socialist" defectors from the Labour Party

102 'Ādil Ḥusayn, "Bay' miṣr fī al-mazād wa qaḍīyat al-qiṭā' al-'āmm", *al-Sha'b*, 12 December 1989.

103 Aḥmad al-Suyūfī, "Al-qānūn al-jadīd yaḥmī ḥuqūq al-mūdi'īn am yuhdir amwālahum", *al-Sha'b*, 5 July 1988.

104 'Abd al-Ḥamīd al-Ghazālī, "Sharikāt tawẓīf al-amwāl bayna al-maraḍ al-hūlandī wal-maraḍ al-miṣrī wal-maraḍ al-bākistānī", *al-Sha'b*, 13 December 1988.

105 'Ādil Ḥusayn, "Aḥmad Bahā' al-Dīn wa miḥnat sharikāt al-amwāl", *al-Sha'b*, 29 November 1988.

106 *MMS*, F5, 3–29, ṭm, pp. 3–12.

were far more critical of the IICs and tended to toe the government line. Gamāl As'ad, the Coptic Labour Party MP from Asyūṭ, hailed the proposed law as necessary to protect the depositors' interests, and stated that the companies harmed national security by engaging in speculation in currency and precious metals. According to the constitution we are supposed to be a socialist country, he said, and therefore only the banks should collect people's savings. For this he earned massive applause from the NDP deputies.[107]

We might also detect a slight difference between 'Ādil Ḥusayn and leading Muslim Brothers in their attitudes towards the IICs. Perhaps somewhat surprising, it is the latter who show the most critical attitude towards the companies. In December 1987 Sayf al-Islām al-Bannā argued in the People's Assembly that the state had more right to the money that the IICs had collected since it needed it for development, which it could effect if it turned the national banks over to Islamic banking and established a government *zakāt* system.[108] In contrast 'Ādil Ḥusayn argued for the positive effect of having a large privately owned financial sector that could break the government monopoly. As has been seen, 'Abd al-Ḥamīd al-Ghazālī pronounced harshly on the speculative companies. In December 1988 he argued that the government must strike with an iron fist against the swindlers among the companies,[109] while 'Ādil Ḥusayn strongly questioned the idea that swindling had been a common feature.

To a great extent these may be differences in tactical approach, with 'Ādil Ḥusayn following a more confrontational style towards the government and its defenders. In some measure it may also reflect the fact that the Muslim Brothers were more closely attached to the Islamic Banks who felt hemmed in by government regulations and harboured envy at the success of the IICs. The exception here is Ḥusayn Shaḥḥāta, who had been working for several IICs.

Islamic banks

Alongside the Islamic investment companies, and in the Egyptian case in the shadow of them, there had since the 1970s existed a number of "Islamic banks" operating as regular banks, but on a non-*ribā* basis.

In 1986 the independent Islamic thinker Gamāl al-Dīn 'Aṭīya published a study of Islamic banks,[110] which, in contrast to 'Abd al-Faḍīl's work on

107 7 June 1988, *MMS*, F5, 1–104, pp. 8482–516.
108 *MMS*, F5, 1–47, pp. 4259–85.
109 'Abd al-Ḥamīd al-Ghazālī, "Sharikāt tawẓīf al-amwāl bayna al-maraḍ al-hūlandī wal-maraḍ al-miṣrī wal-maraḍ al-bākistānī", *al-Sha'b*, 13 December 1988.
110 Gamāl al-Dīn'Aṭīya, *Al-bunūk al-islāmiyya* [Islamic banks], Kitāb al-Umma, Qatar, 1987.

investment companies, was written from a viewpoint sympathetic to the Islamic revival by one who supported the idea of Islamic banks and had worked within the Islamic financial institutions. However, his study is a critical one, examining the relation between the practice of the banks and the rulings of the *Sharī'a*.

The first Islamic banks in the proper sense to be recognised by state authorities were the Dubai Islamic Bank in 1975 and the Sudanese and Egyptian branches of the Bank Fayṣal al-Islāmī in 1977. This was an expression of the rising tide of Islamic revival. Because of their religious convictions many citizens would only very reluctantly, or not at all, deal with the ordinary banking system. Accepting the emergence of Islamic banks meant that the governments allowed these people access to an alternative *ḥalāl* financial system, 'Aṭīya wrote.[111]

The basic principle of the Islamic banks were of course the same as that of the investment companies. *Ribā*, understood as the paying or receiving of a fixed interest rate, was replaced with the principle of *mushāraka*, that is partnership in profit or loss (the term *mushāraka* may also be applied to one particular form of this partnership, in contrast to others like *muḍāraba, murābaḥa* etc., cf. pp. 201–2, notes 43–45).

How did it all turn out in practice? 'Aṭīya's book was published in 1987 and from the experience gathered to that point, he saw an important problem in the development from a varied set of ideas on Islamic banking to one dominant practice. Early writers who theorised on an Islamic alternative to the "modern" banking system had presented a variety of suggestions like cooperative societies, government banks offering free services, specialised banks within agriculture, industry, housing, commerce etc., local savings banks and international banks for development and investment. Yet until the time of writing, 'Aṭīya said, the dominant tendency had been the creation of commercial banks in the form of joint stock companies. The only exceptions to this rule were the Islamic Development Bank, an international institution with governments of Islamic countries as participants and basically concerned with financing infrastructural projects against a service fee to cover costs, the Nāṣir Social Bank in Egypt, a governmental institution concerned primarily with social services like collecting and distributing the *zakāt* and offering loans, and Pakistani and Iranian state-owned banks, but they offered their services for a compensation (*bi-muqābil*) like the joint stock commercial banks.

Now, he said, there were those who justified the actual one-sidedness of Islamic banks with a reference to the comprehensiveness and integration of Islam as a system. Some claimed that the specialisation of varied

[111] *Ibid.*, p. 18. Cf. Mohamed Ariff, "Islamic banking", *Asian-Pacific Economic Literature*, vol. 2, no. 2 (September 1988), p. 1.

financial institutions would contradict this Islamic principle, but in 'Aṭīya's view this was neither confirmed by any text from the scriptures, nor was it in the interest of society.[112]

He pointed to the deplorable absence of Islamic institutions in several important fields:

— There was a lack of cooperative banks. The positive aspect of such banks was that there would be no clash of interests between the stock holders and the depositors and clients. In the statutes of some of the joint stock commercial Islamic banks various attempts had been made to put the depositors and the stock holders on equal terms, but this had not succeeded since the clash of interests was fundamental.

In fact the early writings on Islamic banks had suggested that the banks should be formed as cooperative societies. The problem was that the laws of the Arab countries permitted only joint stock companies to conduct business in the fields of banking, insurance and investment. This was all the worse since the laws of European countries, which were the model of most Arab laws, carried no ban against cooperative societies working in these fields, and indeed many large financial institutions were cooperative in nature.

Another advantage to cooperative societies, said 'Aṭīya, was the fact that in such a society every member would have one vote, whatever the size of his or her deposit, whereas in a joint stock company the number of votes would depend on the size of the portfolio, which meant that the large stock holders could in practice direct the bank as they pleased. Some writers had even said that the cooperative form was the only possible form of a truly Islamic bank, and that other forms were in reality nothing but a capitalist entity bearing an Islamic name.

— There was a lack of government banks offering services free or for a nominal service charge like that charged for other public services. This was not to be expected from private joint stock companies where the stock holders would expect a profit on their invested capital. But it was a problem that states that had turned their entire banking system into an Islamic system, mostly state-owned, did not implement such services.

— There was a lack of local development banks and specialised investment banks, with the sole exception of the Islamic Development Bank. There were no Islamic banks financing the development of small-scale productive projects initiated by individuals, companies, or for that matter public agencies. The private joint stock banks generally shied away from this for good reasons, since their assets were composed pri-

[112] 'Aṭīya, [Islamic banks], pp. 175–6.

marily of short term deposits and current accounts, while these kinds of projects would often either need a long time to pay back a loan or be in need of permanent investment.

— There was a lack of international banks that might coordinate the activities of Islamic banks and help to arrange mutual assistance in the case of funds shortages in some banks. Some had even suggested that such banks might perform central bank services to Islamic banks around the world, said 'Aṭīya, but this would violate state sovereignty and was not advisable.[113]

'Aṭīya then discussed the problem of the capital of the Islamic banks being invested outside the Islamic world. One of the main criticisms of the traditional banks made by the theoreticians of Islamic banking, he says, was that the system of interest made the banks mere middle-men for the collection of capital and its transport to wherever the highest interest rate was. Thereby the link between the owner of the capital and his capital was severed, and he was left with no control over where his capital was used. It might even be by his enemy or for some purpose that he would not condone. So Islamic banking would use the principle of direct investment. This way the link would be restored. Therefore it was expected that in light of the fact that most Islamic countries were developing countries in bad need of capital for investment, the capital of Islamic banks would primarily cover the needs of local productive projects, in the next place go to investment in other Islamic countries if there was a surplus left. Placing capital outside the Islamic world would only be done with a small fraction necessary for securing access to foreign currency. But the result, he said, was different. For the year 1984 the Kuwayti Bayt al-Tamwil placed 18 per cent of its capital outside the Islamic world, the Sudanese Bank Fayṣal 19 per cent and Bank Fayṣal of Egypt 43 per cent. It was true that the last figure had been declining, but still the figure was extremely high in view of the extreme need for investment capital in Egypt. This problem must be solved by expanding opportunities and channels for investing in Egypt and making the financial and monetary regime more flexible. "We must stop the current flow of money towards the West, not only from the Gulf countries but from a definitely non-capital-exporting country like Egypt", 'Aṭīya wrote. The banks of the West were now like the 'Abbāsī caliph in Baghdad who said: "if you are in the East or in the West, your tax will come to me".[114]

Another problem related to the relative weight given to the practice of *murābaḥa* to the detriment of *mushāraka* and *muḍāraba* in the banks' reinvestment of their deposits. In 1984 it ranged from 22 per cent of the placement of funds at the Bayt al-Tamwīl to 80 per cent at the Dubai

[113] *Ibid.*, pp. 176–9.
[114] *Ibid.*, pp. 180–3.

Islamic Bank, but most banks did not show the percentage in their published accounts. *Murābaḥa* was really no better than traditional interest, said ʻAṭīya, in that it did not expose the invested capital to risk, since the mark-up was agreed beforehand, irrespective of the outcome of the activity into which the purchased goods were put by the client. Another problem was that that activity was mostly import trade, and it would be hoped that the Islamic banks would give preference to productive projects, and within the field of trade to facilitating export.[115]

ʻAṭīya went on to show that while the initial priority given by the theoreticians of Islamic Banking was to facilitate credit flows to small scale industry and artisans, in reality it had come to be an additional source of finance to the rich.[116] He concluded by criticising the Islamic banking system for tending to become a group of institutions serving the existing capitalist system in stead of the vanguard of a distinct Islamic economy.[117]

As for pronouncements on the Islamic banks from members of the political organisations under scrutiny here, four years after ʻAṭīya's book was published, his critical views were reflected by Yūsuf Kamāl, leading Muslim Brother spokesman on economic questions. Kamāl claimed that the problems of the Islamic banks were created by their tendency to let action and application precede thinking and theory. He criticised the dominance of *murābaḥa*, a *ḥīla* (cf. p. 202, n. 45) with mainly negative effects, taking up 75 per cent of transactions by the banks. This turned the Islamic banks into commercial banks under the cover of being investment banks. The Islamic banks also neglected the financing of small projects, for instance among artisans.[118] Nevertheless Kamāl emphasised that his critique did not mean he put them on a par with the *ribā* banks. And when the Islamic banks came under attack from government and leftist circles, the Islamists took up a vivid defence.

In March 1987 Ḥusayn Shaḥḥāta wrote an article in *al-Nūr* devoted to a defence of Islamic banks against what he considered slanderous attacks. Not before have the *ʻulamāʼ* and *fuqahāʼ* found an Islamic alternative to the *ribawī* banking system, Shaḥḥāta writes, an alternative that brings a light in the darkness of the present *Jāhiliyya*, before the enemies of the Muslims try to slander the Islamic banks, and kill them off in the early phase of this great experiment. Small mistakes, he says, are being used by the media. He gives a list of the slanders, and provides answers to them:

— "The services are not good enough." Some clients have complained about bad and slow service and have moved to other banks. This inade-

[115] *Ibid.*, pp. 184–7.
[116] *Ibid.*, pp. 188–90.
[117] *Ibid.*, pp. 190–3.
[118] Magdī Muṣṭafā, "Miḥnat al-bunūk al-islāmiyya fī al-fikra am fī al-taṭbīq", *Liwāʼ al-islām*, 28 January 1990.

quate service, Shaḥḥāta says, stems from the problem of having to acquire trained and trustworthy personnel in a short time, the result of the banks' rapid success. The banks have also been too slow in introducing modern equipment.

It is noticeable that when talking about people withdrawing their money the word he uses is "*irtadda*", a verb also implying the act of committing the mortal sin of apostasy. Thereby Shaḥḥāta is at the very least hinting at a sacred character for the Islamic Banks.

— Some say that "*murābaḥa* sales are not really Islamic but an avoidance of God's law". But many contemporary *fuqahā'* have declared this to be approved by the *Sharī'a*, says Shaḥḥāta. He cites a conference of Islamic legal experts recently held in Kuwait, which pronounced that *murābaḥa* is licit, provided that the bank should bear responsibility for any wear on the merchandise subject to the transaction.

On this point Shaḥḥāta provides an example of a style of reasoning not atypical for some Muslim Brothers in the 1980s, and influenced by the Azhar, of which he himself was a professor. The argument is conducted basically by invoking some authority for the view preferred, rather than proceeding by way of logical argument. It thus in a sense makes part of a closed discourse.

— The Islamic banks are criticised for dealing with *ribā* banks. This is true, says Shaḥḥāta, and has been necessary because in some countries where there are customers there are no Islamic banks. However, the Islamic banks in these cases do not add the interest received to their capital, but use it for good public purposes. In any case these kinds of deals will disappear when the Islamic banks expand to more countries.
— Some also criticise the banks for investing in non-Muslim countries. This is done to spread risks, says Shaḥḥāta. In addition investment fields were in the early years of Islamic banking not sufficiently available or attractive in some Muslim countries, due not least to unstable economic policies.
— Critics complain of low return and high costs. Here Shaḥḥāta presents a double argument. First he says that depositors and businessmen are raised in *ribā* thinking and expect the same or better conditions when dealing with Islamic Banks as those encountered in traditional banks. They should be educated and think also of the spiritual and moral return, Shaḥḥāta says. But then he hurries to state that many Islamic banks do in fact distribute far higher returns than the *ribā* banks!
— "The banks have been dealing with immoral people." Yes, this can happen to all Muslims, Shaḥḥāta says. But it could be avoided by

improving the information gathering of the banks and by treating people "objectively" not sentimentally.

Shaḥḥāta finishes his article with Koranic verses and *Ḥadīth* that serve the purpose of telling Muslims not to pass on slanderous lies about these banks that will liberate them from the oppression of *ribā*.[119]

Whether the obvious contradictions between the cited statements of 'Aṭīya and Shaḥḥāta, not least on the question of *murābaḥa*, merely reflect the different purposes and occasions of their respective pronouncements on the Islamic banks is hard to judge with certainty. To some extent it may be connected to Shaḥḥāta's close practical involvement in Islamic finance. In any case the Islamists several times complained that the government created obstacles for the Islamic banks[120] and refused to cooperate with them constructively.

In January 1988 Ma'mūn al-Huḍaybī took up the issue of the government's reluctance to accept loans from Islamic banks while drowning the country in debts to Western countries. The so-called investment crisis, the lack of means for investment, must be considered an artificial crisis, said Huḍaybī, since there was no doubt that money was available. Recently in Alexandria there had been no problem getting buyers for apartments at 50–60,000 LE a piece. Egyptians also held 120 billion dollars abroad. The problem was that the policies of the government did not encourage a return of this money. For instance the government had turned down an offer from Bank Fayṣal for financing the reclamation of one million *faddān*, and a similar reduced offer for 100,000 *faddān*. The same had happened to an offer from the Bank al-Taqwā for the financing of 15,000 housing units and the reclaiming of 10,000 *faddān*, an offer that had been accepted by five other Islamic countries. These loans were not suitable, said the government, but, Huḍaybī wanted to know, was it more suitable to accept *ribā* loans from the West? It was unacceptable that Egypt continue to live under the supervision of the "food creditors". Every four out of five loaves of bread came from "mild donors". But if the doors were opened for Islamic investors, Egyptian capital held abroad would return and make real independence possible, he ended.[121]

The Islamists and "Islamic finance"

There is not a one-to-one relationship between the Islamic Alliance partners on the one hand and the so-called Islamic financial institutions

[119] Ḥusayn Shaḥḥāta, "Al-maṣārif al-islāmiyya wal-iftirā'āt al-saba'", *al-Nūr*, 4 March 1987.

[120] See for instance statements to this effect by 'Abd al-Ḥamīd al-Ghazālī in Ḥamdī al-Baṣīr, "Munāqasha sākhina ḥawla miṣdāqiyyat sharikāt tawẓīf al-amwāl", *al-Nūr*, 6 July 1988.

[121] People's Assembly, 9 January 1988, *MMS*, F5, 1–51, pp. 4447–72.

on the other. Therefore we cannot in any direct sense consider the activities of these institutions as a test for the policies of the Labour Party and the Muslim Brothers put into practice. Maḥmūd ʿAbd al-Faḍīl is obviously right when he says that the Alliance's heated defence of the Islamic investment companies against the state's intervention came not least because the Islamists considered these companies an important breach in the state monopoly over the economic life. In particular this was true of ʿĀdil Ḥusayn. A slight change in Ḥusayn's attitude from the time of writing *Towards a New Arab Thinking* is noticeable here in the sense that he argues positively for the existence of powerful economic actors outside the state, deciding the allocation of resources outside the state, although he maintained the idea of the necessity of a grand strategy informing the activities of private capital, speaking of a "mixed economy" as the ideal. He even positively defended the money dealers on the black, or "unofficial", market, lauding their efforts and implicitly arguing for letting the pound float, something he had otherwise been against. In a way we may suspect that this apparent contradiction springs from the fact that Ḥusayn was in opposition to the policies of the present state, and that the question of the relationship between private and public direction of the economy might look different in his view of the ideal Islamic state.

The Islamists definitely did not defend every move taken by the Islamic investment companies. They criticised their accounting practices for being grossly inadequate considering the amount of capital controlled by the companies in the late 1980s. And they took the companies to task for channelling their investments into speculative trade dealings instead of into production in agriculture or industry, in defiance of "Islamic priorities". This last critique was also directed at the Islamic banks.

On the other hand both the banks and the companies were seen as a positive attempt to develop channels of investment free from the *ribā* prohibited by the Koran. In particular this was emphasised by Muslim Brother commentators. The state was criticised for obstructing their positive development, rather than encouraging it.

Did the Islamists view the Islamic financial institutions as truly Islamic? ʿĀdil Ḥusayn's answer was equivocal. He emphasised that running without interest was not enough to claim this honour, although it was indeed an Islamic feature. To be classified as Islamic the whole business would have to follow Islamic guidelines. The companies and banks certainly did not represent an Islamic economy, for that could only exist within an Islamic state and society governed by the *Sharīʿa*.[122] Especially

[122] ʿĀdil Ḥusayn, "Fī sharikāt al-amwāl: kayfa badaʾa al-musalsal wa kayfa sa-yantahī", *al-Shaʿb*, 22 November 1988.

regarding the investment companies Muslim Brothers have also made harshly critical assessments.

A few more general observations are in place. One is that the whole range of Islamising economic and welfare institutions, through their viability and success, has the effect of demonstrating to the public that the Islamists and their sympathisers were perfectly capable, if anyone doubted it, of running modern economic institutions. In several respects they showed far greater efficiency than state institutions or those run by other private interests. Another is that the very fact of carrying the name Islamic had a powerful appeal to many people fearing involvement in business not condoned by Islam. In this way savings not otherwise mobilised were brought into the credit system. However, the third observation must be that although an institution carried the name Islamic or even abided by formally Islamic rules, there was no guarantee that it would concentrate its investments on those purposes that were most important for society, and which both the programmes of the Muslim Brothers and of the Labour Party determined as the true Islamic priority, namely development of the country's productive capacity and securing of the people's basic needs. Apparently securing a profit was the dominant urge among the Islamic banks and investment companies, as both 'Abd al-Faḍīl and 'Aṭīya argue, from quite opposite ideological points of view.

The model: Islamic regimes or South Korea? Success prevailing over religion

In the period being studied two Middle Eastern countries saw Islamists in power, Iran from 1979 and Sudan from 1989. The almost total lack of interest exhibited by Egyptian Islamists towards the Iranian and Sudanese economic experience is interesting compared with their attitudes towards the non-Muslim "newly industrialising countries of East Asia."

On several occasions, and with increasing frequency towards the end of the 1980s, 'Ādil Ḥusayn in particular held forth the East Asian countries, China and not least South Korea and the other "little NIC tigers", as positive models for independent development. "We agree with the IMF and IBRD when they urge a solution [to Egypt's economic problems]", he wrote on one occasion, "but at the same time we say that *we* must be the masters of that solution". A surgical operation was called for, Ḥusayn said, and the solution the Americans proposed was not wrong because it was cruel, but because it was detrimental. What was needed was a national program for reform that would strengthen independence. This would demand hard work and increased productivity in a situation where there was a lack of money and goods. The Egyptian people must follow the line of God's commands, not the line advised by Satan. God's commands must be translated into a long term strategic program for development, he declared.[123]

This is a typical example of the way in which Ḥusayn weaves an appeal to religious values into his discourse, which is in substance a rationalist discussion and mostly uses modern economic and political concepts taken from the international debate.

In China they had an *infitāḥ* in 1977/8, but they also had a government, Ḥusayn stated ironically. When import demand far exceeded export earnings, they regulated it. The Chinese had not followed Egypt's way, as some people claimed. They made their exports grow by 22 per cent yearly. At the same time they did not import food, which meant the currency earned could be used to increase productive capacity. Living standards increased, but under control, so the saving level held at 30 per cent.

China was big, but South Korea had made similar achievements. In South Korea they directed the private sector. The state forced the Hyundai company to go into ship building, but also supported it, by persuading importers to use Korean-built ships. Now South Korea had become a leading ship builder in the world market.

China and South Korea were very different but Ḥusayn considered they had in common an insistence on following their own thinking and cultural identity. In contrast Egyptian politicians had been possessed by an idea that contradicted experience: the foreigners only wished the country well and could be trusted with the keys to the national economy. Those who demanded Egyptianisation were ridiculed. South Korea received a lot of American aid and credit up to 1970, but far less that Egypt had now been receiving for some time. But the Koreans had concentrated on developing their own productive capability and were no longer in need of help. They had always been wary of the debts, and even more of direct foreign investment. On this point an extremely restrictive line had also been followed not only by Communist China, but by Japan and Taiwan as well.[124]

Later Ḥusayn summarised the positive experience of the "four tigers" South Korea, Taiwan, Hong Kong and Singapore, saying that the East Asian model involved a determined struggle to maximise exports, and an opening for foreign capital. The opening, however, was always selective and restrictive. It was guided by the state, and involved an intimate cooperation between state and private capital, a liberation of private initiative within the framework of a national plan. On occasion the state would

[123] ʻĀdil Ḥusayn, "Raddan ʻalā 'muḥarrir al-ahrām' alladhī taṭāwala ʻalaynā" *al-Shaʻb*, 23 December 1986.

[124] *Ibid.*

intervene directly. The model also involved upholding full employment, and wages rose steadily, so extreme income gaps were avoided.[125] Isolation on the Albanian model was out of the question in the late nineteenth century, Ḥusayn wrote. It was necessary to enter the world market, but this should be done with care and planning, not by removing all control and protection. What South Korea had done was to enter the world market from a position of strength.[126]

There were several misconceptions about the South Korean model, Ḥusayn stated in June 1989. For instance the story that Korea's development effort had been focused on the establishment of economic free zones, and on the attraction of investment from multinational companies, was quite false. Both these factors had played a minor role. All along the export industry had been overwhelmingly dominated by companies one hundred per cent owned by Koreans. A similar contradiction was present in the belief that the state played an insignificant role in Korean development. On the contrary the government planning institutions directed the whole process through long and medium term planning, defining the desired fields of investment and working closely with private management.

A positive feature of the Korean experience was how they in every phase of development had tailored their export ventures to the conditions at home and abroad. In the catching-up phase the Koreans would typically export industrial goods from their labour intensive industries to the West, and goods from more capital intensive industries to the developing countries of the South.[127]

The Korean model, Ḥusayn stated, was in flagrant contradiction of IMF guidelines, since it involved state intervention in the economy, for instance through subsidising companies, manipulating prices and restricting import to protect local industry. The model represented a third way between bureaucratic monopoly and anarchic chaos and injustice, and this was what the Labour Party wanted for Egypt.[128] On occasion the "Asian tigers" were held up as a positive example by Muslim Brothers as well, although the Brothers never elaborated on the implications of this model as did ʻĀdil Ḥusayn.[129]

[125] ʻĀdil Ḥusayn, "ʻAn al-iqtiṣād wa al-sharīʻa wa al-ḥiwār al-qawmī", *al-Shaʻb*, 6 June 1989.

[126] ʻĀdil Ḥusayn, "Qānūn al-istithmār al-jadīd", *al-Shaʻb*, 20 June 1989. Cf. his article "Bal tuṣaffūn al-sharikāt wa li-maṣlaḥat al-ajānib", *al-Shaʻb*, 28 June 1988.

[127] ʻĀdil Ḥusayn, "Qānūn al-istithmār al-jadīd", *al-Shaʻb*, 20 June 1989.

[128] ʻĀdil Ḥusayn, "Tasāʼulāt ʻan al-qiṭāʻ al-ʻāmm baʻda khiṭāb awwal māyū", *al-Shaʻb*, 8 May 1990.

[129] ʻIṣām al-ʻIryān, People's Assembly, 28 January 1990, *MMS*, F5, 3–24, ṭm, pp. 3–20. Cf. Lāshīn Shanab, 25 February 1990, *MMS*, F5, 3–36, ṭm, pp. 31–44.

Ḥusayn had just come out of a long process away from Marxism. At the same time socialist ideas were on the defensive internationally, which was also felt within Egypt. In this situation we may discern a noticeable move away from talk of socialism on the part of the Labour Party in general, and of 'Ādil Ḥusayn in particular. The move is towards a position where independence is what counts, and the character of the economic system is less important, somewhat like the famous formula of Deng Hsiaoping: it matters not whether the cat is black or white, as long as it catches mice. From this position the East Asian countries are held forth as having succeeded in breaking out of backwardness, and the key to their success is that whether dominated by state or private ownership, they have protected themselves from outside control, and followed a tightly knit strategy for development guided by a strong state.

CONCLUSION

A MODERNISING MORAL NATIONALISM

"Independence" and "development" have emerged from this investigation as the two main concerns directing Islamist intervention into the issues of economic policy. Before revisiting the general question of how to understand Islamism, it is therefore useful to consider more closely the relation of the Egyptian Islamist movement to nationalism and modernisation, respectively.

Nationalists despite themselves?

Is Islamism at root merely an alternative incarnation of the same radical nationalist spirit that produced Nasserism? The Islamists, in common with nationalists, stress as a major goal—perhaps *the* major goal—independence from the West in the economic field as in others. They see the desired result of the development effort as strength and glory for the nation, and although the talk is often of the *umma*, which may refer to the community of all Muslims, the concentration is usually on the problems of *Egypt* in particular, and on those of the *Arab* world in general. On the subject of inter-*Muslim* solidarity, the concrete examples given refer to the wish for cooperation and economic integration with other *Arab* countries. The rather eclectic agglomeration of ideas presented by the Islamists on how to achieve economic independence are drawn from various schools which have in common a search for alternatives to the neo-liberal gospel preached by the IMF. Though many of the theorists in question would hardly consider themselves nationalists, they have certainly been concerned with the conditions for independent development for nations, states and regions in the South. Generally the Islamists would prefer a greater role for private capital and a greater degree of deregulation of the internal market than that allowed by the Nasser regime, and seem to be aware of the dangers inherent in a pure import substitution strategy. Yet in their wish to establish Egypt as an independent and strong market economy in the world market place, they might well be seen as promoters, perhaps *post mortem*, of the "project of the national bourgeoisie". They use the East Asian development success stories to argue that direct foreign investment should be kept to a minimum and that private capital must be firmly guided by national strategy.

It is significant that the goal of independence seems to be a more basic reference for the formulation of economic policies than Islam. For one thing independence is taken as a goal in itself with no apparent need to be legitimised with Islamic references. For another the call for independence seems to have priority over Islam as a basis from which to criticise government policies, and indeed self-professedly Islamic institutions are evaluated more according to whether or not they can be seen to promote independence than by their formal compliance with Islamic norms. In debates over the contracting of foreign loans the Islamists very rarely raise the issue of *ribā* transactions being unlawful, while they warn time and again that reliance on outside sources of finance undermines national sovereignty. Population control is considered suspect not because of ethical considerations but because it would undermine Arab and Muslim strength *vis-à-vis* the West. Development financing from the ostensibly Islamic-oriented Gulf countries is criticised for operating in league with the IMF and the United States, and Islamic banks are castigated for not investing their funds according to national priorities for investment.

When Islamic phraseology is used in the discussion of independence, it is to add flavour to an argument, as when the interest paid by Muslim states to Western creditors is compared to the *jizya*. And historical references almost invariably pass over the golden ages of Islam, but instead draw from the nationalist history book of struggle against Western dominance since the 19th century, as in the frequent references to the haunting spectre of the *Caisse de la Dette Publique* of the 1870s.

As Immanuel Wallerstein has remarked, as "Western civilization sought to transform itself into civilization pure and simple", instead "everywhere, and more and more, nationalist particularism has been asserting itself".[1] The old idea of romantic nationalism, that each people has its distinct "soul", giving their nation a specific character and moulding its customs, morals, cultural production, political system and world view, proved an efficient tool in providing cohesion to defensive actions against Western dominance. The concept of civilisation as discussed by Renan in the 19th century and Toynbee in the 20th century was taken up by people in non-European parts of the world, and it was asserted that each civilisation can only prosper as long as it remains "true to itself". Islamism, in

[1] Immanuel Wallerstein, "Civilizations and Modes of Production", *Theory and Society*, no. 5, 1978, p. 7, quoted here from Fouad Ajami, *The Arab Predicament: Arab Political Thought and Practice Since 1967*, Cambridge University Press, 1992.

some of its aspects, should clearly be seen as part of this worldwide anti-Western intellectual, cultural and political reaction. Readily discernible in the discourse of the Muslim Brothers, with 'Ādil Ḥusayn this quest for civilisational authenticity becomes explicit. Time and again he speaks of the need for civilisational independence, citing Japan, China and Korea as positive examples of what such independence can achieve. He stresses the need for renewal must come from within the Islamic tradition, not by copying the West. Consumptive tastes and productive technology must be made to suit the social and natural environment of Egypt, he says, and should not be unthinkingly imported from Europe or the United States.

However, Ernest Gellner has claimed that what is celebrated by "Islamic revivalists", "fundamentalists" included, is not the mystical depths of popular belief and ritual practice, but the "high religion" of the *'ulamā'*. Throughout history this "high Islam" has repeatedly served as a platform for reform movements seeking, as it were, to "restore" the pure religion, cleansing it of the popular accretions and syncretism expressed through Sufi beliefs and practices. "High Islam" is also a fairly flexible belief system with a relatively simple ritual and doctrine, easily adaptable to changing circumstances of time and place.[2]

A closer examination would show the relationship between Islamism and Sufism to be far more ambiguous. Occasionally Islamists may use very harsh language to denounce Sufi magic practice and saint-worship, and in the Egyptian case not least to condemn the political quietism of the Sufis. On the other hand there are distinct positive links. Ḥasan al-Bannā was an active Sufi for much of his life. And, more important, the Sufi heritage is easily discernible in the organisational style of the Islamists, and above all in their emphasis on the fostering of spiritual discipline among their followers.[3] Islamism, as basically a movement of lay people, is thus not identical to the Islam of the present day *'ulamā'*. Yet when Egyptian Islamists formulate their economic views, there is virtually no evidence of a search for solutions among the traditional economic or religious practices of the people in towns and villages. The Islamist economic discourse draws its symbols and language from within the discourse upheld by the *'ulamā'*. It may at times challenge the prevalent interpretations among the "men of religion", but overwhelmingly the tendency is to base those challenges on alternative readings of the same masters of religion that the *'ulamā'* venerate.

[2] Ernest Gellner, "Marxism and Islam: Failure and Success" in Azzam Tamimi (ed.), *Power-sharing Islam*?, Liberty for Muslim World Publications, London, 1993, pp. 38 ff.

[3] See for instance the discussion of Sufi elements in the organisational style of the early Society of Muslim Brothers in Brynjar Lia, *The Society of the Muslim Brothers in Egypt*, pp. 11 ff. Cf. John O. Voll, "Fundamentalism in the Sunni Arab World", pp. 360–1.

It follows that if Islamism represents a quest for authenticity, this does not mean an authenticity growing out of the soil of Egypt, as it were. True, it is argued that economic independence should not only be freedom from directly relying on Western sources of finance or of essential goods, but should go beyond this to mean building an economy that creates relations between people for production and distribution different from those prevailing in the West. However, the precise point of the difference is not always clear and may vary from one Islamist group to the other.

More important, the Islamists do not go looking for traditional forms of economic activity peculiar to their own country, in the sense for instance of the Narodniki propagation of the example of the Russian village community, the *mir* in the nineteenth century. Traditional local forms of economic practice are only of interest as positive examples to the degree that they are, or can be construed to be, in greater harmony with the letter or spirit of the *Sharī'a* than modern Western practices. In the same vein the unfolding history of the Muslim world is nearly absent in Islamist discourse. We find the occasional reference to a classical institution like the market inspector, or *muḥtasib*, but its function is merely to illustrate the moral force of the Islamic system. In general the Islamic reference of the Islamists is linked to the idealised picture of the earliest Muslim state in Medina as related by *fiqh* tradition, although Islamists emphasise the need for reinterpretation through direct study of the Koran and *Ḥadīth*.

Islam is the spirit of the community of believers, the ideal towards which it yearns. And in Egypt, having belonged to this community since the time of Amr ibn al-'Āṣ, the Arab general who conquered the country for the Caliph in 641 (even if the majority of the local population did not convert till centuries later), Islam is the spirit of the Egyptian people. So perhaps the authenticity sought is an ideal or moral one, rather than a real one: acting as the fathers should have done, and aspired to do, rather than as they did. Thus it may serve as a platform for critique of inherited practices both in the circles of power and among the people at large.

Islamism does not focus on loyalty to a certain people in the sense of an ethnic group bound by common ancestry, language or even culture. Theoretically the call is for the unity of all Muslims of the world, a much wider community and one which is in principle open to all mankind. However, this highlights a basic enigma of the Islamist movement, its prevarication between Islamic universalism and civilisational relativism. On the one hand the Islamists, and especially those of the Labour Party, claim that every civilisation can only flourish so long as it remains true to its own roots, to its indigenous beliefs and customs.[4] The Muslim Community in

[4] The reference to European civilisation theorists like Arnold Toynbee is explicit. See for instance 'Ādil Ḥusayn, *Naḥwa fikr 'arabī jadīd*, p. 230.

its golden ages, the expanding West, and Israel are cited as proof of this (something that would incidentally be fiercely denied by Israeli ultra-orthodox Jews, who have fought a drawn-out battle against dominant secularist Zionism). What is seen as the present decline of the West is understood in terms of its losing touch with the religious roots of its civilisation. And while the Islamists consistently stress the importance of faith as vital to a successful development effort it is not always obvious why this faith must be Islamic, apart from the fact that this happens to be the inherited religion of the majority in Egypt. At times, when national unity with the Christians is in focus, the talk is of "the heavenly religions" in general.

On the other hand the particular civilisation that is indigenous to the Middle East, Islam, is based on a religion with universalist claims. And certainly the Islamists will say that Islam is the right solution not only for those who are Muslims today, but for all of mankind, both because there is only one God and the Koran and Sunna contain his eternal guidance for all mankind, and because Islam is the natural religion of man, consistent with his nature. From the discourse of the Islamists in propagation of Islam, it also follows that success on this earth is a sign of God's grace, of following his guidance and practising His Law. How then could this be harmonised with the idea that people on earth will be successful only if they follow their own beliefs, as the civilisationist thesis goes? For in the case of most of Europe these beliefs would not be Islamic, nor would they be so in the case of India, China or South Korea, so often heralded as a development success by the Islamists. For Europe's part it could of course be said that Muslims recognise Christianity and the Gospel as representing one of the heavenly religions having received a message from God. But Christians are seen to have distorted the original message, so it is hard to see why they should be successful even if living by their religion.

We would argue that the dilemma is a fruit of the uneasy marriage between Islam's claim to universal truth and the relativist inclination of romantic nationalism. In the concept of civilisational independence promoted by 'Ādil Ḥusayn there is certainly an affinity to the ideas of nineteenth-century romantic European nationalism, on the line of Herder for instance, which was in part a reaction against the universalist claims of the French revolution and the Enlightenment. But while Ba'thism is probably the most licit Arab child of Herder with its idea of the eternal mission of the Arab race, Islamism is in a sense a hybrid. It does not place at the heart of its doctrine the glory and greatness of a people or a race, but that of a universalist religion. Still the distinction is easily blurred as long as the foreign enemy is of another religion, and it is even more blurred in the Arab world because of the privileged role of the Arabs in the genesis of

Dār al-Islām. The Arabs were the first to receive God's final revelation through Muhammad, and the guardians of the language of the Koran. Without an Arab renaissance there could be no global Islamic revival. Ḥasan al-Bannā found no contradiction in fighting for Egypt (as the heart of the Arab world), for Arabism and for Islam. The Labour Party, and its forerunner Young Egypt, has always combined the two loyalties with the relative emphasis shifting according to political circumstances. It is an expression of this dualism when 'Ādil Ḥusayn in his theoretical works expounds the doctrine that every people should stay true to its own culture, while in writings for more popular consumption he uses the idea of Islam's universal truth to mobilise Muslims for the fight against the intrusions of the infidel Franks of the Northern powers.

In an important sense Islamism, in its ideas on economic policy, fits well into the general picture of formerly colonised areas struggling to establish a modicum of real independence. From Ḥasan al-Bannā through Sayyid Quṭb to 'Iṣām al-'Iryān and 'Ādil Ḥusayn it is not uncommon to find references to a general solidarity with the struggle of the South against the imperialist North. But this solidarity remains secondary and contingent, always subordinate to the imperative of solidarity among Muslims, and is never given a firm grounding in Islamist ideology itself. Perhaps it could be said that as Islamism takes the place of diverse interpretations of Marxism as the ideology for combating Western dominance, the struggle for independence gains in popular appeal, but loses in its ability to forge links with people engaged in the same struggle outside the Muslim world. This is not to deny the possibility that Islamists may develop a more coherent platform for cross-cultural solidarity in the future, but it points to an unresolved issue in Islamist ideology as it now stands.

Despite the programmatic effort to establish distance from the West and Western ideas, the Islamist attitude is not unambiguous. True, at the level of rhetoric, the Egyptian Islamists are very hesitant to identify themselves with for instance the concept of "modernisation", on the grounds that it has become synonymous with Westernisation. They would certainly emphasise the need for economic, social, political and intellectual change, but would discard the Arab translation for modernisation, *taḥdīth*, in favour of *tajaddud dhātī*, "self renewal", the implication being that modern Muslim society should evolve from indigenous culture and tradition rather than through imitation of the West. Yet a whole range of ideas and values propagated by the Islamists have a Western heritage, or at least a well established Western counterpart, and more often than not aspects of Western society are used explicitly as positive models of emulation for Egypt. Even the choice of alternative "Islamic" terms in discussing socioeconomic issues is not consequent.

When the Islamists encourage the believers to make purposeful use of their time, they echo the Western ethos of work and efficiency whose roots stretch back to early-modern Christian Protestant movements. In a similar way the call for impersonal relations to dominate in public and market affairs strikes a deep resonance in the West. When Yūsuf Kamāl talks of the advantages of the free movement of supply and demand in setting commodity prices he is spreading ideas of a Western origin, no less than ʻĀdil Ḥusayn does when discussing the vices of a dependent economic relation *vis-à-vis* the West.[5] Indeed, the very focus, common to the Egyptian Islamists, on the need for rapid economic development has as its starting point a wish to emulate the West in this regard, to make Egypt "join the developed world", as Muḥammad Ḥilmī Murād once expressed it.[6] More explicitly Western society is praised for its strong emphasis on productivity and on education, and for the way the rich voluntarily contribute to social redistribution through the tax system, because they grasp that it is in their own interest to do so. And Western economic theorists of diverse persuasions are often quoted approvingly in support of one argument or another.

Finally although Islamist discourse on economic questions is interspersed with positive and negative terms from the Koran, Sunna and more broadly from Islamic history—*ribā, zakāt, fasād, muḥtasib* etc.—overwhelmingly the conceptual apparatus consists of Arabic translations for the terminology used in Western (including Marxist) economic theory. Sometimes distinctly Koranic terms, with scarce regard for their original set of connotations, are used by the Islamists in a manner that nearly reduces them to translations for modern phenomena or concepts originating in the West: witness how *ribā* comes to mean interest, and *fasād* is used for corruption in the modern sense.

We should remind ourselves here that, as Fouad Ajami has noted, when people struggling against Western domination are "busy trying to revalidate once-discredited traditions and revive once-forgotten symbols", they tend at one and the same time to "embrace the dominant model for fear of being left behind and denounce it to affirm their uniqueness at the moment that they feel swept [up] by the current".[7] Discussing what he terms "Orientalism-in-reverse", Mehrzad Boroujerdi writes that "even in their newly acquired capacity as speakers, authors and actors the

[5] Many non-Western scholars have made important contributions to the criticism of modernisation theory, but overwhelmingly they operate within the conceptual framework of Western economic science.

[6] Muḥammad Ḥilmī Murād, "Fal-mashākil madrūsa wal-ḥulūl maʻrūfa", *al-Shaʻb*, 20 January 1987.

[7] Ajami, *The Arab Predicament*, p. 208.

'Orientals' continue to be overdetermined by the occidental listener, text and audience."[8]

Having an arch enemy may at times be a lethal relationship, but it is always a strong one, and long-time enemies often come to resemble one another; in particular the weaker part consciously or unconsciously tends to learn from the stronger. Even if Islamists insist (though not exclusively) on tapping the rich reservoir of the Islamic heritage for symbols and concepts to formulate their ideology, and dispensing with Western linguistic imports, their discourse is still *structured* by that of the enemy. Being the first moderniser, the West has formulated answers to the challenges posed by modernity. And since Islamists do not intend to dismantle modernity but to Islamise it, to create an alternative modernity, as it were, they must answer the same challenges and provide alternative answers to those of the West. These are questions of economic development, of social welfare, of gender relations, of democracy and of human rights. It is interesting, then, to notice that in important fields Islamist solutions often come to closely resemble ideas known from Western societies, but, especially in theoretical works and in programmatic documents, are frequently expressed through an Islamic idiom and legitimised with references to the Koran and the Sunna.

Back to the future: Islamist developmentalism

In the light of all this, is it still possible to consider that the Islamist call for cultural and intellectual authenticity, and the efforts to recreate the perceived ideal moral society of the Rightly Guided Caliphs, amounts to a wish to turn back the clock, or at least to resist the progress of modernisation and change?

From the time of Ḥasan al-Bannā the Egyptian Islamists have been unequivocal advocates of modernisation in its technological sense. As the present study shows the call for technological and economic development continued to be central in the political agenda of the Egyptian Islamists of the late 1980s: rapid industrialisation, improved communications, upgrading basic infrastructure and services in the villages etc. The call for modernising the economy has even been given priority over the formal fulfilment of tenets of *fiqh*, for example the Islamist criticism of "Islamic" investment companies and banks for not investing in projects that would contribute to the development of production. Yet it is commonly stated that while the Islamists cherish the material products of modern Western civilisation, they want to block the influence of Western philosophical and

[8] Mehrzad Boroujerdi, *Iranian Intellectuals and the West: The Tormented Triumph of Nativism*, Syracuse University Press, 1996, p. 13.

political thought. Consequently, a slightly broader discussion of the relationship between Islamism and modernity is expedient.

Does for instance the economic discourse of the Egyptian Islamists represent a move away from rationalism? There is no single answer to this. It is true that Islamist economic discourse is in many respects a moral one. And it is true that there is a tendency, as Samir Amin has argued, especially in the writings of the Muslim Brothers, to provide justification for particular positions by paraphrasing the text of the Koran and Sunna, rather than by substantial argument.[9] The style is often apologetic rather than probing.

On the other hand, there need hardly be a contradiction between a moral discourse as such and a rational one. The proponents of a "scientific" economic thinking in the eighteenth century (and certainly in later centuries) were (in most cases at least) influenced by the mores (and interests) of certain classes, which determined the angle from which their "neutral, objective" observations were made. This does not in the least reduce their importance as pioneers of a rationalist approach to economic questions. It is commonly understood that no social scientist can conduct her or his inquiry into a given subject totally uninfluenced by social background, inherited belief structures and ideological leanings. Given such influence on questions asked, approach chosen and targets set, the distinguishing mark of a rationalist discourse would rather be that the investigation should proceed by the use of logical argument and testable empirical evidence.

In this regard, the Islamist discourse on Islamic economics, or on the solutions to economic problems in an Islamic state, would seem to fall into two categories. One tendency is to proceed from Koranic and Sunna injunctions on economic matters and discuss their superiority to capitalist and socialist solutions. The emphasis here is on orthodoxy as shown through frequent references to the Koran, *Aḥādīth* and the viewpoints of exegetists and experts on jurisprudence through the centuries. For although it is a general Islamist belief that the door of *ijtihād* is open (given certain conditions), in many of the theoretical writings on an Islamic economic alternative produced by Muslim Brothers in the 1980s considerable deference is shown to the old masters, like the founders of the four *Sunnī* legal schools. This tendency is explicitly apologetic in that it takes the economic elements of the *Sharī'a* as given and proceeds to a rational argumentation for their superiority in producing a stable, prospering and just society. In both these aspects this tendency is reminiscent of the discourse of Azhar scholars who from time to time deliver *fatwās* on eco-

[9] Samir Amin, *Delinking*, p. 181.

nomic issues in the Egyptian press.[10] The typical style in the writings of the Brothers is to proceed from traditional Islamic precepts like *zakāt*, prohibition of *ribā* and so on, which they discuss in the abstract with numerous references to authorities of Islamic jurisprudence (*fiqh*) throughout the ages. In accordance with this in the mid-1980s there seems to have been little effort from the Brothers to present their views on current economic affairs. A magazine like *al-I'tiṣām*, close to the Brothers, would scarcely raise questions of current economic policy. The few articles that did were typically concerned with for example a campaign against importation of foodstuffs suspected of containing pig's fat.[11]

The other tendency, 'Ādil Ḥusayn being one of its foremost representatives, to a much greater extent proceeds on the one hand from an analysis of the actual state of the economy, and on the other from general principles defined as Islamic, such as self-reliance. Throughout its lifespan *al-Sha'b* newspaper gave broad coverage to current economic issues. In this type of discourse Islam is seen not so much as offering ready-made solutions, but as the moral force that will unite the population in enduring the effort and hardships of independent development, and as offering broad principles of social justice and harmony. Based on those principles the concrete strategies for progress are developed with reference to modern economic and political theory as formulated both by Westerners and by theorists from the Third World, more than with constant reference to the Koran or models from Islamic history. In fact the Labour Party, in its ideas about the conditions for development, was quite close to the delinking strategy proposed by the Egyptian economist Samir Amin.

Of course it could be said that Ḥusayn is atypical of Islamists in that the formative years of his political career were spent in the communist movement, and he seems to have approached Islamism from the outside in search more of a source of political energy and legitimacy than particular political or economic precepts. But also among some Muslim Brothers a more modernist style could be observed towards the end of the period under discussion. In the latter half of the 1980s the Brothers became more active in presenting their economic views through the press and the People's Assembly, especially from 1987 when they entered parliament with a sizable group of deputies. A number of those representing the younger generation recruited from the student movement in the 1970s, like 'Iṣām al-'Iryān and Mukhtār Nūḥ, would discuss economic issues in a way that both in style and content was much closer to 'Ādil Ḥusayn than the old

10 See for example the series of articles in *al-Ahrām al-Iqtiṣādī* in August 1991 by the Muftī of Egypt, Muḥammad Sayyid al-Ṭanṭāwī, on the question of what constitutes *ribā*.

11 See *al-I'tiṣām*, November/December 1986, p. 36.

guard represented by Ma'mūn al-Huḍaybī,[12] who remained closer to the more conservative style described above.

While appealing to the Koran and the Sunna as sources of legitimacy for their policies, the Labour Party and the younger Muslim Brother leaders seem to represent a modernisation of Islamist political discourse, and a decidedly rationalist style in argument.

The two tendencies described here are of course not mutually exclusive, but there is a marked difference in emphasis and in the manner of approaching the problematic. An example of this is apparent in the differing approaches to the *zakāt*. Yūsuf Kamāl and Ḥusayn Shaḥḥāta see the collection of *zakāt* from every able citizen according to the rates established in classical *fiqh* as an important task of the state. They also see it as the mainstay of public finances and of social security in an Islamic state. In contrast, 'Ādil Ḥusayn would prefer it to remain a voluntary contribution by the pious. The Islamic state, for its part, must construct an efficient and just system for securing the revenue necessary for the development effort, for national security and for social redistribution. This system of taxation must be guided by general Islamic principles of justice, but should not be bound by particular historic interpretations or implementations of those principles.

In any case it must be noted that generally, when dealing with real economic issues, for instance in the People's Assembly, the Islamists are hardly distinguishable from others in the way they use factual arguments for concrete solutions. Conversely older MPs from across the political board, including Wafdists and NDP representatives, would intersperse their speeches with Koranic quotations. In some cases no doubt this would be their habitual way of speaking on formal occasions, in others there was a conscious attempt to give one's discourse an air of Islamic piety and respectability. In either case this is an indication of the lingering force of Islam as the ultimate source of legitimacy for the bulk of the population.

Even Muslim Brother writers like Kamāl and Shaḥḥāta would not unambiguously belong in the scripturalist category, and it is debatable indeed whether they could be said to represent an anti-rationalist trend. For one thing, apologetics is a hybrid genre in this regard. Its aim is to defend the correctness of the divine truth of the texts. But to do so it has to enter into a discussion of reality, and thereby comes to contain elements both of rationalist and non-rationalist exegesis of Scripture, although its a *priori* goals blunt its critical edge.[13]

[12] Son of longtime Muslim Brother leader Ḥasan al-Huḍaybi and later (2002) himself Supreme Guide.

[13] Cf. Roy, *L'échec de l'islam politique*, p. 36.

For another, it must be emphasised that even though the writers in question underpin their views with frequent quotations from the Koran and Sunna and with references to classical *fiqh*, theirs is of course a *selective* reading of the divine texts and of the old masters. An example may be found in the question of the place of non-Muslims in Muslim society. With regard to the accepted religions of Jews, Christians and Zoroastrians, the holy scriptures contain an abundance of material, sometimes expressing respect for the "People of the Book", sometimes harsh censure. In the discourse on economic questions surveyed here, the Islamists consistently tend to point to the positive aspect, and call for equality in the service of national unity. The special tax of *jizya* is understood to be equal in size and social purpose to the *zakāt*, except for a part that compensates the exemption of non-Muslims from military service, and the option of doing service is left open. A more important example, perhaps, is found in the discussion of private property and its limits. While all accept the general idea of the legitimacy of private property within limits defined by God, Koranic and Prophetic quotations are selected in widely varying combinations, according to the individual writer or speaker's intent to emphasise the sanctity or the boundaries of private property rights. The near total absence of any reference to the issue of slavery, which was regulated by the great *fuqahā*' of classical times, would seem natural of course, but still points to the fact that what directs the choice of sacred references is the problems of current society. In this context Koran-quoting may well be a way of blurring the fact that the idea of developing an Islamic economy is really something quite new, and that it is being constructed by people outside the corps of *ulamā*'.

Finally, even with Kamāl and Shaḥḥāta, and *a fortiori* with 'Abd al-Ḥamīd al-Ghazālī, there is towards the turn of the decade a discernible move away from the scripturalist approach. This is clearly visible in Kamāl's 1990 book *Fiqh al-iqtiṣāḍ al-'āmm*, which includes extended excursions into the real problems of the current Egyptian economy, like the huge public debt, the crisis of the public sector etc. Classical *fiqh* is used as one reference in discussing these issues, but not as the starting point. In the same work Kamāl clearly gives secular economic science the role of analysing the workings of the economy, given the choice by society of a certain guiding ideology. The difference to 'Ādil Ḥusayn is then mainly in Kamāl's use of mainstream liberal Western economic theory, versus Ḥusayn's proximity to dependency theory and other critical trends. As for the Islamic principles supposed to guide the economy Kamāl declares the purpose of his book is to "connect the present with the [sacred] text" as a basis for developing a contemporary interpretation through *ijtihād* (although he modestly declares himself unqualified to act as *mujtahid*).

In the same vein we may point to the criticism raised by Shaḥḥāta and others against the "Islamic" financial institutions, which reveals these authors are more concerned with what is required to achieve economic progress for the country, than with the subtleties of what constitutes *ribā* in classical *fiqh*. The remark by 'Abd al-Ḥamīd al-Ghazālī that God's will is found in that which serves the public interest, is only the most pronounced expression of this tendency.[14]

The tendency towards a more "free" Islamist thought is, however, to a certain extent contravened by another which strengthens the hold of the traditional *fiqh* of the *'ulamā'*. The Islamist movement, as defined above, may have narrowed somewhat the scope of interpretations of God's message by raising the slogan of the *Sharī'a* as their foremost issue. For even if the Islamists defend the right to fresh *ijtihād* on the basis of Scripture, they cannot avoid the weight of the historical traditions of *fiqh* scholarship. This is true even if 'Ādil Ḥusayn for instance makes an interesting distinction between the *Sharī'a* as God's eternal guidance for mankind and *fiqh* as the concrete human efforts at interpreting God's message in line with the changing circumstance of time and place.

The *'ulamā'*, originally more a target of attack from the Islamist movement than a participant, have begun to seize the opportunity for regaining some of their lost status in society by capitalising on their traditional role as the protectors and transmitters of the *Sharī'a*. "You want the *Sharī'a*", they say, "that's us!". As they jump on the bandwagon of Islamic revival they bring with them the juggernaut of scholarly interpretations of the Law accumulated over the previous 1400 odd *hijra* years, on the way inducing in the Islamist discourse a fair amount of conservatism, for instance on the question of property.[15]

Although in general Sunni Islamists would not confer on the *'ulamā'* any monopoly over the interpretation of the faith, the Islamist movement has never had a clear-cut attitude towards the role of "the learned men of religion" in the true Islamic society they seek to create. On the one hand they call for the question of *ribā* to be settled by trained *fuqahā'* and not by politicians, and demand the convening of the Azharī Islamic Research Academy (*Majma' al-buḥūth al-islāmiyya*) to pronounce on the issue. On the other hand the Islamist politicians and ideologues are living examples of laymen venturing into the field of *ijtihād* and taking it upon themselves to proclaim how the sacred texts should properly be understood.

[14] See above, p. 201.

[15] The contention that Azharī *ulamā'* were exercising a conservative influence on Islamist discourse does of course not mean that al-Azhar should be seen as a static and monolithic ideological bloc. For a recent study of al-Azhar see Malika Zeghal, *Gardiens de l'islam: Les oulémas d'Al Azhar dans l'Égypte contemporaine* , Presses de Sciences Po, Paris, 1996.

The resulting interpretation of the social message of Islam is conducive to supporting economic development. The furtherance of public interest, *maṣlaḥa*, is held up as equal to fulfilling God's will. A glance at the set of values presented as those that should guide a true Islamic economic system points in the same direction. A central tenet is that of the economic development effort as a collective duty (*farḍ kifāya*) on the Muslim society, and even as a *jihād*. The perfection of one's work is an integral part of the service of God, on a level with the fulfilment of the ritual duties. Finally there is the sacred duty to exploit natural resources to the full for the increase of the material wealth of society. More generally this is linked to the idea that a true Muslim is involved in an unceasing battle for good against evil, and should use her or his measured time in this world in a disciplined and purposeful way. When the energy of the believer through the values listed above is directed towards the increase of material production, Islamist doctrine would seem to possess a substantial potential for economic mobilisation. Not least this is true since there is an emphasis not only on an Islamic state enforcing these values, but ultimately on them being internalised as natural instincts by believers, somewhat reminiscent of the way Max Weber saw the Protestant ethic as beneficial to capitalist development in Europe.[16]

Contrast this with Timur Kuran's reading of the contemporary discourse on Islamic economics.[17] To Kuran the core of the ideal Islamic economy presented in the works he has studied is a notion of justice based on the two principles of equality in distribution and fairness in productive, commercial and financial interaction. The realisation of these principles is presented as flowing naturally from the implementation of the Islamic procedures of *zakāt* (which secures equality), and the prohibition of *ribā* (which secures fairness). Kuran argues that this is an illusion based on unrealistic presumptions about the workings of a modern market economy.[18] The literature analysed by Kuran stems mainly from the South Asian Islamic region, and is mostly not produced by political Islamists. These writings probably also tend to be of a more technical and scripturalist nature than the texts analysed here. Yet this can at best only partially account for Kuran's inclination to reduce Islamic economic thought to a misguided belief in the miraculous effect of reintroducing medieval economic principles (albeit in a selective way).

16 Max Weber, *The Protestant Ethic and the Spirit of Capitalism*, HarperCollins, London, 1991, for instance pp. 180 ff.

17 See above p. 44, n. 2.

18 Timur Kuran, "On the notion of economic justice in contemporary Islamic thought", pp. 172–8.

It would seem that in his effort to disprove the "workability" of Islamist economic prescriptions, Kuran becomes insensitive to the dynamic aspect of Islamist reformulations of Islam. He does acknowledge that equality and justice are part of a wider set of moral injunctions, but to Kuran these injunctions can be summed up as a general call for altruistic behaviour, and this he summarily dismisses as unworkable, since altruism can only work within small social units, such as the family, and not on the scale of a nationwide market.[19] This statement in itself is certainly debatable. But more important Kuran fails to notice that Islamist advocacy of hard and conscientious work, the establishment of merit as the sole criterion for economic decisions, and the urgency of economic development as central Islamic values, gives a thoroughly modernising flavour to the "package" of values presented as those guiding an Islamic economy. Furthermore, and precisely for this reason, the fact that efficiency, growth, employment and industrialisation are held forth as important goals, stands for Kuran as somehow isolated from, and partly in contradiction to, the "moral economy" otherwise propagated.[20] A careful reading of this same moral economy would actually show consistency between the moral principles advocated and the practical economic goals. Instead Kuran ends up suggesting that the only link between Islamism and modernisation would spring from social reaction *against* "fundamentalist" Islamic regimes.[21]

Kuran concentrates on discussing the feasibility of the solutions proposed by the "Islamic economics" literature. This leads him to disregard the possibility that the inconsistencies he points to might be understood as expressing a tension between the resolve to promote a reading of the Islamic message relevant to the problems of modernising society, and the equally strongly felt need to guard the sanctity of the scriptures. The tension in question reflects precisely the innovative character of the discourse.

Islamism should be considered as a pro-modern ideology not only in the sense of its stressing the need for economic and technological development, but also in view of the individualising aspects of the Islamist interpretation of the Islamic message. There is a strong focus on the individual as responsible not only for his own conduct but for all the affairs of society and state, which contrasts with more traditional communalist attitudes and a traditional division of roles where politics would be the domain of notables and religion that of the clerical leaders. Especially with the Muslim Brothers the focus on individual duties is coupled with a

[19] Timur Kuran, "The Economic Impact of Islamic Fundamentalism", p. 328.
[20] Timur Kuran, "On the notion of economic justice", p. 181. Cf. "The Economic Impact of Islamic Fundamentalism", p. 305.
[21] Kuran, "The Economic Impact of Islamic Fundamentalism", p. 332.

strong defence of individual rights against the encroachment of the state. Common to all Islamists is a strong emphasis on merit, that is the idea that there should be full access to social mobility for every individual regardless of family background, and that all promotions should take place based on consideration of individual merit in piety and in efficient and good work. This would require equal access to education and employment and an end to age-old practices of nepotism and favouritism in public and business life.

The stress on merit is therefore closely linked to the Islamists' frenetic campaigning against corruption. The main target is the misuse of public office to further personal interests or those of individual or groups close to the office holder. The Islamists criticise officials taking bribes and illegitimate charges for exercising their duties, and denounce the misappropriation of funds for buying votes and for paying commissions to cronies of people in office, or by awarding public contracts to other than the one presenting the best tender. A modernising aspect can also be seen in this, in that the border between corruption and traditional patron-client relations is very thin and vague. One might say that corruption thrives in the confrontation between inherited social structures based on the reciprocal solidaric obligations of kinship and client networks, and the institutions of a modern market and a modern state. The Islamists seem not only in their campaigning against corruption, but also to the extent that they are involved in business, to favour a detached impersonal style focused on economic efficiency.[22]

The Islamists may be seen historically as a force for also *political* modernisation.[23] Precisely through their focus on individual responsibility and individual merit, they have contributed in important ways to make politics a business for people outside the old "political classes" of notables and *'ulamā'* and the new state élites. Their constant emphasis on the furthering of education and their promotion of new political techniques has contributed in preparing the ground for modern mass politics.

Part of the modernising aspect of Islamism is also its emphasis on the state. Egyptian Islamists are certainly critical of the totalitarian power of the state and they stress the need for the reform of the Muslim individual in order to achieve a true Islamic state of affairs. Nevertheless it is a crucial feature of their ideology, setting them apart from earlier Islamic reform movements, that the virtuous society they seek can ultimately only

[22] An indication of this is found in Nefissa N. A. Naguib, *Men of Commitment: An Anthropological Study about Top Norwegian Business Executives*, University of Oslo, 1989, p. 105.

[23] For an elaboration, cf. Utvik, "'A pervasive seriousness invaded the country …'".

come about through the agency of an Islamic *state*. This is apparent in their central demand, which is for the reintroduction of the Islamic law, the *Sharī'a*, as supreme law. It is important to notice that for the Islamists this involves the codification of the *Sharī'a* into modern law texts by an elected assembly. This is very different from the traditional situation in which the *Sharī'a* was nothing but the Koran and the Sunna as interpreted by experts on religious law. The Islamist version of the *Sharī'a* ties it to the state and its judicial bureaucracy, and to the representatives of the people, rather than to the religious class, the *'ulamā'*.[24]

In search of a place in the modern world: return to a new Islam

A reasonably clear picture emerges: Gauged from the views they have expressed on economic questions, the Egyptian Islamists could, as indicated above, be seen to be picking up the rag-torn "project of the national bourgeoisie", that is, a quest for establishing Egypt as an independent actor on the world market. As in Nasser's time this project involved an emphasis on economic independence and on rapid industrialisation. It also involved a call for social justice in the sense of ameliorating the conditions of the poor majority of the population, but appeals for class struggle were condemned as dangerously divisive. There is clearly a similarity to the social-democrat position in opposition to communism, the idea being that without changing the basic capitalist relations of production it was still possible to create a sort of socialism in the sphere of distribution.

The main difference between the Islamist version of the "project of the national bourgeoisie" and the one promoted by Nasser in his heyday, would be found at one level in the Islamist stress on the need for liberalising the internal economic life of the country, and giving the private sector an active role in the development effort. The Muslim Brothers were strongest in their commitment to private enterprise, while the Labour Party remained more pro-statist. Yet they held in common the view that the collective welfare of society must be given priority and that the state must secure this through the guidance of the private sector by an effective planning apparatus possessing the means to move private investment in the desired direction. At another level, of course, the Islamists differed from the Nasserism of the 1960s in the linking of their programme for independent development to a call for a general re-Islamisation of state and society.

However, only in very general terms is the economic programme of the Islamists linked to the sacred texts, and still less to actual Islamic history.

[24] Cf. Guazzone, *The Islamist Dilemma*, pp. 10–11.

Concerning the most central point of the Islamist programme, the call for independence, virtually no effort is made to deduce it from Islamic precepts. Furthermore the Islamists emphasise the need for an open-minded attitude towards economic ideas emanating from outside the Islamic world. They stress the necessity of a new *ijtihād* and they constantly refer to public interest, *maṣlaḥa*, as the paramount determinant of correct policies. These aspects of Islamist discourse easily convey the impression that this is primarily a movement for independence, economic development and (a modicum of) social justice, and that the reference to Islam is merely used for legitimising the struggle for these goals in the eyes of a religious populace. When this is combined with the strong emphasis of the Islamists on Arab unity and economic integration it is an indication that instead of talking of Arab nationalism versus (pan)-Islamism, it might be better to talk of Arab nationalism in a secular or semi-secular version like Nasserism and Ba'thism versus an Islamic version now dominant in stirring popular feeling.

One of the initial assumptions of this study (see p. 40) of Islamism as a sort of cultural nationalism, would thus seem to be confirmed by the Islamist discourse on economic issues. This framework of understanding is supported by the fact that within the discourse surveyed the Islamic heritage appears more important as a source of legitimising vocabulary, than as a provider of specific substantial solutions to economic problems. But it is striking that even at the level of terminology the Islamists were mostly operating well within the established Western-developed idiom. While the case may be different in other fields of Islamist discourse, the fact that the West is not infrequently implicitly or explicitly used as a positive model would strongly indicate that, more than a total negation of Western ideas and practices, the appeal to Islam as an alternative represents first and foremost a quest for increased freedom of thought and action *vis-à-vis* the dominant powers.

If the importance of religion in forming Islamist programmes of reform to a large extent remained on the symbolic level, one might expect to find under the umbrella of a common Islamic vocabulary a broad range of views on economic policies across the scale from left to right. Indeed quite a spectrum of opinion can be found within the Islamist movement of Egypt, both now and in the past, ranging for instance from the attack on the property-owning classes by Sayyid Quṭb and Ḥasan al-Bannā to the strong defence of private property by Yūsuf Kamāl, and from the central planning envisaged by 'Ādil Ḥusayn to the aversion towards price controls on the part of the Muslim Brothers.

On the other hand there seems to be Islamist *ijmā'* on certain important issues. First of all, as indicated, this consensus covers the call for economic independence, for reducing the influence of Western capital and the world market. The Islamists are also in total agreement in seeing rapid and comprehensive economic development as an imperative. Beyond this, there is a shared emphasis on private property as the basis of an Islamic economy, although the Islamists differ in the scope allowed for state intervention, and in the models presented by writers like Sayyid Quṭb and later ʻĀdil Ḥusayn, the state is given wide powers. Finally there is a common abhorrence for class struggle, and an emphasis on harmony. The ideal society is not one without social differences, but one of solidarity and cooperation, where the rich give to the poor.

Of course it is a limitation that only two parties have been examined, albeit that in combination the two make up most of what might be termed organised mainstream Islamism in Egypt. For lack of material, the economic line of the more militant groups, with a "lower" social basis, like the *Jamāʻa Islāmiyya*, who some observers claim tended towards more radical economic views,[25] has not been discussed. Nor have the independent Islamist thinkers like Yūsuf al-Qaraḍāwī or Muḥammad ʻImāra, nor the philosopher Ḥasan Ḥanafī, who has endeavoured to promote something he terms an "Islamic left" been included. Of course it can not be denied, in the light of the historically proven ideological fertility of religions, that there might emerge from these circles, or from elsewhere in *Dār al-Islām*, innovative interpretations of the economic message of Islam.

But whatever the plurality of economic options that might conceivably be reconciled with Islamic precepts, the economic vision held by dominant groups within the Islamist movement will unavoidably tend to gain a strong legitimacy as *the* Islamist view. Of course this does not mean that the established doctrine may neither be challenged nor substantially modified over time. Islamist proposals for *political* reform, for example, have changed dramatically from the "no-party" view often expressed by early Islamists like Ḥasan al-Bannā,[26] to the Muslim Brothers' advocacy of parliamentary multi-party democracy in the 1990s.[27] Nevertheless, it is clear that in economic matters there is by now a constituted quasi-consensus, for instance on the issue of private property, which poses a formidable ideological obstacle for those wanting to promote another view as Islamist *within* the existing movement. The *fiqh* tradition has gained in prestige with the increasing influence of Azharī scholars especially in the Muslim Brothers. On the other hand the social constituency of the

[25] This is flatly rejected by Nazih Ayubi who claims there is no known evidence to support such a view, and it is certainly true that such evidence has not been presented. See Ayubi, *Political Islam*, p. 232.

[26] Mitchell, *The Society of Muslim Brothers*, pp. 219, 261.

[27] Al-ikhwān al-muslimūn, "Mūjaz ʻan al-shūrā fī al-islām", *al-Shaʻb*, 19 May 1994.

Islamists seems, as far as it can be gauged, to be a coalition of groups seeing their progress hindered by the dependent situation of Egypt and the entrenched ruling class whose interests have become tied to the country's dependent insertion in the world market. The coalition includes most prominently a large segment of the educated groups: doctors, lawyers, engineers and other professionals, teachers, *muwaẓẓafīn* of all sorts and students, but also small and medium-sized, and some large, private entrepreneurs. While the big business element within the Muslim Brothers might be less anxious for social change, and favourable towards the conservative Azhar influence, the younger leadership recruited from the student movement of the 1970s and '80s, as well as the Labour Party, lean towards a somewhat more "social-democrat" and statist view. The tensions and struggle between these conflicting tendencies within the "alternative Islamic élite" seem to be a main determinant of future developments, in line with the third assumption made at the beginning of this study.

The significance of the Islamic reference

The above analysis does not convey an untrue picture of the Islamists and their economic ideas. But for all its merit, if left standing alone it would represent an impoverished and lop-sided understanding of Islamism, a sort of socio-economic reductionism. For despite the contention that the theoretical outlines of an Islamic economy are so general and vague that it is difficult to pinpoint the specific "Islamic" elements in the concrete economic policies of the Egyptian Islamists, this is not to say "Islam has nothing to do with it". Indeed, another of the initial assumptions of this study, that Islamism represents an effort "to impose a moral cohesion on modernising society", has been abundantly confirmed.

For one thing the choice of Islam as an ideological reference by important social segments is not fortuitous. For another it is insignificant neither in its mobilising effects, nor in its political implications. Thirdly, rather than seeing Islamists as people appropriating Islamic references for secular political purposes, we may view their activism as springing from a genuine religious conviction and thus gain access to alternative perspectives. Finally, if Islamism is indeed a sort of nationalism, then precisely its peculiarity, its moralising nature, could be said to make it an apt tool for an attack on tradition.

The choice of Islam as framework and reference for the construction of political ideology is not fortuitous, because the social constituency described above is comprised of those (majority) elements within the educated groups and the entrepreneurial class who are rooted in a social environment where the Islamic symbolic universe continues to be dominant. Therefore, for the individuals concerned, Islam easily becomes the natural identity marker in their struggle both against Western dominance of their country and against the more Westernised indigenous elements monopolising positions of power. More than that, when trying to impose order and security on a life and world in chaotic change, Islam becomes their natural moral reservoir.

By the same token the choice of Islam is not insignificant. On one level the possible mobilising effects of the fact that Islamist political discourse is couched in an idiom drawn from Islamic tradition must be considered. By tying their economic programme to Islam, to the values cherished by the mass of the people, it is not inconceivable that were the Islamists to gain power, they might be able to mobilise a popular enthusiasm that would make people willing to endure hardships in the struggle for development. By appealing to the Egyptians' strong faith in God, they might hope to reduce corrupt practices in government, at least for a "grace period".

At another level, if it is not fortuitous that certain social segments are drawn towards Islamist ideology in their struggle for independence and social progress, neither is it fortuitous which options they come to favour in economic policy once the "Islamic choice" is made. For while the Islamist call for a return to the true Islam may *potentially* be flexible enough to accommodate the whole range of existing ideas on structuring socio-economic relations, as Islamism unfolds as a real movement in concrete societies, on at least two points there are imperatives steering its discourse on the economy in certain broad directions.

The first and perhaps the strongest is the demand for independence. The whole inner logic of the quest for authenticity leads in the direction of such a demand, since this quest has developed in response to the heavy dominance of the West on the cultural and ideological level. Since the major threats to the independence of Egypt are today seen to be the military power of the United States and Israel, and the economic power of the West as spearheaded by the International Monetary Fund, the Islamists cannot hope to be taken seriously if they do not present themselves as an alternative to what is widely seen as the present regime's subservience to the West and the IMF. This implies both directing criticism against IMF policies, and presenting ideas of a possible strategy for independent development.

The second point concerns the welfare of the population. It has been argued here that Islamism should not be understood simplistically as an expression of economic discontent. But if the analysis of the "social impulse" behind Islamism is correct, the Islamists would be searching for ways to recreate a social cohesion by forging strong ideological links, sanctified by Islam, between the rulers and the ruled in a future Islamic state. Then a salient point in their programme would naturally be to secure an economic system that will produce a feeling of common interest among the various layers of the population and between the population and the state apparatus. This imperative is underscored by the fact that undoubtedly a lot of the force of popular support for the movement springs from the economic misery faced by millions of pauperised people in town and countryside.

Beyond this, there are severe problems facing the contention that if the impetus behind Islamist movements is of a social and political nature, Islamism has only a weak link to religion, and its relation to Islam must be of a rather instrumental kind. First of all this view presupposes an isolation of religion as something concerned with spiritual matters and not with social and political affairs. But that is an over-generalisation of something that could (and only with some hesitation) be said to hold true for some modern Western societies, and is precisely what the Islamists deny. Rafīq Ḥabīb has argued that Islamism should be analysed as a movement springing from religious zeal. If not, he says, it will be hard to understand how these movements may oscillate between political activism and a concentration on spiritual revival.[28] Certainly this would hold true for the Muslim Brothers. The story of the Labour Party is a bit different, since this organisation moved to an Islamist position only in the late 1980s. However, the Young Egypt tradition from which the party sprang always held religion in high esteem. The split over the party's Islamisation was not between the pious and the non-religious, but a split among believers over the question of the explicit politicising of religion. Even in the case of the former communist ʿĀdil Ḥusayn we may talk of a *return* to the religious fold, since in early youth his first activism was as a member of the Young Egypt, whose nationalist ideology contained strong Islamic elements. That Ḥusayn argues for Islam as the only force able to mobilise the Egyptian people in the struggles ahead does not necessarily reveal any shallowness in his religiosity. It cannot be ruled out that there might be individuals inside the movements under discussion for whom religion is a political tool and not a faith, although it would be hard to ascertain. But there is hardly any doubt that the membership of the movements consists overwhelmingly of sincere believers who view their political struggle as part and parcel of the defence and advancement of the true faith.

The modernising revolt of the pious

From this point of view the Islamists may be seen as people acting from within religion, as it were, to defend their individual and collective

[28] Rafīq Ḥabīb, *Al-iḥtijāj al-dīnī wal-ṣirāʿ al-ṭabaqī fī miṣr* [Religious Protest and Class Struggle in Egypt], Sinā lil-nashr, Cairo, 1989, pp. 15, 18.

identity against a perceived Western onslaught, and to effect a moral and material regeneration in their society. Accordingly the message that they preach stresses two aspects of Islam. One concern is with the manifestation of identity through an open profession of faith and piety and the upholding of ritual duties and Islamic rules of conduct. This concern also prompts an (albeit only partial) return to an Islamic symbolic universe as a reservoir for legitimation and meaningful references. Secondly the Islamists present a set of Islamic moral norms. The holy scriptures and traditional *fiqh* here become sources of general principles, which are selected and reinterpreted so that a set of values are produced that are more adaptable to modern conditions than traditional customs and quite conducive to economic development. For as Richard Mitchell writes of the Egyptian Muslim Brothers of the 1940s and '50s, in "the very process of reaffirming the old, the old is newly conceived and formulated in a way which inevitably reflects the forces which helped to undermine it".[29] Yet the fact that the Islamist version of religion differs from traditional *fiqh* can only with a very static view of religion be said to make them less genuinely Islamic. Religions, as life itself, are ever changing.

In fact, if Islamism could be considered a kind of nationalism, it is precisely its attachment to a religious ideal, its moralising character, that gives it a cutting edge against inherited traditions and customs, and a powerful modernising potential, as shown not least in its frenetic struggle against the corruption and nepotism so interwoven with traditional patron-client relations in Egyptian society.

[29] Mitchell, *The Society of Muslim Brothers*, p. 331.

BIBLIOGRAPHY

PRIMARY SOURCES

Works by Islamists on an "Islamic economic model"

'Awda, 'Abd al-Qādir, *Al-māl wal-ḥukm fī al-islām* [Wealth and Government in Islam], Al-dār al-su'ūdiyya lil-nashr wal-tawzī', Jidda, 1984.

Ḥusayn, 'Ādil, *Naḥwa fikr 'arabī jadīd—al-nāṣiriyya wal-tanmīya wal-dīmuqrāṭīya* [Towards a New Arab Thinking: Nasserism, Development and Democracy], Dār al-mustaqbal al-'arabī, Cairo, 1985.

——— "Mashrū' lil-mustaqbal" [A Project for the Future], Minbar al-ḥiwār, no. 13, 1989.

——— *Al-islām dīn wa ḥaḍāra—mashrū' lil-mustaqbal* [Islam: Religion and Civilisation: A Project for the Future], Al-manār al-'arabī, Giza, 1990.

Kamāl, Yūsuf, *Al-islām wal-madhāhib al-iqtiṣādiyya al-mu'āṣira* [Islam and Contemporary Schools of Economic Thought], Dār al-wafā', Manṣūra, 1986.

——— *Fiqh al-iqtiṣād al-'āmm*, Stābrus lil-ṭibā'a wal-nashr, Cairo, 1990.

Mawdūdī, Abū al-A'lā, *Al-ribā* [Usury], Al-dār al-su'ūdiyya lil-nashr wal-tawzī', Jidda, 1987.

——— *Mafāhīm islāmiyya ḥawla al-dīn wal-dawla* [Islamic Concepts on Religion and State], Al-dār al-su'ūdiyya lil-nashr wal-tawzī', Jidda, 1987.

——— *Niẓām al-ḥayāt fī al-islām* [The Organisation of Life in Islam], Al-dār al-su'ūdiyya lil-nashr wal-tawzī', Jidda, 1987.

Quṭb, Sayyid, *Ma'rakat al-islām wal-ra'smāliyya* [The Struggle between Islam and Capitalism], Dār al-shurūq, Cairo, 1987.

——— *Al-'adāla al-ijtimā'iyya fī al-islām* [Social Justice in Islam], Dār al-shurūq, Cairo, 1989.

Al-Ṣadr Muḥammad Bāqir, *Iqtiṣādunā* [Our Economy], Dār al-ta'āruf, Beirut, 1987.

Shaḥḥāta, Ḥusayn, *Al-minhaj al-islāmī lil-amn wal-tanmīya* [The Islamic Road to Security and Development], Dār al-tawzī' wal-nashr al-islāmiyya, 10th of Ramaḍān city, 1990.

Programmatic documents

Ḥizb al-'amal al-ishtirākī, "Taqrīr ḥizb al-'amal al-ishtirākī ilā al-mu'tamar al-iqtiṣādī 'an al-mashākil al-iqtiṣādiyya wa ṭarīqat ḥalliha", *Al-'amal al-ishtirākī*, no. 19, Cairo, 1981.

——— *Da'ā'im al-iṣlāḥ al-iqtiṣādī*, Cairo, 1982.

——— *Al-da'm bayna al-ilghā' wal-tarshīd*, Cairo, 1984.
Ḥizb al-'amal, "Al-barnāmaj al-intikhābī 'alā qā'imat ḥizb al-'amal", *al-Sha'b*, 17 March 1987.
——— *Maḥāwir islāmiyya lil-iṣlāḥ al-iqtiṣādī*, Cairo, 1989.
——— *Maḥāwir islāmiyya lil-iṣlāḥ al-siyāsī*, Cairo, 1989.
Shaḥḥāta, Ḥusayn, *Al-minhaj al-islāmī lil-iṣlāḥ al-iqtiṣādī* [The Islamic Road to Economic Reform], n.p., Cairo, 1991.
Shukrī, Ibrāhīm, *Al-taqrīr al-siyāsī li-ḥizb al-'amal al-ishtirākī*, Cairo, 1987.

Minutes of the People's Assembly

Maḍābiṭ majlis al-sha'b, al-faṣl al-tashrī'ī al-rābi':
Dawr al-in'iqād al-awwal, al-ijtimā'āt 1–99.
Dawr al-in'iqād al-thānī, al-ijtimā'āt 17–20.
Dawr al-in'iqād al-thālith, al-ijtimā'āt 1–3.
Maḍābit majlis al-sha'b, al-faṣl al-tashrī'ī al-khāmis:
Dawr al-in'iqād al-awwal, al-ijtimā'āt 1–62 wa 104–5.
Dawr al-in'iqād al-thānī, al-ijtimā'āt 91–4.
Dawr al-in'iqād al-thālith, al-ijtimā'āt 9–47.

Articles from the Islamist press

Al-Tilmisānī, 'Umar, "Idhā jā'a al-muslimūn fa-lā māl li-aḥad", *Al-Da'wa*, 383, February 1977.
Kamāl, Yūsuf, "Qaḍīyat al-da'm min khilāl naẓara islāmiyya", *Al-Da'wa*, 394, January 1978.
'Abd al-Quddūs, Muḥammad, "Ḥadīth ṣarīḥ ma'a al-duktūr Muḥammad Ḥilmī Murād", *Al-I'tiṣām*, July 1980.
Al-Suyūfī, Aḥmad, "Al-islām huwa al-ḥall, kayfa? Qaḍīyat al-iqtiṣād al-islāmī—al-iṭār wal-huwīya", *Liwā' al-islām*, July–August 1982.
Durra, Muḥammad Ḥasan, "Al-tamlīk lil-qādir wal-ta'jīr li-man lā yastaṭī'", *Al-Sha'b*, 24 January 1984.
Murād, Muḥammad Ḥilmī, "Aghniyā' al-infitāḥ ya'īshūn bi-amn al-muwāṭinīn", *Al-Sha'b*, 14 February 1984.
Durra, Muḥammad Ḥasan, "10 as'ila ḥawla azmat al-iskān", *Al-Sha'b*, 12 August 1984.
Murād, Muḥammad Ḥilmī, "Fawḍā al-as'ār wa-khuṭūrat tarkaha bi-lā ḍābit", *Al-Sha'b*, 11 September 1984.
Durra, Muḥammad Ḥasan, "Ilghā' al-istithnā'āt wal-imtiyāzāt al-khāṣṣa amr ḥatmī", *Al-Sha'b*, 12 October 1984.
Al-Tilmisānī, 'Umar, "Ziyādat al-intāj", *Al-Sha'b*, 19 October 1984.
Zaydān, Ḥāmid, "'Alā wazīr al-iqtiṣād an yujīb aw yarḥal", *Al-Sha'b*, 23 October 1984.
Durra, Muḥammad Ḥasan, "Ma'sāt al-da'm wa subul al-'ilāj", *Al-Sha'b*, 11 December 1984.
Durra, Muḥammad Ḥasan, "Qirā'a fī milaff al-iskān (1)", *Al-Sha'b*, 22 January 1985.

Murād, Muḥammad Ḥilmī, "Iḥdharū makhāṭir al-i'timād 'alā al-ma'ūna", *Al-Sha'b*, 29 January 1985.

Zaydān, Ḥāmid, "Khaṭar al-ḥarb al-'ālamiyya al-thālitha fī 3 mu'tamarāt duwaliyya fī usbū' wāḥid", *Al-Sha'b*, 5 February 1985.

Murād, Muḥammad Ḥilmī, "Al-junayh al-miṣrī fī miḥna wal-'ilāj bayna aydīnā", *Al-Sha'b*, 12 February 1985.

Durra, Muḥammad Ḥasan, "Qirā'a fī milaff al-iskān (2)", *Al-Sha'b*, 12 February 1985.

Durra, Muḥammad Ḥasan, "Dawr al-dawla wa al-tawāzun al-mafqūd", *Al-Sha'b*, 19 March 1985.

Zaydān, Ḥāmid, "Lan takūn al-iqāla aw al-istiqāla wasīla lil-hurūb min al-musā'ala", *Al-Sha'b*, 2 April 1985.

Murād, Muḥammad Ḥilmī, "Wujūb tawsī' dā'irat al-musā'ala fī-mā sammathu al-maḥkama bil-nakba al-iqtiṣādiyya", *Al-Sha'b*, 2 April 1985.

Durra, Muḥammad Ḥasan, "Al-arḍ miftāḥ al-qaḍīya", *Al-Sha'b*, 12 April 1985.

Murād, Muḥammad Ḥilmī, "Idārat qiṭā' al-bitrūl fī ḥāja ilā murāja'a", *Al-Sha'b*, 23 April 1985.

Shukrī, Ibrāhīm, "Al-siyāsāt al-iqtiṣādiyya tad'afnā fī muwājahat amrīkā wa-isrā'īl wa tushī' al-maẓālim al-ijtimā'iyya", *Al-Sha'b*, 23 April 1985.

Ḥusayn, 'Ādil, "Kayfa ḥawwala al-infitāḥ iqtiṣād miṣr ilā haykal hashsh?", *Al-Sha'b*, 23 April 1985.

Ḥusayn, 'Ādil, "Al-taṭbī' mas'ā lil-haymana al-isrā'īliyya min al-dākhil", *Al-Sha'b*, 30 April 1985.

Sulaymān, 'Iṣām, "Ibrāhīm Shukrī: al-duyūn al-khārijiyya tuhaddid istiqlālnā al-waṭanī", *Al-Sha'b*, 30 April 1985.

Author unknown, "Mamdūḥ Qināwī yujaddid istijwābahu lil-ḥukūma 'an al-iḍṭirābāt fī al-siyāsa al-iqtiṣādiyya", *Al-Sha'b*, 30 April 1985.

Murād, Muḥammad Ḥilmī, "Man alladhī yatasattar 'alā al-inḥirāfāt fī hay'at al-bitrūl?", *Al-Sha'b*, 4 June 1985.

Murād, Muḥammad Ḥilmī, "Maṭlūb ittikhādh al-qarārāt al-sarī'a al-ḥāsima qabla tafāqum al-mashākil", *Al-Sha'b*, 16 July 1985.

Murād, Muḥammad Ḥilmī, "Hal tattafiq al-qurūḍ al-jadīda bi-miṣr lil-ṭayrān ma'a al-ṣaḥwa al-kubrā?!", *Al-Sha'b*, 26 November 1985.

Ḥusayn, 'Ādil, "Hādha ḥadīth ghayr muwaffaq li-ustādh iqtiṣād—wa laysa bayānan li-ḥukūma", *Al-Sha'b*, 3 December 1985.

Ḥusayn, 'Ādil, "Al-azma al-iqtiṣādiyya: la'allahu khayr la'allanā nufiq", *Al-Sha'b*, 28 January 1986.

Ḥusayn, 'Ādil, "'An al-sharī'a wal-iqtiṣād wal-bunūk al-islāmiyya", *Al-Sha'b*, 13 May 1986.

Murād, Muḥammad Ḥilmī, "Li-mādha yabqī Wālī wazīran lil-zirā'a wal-amn al-ghadhā'ī raghma fashlihi?", *Al-Sha'b*, 30 September 1986.

Ḥusayn, Magdī Aḥmad, "Matā nuwaqqif ṣandūq al-naqd al-amrīkī—'inda ḥad-dihi?", *Al-Sha'b*, 25 November 1986.

Ḥusayn, 'Ādil, "Mādhā jarā fī mubāḥathāt al-ra'īs?", *Al-Sha'b*, 16 December 1986.

Ḥusayn, ʻĀdil, "Raddan ʻalā "muḥarrir al-Ahrām" alladhī taṭāwala ʻalaynā", *Al-Shaʻb*, 23 December 1986.

Ḥusayn, Magdī Aḥmad, "Miṣr—sharika amrīkiyya", *Al-Shaʻb*, 12 January 1987.

Murād, Muḥammad Ḥilmī, "Fal-mashākil madrūsa wal-ḥulūl maʻrūfa", *Al-Shaʻb*, 20 January 1987.

Ḥusayn, ʻĀdil, "Ayna ra'īs al-ḥukūma?", *Al-Shaʻb*, 10 February 1987.

Shaḥḥāta, Ḥusayn, "Al-maṣārif al-islāmīyya wal-iftirā'āt al-sabaʻ", *Al-Nūr*, 4 March 1987.

Ḥusayn, ʻĀdil, "Kayfa yaḥkumūnanā wa kayfa tuṣdar al-qarārāt?", *Al-Shaʻb*, 17 March 1987.

Murād, Muḥammad Ḥilmī, "Man huwa "Abū Lamʻa" muqaddim bayānāt khiṭāb ʻīd al-ʻummāl?", *Al-Shaʻb*, 5 May 1987.

Bakrī, Maḥmūd and Muḥammad Gamāl ʻArafa, "Al-ittifāq maʻa ṣandūq al-naqd", *Al-Shaʻb*, 12 May 1987.

Ḥusayn, ʻĀdil, "Al-islāmiyyūn wal-ittifāq maʻa ṣandūq al-naqd", *Al-Shaʻb*, 12 May 1987.

Murād, Muḥammad Ḥilmī, "Istimrār duwwāmat al-qurūḍ al-ajnabiyya wa tijārat al-ʻumla", *Al-Shaʻb*, 26 May 1987.

Ḥusayn, ʻĀdil, "Kārithat al-ittifāq al-sirrī maʻa amrīka wa ṣandūq al-naqd", *Al-Shaʻb*, 26 May 1987.

Shaḥḥāta, Ḥusayn, "Al-tandīd bil-mutaʻāmilīn bil-ribā fī ḍaw' al-qur'ān wal-sunna", *Al-Nūr*, 27 May 1987.

Ḥusayn, ʻĀdil, "Hā'ulā'i al-mufāwidūn yuhdirūn ḥuqūq miṣr", *Al-Shaʻb*, 2 June 1987.

Ḥusayn, Magdī Aḥmad, "Al-tawassuʻ fī al-minaḥ al-ajnabiyya niʻma am naqma?", *Al-Shaʻb*, 23 June 1987.

Ḥusayn, Magdī Aḥmad, "Al-ra'īs wal-qamḥ wal-sūfyat", *Al-Shaʻb*, 1 September 1987.

Ḥusayn, ʻĀdil, "9 ittihāmāt ḍidda sharikāt tawẓīf al-amwāl", *Al-Shaʻb*, 15 September 1987.

Ḥusayn, ʻĀdil, "Sharikāt tawẓīf al-amwāl al-mushkila wal-ḥall", *Al-Shaʻb*, 22 September 1987.

Ḥusayn, Magdī Aḥmad, "Ilā wazīr al-iqtiṣād: nuṭālibuka bil-ṣumūd", *Al-Shaʻb*, 22 September 1987.

Murād, Muḥammad Ḥilmī, "Wa mādhā ʻan al tasattur ʻalā al-inḥirāf fī qiṭāʻ al-bitrūl?", *Al-Shaʻb*, 29 September 1987.

Murād, Muḥammad Ḥilmī, "Innā uttahim wazīr al-bitrūl shakhṣiyyan", *Al-Shaʻb*, 6 October 1987.

Murād, Muḥammad Ḥilmī, "Qiṭāʻ al-bitrūl fī ḥāja ilā ṣaḥwa qawmiyya", *Al-Shaʻb*, 13 October 1987.

Murād, Muḥammad Ḥilmī, "Faḍīḥat maʻmal takrīr al-bitrūl bi-Asyuṭ", *Al-Shaʻb*, 27 October 1987.

Ḥusayn, ʻĀdil, "Al-ithnayn al-aswad wa mu'tamar al-intāj", *Al-Shaʻb*, 10 November 1987.

Murād, Muḥammad Ḥilmī, "Al-ḍajja al-khādiʻa ḥawla ittifāqiyyāt al-baḥth ʻan al-bitrūl", *Al-Shaʻb*, 17 November 1987.

Hadīya, Fu'ād, "Takhṭīt bilā ḥisāb walā dīmuqrāṭīya", *Al-Sha'b*, 25 November 1987.

Ḥusayn, 'Ādil, "Al-baṭāla wal-siyāḥa wa sharikāt tawẓīf al-amwāl", *Al-Sha'b*, 8 December 1987.

Ḥusayn, 'Ādil, "Al-shabāb wal-baṭāla wal-ḥall al-islāmī", *Al-Sha'b*, 15 December 1987.

Murād, Muḥammad Ḥilmī, "I'tirāfāt kādhiba bi-irtikāb jināya lam yuḥāsab al-mas'ūlūn 'an ṣudūriha", *Al-Sha'b*, 22 December 1987.

Ḥusayn, Magdī Aḥmad, "Wa ishta'alat nīrān al-as'ār!", *Al-Sha'b*, 19 January 1988.

Murād, Muḥammad Ḥilmī, "Mulābasāt hurūb wazīr al-bitrūl", *Al-Sha'b*, 26 January 1988.

Murād, Muḥammad Ḥilmī, "Mā ra'y wazīr al-bitrūl fī al-ḥukm 'alā dhī al-ri'āsatayn?", *Al-Sha'b*, 26 January 1988.

Al-Suyūfī, Aḥmad, "Al-sharikāt mushkila tuhimm kull bayt", *Al-Sha'b*, 16 February 1988.

Ḥusayn, 'Ādil, "Kānat hunāka nawāqiṣ wa-inḥirāfāt wa-lākin lam takun al-mas'ala mujarrad 'amaliyyat naṣṣāb", *Al-Sha'b*, 29 February 1988.

Ḥusayn, 'Ādil, "Ḍidda al-fasād aynamā kāna", *Al-Sha'b*, 29 February 1988.

Ḥusayn, 'Ādil, "Mas'alat al-'umran al-basharī aw al-tanmīya al-mustaqilla al-murakkaba", *Al-Sha'b*, 1 March 1988.

Al-Hawārī, Anwar, "Al-gharb yanhab 'awā'id nafṭ al-muslimīn", *Liwā' al-islām*, 17 May 1988.

Ḥusayn, 'Ādil, "Al-mushīr Abū Ghazāla wa kuttāb al-ḥukūma wal-ḥamla ḍidda sharikāt tawẓīf al-amwāl", *Al-Sha'b*, 17 May 1988.

Zahrān, Sayyid, "Miṣr ilā ayn?", *Ṣawt al-'arab*, 29 May 1988.

Ḥusayn, 'Ādil, "Mādhā yaqūl al-qānūn al-ghādir al-ẓālim?", *Al-Sha'b*, 7 Junc 1988.

Al-Suyūfī, Aḥmad, "Innahū qānūn lil-ṭawāri' fī majāl al-iqtiṣād", *Al-Sha'b*, 14 June 1988.

Gamāl al-Dīn, Maḥmūd, "Aṣḥāb sharikāt tawẓīf al-amwāl bayna al-mūdi'īn wa ḍughūṭ al-ḥukūma", *Al-Sha'b*, 14 June 1988.

Murād, Muḥammad Ḥilmī, "Al-niẓām al-ḥākim yuqarrir iḥtikār al-majālis al-maḥalliyya wa khanq sharikāt tawẓīf al-amwāl", *Al-Sha'b*, 14 June 1988.

Al-Baṣīr, Ḥamdī, "Thalāthūna khabīran iqtiṣādiyyan yunāqishūn ḥāḍir al-sharikāt wa mustaqbalaha", *Al-Nūr*, 15 June 1988.

Al-Baṣīr, Ḥamdī, "Akbar tajammu' iqtiṣādī miṣrī yuṭālib bi-ilghā' al-ribā", *Al-Nūr*, 15 June 1988.

Al-Suyūfī, Aḥmad, "Mukhālifāt dustūriyya wa akhṭā' qānūniyya wa makhāṭir iqtiṣādiyya fī qānūn tawẓīf al-amwāl", *Al-Sha'b*, 21 June 1988.

Ḥusayn, 'Ādil, "Bal tuṣaffūn al-sharikāt wa li-maṣlaḥat al-ajānib", *Al-Sha'b*, 28 June 1988.

Al-Suyūfī, Aḥmad, "Al-qānūn al-jadid yaḥmī ḥuqūq al-mūdi'īn am yuhdir amwālihim?", *Al-Sha'b*, 5 July 1988.

Al-Baṣīr, Ḥamdī, "Munāqasha sākhina ḥawla miṣdāqiyyat sharikāt tawẓīf al-amwāl", *Al-Nūr*, 6 July 1988.

Author unknown, "Munāqashāt sākhina fī al-nadwa al-'ilmiyya li-tawẓif al-amwāl", *Liwā' al-islām*, 15 July 1988.
Author unknown, "Qānūn tawẓīf al-amwāl yadkhul dā'irat al-khilāf al-ḥizbī", *Al-Hawādith*, 19 August 1988.
Ḥusayn, 'Ādil, "Ta'jīr miṣr li-ḥall al-azma al-iqtiṣādiyya", *Al-Sha'b*, 30 August 1988.
Ḥusayn, 'Ādil, "Miḥnat al-muwaẓẓafīn wa ḥukm al-aghbiyā'!", *Al-Sha'b*, 6 September 1988.
Ḥusayn, 'Ādil, "Li-narfuḍ al-dhull wa nu'lin al-jihād", *Al-Sha'b*, 20 September 1988.
Ḥusayn, 'Ādil, "Al-ghalā' wal-amn al-markazī wal-qamar al-isrā'īlī", *Al-Sha'b*, 27 September 1988.
Murād, Muḥammad Ḥilmī, "Lā takhda'ūnā: azmatunā lan yuḥilliha ta'jīl al-qurūḍ al-ajnabiyya", *Al-Sha'b*, 4 October 1988.
Ḥusayn, 'Ādil, "Kārithat al-mūdi'īn fī sharikāt al-tawẓīf", *Al-Sha'b*, 1 November 1988.
Ḥusayn, 'Ādil, "Ḥukūmāt 'ājiza 'an binā' al-qūwa al-iqtiṣādiyya", *Al-Sha'b*, 8 November 1988.
Ḥusayn, 'Ādil, "Fī sharikāt al-amwāl: kayfa bada'a al-musalsal wa kayfa sa-yantahī?", *Al-Sha'b*, 22 November 1988.
Murād, Muḥammad Ḥilmī, "Min i'ṣār sharikat al-Rayyān ilā mufāja'at tamāthīl al-ḥukkām", *Al-Sha'b*, 22 November 1988.
Ḥusayn, 'Ādil, "Aḥmad Bahā' al-Dīn wa miḥnat sharikāt al-amwāl", *Al-Sha'b*, 29 November 1988.
Ḥusayn, 'Ādil, "Ittaqi allāh yā Bahā'!", *Al-Sha'b*, 6 December 1988.
Al-Baṣīr, Ḥamdī, "Al-insān wal-minhaj al-islāmī fī al-tanmīya al-iqtiṣādiyya", *Al-Nūr*, 7 December 1988.
Al-Ghazālī, 'Abd al-Ḥamīd, "Sharikāt tawẓīf al-amwāl bayna al-maraḍ al-hūlandī wal-maraḍ al-miṣrī wal-maraḍ al-bākistānī", *Al-Sha'b*, 13 December 1988.
Shaḥḥāta, Ḥusayn, "Al-ḥaqā'iq al-tā'iha wal-awrāq al-mukhtaliṭa fī qaḍīyat sharikāt tawẓīf al-amwāl", *Liwā' al-islām*, 9 January 1989.
Al-Ghazālī, 'Abd al-Ḥamīd, "Sharikāt tawẓīf al-amwāl bayna islāmiyyat al-tawajjuh wa khaṭa' al-mumārasa (1)", *Al-Nūr*, 25 January 1989.
Al-Ghazālī, 'Abd al-Ḥamīd, "Sharikāt tawẓīf al-amwāl bayna islāmiyyat al-tawajjuh wa khaṭa' al-mumārasa (2)", *Al-Nūr*, 25 January 1989.
Author unknown, "Al-zakāt rakīza iqtiṣādiyya ḥaḍāriyya tanammuwiyya yajib al-akhdh bi-hā fī al-tawajjuh al-iqtiṣādi", *Liwā' al-islām*, 5 June 1989.
Ḥusayn, 'Ādil, "'An al-iqtiṣād wa al-sharī'a wa al-ḥiwār al-qawmī", *Al-Sha'b*, 6 June 1989.
Ḥusayn, 'Ādil, "Qānūn al-istithmār al-jadīd", *Al-Sha'b*, 20 June 1989.
Al-Ghazālī, Muḥammad, "Hādhā dīnunā", *Al-Sha'b*, 20 June 1989.
Murād, Muḥammad Ḥilmī, "Min istijdā' raghīf al-khubz ilā iḥtiḍān al-Numayrī", *Al-Sha'b*, 27 June 1989.
Ḥusayn, 'Ādil, "I'linū al-ittifāqiyyāt al-sirriyya ma'a ṣandūq al-naqd", *Al-Sha'b*, 4 July 1989.

Muṣṭafā, Magdī, "Al-qiṭā‘ al-‘āmm ‘alā al-ṭarīqa al-miṣriyya", *Liwā' al-islām*, 5 July 1989.
Ḥusayn, ‘Ādil, "Al-ḥiwār al-qawmī bayna al-ḍaghṭ al-amrīkī wa ḍarūrat al-iṣlāḥ al-shāmil", *Al-Sha‘b*, 1 August 1989.
Maṭar, Zakarīya, "Ṣandūq al-naqd wal-ghalā' al-qādim", *Liwā' al-islām*, 3 August 1989.
Ḥusayn, ‘Ādil, "Innahum yuwarriṭūnaka yā faḍīlat al-muftī", *Al-Sha‘b*, 8 August 1989.
Shaḥḥāta, Ḥusayn, "Al-fā'ida al-ribawiyya wuqūd al-taḍakhkhum al-naqdī wa laysat ta‘wīḍan ‘anhu", *Al-Nūr*, 23 August 1989.
Author unknown, "‘Ulamā' al-sharī‘a wa asātidhat al-iqtiṣād al-islāmī yunāqishūn al-fawā'id al-maṣrafiyya bayna al-ibāḥa wal-taḥrīm", *Al-Qabas*, 25 August 1989.
Muṣṭafā, Magdī, "Al-fawā'id al-maṣrafiyya hiya ‘ayn al-ribā", *Liwā' al-islām*, 1 September 1989.
Author unknown, "Fiqh al mu‘āmalāt: al-muḍāraba", *Liwā' al-islām*, 1 September 1989.
Ḥusayn, ‘Ādil, "Al-ḥukūma tasriqnā yā faḍīlat al-muftī", *Al-Sha‘b*, 12 September 1989.
Ḥusayn, ‘Ādil, "‘An al-fawā'id al-maṣrafiyya marra ukhrā", *Al-Sha‘b*, 19 September 1989.
Al-Baṣīr, Ḥamdī, "Wa-khubarā' al-iqtiṣād al-islāmī yu‘āriḍūn al-muftī", *Al-Nūr*, 27 September 1989.
Al-Ghazālī, ‘Abd al-Ḥamīd, "Ḥawla al-fawā'id al-maṣrafiyya: min al-aghlabiyya al-ṣāmita ilā jumhūr al-iqtiṣādiyyin", *Al-Ahrām al-Iqtiṣādī*, 9 October 1989.
Al-Ghazālī, Muḥammad, "Hādhā dīnunā", *Al-Sha‘b*, 10 October 1989.
Al-Ghazālī, ‘Abd al-Ḥamīd, "Al-fawā'id al-maṣrafiyya: min al-aghlabiyya al-ṣāmita ilā jumhūr al-iqtiṣādiyyin", *Al-Nūr*, 11 October 1989.
Ḥusayn, ‘Ādil, "Awqifū munāqashat al-fawā'id fa-hunāka su'āl akhṭar", *Al-Sha‘b*, 17 October 1989.
Muṣṭafā, Magdī, "La‘bat al-iṣdār al-naqdī ta‘nī mazīdan min al-taḍakhkhum wa ghalā' al-as‘ār", *Liwā' al-islām*, 1 November 1989.
Al-Mut‘inī, ‘Abd al-‘Aẓīm, "Naksa fī al-iftā' wa ‘awda li-ribā al-jāhiliyya", *Liwā' al-islām*, 1 November 1989.
Ḥusayn, ‘Ādil, "Bay‘ miṣr fī al-mazād wa qaḍīyat al-qiṭā‘ al ‘āmm", *Al-Sha‘b*, 12 December 1989.
Shaḥḥāta, Ḥusayn, "Al-ta'mīn al-ta‘āwunī badīl lil-ta'mīn al-tijārī", *Al-Nūr*, 27 December 1989.
Al-Shīwī, ‘Imād, "Wal-sanadāt al-dūlāriyya aydan ghayr shar‘iyya", *Al-Nūr*, 27 December 1989.
Badr, Badr Muḥammad, "Matā yastaridd al-mūdi‘ūn amwālihim?", *Liwā' al-islām*, 30 December 1989.
Ḥusayn, ‘Ādil, "Al-tisa‘īnāt ‘aqd al-nahḍa al-islāmiyya", *Al-Sha‘b*, 23 January 1990.
Al-Ghazālī, ‘Abd al-Ḥamīd, "Sanat al-taghyīr wa irādat al-binā' amama ma‘āwil al-hadm wa quwā al-jumūd (1)", *Al-Nūr*, 24 January 1990.

Muṣṭafā, Magdī, "Miḥnat al-bunūk al-islāmiyya fī al-fikra am fī al-taṭbīq?", *Liwā' al-islām*, 28 January 1990.

Al-Ghazālī, 'Abd al-Ḥamīd, "Sanat al-taghyīr wa irādat al-binā' amama ma'āwil al-hadm wa quwā al-jumūd (2)", *Al-Nūr*, 31 January 1990.

Al-Baṣīr, Ḥamdī, Muḥammad Fatḥallāh and Muḥammad Sālimān. "Mashrū' wazīr al-iqtiṣād khud'a i'lāmiyya", *Al-Nūr*, 31 January 1990.

Shaḥḥāta, Ḥusayn, "Hākadhā takūn al-tanmīya", *Al-Nūr*, 21 February 1990.

Muṣṭafā, Magdī, "Kayfa yu'ālij al-islām al-taḍakhkhum?", *Liwā' al-islām*, 28 March 1990.

Shu'ayr, Aḥmad, "Wa ba'da muḥākamat al-Rayyān hal ta'ūd amwāl al-mūdi'īn?", *Liwā' al-islām*, 28 March 1990.

Ḥusayn, 'Ādil, "Al-qiṭā' al-'āmm yubā' lil-ajānib, taḥarrakū li-man' al-jarīma", *Al-Sha'b*, 10 April 1990.

Ga'far, Aḥmad, "Al-taqyīm al-islāmī li-sharikāt tawẓīf al-amwāl wa ḥimāyat ḥuqūq al-mūdi'īn", *Al-Nūr*, 18 April 1990.

Al-Aḥmadī, 'Abd al-Mun'im, "Nuwwāb al-ikhwān bi-majlis al-sha'b yu'akkidūn: qānūn al-tijāra al-baḥriyya mukhālif lil-sharī'a al-islāmiyya", *Al-Nūr*, 18 April 1990.

Shaḥḥāta, Ḥusayn, "Asās al-tanmīya fī al-mujtama'", *Al-Nūr*, 25 April 1990.

Muṣṭafā, Magdī, "Aṣwāt tad'ū li-ḍarūrat dukhūl al-bunūk al-islāmiyya majāl al-tanmīya", *Liwā' al-islām*, 26 April 1990.

Muṣṭafā, Magdī, "Al-mushkila al-sukkāniyya shammā'at al-ḥukūma li-tabrīr 'ajziha", *Liwā' al-islām*, 26 April 1990.

Shaḥḥāta, Ḥusayn, "Khawāṭir ḥawla al-minhaj al-islāmī lil-amn wal-tanmīya", *Al-Nūr*, 2 May 1990.

Ḥusayn, 'Ādil, "Tasā'ulāt 'an al-qiṭā' al-'āmm ba'da khiṭāb awwal māyū", *Al-Sha'b*, 8 May 1990.

Murād, Muḥammad Ḥilmī, "Raf' al-as'ār aswa' al-ḥulūl li-mu'ālajat azmat al-ḥukūma", *Al-Sha'b*, 15 May 1990.

'Abd al-Quddūs, Muḥammad, "'Ajā'ib", *Al-Nūr*, 16 May 1990.

Al-Ghazalī al-Jubaylī, Zaynab, "Hal yakill al-mujāhid?", *Al-Nūr*, 16 May 1990.

Abū Dāwud, Al-Sayyid, "Al-qiṭā' al-'āmm min wijhat naẓar islāmiyya fī ḥiwār ma'a Yūsuf Kamāl khabīr al-iqtiṣād al-islāmī", *Al-Nūr*, 16 May 1990.

Al-Ṣādiq, Aḥmad and Muḥammad 'Alā' al-Dīn, "Al-as'ār tashta'il wal-badhakh al-ḥukūmī mustamirr", *Al-Nūr*, 16 May 1990.

Shaḥḥāta, Ḥusayn, "Al-ḍawābiṭ al-islāmiyya li-tarshīd al-qiṭā' al-'āmm", *Liwā' al-islām*, 25 May 1990.

Author unknown, "Mudīr 'āmm al-mu'āmalāt al-islāmiyya bi-bunūk al-qarya yad'ū li-inshā' sharikāt ta'mīn islāmiyya", *Liwā' al-islām*, 25 May 1990.

'Abd al-'Alīm, 'Abduh, "Dirāsa khaṭīra li-hay'at sūq al-māl tad'ū li-'amal aw'iyat iddikhār islāmiyya li-khidmat khiṭṭat al-tanmīya", *Liwā' al-islām*, 25 May 1990.

Author unknown, "Tadakhkhul al-dawla fī al-nishāṭ al-iqtiṣādī", *Liwā' al-islām*, 23 June 1990.

Muṣṭafā, Magdī, "Waraqa mansīya min milaff al-bunūk al-islāmiyya", *Liwā' al-islām*, 23 June 1990.

Murād, Muḥammad Ḥilmī, "'Alā al-ra'īs Mubārak an yuwaqqif nahb bitrūlna li-ṣāliḥ sharikat shil", *Al-Sha'b*, 26 June 1990.

Muṣṭafā, Magdī, "Al-tahrīb al-ḍarībī wa al-'ab' alladhī yataḥammaluhū al-fuqarā' wa maḥdūdī al-dakhl", *Liwā' al-islām*, 23 July 1990.

Fawda, Ṣubḥī 'Abd al-Mun'im, "Idārat wa tanẓīm al-waqt ḍarūra li-taḥqīq al-iqtiṣād al-nājiḥ", *Liwā' al-islām*, 21 September 1990.

Author unknown, "Qāfila ṭibbiyya nājiḥa tuqīmuhā jam'iyyat al-zahrā' bi-miṣr al-qadīma", *Al-Nūr*, 26 September 1990.

Al-Ghazālī, 'Abd al-Ḥamīd, "Al-bu'd al-iqtiṣādī al-duwalī lil-kāritha wal-wāqi' al-siyāsī", *Al-Nūr*, 3 October 1990.

Author unknown, "Mudakhkharāt al-'āmilīn bil-khārij—kayfa yatimm jadhbuha lil-istithmār?", *Liwā' al-islām*, 20 October 1990.

Muṣṭafā, Magdī, "Kayfa tajid tharwāt al-muslimīn ṭarīqaha lil-istithmār fi bilādihim?", *Liwā' al-islām*, 20 October 1990.

Khalīl, Sayyid, "Mawākib al-isrāf al-ḥukūmī mustamirra", *Liwā' al-islām*, 1 November 1990.

Muṣṭafā, Magdī, "Al-isqāṭ al-juz'ī li-madyūniyyat miṣr al-khārijiyya hal yakūn furṣa li-murāja'a shāmila wa iṣlāḥ haykal al-iqtiṣād al-miṣrī?", *Liwā' al-islām*, 19 November 1990.

Author unknown, "Shirā' mumtalakāt al-Rayyān", *Liwā' al-islām*, 19 November 1990.

Muṣṭafā, Magdī, "Da'wa 'ilmiyya li-iḥyā' farīḍat al-zakāt", *Liwā' al-islām*, 18 December 1990.

Murād, Muḥammad Ḥilmī, "Mukhaddir jadīd ismuhu "mashrū' al-alf yawm"", *Al-Sha'b*, 25 December 1990.

Author unknown, "Al-mushkila al-iqtiṣādiyya wa 'ilājuhā fī al-islām", *Liwā' al-islām*, 17 January 1991.

Ḥusayn, Magdī Aḥmad, "Taḥdīd al-nasl: siyāsat al-gharb naḥwa 'ālam al-mustaḍ'afīn" [Birth Control: The Policy of the West towards the Oppressed], *Minbar al-Sharq*, no. 1, 1992.

Ḥusayn, 'Ādil, "Al-thawra al-islāmiyya fī al-sūdān: ḥurriyya kāmila lil-sūq wal-as'ār ma'a takāful yaḥmī al-mustaḍ'afīn wa tanmīyat al-i'timād 'alā al-nafs", *Al-Sha'b*, 10 March 1992.

Ḥusayn, 'Ādil, "Durūs fī al-iqtiṣād al-siyāsī nata'allamuhā min al-sūdān al-islāmī", *Al-Sha'b*, 17 March 1992.

Imbābī, Gamāl, "Dayrūṭ wal-Qūṣīya al-asbāb wal-ḥulūl wa ahamm al-mashākil", *Al-Sha'b*, 10 May 1994.

Budaywī, Salāh, "Miṣr taḥta khaṭṭ al-faqr", *Al-Sha'b*, 17 May 1994.

Ḥusayn, 'Ādil, "Lā budda min shahādat ṣidq fī ḥaqq thawrat yūlyū ḥattā nastafīd min tajāribihā", *Al-Sha'b*, 22 July 1994.

SECONDARY SOURCES

'Abd al-Faḍīl, Maḥmūd, *Al-khadī'a al-māliyya al-kubrā. Al-iqtiṣād al-siyāsī li-sharikāt tawẓīf al-amwāl* [The Great Financial Deception: The Political

Economy of the Investment Companies], Dār al-mustaqbal al-'arabī, Cairo, 1989.

——— "Fī al-iqtiṣād al-islāmī" [On Islamic Economics], *Qaḍāyā Fikriyya*, October 1989, Cairo.

'Abd al-Ḥalīm, Maḥmūd, *Al-ikhwān al-muslimūn—aḥdāth ṣana'at al-tārīkh* [The Muslim Brothers: Events that Made History], 3 vols, Dār al-da'wa, Alexandria, 1979.

'Abd al-Ḥamīd, Muḥsin, *Tajdīd al-fikr al-islāmī* [The Renewal of Islamic Thinking], Dār al-ṣāḥwa, Cairo, 1985.

'Abd al-Karīm, Khalīl, *Li-taṭbīq al-sharī'a lā lil-ḥukm* [For the Application of the Sharī'a, not for Power], Al-ahālī, Cairo, 1987.

'Abdallāh, Aḥmad, *The Student Movement and National Politics in Egypt*, Al Saqi Books, London, 1985.

——— "Sie schaffen eine Atmosphäre konstanter Instabilität", interview with Ahmad Abdallah, *TAZ*, 26 March 1993.

——— "Representing Youth in all its Glory", *Al-Ahram Weekly*, 2 May 1994.

——— and Jūrj 'Ajāyibī (eds), *Al-ḥiwār al-waṭanī* [National Dialogue], Al-lajna al-miṣriyya lil-'adāla wal-salām, Cairo, 1994.

'Abd al-Majīd, Waḥīd, *Al-aḥzāb al-miṣriyya min al-dākhil 1907–1992* [Egyptian Parties from Within 1907–92], Markaz al-Maḥrūsa lil-nashr wal-khidmāt al-ṣuḥufiyya, Cairo, 1993.

Abdel-Malek, Anwar (ed.), *Contemporary Arab Political Thought*, Zed Books, London, 1983.

——— *Al-ibdā' wal-mashrū' al-ḥaḍārī* [Innovation and the Civilisational Project], Al-hilāl, Cairo, 1991.

'Abduh, Muḥammad, *Al-islām dīn al-'ilm wal-madaniyya* [Islam, the Religion of Science and Civilisation], Sinā lil-nashr, Cairo, 1990.

Abou-Mandour, Mohamed, "The State of Egyptian Agriculture: Perspectives and Problems in Future Development", paper presented at Danida seminar on Egyptian development, Copenhagen, June 15–16 1990.

Abrahamian, Ervand, *Radical Islam: The Iranian Mojahedin*, I. B. Tauris, London, 1989.

——— *Khomeinism*, I. B. Tauris, London, 1993.

Abu Zayd, Naṣr Ḥāmid, *Mafhūm al-naṣṣ* [The Meaning of the Text], Al-hay'a al-miṣriyya lil-kitāb, Cairo, 1990.

Abū Zayd, Ṣabrī Aḥmad, "Al-taḥawwulāt al-haykaliyya fī al-ṣinā'a al-taḥwīliyya fī miṣr 1959/60–1980/81" [Structural Changes in Egyptian Manufacturing Industries 1959/60–1980/81], *L'Egypte Contemporaine/Miṣr al-mu'āṣira*, no. 403, Cairo, January 1986.

Aḥmad, Rif'at Sayyid, *Al-nabī al-musallaḥ (1)—al-rāfiḍūn*, Riad El-Rayyes Books, London, 1991.

——— *Al-nabī al-musallaḥ (2)—al-thā'irūn*, Riad El-Rayyes Books, London, 1991.

——— "La problematique du nationalisme dans la pensée islamique contemporaine en référence au modèle égyptien", *Egypte Monde Arabe*, no. 15/16, Cairo, 1993.

Ajami, Fouad, *The Arab Predicament: Arab Political Thought and Practice Since 1967*, Cambridge University Press, 1992.

Al-'Alawī, Hādī, "Naẓara mujmala fī iqtiṣādiyyāt al-islām" [An Overview of the Economics of Islam], *Qaḍāyā Fikriyya*, October 1989, Cairo.

Aly, Abdel Monem Said, "Democratization in Egypt", *American-Arab Affairs*, no. 29.

'Āmil, Mahdī, *Naqd al-fikr al-yawmī* [Critique of Contemporary Thought], Dār al-Farābī, Beirut, 1988.

Amīn, Galāl, *Al-iqtiṣād wal-siyāsa wal-mujtama' fī 'aṣr al-infitāḥ* [Economy, Politics and Society in the Era of infitāḥ], Maktabat Madbūlī, Cairo, 1984.

——— "Foreign Aid, Foreign Investment and Economic Development in Egypt 1975–1990", paper presented at Danida seminar on Egyptian development, Copenhagen, June 15–16 1990.

——— *Ma'ḍalat al-iqtiṣād al-miṣrī* [The Dilemma of the Egyptian Economy], Miṣr al-'arabiyya lil-nashr wal-tawzī', Cairo, 1994.

Amin, Samir, *Accumulation on a World Scale*, Monthly Review Press, New York, 1974.

——— *The Arab Economy Today*, Zed Books, London, 1982.

——— "Syd kan inte vänta" [The South Cannot Wait], *Ligan*, no. 1, 1985, Stockholm.

——— "Bandung—Thirty Years Later", paper presented at a conference convened by the Egyptian Diplomatic Institute on the occasion of the Thirtieth Anniversary of the Bandung Conference, Cairo, April 1985.

——— *Eurocentrism*, Zed Books, London, 1989.

——— "Al-ijtihād wal-ibdā' fī al-thaqāfa al-'arabiyya wa amāma taḥaddīyāt al-'aṣr" [Interpretation and Innovation in Arab Culture and Facing the Challenges of Our Time], *Qaḍāyā Fikriyya*, October 1989, Cairo.

——— *Delinking: Towards a Polycentric World*, Zed Books, London, 1990.

——— and Andre Gunder Frank, *På vei mot 1984* [Towards 1984], Gyldendal, Oslo, 1979.

Anderson, Lisa, "Fulfilling Prophecies: State Policies and Islamist Radicalism" in John L. Esposito (ed.), *Political Islam: Revolution, Radicalism or Reform?*, Lynne Rienner, Boulder, CO and London, 1997.

Aoude, Ibrahim G., "From National Bourgeois Development to Infitah: Egypt 1952–1992", *Arab Studies Quarterly*, vol. 16, no. 1 (winter 1994).

Ariff, Mohamed, "Islamic banking", *Aslan-Pacific Economic Literature*, vol. 2, no. 2, September 1988.

Asad, Talal, "Politics and Religion in Islamic Reform: A Critique of Kedourie's Afghani and Abduh", *Review of Middle East Studies*, no. 2, Ithaca Press, London, 1976.

Al-'Ashmāwī, Muḥammad Sa'īd, *Uṣūl al-sharī'a* [The Bases of the Sharī'a], Sinā lil-nashr, Cairo, 1992.

'Aṭīya, Gamāl al-Dīn, *Al-bunūk al-islāmiyya* [Islamic Banks], Kitāb al-Umma, Qatar, 1987.

Auda, Gehad, "An Uncertain Response: The Islamic Movement in Egypt" in James Piscatori (ed.), *Islamic Fundamentalisms and the Gulf Crisis*, The American Academy of Arts and Sciences, Chicago, IL, 1991.

Ayubi, Nazih, *Political Islam: Religion and Politics in the Arab World*, Routledge, London, 1991.

Azzam, Maha, "Egypt: The Islamists and the State under Mubarak" in Abdel Salam Sidahmed and Anoushiravan Ehteshami (eds), *Islamic Fundamentalism*, Westview Press, Boulder, CO and Oxford, 1996.

Aziz, T. M., "The Role of Muḥammad Baqir al-Sadr in Shi'i Political Activism in Iraq from 1958 to 1980", *IJMES*, no. 2, 1993.

Baer, Gabriel, *Studies in the Social History of Modern Egypt*, University of Chicago Press, 1969.

Bajazet, "La tradition? Quelle tradition?", *Maghreb-Machrek*, no. 151, January–March 1996.

Baker, Raymond William, *Sadat And After: Struggles For Egypt's Political Soul*, Harvard University Press, 1990.

——— "Invidious Comparisons: Realism, Postmodern Globalism, and Centrist Islamic Movements in Egypt" in John L. Esposito (ed.), *Political Islam: Revolution, Radicalism or Reform?*, Lynne Rienner Publishers, Boulder, CO, 1997.

——— *Islam Without Fear: Egypt and the New Islamists*, Harvard University Press, 2003.

Bakhash, Shaul, *The Reign of the Ayatollahs*, Counterpoint, London, 1985.

Al-Bannā, Ḥasan, *Five Tracts*, University of California Press, 1978.

Barbūtī, Ḥaqqī Ismā'īl, "Al-waḥda al-'arabiyya wal-āfāq al-fikriyya al-muta'āriḍa lil-'aql al-'arabī" [Arab Unity and Conflicting Horizons of Thought in the Arab Mind], *Al-Waḥda*, no. 89, February 1992.

Bari, Zohurul, *Re-emergence of the Muslim Brothers in Egypt*, Lancer Books, New Delhi, 1995.

Bayart, Jean-François, "Le politique par le bas en Afrique noire. Questions de méthode" in Jean-François Bayart, Achille Mbembe and Comi Toulabor, *Le politique par le bas en Afrique noire*, Karthala, Paris, 1992.

Bayat, Assef, "Marx and Shariati: A Critique of the 'Islamic' Critique of Marxism", *Alif*, no. 10, 1990.

Beedham, Brian, "Not Again, for Heaven's Sake: A Survey of Islam", *The Economist*, August 6, 1994.

Beinin, Joel, *Islamic Response to Capitalist Penetration*, Monthly Review Press, New York, 1980.

Beck, Lois and Nikki Keddie (ed.), *Women in the Muslim World*, Harvard University Press, 1978.

Belkaïd, Akram, "Introuvable modèle pour l'économie algérienne", *Le Monde Diplomatique*, December 1993.

Ben Néfissa, Sarah, "Associations égyptiennes: une libéralisation sous contrôle", *Maghreb-Machrek*, no. 150, October–December 1995.

Binder, Leonard, *Islamic Liberalism: A Critique of Development Ideologies*, University of Chicago Press, 1988.

Al-Bishrī, Ṭāriq, *Al-ḥaraka al-siyāsiyya fī miṣr 1945–1952* [The Political Movement in Egypt 1945–1952], Dār al-shurūq, Beirut and Cairo, 1983.

——— "'Anāṣir al-thabāt wal-taghyīr" [The Elements of Continuity and of Change], *Minbar al-ḥiwār*, no. 13, 1989.

——— and ‘Alā al-Dīn Hilāl, “Ḥiwār hawla mu’assasāt al-dawla fī al-nuẓum al-islāmiyya” [Dialogue on State Institutions in Islamic Regimes], *Minbar al-ḥiwār*, no. 14, 1989.

Bjorvatn, Kjetil, “Islamic Economics and Economic Development”, *Forum for Development Studies*, 2/98.

Blin, Louis, “Un trimestre d’informations economiques”, *Egypte Monde Arabe*, no. 6, 1991.

——— “Le renouvellement de l’accord entre l’Egypte et le Fonds Monétaire International et ses conséquences”, *Egypte Monde Arabe*, no. 15–16.

Boroujerdi, Mehrzad, *Iranian Intellectuals and the West: The Tormented Triumph of Nativism*, Syracuse University Press, 1996.

Botiveau, Bernard, “Egypte: crise de l’Ordre des avocats et normalisation des syndicats professionels”, *Maghreb-Machrek*, no. 142, 1993.

Boulby, Marion, “The Islamic challenge: Tunisia since independence”, *Third World Quarterly*, vol. 10, no. 2, April 1988, London.

Bourdieu, Pierre, *Ce que parler veut dire. L’économie des échanges linguistiques*, Fayard, Paris, 1982.

——— *In Other Words: Essays Towards a Reflexive Sociology*, Stanford University Press, 1990.

——— *Language and Symbolic Power*, Polity Press, Cambridge, 1991.

——— *Kultursociologiska texter* [Texts in Cultural Sociology], Brutus Östlings Bokförlag, Stockholm/Stehag, 1993.

——— and Loïc Wacquant, *Den kritiske ettertanke. Grunnlag for samfunnsanalyse* [Critical Reflection: A Basis for Social Analysis], Samlaget, Oslo, 1993.

Braanen, Bjørgulv and Per Lund, “Islam og marxismen” [Islam and Marxism], interview with Trond Linstad and Bjørn Olav Utvik, *Røde Fane*, no. 3/86.

Brewer, Anthony, *Marxist Theories of Imperialism*, Routledge & Kegan Paul, London, 1980.

Bromley, Simon, *Rethinking Middle East Politics*, Polity Press, Cambridge, 1994.

Brown, Nathan J., “Shari‘a and State in the Modern Muslim Middle East”, *IJMES*, no. 3, 1997.

——— *The Rule of Law in the Arab World: Courts in Egypt and the Gulf*, Cambridge University Press, 1997.

Burgat, François, *L’Islamisme au Maghreb*, Karthala, Paris, 1988.

——— “Communisme, nationalisme, islamisme: itinéraire d’un intellectuel égyptien, Adil Husayn”, *Egypte Monde Arabe*, no. 5, Cairo, 1991.

——— “Les conditions d’un dialogue avec l’occident, entretien avec Tariq al-Bichri”, *Egypte Monde Arabe*, no. 7, Cairo, 1991.

——— “L’Algerie, des ‘fellaghas’ aux ‘intégristes’”, *Le genre humain*, no. 23, Seuil, Paris, 1991.

——— “La dynamique de réislamisation”, *Geopolitique*, no. 34, Paris, 1991.

——— “Islam, nationalisme et islamisme”, interview with Rachid Ghannouchi, *Egypte Mond Arabe*, no. 10, Cairo, 1992.

——— and William Dowell, *The Islamic Movement in North Africa*, Center for Middle Eastern Studies, University of Texas at Austin, 1993.

——— with the collaboration of Baudouin Dupret: "Cacher le politique. Les représentations de la violence en Egypte", *Maghreb-Machrek*, no. 142, 1993.

——— *L'islamisme en face*, La Découverte, Paris, 1995.

——— and John Esposito (eds), *Modernizing Islam: Religion and the Public Sphere in the Middle East and Europe*, Hurst, London/Rutgers University Press, Piscataway, NJ, 2002.

——— *Face to Face with Political Islam*, I. B. Tauris, London, 2003.

Bush, Ray, "Egypt's Agricultural Strategy in the Nineties", *The Middle East*, May 1992.

——— "Er Egypt neste land på listen?" [Is Egypt the Next Country on the List?], *Aftenposten*, 11 May 1992.

Būttner, Friedemann, "The Fundamentalist Impulse and the Challenge of Modernity", *Law and State*, vol. 55, Tūbingen, 1997.

Caldwell, Malcolm, *The Wealth of Some Nations*, Zed Books, London, 1977.

Carré, Olivier, *L'islam laïque ou le retour à la Grande Tradition*, Armand Colin, Paris, 1993.

——— and Gérard Michaud, *Les Frères Musulmans 1928–82*, Gallimard/Juillard, Paris, 1983.

Central Agency for Public Mobilisation and Statistics, *Statistical Yearbook: Arab Republic of Egypt 1952–85*, Cairo, 1986.

Cesari, Jocelyne, "Algérie: contexte et acteurs du combat pour les droits de l'homme", *Maghreb-Machrek*, no. 142, 1993.

Chatterjee, Partha, *Nationalist Thought and the Colonial World*, Zed Books, London, 1986.

Choueiri, Youssef, "The Political Discourse of Contemporary Islamist Movements" in Abdel Salam Sidahmed and Anoushiravan Ehteshami (eds), *Islamic Fundamentalism*, Westview Press, Boulder, CO and Oxford, 1996.

Connaissance de l'Islam, Syros, Paris, 1992.

Davidson, Basil, *Africa in Modern History*, Penguin Books, Harmondswoth, 1978.

Dessouki, Ali E. Hillal, "The Public Sector in Egypt: Organisation, Evolution and Strategies of Reform" in Heba Handoussa and Gillian Potter (eds), *Employment and Structural Adjustment: Egypt in the 1990s*, AUC Press, Cairo, 1991.

——— "L'évolution politique de l'Egypte: pluralisme démocratique ou néo-autoritarisme?", *Maghreb-Machrek*, no. 127, Paris, 1990.

Donohue, John D. and John L. Esposito (eds), *Islam in Transition: Muslim Perspectives*, Oxford University Press, New York, 1982.

Dupret, Baudouin, "La problématique du nationalisme dans la pensée islamique contemporaine. Introduction", *Egypte Monde Arabe*, no. 15/16, Cairo, 1993.

Durán, Khalid, "Islamism: Its Background and Present Status: The Ascendancy of Fascism over Fundamentalism", unpublished paper, Oslo, 1992.

Duwaydār, Muḥammad, "Sharikāt tawẓīf al-amwāl" [The Investment Companies], *Qaḍāyā Fikriyya*, October 1989, Cairo.

Dwyer, Kevin, *Arab Voices: The Human Rights Debate in the Middle East*, University of California Press, 1991.

Ebeid, Mona Makram, "Le rôle de l'opposition officielle en Egypte", *Maghreb-Machrek*, no. 119, Paris, 1988.

Egset, Willy, *Conflict or Accommodation: An Analysis of the Transition to Multiparty System in Egypt and the Political Strategies of the Muslim Brotherhood*, thesis for the cand. polit. degree, University of Oslo, 1998.

Ekelund, Robert B. jr. and Robert F. Hebert, *A History of Economic Theory and Method*, McGraw-Hill, New York, 1990.

Enayat, Hamid, *Modern Islamic Political Thought*, Macmillan, London, 1982.

Esposito, John L., *Islam and Politics*, Syracuse University Press, 1987.

——— *The Islamic Threat: Myth or Reality?*, Oxford University Press, New York, 1992.

——— (ed.), *Political Islam: Revolution, Radicalism or Reform?*, Lynne Rienner, Boulder, CO and London, 1997.

——— "Introduction" in John L. Esposito (ed.), *Political Islam: Revolution, Radicalism or Reform?*, Lynne Rienner, Boulder, CO and London, 1997.

——— and François Burgat (eds), *Modernizing Islam: Religion and the Public Sphere in the Middle East and Europe*, Hurst, London/Rutgers University Press, Piscataway, NJ, 2002.

Etienne, Bruno, *L'islamisme radical*, Hachette, Paris, 1987.

Fahmy, Khaled Mahmoud, *Legislating Infitah: Investment, Currency and Foreign Trade Laws*, Cairo Papers in Social Science, vol. 11, monograph 3, Cairo, 1988.

Fanon, Frantz, *Jordens fordømte* [The Wretched of the Earth], Pax, Oslo, 1967.

Faraj, 'Abd al-Salām, *Al-farīḍa al-ghā'iba* [The Absent Obligation], n.p., Cairo, n.d...

Farhat, Muḥammad Nūr, "'An al-taḥawwulāt al-ijtimā'iyya wal-idiyulūjīya al-islāmiyya" [On Islamic Social and Ideological Transformations], *Qaḍāyā Fikriyya*, October 1989, Cairo.

Farschid, Olaf, "ḥizbiya: Dic NcuOricntierung der Muslimenbruderschaft Ägyptens in der Jahren 1984 bis 1989", *Orient*, 1/89.

Fergany, Nader, "A Characterisation of the Employment Problem in Egypt" in Heba Handoussa and Gillian Potter (eds), *Employment and Structural Adjustment: Egypt in the 1990s*, AUC Press, Cairo, 1991.

Ferrié, Jean-Noël, "Les paradoxes de la réislamisation en Egypte", *Maghreb-Machrek*, no. 151, January–March 1996.

Forstner, Martin, "Auf dem Legalen Weg zur Macht? Zur politische Entwicklung des Muslimenbruderschaft Ägyptens", *Orient*, 3/88.

Frank, Andre Gunder, "Underutviklingens utvikling" [The Development of Underdevelopment] in Tore Linné Eriksen (ed.), *Underutvikling* [Underdevelopment], Gyldendal, Oslo, 1974.

Fu'ād, Ni'mat Aḥmad, *Ṣinā'at al-jahl* [The Manufacture of Ignorance], Dār al-mustaqbal al-'arabī, Cairo, 1985.

Furre, Berge, *Soga om Lars Oftedal* [The Tale of Lars Oftedal], Samlaget, Oslo, 1990.

Gahrton, Per, *Egypten—en arabisk demokrati* [Egypt: An Arab Democracy], Ordfronts förlag, Stockholm, 1987.

Gellner, Ernest, *Postmodernism, Reason and Religion*, Routledge, London, 1992.

——— "Marxism and Islam: Failure and Success" in Azzam Tamimi (ed.), *Power-sharing Islam?*, Liberty for Muslim World Publications, London, 1993.

General Authority for Investment, Arab Republic of Egypt: Investment Law no. 230 for 1989.

George, Susan, *A Fate Worse than Debt*, Penguin Books, London, 1989.

Ghalyūn, Burhān, *Al-mas'ala al-ṭā'ifiyya wa mushkilat al-aqalliyyāt* [The Sectarian Question and the Minority Problem], Sinā lil-nashr, Cairo, 1988.

Ghānim, Ḥusayn, *Al-iqtiṣād al-islāmī* [Islamic Economics], Dar al- wafā', Manṣūra, 1991.

Al-Ghannūshī, Rāshid, *Maqālāt* [Articles], Dār al-karawān, Paris, 1984.

——— "Europe and Islam: Cooperation or Confrontation" in *International Seminar on Islam: Debates on the Rushdie Affair*, Jasmin Publishers, Oslo, n.d.

——— "Mustaqbal al-tayār al-islāmī" [The Future of the Islamic Trend], *Minbar al-Sharq*, 1992.

——— "The Participation of Islamists in a Non-Islamic Government" in Azzam Tamimi (ed.), *Power-sharing Islam?*, Liberty for Muslim World Publications, London, 1993.

Al-Ghazālī, Muḥammad, "Ḥall li-azmat al-isti'mār al-tashrī'ī fī bilādinā" [A Solution to the Crisis of Legislative Colonisation in our Country], *Minbar al-ḥiwār*, no. 13, 1989.

Giddens, Anthony, *Sociology*, Polity Press, Cambridge, 1989.

Giugale, Marcelo M., "The Rationale for Structural Adjustment: A Layman's Guide" in *The Economics and Politics of Structural Adjustment in Egypt, Cairo Papers in Social Science*, vol. 16, no. 3, AUC Press, Cairo, 1993.

Graham, Ronald, *The Aluminium Industry and the Third World*, Zed Books, London, 1982.

Gresh, Alain, "Quand l'islamisme menace le monde ...", *Le Monde Diplomatique*, December 1993.

Guazzone, Laura, "Islamism and Islamists in the Contemporary Arab World" in Laura Guazzone (ed.), *The Islamist Dilemma: The Political Role of Islamist Movements in the Contemporary Arab World*, Ithaca Press, Reading, 1995.

——— *The Islamist Dilemma: The Political Role of Islamist Movements in the Contemporary Arab World*, Ithaca Press, Reading, 1995.

Guenena, Nemat, *The "Jihad": An Islamic Alternative in Egypt, Cairo Papers in Social Science*, vol. 9, AUC Press, Cairo, 1986.

Gule, Lars, "Islam og det moderne" [Islam and Modernity], *Ariadne*, 4, Bergen, May 1990.

Ḥabīb, Rafīq, *Al-iḥtijāj al-dīnī wal-ṣirā' al-ṭabaqī fī miṣr* [Religious Protest and Class Struggle in Egypt], Sinā lil-nashr, Cairo, 1989.

——— *Awrāq ḥizb al-wasaṭ* [The Centre Party Papers], n.p., Cairo, 1996.

Ḥamūda, 'Ādil, *Sayyid Quṭb—min al-qarya ilā al-mishnaqa* [Sayyid Quṭb: From the Village to the Gallows], Sinā lil-nashr, Cairo, 1990.

Ḥamūda, Ḥusayn, "Al-ḥadātha fī mizān al-islām" [Modernity on the Scales of Islam], *Qaḍāyā Fikriyya*, October 1989, Cairo.

Ḥanafī, Ḥasan, *Al-yasār al-islāmī*, Al-Markaz al-'arabī lil-baḥth wal-nashr, Cairo, 1981.

——— *Al-dīn wal-tanmīya al-qawmiyya* [Religion and National Development], Maktabat Madbūlī, Cairo, 1989.

——— and Muḥammad al-Jabiri, "Dialogue entre le Maghreb et le Machreq", *Egypte Monde Arabe*, no. 6, Cairo, 1991.

Handoussa, Heba, "Crisis and Challenge: Prospects for the 1990s" in Heba Handoussa and Gillian Potter (eds), *Employment and Structural Adjustment: Egypt in the 1990s*, AUC Press, Cairo, 1991.

——— "The Role of the State: The Case of Egypt", paper presented at the First Annual Conference on Development Economics, Cairo, June 1993.

——— "Egypt's Structural Adjustment Program and Prospects for Recovery", report prepared for Institute of Developing Economies, Tokyo, March 1993.

——— (ed.), *Economic Transition in the Middle East: Global Challenges and Adjustment Strategies*, AUC Press, Cairo, 1997.

——— and Gillian Potter (eds), *Employment and Structural Adjustment: Egypt in the 1990s*, AUC Press, Cairo, 1991.

Hansen, Bent, *The Political Economy of Poverty, Equity and Growth: Egypt and Turkey*, The World Bank/Oxford University Press, 1991.

Harik, Ilya, "Continuity and Change in Local Development Policies in Egypt: From Nasser to Sadat", *IJMES*, no. 1, 1984.

Harris, Nigel, *The End of the Third World*, Penguin Books, London, 1986.

Hawwa, Saeed, *The Muslim Brotherhood*, International Islamic Federation of Student Organizations, Kuwait, 1985.

Heikal, Mohamed, *Autumn of Fury*, Random House, New York, 1983.

Hilāl, 'Alā al-Dīn (ed.), *Al-niẓām al-siyāsī al-miṣrī: al-taghayyur wal-istimrār* [The Political System in Egypt: Change and Continuity], Markaz al-buḥūth wal-dirāsāt al-siyāsiyya, Kulliyyat al-iqtiṣād wal-'ulūm al-siyāsiyya, Jāmi'at al-Qāhira, Cairo, 1988.

Ḥizb al-tajammu' al-waṭanī al-taqaddumī al-waḥdawī, *Al-barnāmaj al-siyāsī al-'āmm*, Cairo, April 1980.

——— *Mashrū' al-taqrīr al-siyāsī lil-mu'tamar al-'āmm al-thānī*, Cairo, June 1985.

——— "Al-barnāmaj al-intikhābī li-ḥizb al-tajammu'", *al-Ahālī*, 4 March 1987.

Hjärpe, Jan, *Islam som politisk ideologi* [Islam as Political Ideology], Gyldendal, Oslo, 1980.

Holter, Åge, *Arabisk statsreligion* [Arab State Religion], Gyldendal, Oslo, 1976.

Hourani, Albert, *Arabic Thought in the Liberal Age*, Cambridge University Press, 1983.

Hunt, Diana, *Economic Theories of Development: An Analysis of Competing Paradigms*, Harvester Wheatsheaf, London, 1989.

Ḥusayn, 'Ādil, "Islam and Marxism: The Absurd Polarisation of Contemporary Egyptian Politics", *Review of Middle East Studies*, no. 2, Ithaca Press, London, 1976.

——— *Al-iqtiṣād al-miṣrī min al-istiqlāl ilā al-taba'iyya 1974–1979* [The Egyptian Economy from Independence to Dependency 1974–9], 2 vols, Dār al-mustaqbal al-'arabī, Cairo, 1982.

Ḥusayn, Aḥmad, *Al-islām wal-mar'a* [Islam and Women], Dār al-sharq al-awsaṭ lil-nashr, Cairo, 1990.

Huwaydī, Fahmī, "I'ādat al-i'tibār lil-'aql al-islāmī—murāja'at kitāb "Al-sunna al-nabawiyya bayna ahl al-ḥadīth wa-ahl al-fiqh" lil-shaykh Muḥammad al-Ghazālī" [Islamic Reason Reconsidered: review of the book "The Sunna of the Prophet between ahl al-ḥadīth and ahl al-fiqh" by Shaykh Muḥammad al-Ghazālī], *Minbar al-ḥiwār*, no. 13, 1989.

——— *Al-islām wal-dīmuqrāṭīya* [Islam and Democracy], Markaz al-Ahrām lil-tarjama walnashr, Cairo, 1993.

Ibrahim, Saad Eddin, "An Islamic Alternative in Egypt: The Muslim Brotherhood and Sadat", *Arab Studies Quarterly*, vol. 4, no. 1/2, spring 1982.

——— "Anatomy of Egypt's Militant Islamic Groups", *IJMES*, no. 4, 1980.

——— "Egypt's Islamic Activism in the 1980s", *Third World Quarterly*, vol. 10, no. 2, London, April 1988.

——— "Economics, Business Transactions and Ethics in Islam", unpublished paper, 1989.

——— "Islamic Activism and Political Opposition in Egypt", paper presented to the seminar on Aspects of Egyptian Development, Centre for Development Research, Copenhagen, June 1990.

Ibrahimi, Khaoula Taleb, "Algérie: l'arabisation, lieu de conflits multiples", *Maghreb-Machrek*, no. 150, October–December 1995.

Al-ikhwān al-muslimūn, "Mūjaz 'an al-shūrā fī al-islām" [A Short Declaration on Shūrā in Islam], *al-Sha'b*, 19 May 1994.

'Imāra, Muḥammad, "Hal yajūz al-ijtihād ma'a wujūd al-naṣṣ?" [Is Interpretation Legal in the Presence of a Text], *Minbar al-ḥiwār*, no. 13, 1989.

——— "Al-ḥiwār bayna al-islāmiyyīn wal-'almāniyyīn" [Dialogue between Islamists and Secularists], *Minbar al-ḥiwār*, no. 15, 1989.

——— "Naḥwa falsafa islāmiyya mu'āṣira" [Towards a Contemporary Islamic Philosophy], *Minbar al-ḥiwār*, no. 21/22, 1991.

Irfani, Suroosh, "The Progressive Islamic Movement" in Mohammad Asghar Khan (ed.), *Islam, Politics and the State: The Pakistan Experience*, Zed Books, London, 1985.

Al-'Iryān, 'Iṣām, "The Future of Power-sharing in Egypt" in Azzam Tamimi (ed.), *Power-sharing Islam?*, Liberty for Muslim World Publications, London, 1993.

'Īsā, Muḥammad Abd al-Shafī', "Al-taṭawwur al-tiknulūjī wa istrātijīyat al-i'timād 'alā al-dhāt fī al-tajriba al-ṣinā'iyya al-miṣriyya 1970–1980" [Technological Development and the Strategy of Relying on Oneself in the Egyptian Industrial Endeavour 1970–1980], *Al-fikr al-istrātījī al-'arabī*, April 1982.

——— "Al-tiknulūjīya al-ṣinā'iyya al-miṣriyya fī al-thamanīniyyat—wāqi'ha al-ḥālī wa āfāq taṭawwuriha" [The Egyptian Industrial Technology of the 1980s: Its Present State and Horizons for its Development], *Al-fikr al-istrātījī al-'arabī*, October 1986.

Al-'Īsāwī, Ibrāhīm, *Mustaqbal miṣr* [The Future of Egypt], Dār al-thaqāfa al-jadīda, Cairo, 1983.

Ismail, Salwa, "Confronting the Other: Identity, Culture, Politics, and Conservative Islamism in Egypt", *IJMES*, no. 2, 1998.

Issawi, Charles, *An Economic History of the Middle East and North Africa*, Columbia University Press, 1982.

Jabhat al-inqādh al-islāmiyya, *Al-thawra al-islāmiyya fī al-jazā'ir* [The Islamic Revolution in Algeria], Yāfā lil-dirāsāt, Cairo, 1991.

Jankowski, James P., *Egypt's Young Rebels*, Hoover Institution Press, Stanford, 1975.

Jenkins, Rhys, "Divisions over the International Division of Labour", *Capital & Class*, no. 22, London, 1984.

Kamali, Mohammad Hashim, "Fiqh and Adaptation to social Reality", *The Muslim World*, vol. LXXXVI, no. 1, January 1996.

Kepel, Gilles, *The Prophet and Pharaoh: Muslim Extremism in Egypt*, Al Saqi Books, London, 1985.

——— *La Revanche de Dieu. Chrétiens, juifs et musulmans à la reconquête du monde*, Seuil, Paris, 1991.

——— *Jihad: The Trail of Political Islam*, I. B. Tauris, London, 2002.

——— et Yann Richard (eds), *Intellectuels et militants de l'Islam contemporaine*, Seuil, Paris, 1990.

Khan, Mohammad Asghar (ed.), *Islam, Politics and the State: The Pakistan Experience*, Zed Books, London, 1985.

"Kolloqium zur deutsch-französische Forschungsprojekt "Islamische Wirtschaft" 29–30 Oktober 1987", *Orient*, 4/87.

Krämer, Gudrun, "Cross-Links and Double Talk? Islamist Movements in the Political Process", in Laura Guazzone (ed.), *The Islamist Dilemma: The Political Role of Islamist Movements in the Contemporary Arab World*, Ithaca Press, Reading, 1995.

Kuran, Timur, "The Economic System in Contemporary Islamic Thought: Interpretation and Assessment", *IJMES*, no. 2, 1986.

——— "On the Notion of Economic Justice in Contemporary Islamic Thought", *IJMES*, no. 2, 1989.

——— "Fundamentalisms and the Economy" in Martin E. Marty and R. Scott Appleby (eds), *Fundamentalisms and the State: Remaking Polities, Economies, and Militance*, University of Chicago Press, 1993.

——— "The Economic Impact of Islamic Fundamentalism" in Martin E. Marty and R. Scott Appleby (eds), *Fundamentalisms and the State: Remaking Polities, Economies, and Militance*, University of Chicago Press, 1993.

——— "Islamic Economics and the Islamic Subeconomy", *Journal of Economic Perspectives*, vol. 9, 1995.

Kvalsvik, Bjørn Nic., "Skiljemerka mellom folk. Intro-dusere Pierre Bourdieu?" [The Distinctions between People: Introducing Pierre Bourdieu], *LITINORs skriftserie*, no. 2, Norges forskningsråd, Oslo, 1993.

Al-Labbān, Muhy Nāṣir, "Taba'iyyat al-fikr al-iqtiṣādī al-'arabī" [The Dependency of Arab Economic Thinking], *Minbar al-ḥiwār*, no. 12, 1988.

Lapidus, Ira M., *A History of Islamic Societies*, Cambridge University Press, 1988.

Lawrence, Bruce B., *Defenders of God: The Fundamentalist Revolt Against the Modern Age*, I. B. Tauris, London, 1990.

Lewis, Bernard, *The Political Language of Islam*, University of Chicago Press, 1988.

Lia, Brynjar, *The Society of the Muslim Brothers in Egypt: The Rise of an Islamic Mass Movement 1928–1942*, Ithaca Press, Reading, 1998.

Linné Eriksen, Tore (ed.), *Underutvikling* [Underdevelopment], Gyldendal, Oslo, 1974.

Lipietz, Alain, *Mirages and Miracles*, Verso, London, 1987.

Lunden, Kåre, *Norsk grålysing* [Norwegian Dawn], Det Norske Samlaget, Oslo, 1992.

Löfgren, Hans, "Economic Policy in Egypt: Breakdown in Reform resistance?", *IJMES*, no. 3, 1993.

——— "Egypt's Programme for Stabilization and Structural Adjustment: An Assessment" in *The Economics and Politics of Structural Adjustment in Egypt, Cairo Papers in Social Science*, vol. 16, no. 3, AUC Press, Cairo, 1993.

Mahjoub, Azzam (ed.), *Adjustment or Delinking? The African Experience*, Zed Books, London, 1990.

——— and Fawzy Mansour, "Egypt: from the Free Officers' Coup to the Infitah" in Azzam Mahjoub (ed.), *Adjustment or Delinking? The African Experience*, Zed Books, London, 1990.

Mallat, Chibli, *The Renewal of Islamic Law: Muḥammad Baqer as-Sadr, Najaf and the Shi'i International*, Cambridge University Press, 1993.

Mannan, Muḥammad Abdul, *Islamic Economics: Theory and Practice*, Hodder and Stoughton, Cambridge, 1986.

Markaz al-dirāsāt al-siyāsiyya wal-istrātījiyya bil-Ahrām, *Al-taqrīr al-istrātījī al-'arabī 1985* [The Arab Strategic Report 1985], Al-Ahrām, Cairo, 1986.

——— *Al-taqrīr al-istrātījī al-'arabī 1986* [The Arab Strategic Report 1986], Al-Ahrām, Cairo, 1987.

——— *Al-taqrīr al-istrātījī al-'arabī 1987* [The Arab Strategic Report 1987], Al-Ahrām, Cairo, 1988.

——— *Al-taqrīr al-istrātījī al-'arabī 1988* [The Arab Strategic Report 1988], Al-Ahrām, Cairo, 1989.

——— *Al-taqrīr al-istrātījī al-'arabī 1989* [The Arab Strategic Report 1989], Al-Ahrām, Cairo, 1990.

——— *Al-taqrīr al-istrātījī al-'arabī 1990* [The Arab Strategic Report 1990], Al-Ahrām, Cairo, 1991.

——— *Al-taqrīr al-istrātījī al-'arabī 1992* [The Arab Strategic Report 1992], Al-Ahrām, Cairo, 1993.

Marshū, Grīgūwār, "'Awdat al-makbūt: al-islām wal-gharb" [The Return of the Downtrodden: Islam and the West], *Minbar al-ḥiwār*, no. 14, 1989.

Marty, Martin E. and R. Scott Appleby, "Conclusion: An Interim Report on a Hypothetical Family" in Martin E. Marty and R. Scott Appleby (eds), *Fundamentalisms Observed*, The University of Chicago Press, 1991.

——— (eds), *Fundamentalisms Observed*, University of Chicago Press, 1991.

——— "Introduction" in Martin E. Marty and R. Scott Appleby (eds), *Fundamentalisms and the State: Remaking Polities, Economies, and Militance*, University of Chicago Press, 1993.

——— "Conclusion: Remaking the State: The Limits of the Fundamentalist Imagination" in Martin E. Marty and R. Scott Appleby (eds), *Fundamentalisms and the State: Remaking Polities, Economies, and Militance*, University of Chicago Press, 1993.

——— (eds), *Fundamentalisms and the State: Remaking Polities, Economies, and Militance*, University of Chicago Press, 1993.

——— (eds), *Fundamentalisms and Society: Reclaiming the Sciences, the Family, and Education*, University of Chicago Press, 1993.

Al-maṣraf al-islāmī al-duwalī lil-istithmār wal-tanmīya, *Bibliyūjrāfiyā al-iqtiṣād al-islāmī* [Bibliography of Islamic Economics], Al-risāla lil-ṭibā'a wal-nashr, Cairo, 1987.

Al-Maṣrī, Sanā', *Khalfa al-ḥijāb* [Behind the Veil], Sinā lil-nashr, Cairo, 1989.

Al-Mawdūdī, Abū al-A'lā, *Mabādi' al-islām* [The Principles of Islam], Idārat al-buḥūth al-'ilmiyya wal-iftā' wal-da'wa wal-irshād, Riyad, 1984.

Mawsillī, Aḥmad, "Al-islām wal-niẓām al-'ālamī min wijhat naẓar al-uṣūliyya al-islāmiyya" [Islam and the World Order from the Point of View of Islamic Fundamentalism], *Minbar al-ḥiwār*, no. 18, 1990.

Mayer, Ann Elizabeth, *Islam and Human Rights: Tradition and Politics*, Westview Press, Boulder, CO, 1991.

Médard, Jean-François, "Politics from Above, Politics from Below" in Mette Masst, Thomas Hylland Eriksen and Jo Helle-Valle, *State and Locality, Proceedings of the NFU Annual Conference 1993*, Centre for Development and the Environment, University of Oslo, 1994.

Middle East Watch, *Behind Closed Doors: Torture and Detention in Egypt*, New York, June 1992.

Mitchell, Richard, *The Society of Moslem Brothers*, Oxford University Press, 1969.

Moghadam, Valentine M., "Rhetorics and Rights of Identity in Islamist Movements", *Journal of World History*, vol. 4, no. 2, 1993.

Momen, Moojan, *An Introduction to Shi'i Islam*, Yale University Press, New Haven, 1985.

Moore, Clement H., "Islamic Banks: Financial and Political Intermediation in Arab Countries", *Orient*, 1/88.

Mortimer, Edward, *Faith and Power*, New York, 1982.

Mottahedeh, Roy, *The Mantle of the Prophet: Religion and Politics in Iran*, Pantheon Books, New York, 1985.

Muṣṭafā, Hāla, *Al-islām al-siyāsī fī miṣr* [Political Islam in Egypt], Markaz al-dirāsāt al-siyāsiyya wal-istrātījiyya bil-Ahrām, Cairo, 1992.

——— *Al-dawla wal-ḥarakāt al-islāmiyya al-mu'āriḍa bayn al-muhādana wal-muwājaha fī 'ahday al-Sādāt wa Mubārak* [The State and the Oppositional Islamist Movements in the Time of Sadat and Mubarak], Markaz al-Maḥrūsa lil-nashr wal-khidmāt al-ṣuḥufiyya, Cairo, 1995.

——— "The Islamist Movements under Mubarak" in Laura Guazzone (ed.), *The Islamist Dilemma: The Political Role of Islamist Movements in the Contemporary Arab World*, Ithaca Press, Reading, 1995.

An-Na'im, Abdullahi Ahmed, *Toward an Islamic Reformation*, Syracuse University Press, 1990.

Al-Nafīsī, 'Abdallāh (ed.), *Al-ḥaraka al-islāmiyya: ru'ya mustaqbaliyya* [The Islamist Movement: Looking to the Future], Maktabat Madbūlī, Cairo, 1989.

Naguib, Nefissa N. A., *Men of Commitment: An Anthropological Study about Top Norwegian Business Executives*, thesis for the cand. polit. degree, University of Oslo, 1989.

Najjar, Fauzi M., "The Application of Sharia Laws in Egypt", *Middle East Policy*, vol. 1, no. 3, 1992.

Nord, Erik, "Underutvikling og utvikling: et historisk perspektiv" [Underdevelopment and Development: A Historical Perspective] in Tore Linné Eriksen (ed.), *Underutvikling*, Gyldendal, Oslo, 1974.

Noreng, Øystein, *Oil and Islam: Social and Economic Issues*, John Wiley & Sons, Chichester, 1997.

Owen, Roger, "Egypt og Europa: fra fransk ekspedisjon til britisk okkupasjon" [Egypt and Europe: From French Expedition to British Occupation] in Tore Linné Eriksen (ed.), *Underutvikling* [Underdevelopment], Gyldendal, Oslo, 1974.

——— "Islam and Capitalism: A Critique of Rodinson", *Review of Middle East Studies*, no. 2, Ithaca Press, London, 1976.

——— *The Middle East in the World Economy 1800–1914*, Methuen, London, 1981.

——— *State, Power & Politics in the Making of the Modern Middle East*, Routledge, London, 1992.

Parfitt, Trevor, "The Politics of Adjustment in Africa with Special Reference to Egypt" in *The Economics and Politics of Structural Adjustment in Egypt, Cairo Papers in Social Science*, vol. 16, no. 3, AUC Press, Cairo, 1993.

Payer, Cheryl, *The Debt Trap: The International Monetary Fund and the Third World*, Monthly Review Press, New York, 1974.

Piscatori, James P. (ed.), *Islam in the Political Process*, Cambridge University Press, 1983.

——— "Religion and Realpolitik: Islamic Responses to the Gulf War" in James Piscatori (ed.), *Islamic Fundamentalisms and the Gulf Crisis*, The American Academy of Arts and Sciences, Chicago, 1991.

Price, Pamela, Retaining *the Past in Tamil Political Practice*, unpublished paper, Oslo, 1994.

Qaḍāyā Fikriyya, October 1989, Special issue on "Al-islām al-siyāsī—al-usus al-fikriyya wal-ahdāf al-'amaliyya" [Political Islam: Ideological Bases and Practical Goals].

Qaḥf, Muḥammad Mundhir, *Al-iqtiṣād al-islāmī* [Islamic Economics], Dār al-qalam, Kuwait, 1979.

Qandil, Amani, "Le courant islamique dans les institutions de la société civile: le cas des ordres professionels en Egypte" in *Modernisation et nouvelles formes de mobilisation sociale II—Egypte-Turquie*, CEDEJ, Cairo, 1992.

Al-Qaraḍāwī, Yūsuf, *Al-ḥulūl al-mustawrada wa kayfa janat 'alā ummatinā* [The Imported Solutions and How They Have Harmed Our Community], Mu'assasat al-risāla, Beirut, 1971.

Qāsim, Nawāl, *Taṭawwur al-ṣinā'a al-miṣriyya mundhu 'ahd Muḥammad 'Alī ḥattā 'ahd 'Abd al-Nāṣir* [The Development of Egyptian Industry from the Era of Muḥammad Ali to the Era of Nasser], Maktabat Madbūlī, Cairo, 1987.

Quṭb, Sayyid, *Islam: The Religion of the Future*, International Islamic Federation of Student Organizations, Kuwait, 1984.

Rabī', 'Amr Hāshim, *Adā' majlis al-sha'b al-miṣrī* [The Performance of the Egyptian People's Assembly], Markaz al-dirāsāt al-siyāsiyya wal-istrātījiyya bil-Ahrām, Cairo, 1991.

Rāḍī, Muḥsin, *Al-ikhwān taḥta qubbat al-barlamān* [The Brothers under the Dome of Parliament], 2 vols, Dār al-tawzī' wal-nashr al-islāmiyya, Cairo, 1990 and 1991.

Rahnema, Ali and Farhad Nomani, *The Secular Miracle: Religion, Politics and Economic Policy in Iran*, Zed Books, London, 1990.

——— *Islamic Economic Systems*, Zed Books, London, 1994.

Ramadan, Abdel Azim, "Fundamentalist Influence in Egypt: The Strategies of the Muslim Brotherhood and the Takfir Groups" in Martin E. Marty and R. Scott Appleby (eds), *Fundamentalisms and the State: Remaking Polities, Economies, and Militance*, University of Chicago Press, 1993.

Ramonet, Ignacio, "Algérie panique", *Le Monde Diplomatique*, no. 486, September 1994.

Repstad, Pål, *Mellom himmel og jord—en innføring i religionssosiologi* [Between Heaven and Earth: An Introduction to the Sociology of Religion], Gyldendal, Oslo, 1984.

Richards, Alan, "Agricultural Employment, Wages and Government Policy in Egypt during and after the Oil Boom" in Heba Handoussa and Gillian Potter (eds), *Employment and Structural Adjustment: Egypt in the 1990s*, AUC Press, Cairo, 1991.

——— and John Waterbury, *A Political Economy of the Middle East*, Westview Press, Boulder, CO and Oxford, 1996.

Rif'at, 'Iṣām, "Al-ujūr al-khafiya wa takālīf al-ḥayāt", *al-Ahrām al-Iqtiṣādī*, no. 1191, 11 November 1991.

Rodinson, Maxime, *Islam and Capitalism*, Penguin Books, Harmondsworth, 1977.

——— *Marxism and the Muslim World*, Monthly Review Press, New York, 1981.

Rosenthal, E. I. J., *Islam in the Modern National State*, Cambridge University Press, 1965.

Roussillon, Alain, *Societés islamiques de placements de fonds et "ouverture économique"*, CEDEJ, Cairo, 1988.

——— "Entre al-Jihâd et al-Rayyân: Phénoménologie de l'islamisme égyptien", *Maghreb-Machrek*, no. 127, Paris, 1990.

——— "Intellectuels en crise dans l'Egypte contemporaine" in Gilles Kepel et Yann Richard (eds), *Intellectuels et militants de l'Islam contemporaine*, Seuil, Paris, 1990.

——— "Trajectoires reformistes: Sayyid Qutb et Sayyid Uways", *Egypte Monde Arabe*, no. 6, Cairo, 1991.

——— *L'Égypte et l'Algérie au péril de la libéralisation* , CEDEJ, Cairo, 1996.

Roy, Olivier, *Islam and Resistance in Afghanistan*, Cambridge University Press, 1986.

——— *L'échec de l'islam politique* , Editions du Seuil, Paris, 1992.

——— *The Failure of Political Islam*, Harvard University Press, 1994.

Rugh, Andrea B., "Reshaping Personal Relations in Egypt" in Martin E. Marty and R. Scott Appleby (eds), *Fundamentalisms and Society: Reclaiming the Sciences, the Family, and Education*, The University of Chicago Press, 1993.

Rumayḥ, Ṭal'at, *Al-wasaṭ wal-ikhwān* [The Centre and the Brothers], Markaz Yāfā lil-dirāsāt wal-abḥāth, Cairo, 1997.

Ruthven, Malise, *Islam in the World*, Penguin Books, Harmondsworth, 1984.

Saad ad-Din, Omar, *The Role of State, Private and Foreign Capital in Law 43 of 1974 Projects*, MA thesis in Political Economy, the American University in Cairo, May 1984.

Said, Mona, Ha-Joon Chang and Khaled Sakr, "Industrial Policy and the Role of the State in Egypt: The Relevance of the East Asian Experience" in Heba Handoussa (ed.), *Economic Transition in the Middle East: Global Challenges and Adjustment Strategies*, AUC Press, Cairo, 1997.

Sa'īd, Muḥammad al-Sayyid, *Mustaqbal al-niẓām al-'arabī ba'da azmat al-khalīj* [The Future of the Arab Order after the Gulf Crisis], Al-majlis al-waṭanī lil-thaqāfa wal-funūn wal-adab, Kuwait, 1992.

Al-Sa'īd, Rif'at, *Ḥasan al-Bannā—matā kayfa wa limādhā?* [Ḥasan al-Bannā: When, How and Why?], Al-ahālī, Cairo, 1990.

——— *Mādhā jarā li-miṣr muslimīn wa-aqbāṭ* [What happened to Egypt—Muslims and Copts?], Al-ahālī, Cairo, 1991.

Ṣaliḥ, Amānī 'Abd al-Raḥmān, "Al-ta'addudiyya al-siyāsiyya fī al-waṭan al-'arabī" [Political Pluralism in the Arab Nation], *Al-fikr al-istrātījī al-'arabī*, no. 38, October 1991.

Salvatore, Armando, *Islam and the Political Discourse of Modernity*, Ithaca Press, Reading, 1997.

Al-Sarrāf, Shīmā, "Waḍ' al-mar'a fī al-sharī'a al-islāmiyya", [The Position of Women in the Islamic Sharī'a], *Minbar al-ḥiwār*, no. 13, 1989.

——— "'Amal al-mar'a bayna al-qur'ān wal-sunna wa-mawqif fuqahā' al-ams wal-yawm" [Women's Work between the Koran, the Sunna and the Position of the fuqahā' of Today and Yesterday], *Minbar al-ḥiwār*, no. 15, 1989.

Al-Sayyid, Mustafa Kamel, *Privatization: The Egyptian Debate, Cairo Papers in Social Science*, vol. 13, monograph 4, AUC Press, Cairo, 1990.

Schacht, Joseph, *An Introduction to Islamic Law*, Clarendon Press, Oxford, 1982.

Senghaas, Dieter, *The European Experience: A Historical Critique of Development Theory*, Berg Publishers, Leamington Spa, 1985.

Shafīq, Munīr, "Two societies" in Anwar Abdel-Malek (ed.), *Contemporary Arab Political Thought*, Zed Books, London, 1983.

Sidahmed, Abdel Salam and Anoushiravan Ehteshami (eds), *Islamic Fundamentalism*, Westview Press, Boulder, CO and Oxford, 1996.

——— "Introduction" in Abdel Salam Sidahmed and Anoushiravan Ehteshami (eds), *Islamic Fundamentalism*, Westview Press, Boulder, CO and Oxford, 1996.

Siegel, Paul N., *The Meek and the Militant: Religion and Politics Across the World*, Zed Books, London, 1986.

Singer, Hanaa Fikri, *The Socialist Labor Party: A Case Study of a Contemporary Egyptian Opposition Party*, MA Thesis in Sociology, American University in Cairo, May 1990.

——— *The Socialist Labor Party: A Case Study of a Contemporary Egyptian Opposition Party, Cairo Papers in Social Science*, vol. 16, no. 1, AUC Press, Cairo, 1993.

Singerman, Diane, *Avenues of Participation: Family, Politics and Networks in Urban Quarters of Cairo*, Princeton University Press, 1995.

Smith, Anthony D., *Theories of Nationalism*, Holmes and Meier, New York, 1983.

——— *National Identity*, Penguin Books, London, 1991.

Springborg, Robert, *Family, Power and Politics in Egypt*, University of Pennsylvania Press, 1982.

——— *Mubarak's Egypt: Fragmentation of the Political Order*, Westview Press, Boulder, CO and London, 1989.

——— "State-Society Relations in Egypt: The Debate over Owner-Tenant Relations", *Middle East Journal*, vol. 45, no. 2, spring 1991.

Sullivan, Denis J., *Private Voluntary Organizations in Egypt: Islamic Development, Private Initiative, and State Control*, University Press of Florida, Gainesville, FL, 1994.

Taha, Mahmoud M., *Islams annet budskap* [The Other Message of Islam], Universitetsforlaget, Oslo, 1983.

Tamimi, Azzam (ed.), *Power-sharing Islam?*, Liberty for Muslim World Publications, London, 1993.

Ṭanṭāwī, Muḥammad Sayyid, "Al-ribā ḥarām ḥarām wa-lākin mā al-ribā?" [Ribā is Forbidden, but What is Ribā?], *al-Ahrām al-Iqtiṣādī*, 5 August 1991.

——— "Al-qurūḍ, al-duyūn, al-wadā'i', al-istithmār" [Loans, Debts, Deposits, Investment], *al-Ahrām al-Iqtiṣādī*, 12 August 1991.

——— "Hal taḥdīd al-ribḥ muqaddiman yajūz shar'an?" [Is it Legal to Determine Profit in Advance?], *al-Ahrām al-Iqtiṣādī*, 19 August 1991.

——— "Amthila wa taṭbīqāt li-ba'ḍ al-mu'āmālāt" [Examples and Applications of Some Mu'āmalāt], *al-Ahrām al-Iqtiṣādī*, 26 August 1991.

Al-Tawātī, Muṣṭafā, "Al-ḥaraka al-islāmiyya fī tūnis" [The Islamic Movement in Tunisia], *Qaḍāyā Fikriyya*, October 1989, Cairo.

Al-Ṭawīl, Muḥammad, *Al-ikhwān fī al-barlamān* [The Brothers in Parliament], Dār al tawzī' wal-nashr al-islāmiyya, Cairo, 1994.

Third World Quarterly, vol. 10, no. 2. Special issue on "Islam & Politics", London, April 1988.

Thompson, E. P., "The Moral Economy of the English Crowd in the 18th Century", *Past and Present*, no. 50, 1971.

Tlemcani, Rachid, *State and Revolution in Algeria*, Zed Books, London, 1986.

Tjomsland, Marit, "“The Educated Way of Thinking”: Individualisation and Islamism in Tunisia" in Mette Masst, Thomas Hylland Eriksen and Jo Helle-Valle, *State and Locality, Proceedings of the NFU Annual Conference 1993*, Centre for Development and the Environment, University of Oslo, 1994.

Tripp, Charles, "Islam and the Secular Logic of the State in the Middle East" in Abdel Salam Sidahmed and Anoushiravan Ehteshami (eds), *Islamic Fundamentalism*, Westview Press, Boulder, CO and Oxford, 1996.

Al-Turābī, Ḥasan 'Abdallāh, *Al-ḥaraka al-islāmiyya fī al-sūdān* [The Islamic Movement in Sudan], n.p., Khartoum, 1990.

——— "Awlawiyyāt al-tayār al-islāmī" [Priorities of the Islamic Trend], *Minbar al-Sharq*, no. 1, 1992.

Tvedt, Terje, *Bilder av "de andre"* [Images of "The Others"], Universitetsforlaget, Oslo, 1990.

Tønnesson, Stein, "From Confucianism to Communism, and Back? Vietnam 1925–95", paper presented at the Annual Conference of the Norwegian Association of Development Studies, June 1993.

Urvoy, Dominique, *Ibn Rushd (Averroes)*, Routledge, London, 1991.

Utvik, Bjørn Olav, *Kva kom inn den opne døra? Industrien i Egypt under Sadats nye økonomiske politikk. 1970–83* [What Came in the Open Door? The Egyptian Industry under Sadat's New Economic Policy 1970–83], University of Oslo, 1990.

——— "Kommunistar og Gud" [Communists and God], *Røde Fane*, no. 3/89.

——— "Bilder av Egypt. Terje Tvedts oppgjer med avhengighetsteorien" [Images of Egypt: Terje Tvedt's Critique of Dependency Theory], *Forum for utviklingsstudier*, no. 2/90.

——— "Hasan al-Banna—ein muslimsk Oftedal?" [Hasan al-Banna: A Muslim Oftedal], *Midtøsten Forum*, 1/93.

——— "The Egyptian Labour Party: A New Brand of Islamism" in Heikki Palva and Knut S. Vikør (eds), *The Middle East: Unity and Diversity, Nordic Proceedings in Asian Studies*, no. 5, Nordic Institute of Asian Studies, Copenhagen, 1993.

——— "Islamism: Digesting Modernity the Islamic Way", *Forum for Development Studies*, 2/93.

——— "Filling the Vacant Throne of Nasser: The Economic Discourse of Egypt's Islamist Opposition", *Arab Studies Quarterly*, vol. 14, no. 4, fall 1995.

——— "“A pervasive seriousness invaded the country …” Islamism: Cromwell's Ghost in the Middle East" in Stein Tønnesson, Juhani Koponen, Niels Steensgaard and Thommy Svensson (eds), *Between National Histories and Global History*, FHS, Helsinki, 1997.

——— *Independence and Development in the Name of God: The Economic Discourse of Egypt's Islamist Opposition 1984–90*, University of Oslo, 2000.

——— "The Modernising Force of Islamism" in François Burgat and John Esposito (eds), *Modernizing Islam: Religion and the Public Sphere in the Middle East and Europe*, Hurst, London/Rutgers University Press, Piscataway, NJ, 2002.

Vikør, Knut S, *Mellom Gud og stat: ei historie om islamsk lov og rettsvesen* [Between God And The State: A History of Islamic Law and Jurisprudence], Spartacus, Oslo, 2003.

Vogt, Kari, *Islams hus. Verdensreligion på fremmarsj* [The House of Islam: An Expanding World Religion], Cappelen, Oslo, 1993.

Voll, John O., "Fundamentalism in the Sunni Arab World: Egypt and the Sudan" in Martin E. Marty and R. Scott Appleby (eds), *Fundamentalisms Observed*, The University of Chicago Press, 1991.

Waardenburg, Jacques, "Fundamentalismus und Aktivismus in der islamisch-arabischen Welt der Gegenwart", *Orient*, 1/89.

Wahba, Mourad Magdi, "The Meaning of "Ishtirakiyya": Arab Perceptions of Socialism in the Nineteenth Century", *Alif*, no. 10, Cairo, 1990.

——— "The Nationalization of the IMF: The Nature and Evolution of the Official Discourse on Economic Reform in Egypt (1987–1991)" in *The Economics and Politics of Structural Adjustment in Egypt, Cairo Papers in Social Science*, vol. 16, no. 3, AUC Press, Cairo, 1993.

Walzer, Michael, *The Revolution of the Saints: A Study in the Origins of Radical Politics*, Weidenfeld and Nicolson, London, 1966.

Al-Wardānī, Ṣāliḥ, *Al-ḥaraka al-islāmiyya fī miṣr—wāqi' al-thamanīnāt* [The Islamist Movement in Egypt: The Situation in the 1980s], Markaz al- ḥaḍāra al-'arabiyya lil-i'lām wal-nashr, Giza, 1991.

Warren, Bill, *Imperialism Pioneer of Capitalism*, Verso, London, 1980.

Waterbury, John, *The Egypt of Nasser and Sadat*, Princeton University Press, 1983.

Watt, William Montgomery, *Islamic Political Thought*, Edinburgh University Press, 1968.

——— *Islamic Fundamentalism and Modernity*, Routledge, London and New York, 1988.

Weber, Max, *The Protestant Ethic and the Spirit of Capitalism*, HarperCollins, London, 1991.

The World Bank, *World Development Report*, 1990.

Yāsīn, Munā, *Al-gharb wal-islām* [The West and Islam], Dār al-jihād lil-nashr wal-tawzī', Cairo, 1994.

Zaalouk, Malak, *Power, Class and Foreign Capital in Egypt*, Zed Books, London, 1989.

Zaki, Moheb, *Civil Society and Democratization in Egypt 1981–1994*, The Ibn Khaldoun Center, Cairo, 1994.

Zeghal, Malika, *Gardiens de l'islam: Les oulémas d'Al Azhar dans l'Égypte contemporaine*, Presses de Sciences Po, Paris, 1996.

Zubaida, Sami, *Islam, the People and the State: Political Ideas and Movements in the Middle East*, I. B. Tauris, London, 1993.

Østerud, Øyvind, *Utviklingsteori og historisk endring* [Development Theory and Historical Change], Gyldendal, Oslo, 1978.

INDEX